What Others Say About Their Facebook Results

"Keith Krance is one of the smartest Facebook ads experts I've ever... Thanks to him we were able to set up our first profitable Facebook ad campaign to our Podcaster's Paradise webinar campaign, which was getting a 6 to 1 ROI, AND helped us ignite our entire new webinar sales funnel!"

—JOHN LEE DUMAS, HOST OF THE #1 BUSINESS PODCAST "ENTREPRENEUR ON FIRE"

"Since becoming a member of Keith and Perry's 80/20 Facebook Express program, I've added over $500,000 in revenue to my company by managing clients' Facebook accounts AND generated over $2,200,000 in sales for my clients in less than six months!"

—SETH GREENE, FOUNDER, MARKET DOMINATION, LLC

"After taking Keith's advice, within just a few days I cut my cost per click and CPM (cost per thousand impressions) by half! If you have a chance to learn from Keith, or work with Keith, DO IT."

—BRIAN BAGNALL, CEO, BAGNALL & ASSOCIATES

"When it comes to Facebook Advertising experts Keith Krance is the best of the best. Over the past few years Keith and his team have helped us generate tens of thousands of quality leads and millions in sales directly from Facebook. His stuff works!"

—BILL HARRISON, BESTSELLERBLUEPRINT.COM

"Keith Krance and his team are incredible! In the short time we've been working together, I have experienced an increase of more than $100,000 in sales for a new service offering on just over $19,000 in ad spend. We expect to reach $200,000 a month very soon (starting from zero). In a world where there seems to be quasi experts on every corner, these guys can actually deliver on their promise. I highly recommend Keith and his team."

—TRAVIS LANE JENKINS, CONSULTANT TO *DOCTORS*, AND HOST OF "THE ENTREPRENEUR'S RADIO SHOW"

"I'm a believer! Not only did Keith Krance take the guesswork out of running Facebook ads, his strategies brought us a flood of new qualified traffic that is now converting straight into the top of our funnel. Thanks to Keith, we're now running promotions regularly with great success."

—LISA WILLIAMS, MARKETING DIRECTOR, THE JACK CANFIELD TRAINING GROUP

"Keith Krance continues to enlighten our community of digital marketers with intelligent and creative traffic advice. As one of the top Facebook advertising experts, Keith is the contact you want to have when setting up, scaling, and simply making money on Facebook."

—MOLLY PITTMAN, SOCIAL MARKETING AND FACEBOOK ADS MANAGER AT RYAN DEISS'S DIGITAL MARKETER

"Perry Marshall has done more to de-mystify Google AdWords for business owners than any person on earth. With this book, he's done the same for Facebook. If you want to cut through the smoke quickly and make money advertising on Facebook, this is the book to read."

—KEN MCCARTHY, THE SYSTEM SEMINAR, TIVOLI NY

"The irony of living in the Information Age is that good info has gotten harder to come by. The lame stuff still manages to clog the pipes, causing chaos and preventing you from discovering the legit specifics that can actually help you in your quest for business success and a bigger bottom line. Perry Marshall has been a first-stop, one-stop resource for the best possible advice on making AdWords work since Google unleashed it on the marketing community . . . and now, Perry's new tome on Facebook's astonishing (and yet-to-be-fully-tapped) power to reach gazillions of targeted, eager prospects (most of whom you'd never even know existed, otherwise) is the first and probably the only book you need to be one of those early adopters who score fastest. Perry's books are always essential. This one is perhaps more so than usual."

—JOHN CARLTON, THE MOST RESPECTED AND RIPPED-OFF VETERAN COPYWRITER ON THE WEB

"Aw, the whole thing makes my head hurt. But other than puffery about 600-million customers, Perry's an honest man in a field rife with charlatans. If anybody can make practical sense of Facebook for marketers, it's Perry. He has his finger on its truth—as advertising media not social media. He also realizes there is a short window of time during which the offers greatest opportunity. He identified this with Google AdWords. Now this book shows how to capitalize on ideal timing with this media. Finally, he is a well-disciplined direct-response practitioner who holds this accountable for ROI. I bestow my 'No B.S. blessing.'"

—DAN S. KENNEDY, LEGENDARY DIRECT MARKETING ADVISOR
AND AUTHOR OF THE *NO B.S.* BOOK SERIES, WWW.NoBSBooks.com

"Perry Marshall is amazing! He reinvented himself from engineer to white paper expert to become the world's leading expert in Google Adwords. Now with his secret weapon, Tom Meloche, he's reinvented himself again, this time as the guru in Facebook advertising . . . through which, he points out, you can access 600 million customers in 10 minutes."

—BOB BLY, AUTHOR OF OVER 60 BOOKS INCLUDING *COMPLETE IDIOT'S GUIDE TO DIRECT MARKETING, THE ONLINE COPYWRITER'S HANDBOOK,* AND *PUBLIC RELATIONS KIT FOR DUMMIES*

"Perry Marshall is a terrific writer who makes wonderful use of stories and analogies to illustrate a concept. He does this exceptionally well in the chapter on ad copy writing, 'The Power of Hidden Psychological Triggers.' That chapter alone is worth the price of this book.

"Many companies have tried Facebook ads and failed for one simple reason: they treated Facebook advertising like search advertising.

"Facebook is social advertising. Social advertising is about understanding and reaching the user. Not the user's behavior; but the actual person. This is where the book shines. It walks you through strategies of reaching your target audience based upon the person's social profile so that you aren't just accumulating 'Likes,' but actually gaining new customers.

"I'd recommend this book to anyone who is advertising, or wants to advertise, on Facebook. Social advertising is unique from most other types of advertising, and this book will teach you the concepts and how-tos you must understand so that your Facebook ads increase your overall profits."

—BRAD GEDDES, AUTHOR OF *ADVANCED GOOGLE ADWORDS*

"One of the things I love about Perry is that he always shoots from the hip. *Ultimate Guide to Facebook Advertising* is written with no holds barred, which means that all the 'juicy' tips that might get left out of other, similar books are all in this book. It's more than just a tactical 'how to.' It goes into the psychological aspects of ad writing specifically suited for Facebook and gives all kinds of practical advice for fan pages. So for anyone who really wants to get serious about Facebook advertising, this book is definitely a must read."

—SHELLEY ELLIS, CONTEXTUAL ADVERTISING EXPERT, WWW.CONTENTNETWORKINSIDER.COM

"Perry Marshall led the pack with Google AdWords back in 2006. He's still leading the pack today with *Ultimate Guide to Facebook Advertising*. Perry and Tom Meloche combine 'insider' knowledge of marketing on Facebook with proven marketing fundamentals for a powerful one-two punch that delivers results. Perry doesn't just theorize about how Facebook marketing works, he does it himself, and he's worked with thousands of others to hone his knowledge of this emerging landscape. If you're thinking of marketing on Facebook, or if you're already doing it, you'd be crazy to not get the *Ultimate Guide to Facebook Advertising*."

—CLATE MASK, PRESIDENT, INFUSIONSOFT

"Hands down, I have never seen a more comprehensive in-depth study of successful Facebook advertising than what you are holding in your hands. Perry has done it again, he's extracted the 'gold' within this amazing system of advertising that every astute marketer should devour and implement."

—ARI GALPER, FOUNDER AND CEO, UNLOCK THE GAME, WWW.UNLOCKTHEGAME.COM

"Perry and Tom not only understand every nuance of the technical aspects of getting Facebook ads to work for your business, they also understand the psychology behind what works and what doesn't when it comes to advertising online. If you're looking for an über-effective way to master the art of driving traffic to your offers through paid advertising, get this book—it truly is the ultimate guide!"

—MARI SMITH, CO-AUTHOR OF *FACEBOOK MARKETING: AN HOUR A DAY*

"*Ultimate Guide to Facebook Advertising* just might be your ultimate guide to earning a ton of money with this social media phenomenon. What you don't know about Facebook could hurt you and what you will learn about Facebook from this book definitely will help you. It's a fun and easy read and a surefire way to seriously increase your income."

—[THE LATE] JAY CONRAD LEVINSON, THE FATHER OF GUERRILLA MARKETING, AUTHOR OF *GUERRILLA MARKETING* SERIES OF BOOKS—OVER 21 MILLION SOLD; NOW IN 62 LANGUAGES

"Facebook advertising appears simple, but it's trickier than search engine marketing. In this book, Perry Marshall and Tom Meloche teach you the secret of 'Right Angle Marketing'—selling based on who people are and what they identify with. This is entirely different from Yahoo! or Google. They help you determine how to prioritize Facebook within your particular marketing mix. Then they take you by the hand and lead you through the minefield, showing you the tools, bidding techniques, and sales cycles of Facebook ads. Without their help, the odds are stacked against you. With their help, your chances of success are excellent."

—ALEX MANDOSSIAN, HERITAGE HOUSE PUBLISHING, AUTHOR OF *THE BUSINESS PODCASTING BIBLE*

"You're getting the *Ultimate Guide to Facebook Advertising* from the ultimate expert in Facebook ads. Keith Krance is a bonafide genius when it comes to advertising on Facebook. Don't walk—run to get a copy of this book."

—RUSS HENNEBERRY, EDITORIAL DIRECTOR AT RYAN DEISS'S DIGITAL MARKETER

"Perry Marshall delivers a huge amount of advertising experience and Keith Krance brings dynamic innovation. Together, they are well established as the leading Facebook marketers on the planet."

—JAMES SCHRAMKO, SUPERFASTBUSINESS.COM

Entrepreneur MAGAZINE'S

ULTIMATE
GUIDE TO
facebook
ADVERTISING
Third Edition

- Access more than a billion potential customers in 10 minutes
- Leverage the latest game-changers to **pinpoint your most profitable audiences**
- Master strategies and techniques of successful Facebook advertisers

PERRY MARSHALL   KEITH KRANCE   THOMAS MELOCHE

EP
Entrepreneur
PRESS®

Entrepreneur Press, Publisher
Cover Design: Andrew Welyczko
Production and Composition: Eliot House Productions

This publication is designed to provide accurate and authoritative information in regard to the
subject matter covered. It is sold with the understanding that the publisher is not engaged in
rendering legal, accounting or other professional services. If legal advice or other expert assistance is
required, the services of a competent professional person should be sought.

Library of Congress Cataloging-in-Publication Data
    Names: Marshall, Perry S., author. | Krance, Keith, author. | Meloche, Thomas, author.
    Title: Ultimate guide to Facebook advertising / by Perry Marshall, Keith Krance, and Thomas
        Meloche.
    Description: Third edition. | Irvine, California : Entrepreneur Media, Inc., [2017] | Series:
        Ultimate guide
    Identifiers: LCCN 2017037285| ISBN 978-1-59918-611-5 (alk. paper) | ISBN 1-59918-611-X
        (alk. paper)
    Subjects: LCSH: Facebook (Electronic resource) | Internet advertising.
    Classification: LCC HF6146.I58 M364 2017 | DDC 659.14/4—dc23
    LC record available at https://lccn.loc.gov/2017037285

Printed in the United States of America

22 21 20 19 18 17   10 9 8 7 6 5 4 3 2 1

Contents

CHAPTER 17

Proven Facebook-Friendly Offers **147**

CHAPTER 18

The Facebook Ad Builder **165**

CHAPTER 19

The 13 Elements of Persuasive Ad Copy by Ralph Burns **175**

CHAPTER 20

How I Know When My Copy Is Ready—Power Questions by Ryan Deiss **195**

CHAPTER 21

Creating Killer Ad Creatives That Reflect Your Hook by Molly Pittman

CHAPTER 22

Three-Step Video Ad Formula

CHAPTER 23

How to Find Your Perfect Audience by Sasha Sibree

Read this First—How to Use this Book

Mastering Facebook ads (or having someone on your team master Facebook ads) will transform your business (and most likely your life) in ways you may not be able to imagine at this stage. That's not a question to me anymore; I've seen too many entrepreneurs' lives change in positive ways to question this statement anymore.

The Ultimate Guide to Google AdWords *is the world's most popular book on Google ads. This book is the sister text for Facebook advertisers. To score your Google compatability visit www. IsAWforme.com.*

After overseeing more than $60 million in ad spending in over 100 different client ad accounts, which has generated several hundred million dollars for businesses of all sizes all over the world, one of the most important lessons I have learned is that it is not about mastering the Facebook ad platform—it is all about mastering the whole selling system, which begins inside Facebook.

Everyone has different levels of knowledge and experience. So, there will be chapters of this book that will be more helpful immediately than other chapters. And there will be chapters of this book that might not make perfect sense until you get more experience. Or, there might be chapters on a topic or strategy you may have already mastered. And that's OK.

This book is not meant to be read from cover to cover, although you can absolutely do that if you wish. However, this book is meant to be used as the ultimate reference guide to winning big with Facebook ads. I want you to feel free to skip around to different chapters that will help you right now. Or, refer back to chapters at a later date, even if you already read that chapter six months earlier because maybe when you first read that chapter you weren't quite ready for that topic.

Maybe you have some campaigns running right now that you would love to add some Facebook video ads to the mix, but you don't know where to start. Then, jump straight to Chapter 22. Or, maybe you recently got started running some simple Facebook ad campaigns, and you would like to get some higher click-through rates and lower cost-per-clicks on your ads—so you jump straight to Chapters 18 to 22, which are all about writing profitable, long-running ads.

Or, maybe you will read the book cover to cover over the next week and then once a month refer back to specific chapters relating to writing ad copy, creating killer ad creatives, "hacking the hook," or one of the other key elements we reveal in this book that can quickly turn a losing campaign into a winning campaign.

This last example is how I would recommend using this book. This book (along with the free online bonuses at www.perrymarshall.com/fbtools) is meant to be that trusted guide you can always turn to when you need a great strategy, an answer, or to just feel more confident about moving forward and hitting "publish" on your campaigns.

And to get the most up-to-date free content, please subscribe to the podcast "Perpetual Traffic," which I co-host with Ralph Burns, CEO of the Dominate Web Media Agency, and Molly Pittman, Vice President, DigitalMarketer, which has over 400 five-star reviews and some of the most cutting-edge strategies out on Facebook advertising today.

—Keith Krance

Go Here Now to Get $99 of Tools,
Videos, and Case Studies, along
with Critical Algorithm, Platform,
and Policy Updates,
FREE

Go to www.perrymarshall.com/fbtools

Chapter 1

Facebook Takes Over Planet Earth

PEOPLE ARE WALKING DOWN THE STREET BANGING INTO LIGHT POLES BECAUSE THEIR FACES ARE BURIED IN FACEBOOK. THEREIN LIES YOUR OPPORTUNITY.

The most precious commodity in the world is attention. Facebook is monopolizing it. Chomping it like a hungry beast. The average American spends five hours per day on Facebook. Wherever you are right now, look up and someone around you is probably on Facebook.

> "*When you give everyone a voice and give people power, the system usually ends up in a really good place. So, what we view our role as, is giving people that power.*"
>
> —Mark Zuckerberg

This book is about how to get in front of those people, get them to open their wallets, and then dominate markets because you're better at this game than all your competitors.

Be warned right this minute that Facebook ads are a serious game. It's a blood sport—not something you just casually dabble in. If you get really good at it, it's a $1,000-per-hour skill and more. It gives you the ability to move mountains and nations. You can literally create cultures and movements at will.

But if you're just going to goof around with it . . . play around . . . try a few experiments—forget it. Go waste your money some other way because 90 percent of Facebook advertisers merely dabble with it, and then Facebook ads amount to nothing more than an expensive tax write-off.

If you're going to take this game seriously, then you bought the right book. **And you should also avail yourself to the online supplement at www.perrymarshall.com/ fbtools.** Go there right now, and download the goodies.

Is Facebook Good or Bad?

I do not think that it is a "good" thing that a billion people are spending this much time on Facebook. I didn't think it was a good thing when the same numbers of people were watching TV for five hours a day, either.

But nobody asked me. And they didn't ask you. That's just what people do.

If you're going to be successful as a marketer or entrepreneur, you must choose to live in the "is" world—not the "should be" world. In the "is" world, 95 percent of people float around in a miasma of mild hypnosis, looking forward to their next hit of "Like" and "Share" happy juice or to extract their pound of flesh out of some bloke who disagrees with them about Donald Trump.

This book is all about how you get inside their head and get them to do what **you** want them to do. Whether you're a church, a school, a winery, a life coach, a car manufacturer, or if you sell aluminum siding, you've got a job to do.

People are going to spend their time and money somewhere. If they spend their time and money with you, you succeed. If they spend it with someone else, you fail.

The fact that people are in a state of partial hypnosis helps you sell them stuff. In this book, you'll learn how to harness that power.

WORKING VS. PLAYING

Now, the very first thing you have to do is get real with yourself and realize that for you, playing around on social media is NOT the same as RUNNING social media or CONTROLLING social media—pulling the puppet strings of the world.

Millions of people quit their jobs to start a business. They're essentially being supported by their spouses. She goes to work every day, and while she's changing bedpans at the hospital, she thinks her husband is working.

When in fact he's just goofing off on Facebook all day. Doing stuff that sorta kinda looks like work.

And making zero money.

That guy is like the chef who, instead of cooking, just stands in the kitchen and shovels food in his mouth all day.

Well, this is a book about making money on Facebook—not screwing around on Facebook. Facebook ads is a serious endeavor. It's a profession. You will get nowhere with those bad habits. You either pull the strings of the Matrix from outside the Matrix . . . or you're in the Matrix being entertained by the Matrix. You can't do both.

I deleted the standard Facebook app from my phone. I hardly ever use Facebook. When I do use Facebook, I use the phone browser instead of the app.

I never log into Facebook as a standard user until after 5:30 P.M. Most days I don't log in at all. But on the very same day I may spend hours in the Facebook interface and Facebook advertising app being the chef and pulling the strings in the Matrix.

Never confuse activity with productivity. The two are not the same.

As a Facebook advertiser, you are tasked with injecting creativity into the system, then measuring and tracking the results. You use your tracking tools. Pay careful attention to what works and what doesn't. Notice stuff. Accept your job, which is to influence the hypnotized masses who are coming to Facebook for their entertainment addiction.

You are not the guy who comes to the restaurant and feeds his face for five hours. You work in the restaurant. You serve up great dishes. You only sample enough of the soup to know whether it tastes good or bad . . . then you go on and create more great cuisine.

Sorry if this sounds preachy. But I have many, many customers and clients whose productivity, sales, profits, and income absolutely skyrocketed after they . . .

- Deleted the Facebook app from their phone (along with Twitter, LinkedIn, and others)
- Realized that the world is in an incessant, never-ending conspiracy to rob them of time, attention, creativity, and mental space
- Closed the Facebook tab in their browser
- Entirely stopped using Facebook in the usual fashion during work hours
- Blocked all email notifications from Facebook and other social media
- Halted ALL smart phone notifications from all social media apps—no banners on the screen, no little red numbers on your app icons, no distractions.

Go on. Do all of the above—now. If you don't, it will be devilishly difficult to master this thing. Instead, it will master you.

Facebook has taken over the world. Facebook is the aquarium that lots of people live in. Facebook is your portal to influencing those people—their behavior, their opinions, their purchases, their relationships. You need to pull the levers without letting Facebook take control of you.

Facebook knows what its members look like, think, enjoy, and visit because they are the world's largest:

- Photo-sharing site,
- Thought-sharing site,
- Liking site,
- Linking site, and
- Demographic and psychographic gathering engine.

Even with Google's gargantuan lead, Facebook will possibly become the world's largest advertising site, especially as the internet continues its trajectory toward easy mobile device access.

FACEBOOK IS THE ONLY COMPANY THAT OWNS THE MOBILE PHONE

The majority of internet use is now via smartphones and tablets. This is bad news for all the old-school internet companies, but it's good news for Facebook. Why?

Because Facebook is the only company that is putting FULL-SCREEN DISPLAY ADS in front of mobile phone users and getting away with it on a daily basis. They have trained people to accept this.

Nearly all other online ads are either in apps or tiny, inconsequential banner ads. Facebook puts display ads and videos right in the middle of the news feed that many people see dozens of every day. People actually share Facebook ads (and good ads will get shared thousands of times!). Plus, many times, those ads don't really seem like ads. Above the ad, the post says "Suzy Smith likes ACME corporation" so the ad has implied endorsement.

This works. On a massive scale.

You can upload a customer phone or email list to Facebook, and Facebook will probably recognize about half of them. You can ask Facebook to target a million people who are just like your customers, and Facebook knows who those people are.

As exciting as all of this is, it is important for advertisers to remember that Facebook did not build the site for us, the advertisers. They built it for regular users and for themselves.

The hottest young college grads Facebook hires from the world's top universities don't say, "I want to work at Facebook to help them maximize ad revenue." Please know that even despite Facebook's massive gains in the ad department, the company doesn't exist simply to send you customers.

Regardless of why Zuckerberg built Facebook or what high ideals his staffers may hold, the personal demographic information Facebook collects is tremendously valuable to us advertisers.

Facebook is not stupid.

It is more closely connected with its advertisers than any other platform on the planet. Facebook visionaries already have years' worth of additional ideas to implement. How do we know this? We see the ideas publicly volunteered every day on Facebook pages by Facebook advertisers.

Facebook knows more about you than your husband or wife. They know what sites you visit, they know a great deal of what you buy, and they have bought data from all kinds of other companies and appended it to their database so they know what you respond to. Facebook even has suicide prevention tools, and AI (artificial intelligence) may detect depression way before doctors or parents.

They know the one million people in the world who are most like you and like the same things you like and buy the same things you buy.

Adult supervision on Facebook is minimal, which is probably why it is so absolutely brilliant. The company aggressively hires fresh college graduates—the brightest college grads on the planet—but still fresh graduates.

These are the smart kids—smarter than you, smarter than us. Some have never had a "real" job outside of Facebook.

They have never tried to live off revenue generated by an ad. They do not feel your pain. Remember that. It is really important.

To use Facebook's paid advertising tools effectively, it is important to understand just how much its creators and designers are not really trying to help you. Fortunately, they do need cash, and we do need clicks, so we can get some great work done together. We focus on the clicks, and they focus on connecting the world.

Facebook has the potential, real potential, to be highly relevant for decades to come. Our rule of thumb is the founder's rule: when you have a dynamic and visionary founder running a business, better to bet on that business continuing to be a success for as long as you see that founder at the helm.

We suggest that as long as you see Mark Zuckerberg engaged at Facebook, you should plan on Facebook being a dynamic and growing, competitive place to advertise.

Oh, Mark was born in 1984.

He will probably be around for a long, long time.

1984? It turns out that Little Brother is the one who's watching you.

ONE TOOL TO RULE THEM ALL, AND IN THE FACEBOOK BIND THEM

One Tool to rule them all,
One Tool to find them,
One Tool to bring them all,
And in the Facebook bind them.

This poem should haunt Google. (I do know for a fact that Google is scared to death of Facebook.) We wrote it as a bit of a taunt in the first edition because so many people were predicting Facebook's early demise. We predicted the opposite and were proved right. Facebook has indeed created one tool to bind the entire world together and Facebook, not Google, is in charge. Facebook currently reports that two billion people connect on Facebook every month. Two billion. Say that number a few times, and let it sink in.

But wait, there's more!

Do you remember when Facebook acquired WhatsApp for 19 billion dollars? WhatsApp now has over a billion users, making it the most popular messaging app of all time. Facebook also acquired Instagram, which now has 700 million users. In addition, Facebook has communities on Messenger and Oculus. Facebook advertising tools are your gateway to all of these communities and more.

Facebook isn't sitting still. If you look closely, you can see their hopes for the future. Facebook has acquired a whole series of smaller technical companies, acquiring technology for fitness tracking, speech and facial recognition, computer vision, augmented reality, video compression, and machine learning. (And some people thought Snapchat really had a fighting chance!)

The Facebook universe will continue to grow larger, more prevalent, and more powerful for years to come. One tool to rule them all, and in the Facebook bind them.

Smartphone Facebook users are usually continually logged in. Facebook reports mobile advertising is 85 percent of the total Facebook advertising revenue. This is no big surprise, as mobile users are connected to Facebook nearly 24/7. Facebook on the phone is the only way to reach some of your customers. Plus, you can find customers you would never have imagined, such as visitors from another State currently travelling through your city within ten miles of your business. You reach them without even knowing it with, "Come in for a special 30 percent discount!"

Facebook users now check into your business when they visit you, without you even asking. No more pathetic "please like me" signs. Mobile makes it easy. When users check into your business, they automatically announce to their friends where they are and what they are doing. Friday nights in the big city need never be lonely again.

But wait, there's more.

Facebook is supporting their community in big ways. They've made it simple to live stream video with Facebook Live, creating a whole new media form. Websites and apps can leverage Facebook's login. This is amazingly powerful now that so many users never log out of Facebook. Capture your customer's attention with live video, collect critical contact information, and get them to call you, register for events, and even donate to you, fast and easy. Literally, it's all at the touch of a button.

One tool to rule them all, and in the Facebook bind them.

YOUR MISSION, SHOULD YOU CHOOSE TO ACCEPT IT

So what do you do with all of this information about Facebook? Simple. Your mission is to buy a click for $1, turn it into $2, and then make more profit than your competitors do from your $2. This is your mission, and it has moved to Facebook. It is a new platform but a very old mission.

The rest is just strategy and tactics. Many existing strategies and tactics that we have taught to over 100,000 Google advertisers work directly in Facebook.

You need to understand your sales funnel, craft a compelling ad, have a focused goal for your landing page, and track and follow up with your leads and your customers. More important, you want to do this automatically.

We will teach you the strategy and tactics required to fulfill your mission: to get those clicks and to turn them into customers.

Some tactics, especially those built around audience targeting and bidding strategies, have changed dramatically for Facebook. Don't worry, we will show you the secrets we have found to be successful on Facebook.

Facebook has dramatically simplified online advertising by making audience targeting and bidding quite easy. Your number one job is creating ads and offers.

Your Mission, a Penny at a Time

Those who like numbers will appreciate how powerful your fundamental mission is. Depending on the size of your market, your mission may also be stated as, "Your mission is to buy a click for $1 and to reliably and repeatedly turn it into $.01 worth of pure profit."

This is how pro gamblers think. If they can find a game where betting a dollar nets them a penny, they are in heaven. They sit there for hours and hours playing round after round trying to bet as much as possible to earn that one percent net.

They even have a name for it. They call it "grinding." The best part about grinding when you're a digital marketer is that you do not have to actually sit at a table in a smoke-filled room. Digital grinding happens in that area of the web now called the "cloud," and clouds are much nicer than smoke-filled rooms.

Also, you do not have to live in Vegas. In the online world, the game comes to you.

Think about this for a moment: a one percent net ROI that may be achieved within a matter of minutes from when the investment was made. What is the return on a dollar, on an annual basis, that can bring one percent every three minutes? The figure is so large it makes even Goldman Sachs blush. A penny, if enough clicks are available, is a fortune. Empires are built on a 1 percent net profit.

Don't despise making a penny, especially if you can make it reliably and repeatedly. Instead, focus on how to make a lot more pennies. Focus on how to get a lot more clicks.

Perhaps it is on Facebook?

For your sake, we hope so. Because advertising on Facebook is actually a lot of fun.

For some advertisers, using Facebook paid advertising to find new customers is also stunningly easy. Take the quiz in Chapter 2 to find out if you are one of the lucky ones. Facebook advertising may be a great fit that will cause new customers to fall into your lap.

■ ■ ■

Get tools, video, and case studies with updates at
www.perrymarshall.com/fbtools.

One Good Ad Can Change the Game

If you're anything like me, when you scan through the Facebook Business Manager, Ads Manager, or Power Editor for the first time, it looks a little like you're reading code or a foreign language. It can even give you cold sweats!

"OK, where do I start?"

"How do I structure my campaigns?"

"How many ads? How many ad sets? How many images? How many versions of the ad copy?"

"How big should my target audience be?"

"And how the heck do I manage this stuff without wasting a bunch of money?"

> *"In the best Thai restaurant in India, the Executive Chef uses two stainless steel skillets, and a torn-up chef's knife that you can buy at Walmart for $20. That's it. You don't need a lot."*
>
> --Tim Ferriss on Accelerated Learning (Meta-Learning)

Do any of those thoughts sound familiar?

The truth is, you shouldn't even be spending that much time inside the Power Editor or the Ads Manager when you first get started.

After overseeing over $58 million in ad spend at the time of this writing (either with our full-service ads management agency or coaching/consulting clients), and now averaging over $2.5 million per month in ad spend in over 100 ad accounts, we've seen a lot of what works, what doesn't work, and where many of the "small hinges that swing big doors" are hidden.

Side note: that $58 million ad spend has generated over 13,000,000,000 impressions, over 400,000,000 video views, over 200,000,000 clicks, millions of leads, and hundreds of millions in revenue. (Yes, that was 13 billion—not million. And YES, mere impressions DO matter, contrary to what some pure direct response marketers might try and tell you—as you will soon discover later in this book.) So, let's talk about how you jump-start this journey with a few related stories.

ACCELERATED LEARNING TECHNIQUES

Let's say you just won a free trip to Beijing, China to tour some of the biggest manufacturing facilities in China. You have a fast-growing home improvement brand with mostly DIY content. You've been looking to add some physical products to your catalog because up to this point most of your sales have been digital products or physical products you promote as an affiliate.

The Problem: The flight to Beijing departs in 26 days, and you don't know an inkling of Mandarin.

Yes, you could get by with only speaking English because most likely the people you will be meeting will speak English, but you also know that if you want to standout and make a great impression, you really need to speak the language.

You need to learn some Mandarin so you can communicate with the leaders over there in their native language—the ultimate sign of respect.

LEARNING A NEW LANGUAGE IN 26 DAYS

If you really want to be able to communicate with the influential Chinese people on your trip, do you think you would start with learning all the slang and the most complex phrases, words, or symbols?

I hope not.

What you should do is use the 80/20 Principle.

If you want to learn any language fast, you need to look for the shortcuts. Focus on the most important building blocks of that language, find the most common words and phrases people use in every day conversation, and spend ALL your time learning *that* stuff. The core elements make it easier for you to have a basic conversation in any environment, as well as give you the foundational components that make it easier to learn all the complexities of that language.

The same goes for quickly learning how to cook great, learning how to play the guitar or the piano, learning to dance, and the list goes on and on. For example: If you can learn how to play the four most popular music chords, then you can already play almost any song at a basic level.

Don't believe me? Do a YouTube search for "Axis of Awesome—4 Chord Song." (The video has over 43 million views.)

Tim Ferriss wrote an entire book on Accelerated Learning: *The 4-Hour Chef: The Simple Path to Cooking Like a Pro, Learning Anything, and Living the Good Life* (New Harvest, 2012).

And Perry Marshall wrote an entire book about how to use the 80/20 Principle to grow your business quickly, *80/20 Sales and Marketing: The Definitive Guide to Working Less and Making More* (Entrepreneur Press, 2013).

FACEBOOK ADS AND FLYING AIRPLANES

After I graduated high school, I went to college at the University of North Dakota ("UND Fighting Sioux"), one of the top aviation schools. I started flying the first semester of my freshman year, but I didn't jump right into flying a Boeing 737 or a CRJ 700 Regional jet, which was the airplane I flew for my last four years at Horizon Air, a subsidiary of Alaska Airlines. I racked up about 3,000 hours in that airplane before I left to pursue my entrepreneurial mission.

But I didn't START flying that airplane.

I started in a Piper Warrior (similar to a Cessna 172). See Figure 2.1.

Even though the Warrior looks a lot smaller and a lot easier to fly around in, that cockpit is still super overwhelming in the beginning.

Just like the Power Editor and the Ads Manager!

When I got ready for my very first flight, I was like: "Wow, what do I do? Where should I start?"

FIGURE 2.1–Piper Warrior

Luckily, my flight instructor, who was there right beside me, said: "Hey Keith! Don't worry, man: I got you. I'll be sitting right beside you with my own yoke and set of rudders—I'll be guiding you the whole time. All you need to do is worry about flying the airplane."

"You only have three main aircraft controls to worry about: The yoke, the rudders, and the throttle and I want you looking outside the airplane 90 percent of the time, focusing on the horizon and other reference points. As for all those instruments in the cockpit—you can forget about almost all of them for right now. There are six primary instruments, but you will only focus on three to four of them for now—the Airspeed Indicator, the Altimeter, the Attitude Indicator (Artificial Horizon), and the Heading Indicator. That's it. Forget everything else until I say not to," he said.

So that's what I did.

About 13 flights later, my instructor endorsed me to take my first "Solo Flight."

And I did it.

I was definitely nervous, but I'm pretty sure my instructor was more nervous than I was watching me from the ground!

The crazy thing is that about 40 hours later I passed my private pilot written test, oral exam, and practical flight exam and received my private pilot certificate.

That was a good feeling.

The funny thing is, flying the Piper Warrior isn't much different than flying a CRJ 700 or a Boeing 747. The cockpit has a lot more dials, there's hundreds more procedures and systems to memorize, but flying the airplane is not really any different.

Ever since I took my first solo flight, I have had this weird fantasy about riding as a passenger in the cabin of a commercial airline flight when they had some crazy emergency and then I come up to the cockpit and help fly the airplane down to safety. I'd be the hero and save the day for everyone on board.

I know, I'm a dork.

But the crazy thing is if that really did happen, and I was on board when I had just gotten my student pilot certificate, I WOULD have been able to fly the airplane down to safety.

Because I had the critical foundation necessary—I knew how to fly the airplane. I couldn't have done it as a career at that point, or handled a bunch of malfunctions, like engine failures or hydraulic failures without a senior pilot walking me through the abnormal or emergency procedures.

But chances are, I really would have been able to fly the airplane down and land it safely on the runway.

THE FACEBOOK FLIGHT PLAN™

The ceiling of your advertising profit, scalability, and the amount of wasted money swallowed up by Facebook, is directly dependent on the quality of ad creation foundation you build.

The skill to be able to create a Facebook ad campaign once and let it run month after month after month, targeting millions of users, generating thousands of leads and customers automatically, all while simultaneously growing your audience and systematically moving people from being completely unaware of the problem your product solves, to being fully aware of the problem and having intent to solve that problem, and finally to having intent to want to buy YOUR product or service, is a beautiful thing.

We call this the Facebook Flight Plan™ (We go through this in detail in Chapters 14 and 15.)

Think of it as your Facebook aeronautical chart: A system where you're perpetually building awareness, building fans, generating leads and customers, and creating goodwill with your audience all along the way. This book will help you build your own FANS™ system.

The ability to build a perpetual system like this is an acquired skill; it does not take raw talent. People are not born into this world as Facebook ad magicians. It takes training, practice, the right tools, the right system, and the right guide or instructor. (Think of the authors of this book as your personal Facebook Flight Instructors.)

The David Copperfields of the world are never natural-born magicians. They are relentless, focused individuals, who will do whatever it takes to master their craft. In fact, I was fortunate to spend a few hours chatting with the coveted 2016 Academy of Magical Arts "Magician of the Year" award winner, master illusionist, and prodigy Derek DelGaudio and the legendary director Frank Oz. I recently spent four days in New York working with Victoria Labalme, an amazing communications and public speaking coach. She happens to be married to Frank Oz, who created *The Muppets*, *Sesame Street*, and dozens of other great movies. (He also played Yoda in *Star Wars*.) While having some drinks and chatting one night, the discussion of mastering your craft came up—and Frank talked about how, at a very young age, Derek would spend countless hours every day in his room alone, practicing card tricks, then progressing to practicing the true art of illusion—today, he is changing the entire industry of magic and illusion. Truly mastering his craft.

David Blaine recently said it best: "Derek isn't just raising the bar, he's moving the whole stadium. He's changing the game—and it's exhilarating to watch."

The Blue Angels pilots were not born with wings on. They were relentless, focused individuals, who got into the best flight training in the world and mastered their craft.

With the right tools, training, and relentless hard work, anyone can become a master craftsman.

The fact that you are reading this book right now tells me that you are on the way to becoming a master craftsman. Just like a Master Illusionist, a Master Chef, a grand Master Martial Artist, a Master Orchestra Conductor or Maestro, a Master Architect, a U.S. Navy Blue Angel pilot, an Airline Chief Pilot—a true Facebook Ads Master.

COPY AND PASTE TEMPLATES OR RARE AND VALUABLE SKILLS?

Everybody wants the copy-and-paste templates. They want paint by numbers. But they also want big profits. They want scalable ad campaigns that don't quickly burn out or take tons and tons of ad rotation. Sorry, you can't have your cake and eat it too. (Sometimes you can for a while, but it will fade, I promise.)

WARNING: If you just want copy-and-paste templates, where there's not much thinking involved at all, then this is not the book for you.

Quit reading right now.

Close the book and go to Google or YouTube and do a search for "Facebook ads for lazy people." I'm sure you will find some great stuff. But if you want to build a masterpiece that's worth 10 to 1,000 times more then what you put into it, in terms of time, energy, and money and you want to build a masterpiece that pays you over and over again—true residual income and wealth that will pay you for the rest of your life—then this book is for you.

I don't necessarily mean monetary wealth. I'm talking about the priceless wealth of knowledge and skills acquired by reading this book, along with taking action and practicing what you learn (both from this book and from our free online bonus content.)

This book will give you plenty of templates, examples, checklists, and step-by-step training, but if you consume the content in this book while simultaneously practicing what you learn, you will train your mind to be able to tackle any given situation and win.

You will have an understanding of the social selling environment, the five critical audience awareness levels, stages of intent, ad building frameworks that set you up for long-running, scalable campaigns, how the algorithm works and why it's important to have a basic understanding of the algorithm, key rules of thumb and when you need to break those rules, troubleshooting procedures, and so much more.

You will crush it. Your brand will be unstoppable. You will "move the stadium" in your industry.

You will develop skills that are rare and VERY valuable.

My mission is not to create marketing robots. My mission is to create architects and engineers who truly understand how to systematically turn a Facebook user from a stranger into a customer without being annoying and overly salesy. These skills will transfer over to all the other social media channels out there as well as the ones that don't even exist yet.

JUST ONE GOOD AD CAN CHANGE THE GAME

Once you really get the principles in this book, it's possible to create ONE great Facebook ad that can blow up your business overnight. I've seen it happen too many times to know for a fact that it is not luck. It is all about having a deeper understanding than you ever thought you would. And it will happen fast—starting with the very next chapter when you see this ridiculous ad I ran for a crazy experiment.

One good ad can literally power the entire Perpetual Traffic System if you get it right. The kind of ad that simultaneously and automatically generates fans, leads, customers, and creates brand awareness and goodwill along the way. This kind of ad also makes it MUCH EASIER to scale out your campaigns without watching your conversion costs skyrocket when you increase ad budgets.

Sound too good to be true?

You be the judge.

In the next chapter, you will see the results of a very risky experiment I ran where I created a new health and fitness brand from scratch, with three divisions: a local personal training gym, a digital product business offering meal plans and workout programs, and an ecommerce division selling physical products. I grew the business using essentially one Facebook ad and recorded the entire process. (In the next chapter, you will see why it was so risky.)

I went to GoDaddy and bought a new domain, installed Wordpress, created a new Facebook page, created a new business manager, and a new ad account. We quickly built some landing pages, created a lead magnet for each business division, and finally— created and published a Facebook ad campaign that is still running today. (And is the ONLY ad running.)

Chapter 3

The Risky One-Ad Experiment

In late 2016, at our company we pre-sold an online Facebook ads course called "Facebook Momentum." It was a course designed for the beginner to intermediate level Facebook advertiser—and we made it available for a discount for pre-orders for a four-day sale about two months before it was live.

This course is also a prerequisite for anybody who wants to attend a signature event—our Facebook Account Manager Certification program, which is held live and in-person. The purpose of this event is to show up at the event with some decent Facebook knowledge or experience, and leave four to five days later as a Facebook ads ninja.

> "You give a poor man a fish, and you feed him for a day. You teach him to fish and you give him an occupation that will feed him for a lifetime."
>
> —Lau Tzu (Chinese Proverb)

We named the course "Facebook Momentum" because we know how important it is to get some quick wins early in the game of running Facebook ads. For example, if you had a lofty goal to own a Gulfstream G6 private jet and be your own pilot, so you could be almost anywhere in the world in just a few hours, unfortunately you cannot start your pilot training in that aircraft. (Maybe you buy the jet with the extra revenue generating from all the ninja strategies we show you in this book!☺) Of

FROM BEGINNER TO NEW CLIENTS IN DAYS

By the way, the case studies of several of our graduates are pretty ridiculous. Some of them landed high-paying clients almost immediately, some quickly built or grew a thriving consultant or agency business, some have become "Advisors" inside one of our coaching programs at Facebook Ads University over at our company, some have become a part-time account managers so they can sharpen their skills on big client accounts and get some cash flow while they build up their own consulting business or "passion business" at the same time. And some graduates are keeping it simple and just crushing it working full time with our agency, so they can leave the stresses of chasing clients and working with difficult or unrealistic clients to someone else—and they can just focus on running ads. (And maybe searching for somewhere fun and exciting to adventure to or work from since the agency team is mostly all virtual . . .)

Our last certification event was in Austin, Texas—and we took those folks who grabbed the first 15 seats on a tour of the Austin Facebook Ads Headquarters, which was really cool. We've been fortunate to build some great relationships with our various Partner Managers over at Facebook's Austin office—at the time of this writing, Ralph Burns and I have visited them or had lunch over there about seven to eight times—we now try and stop in and say hi or have a meeting whenever we are in Austin for any other reason.

course, *you* want to be the pilot so you can fly your own jet—but you can't just start your flying lessons in the G6. You need to start in something smaller, like a Piper Warrior or Cessna 172, and learn how to fly a smaller, simpler airplane first. As you build momentum and gain confidence, you will start adding more complexity, more maneuvers, memorizing more rules and procedures, flying in more adverse conditions, and going on longer flights.

One afternoon, a few weeks after I started working on the content and deliverables for the course, I just finished a great workout and hopped in the idea machine (aka: the shower) to clean up and got back to work. As I rinsed the conditioner out of my hair, an idea hit me like a ton of bricks. I tried to think of some case study examples I could use to demonstrate some of the important points in the course. You see, one of the biggest challenges with teaching Facebook ads strategies to the masses is that the best strategy for one type of business might not work for another type of business. Suddenly, an idea came to me. It was that I should create a new business from scratch—with three divisions: a local personal training gym, a digital product business offering meal plans and workout programs, and an ecommerce division selling physical products. And record the entire process—from getting the new domain to running the Facebook ads, and we would use this new brand as the guinea pig to test, and *hopefully* show proof of how powerful our system is.

If the campaigns bombed then we would eat crow. I would look like the fool offering guidance with his Tarot Cards in the streets . . . The cards he found on the sidewalk in the previous town he rode in on his horse from the week before.

"FACEBOOK MOMENTUM"—THE PROMISE

This course is called "Facebook Momentum," and was built for beginner to intermediate Facebook advertisers. There were two main goals when creating this program. One was to help someone get some quick momentum by getting ads up quickly and getting fast results, thus motivating you to keep going and start getting into the more complex strategies after you get the foundational concepts. The other goal was to show you how to create a foundational ad campaign that will set you up for long-term scale with your campaigns—an ad that will resonate with cold audiences, and generate conversions.

I really wanted to show how big of an impact making ONE GOOD AD can make on a business. So, after we quickly built the landing pages, created the new Business Manager, set up tracking, etc. I created one "Like Ad" campaign with three different images and one "Link Post Ad" long copy Website Conversions campaign with two different images. We did not use video ads for this program because we wanted to prove that you can still get great results without using video as long as you follow the formula. And if a long-copy ad performs well, then you can just use that content as the storyboard for a video ad!

RESULTS AFTER ONE WEEK

After one week, we generated 612 new subscribers and 5,220 new quality fans with an ad spend of $1,011.88 (see Figures 3.1 and 3.2 on page 20).

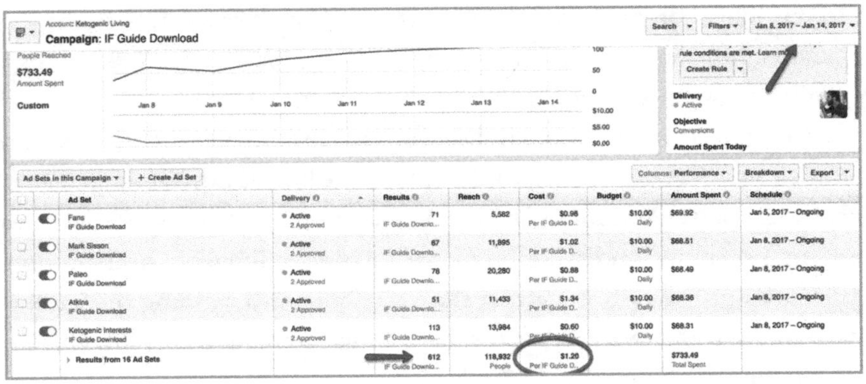

FIGURE 3.1–New Leads After One Week

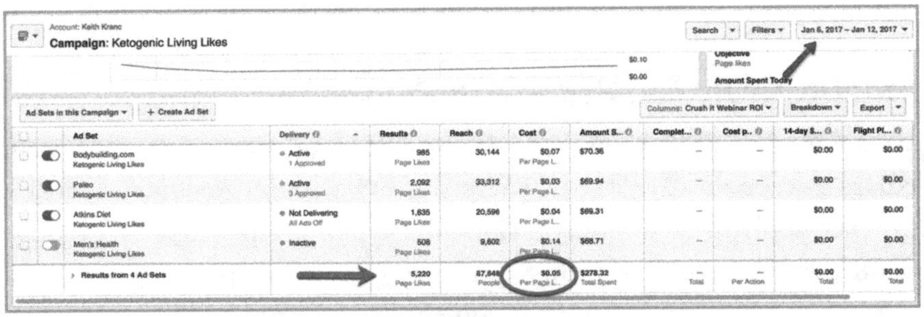

FIGURE 3.2–New Quality Fans After One Week

RESULTS AFTER ONE MONTH

After 30 days and just 15 minutes of optimization (recorded inside the course), and no more ads, we had exactly 3,000 subscribers and 33,000 fans, spending just $100 per day. Without touching anything. No more ads. No more optimization.

After a couple weeks, I felt like I could finally take a breath. It worked even better than we expected it to! If you would like to learn more about this course please visit www.perrymarshall.com/fbtools.

The rest of this book will take you through the exact formula that we used to have this success, along with some of the advanced strategies like video ads, troubleshooting, and scaling out your campaigns.

Please take this book very seriously. And remember this quote from Peter Parker's Uncle Ben, "with great power comes great responsibility." When you get good at this—when you truly master your craft, you can make a big impact on many,

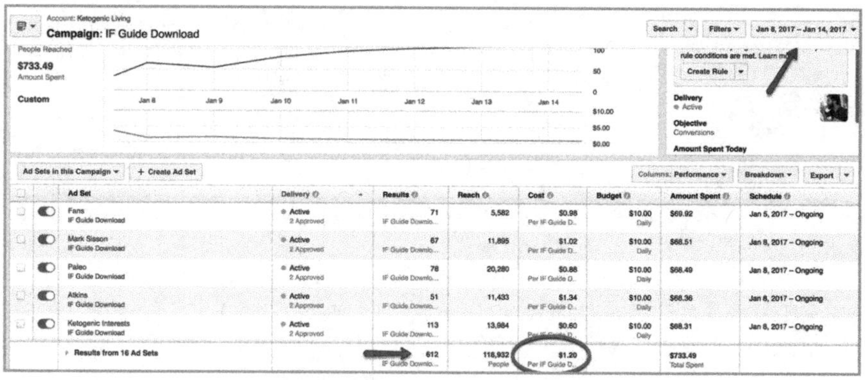

FIGURE 3.3–New Subscribers After 30 Days

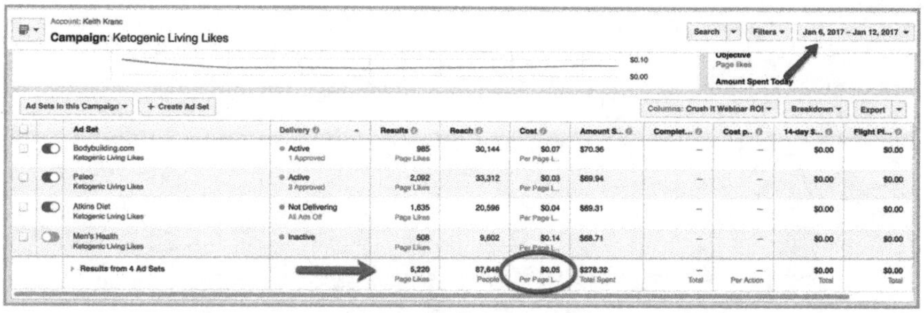

FIGURE 3.4–New Fans After 30 Days

many people. So please be careful with what you choose to promote and how you choose to promote it.

Chapter 4

A Tale of Identical Twins Separated at Birth

TWO TWIN BOYS AND TWO SETS OF PARENTS

It's 1985. The movie *Back the Future* just swept the nation.

Every 16-year-old boy with ten good digits is begging his parents to get him a guitar so he can play like Chuck Berry or maybe more like Eddie Van Halen.

There are no personal computers, internet, or social media.

Separated at birth, identical twins Rick and James never met each other, but somehow both of them grew up to become amazing guitar players. They are 48 years old, and coincidentally, they both transitioned into becoming guitar instructors in each of their respective cities. Must have been that good ole' gut instinct or maybe they have some telepathic connection they don't know about. Either way, they're both guitar instructors now and it's a pretty good time to be a guitar teacher, although competition is fierce.

Rick grew up in New York City with his father and stepmother raising him.

Rick's father was an equities day-trader for a large financial investment firm and his stepmother was an amazing violinist for a popular folk-rock band. The bulk of his father's

> "*R*eady are you? For eight hundred years have I trained Jedi. My own counsel will I keep on who is to be trained. A Jedi must have the deepest commitment, the most serious mind."
>
> —Yoda

pay came from him making bold and swift moves on a minute-by-minute basis every single day. His mother was one of the best violinists on the east coast, if not the best. But she also knew how lucky she was to land a spot with such a talented band at a young age like she did. The lead singer was a super talented songwriter, and they worked with the top producer in the industry the entire time she was with the band. Deep down, she knew that those two factors were huge influences in her success, notoriety, and continual growth throughout her career.

James grew up in a rural town, 25 minutes outside of Seattle, Washington with his mother and stepfather raising him.

James' mother was a sought-after software architect and his stepfather was a conductor of a famous orchestra. His mother's industry-topping fees and high demand came as a result of her reputation, which was that her designs constantly produced amazing products in the marketplace. Software engineers loved working with her because they always knew the end result would be a product that outperformed everything else. Her reputation was based on finished product performance in the marketplace, NOT just on the quality of her designs. She played the long game, and it paid off. By the time James was a teenager, the only calls his mom would even consider were from companies at the Microsoft and Amazon level, companies spending upwards of $12 billion a year just on RandD.

James and Ricky both have similar guitar skills and both are great natural teachers. But for some reason, James has a booming business, and Ricky is struggling to get by.

James has a waiting list a mile long to get lessons from him personally. He also has 12 junior instructors under him who he trained in his teaching methodology, and they all have pretty packed calendars as well.

Most of Ricky's clients come through referrals, along with a little newspaper advertising. He is just as good of a teacher as James—maybe even better. He doesn't get why it's so hard building this business when he knows he is truly one of the best guitar teachers in the country.

The problem is that most people don't know it.

A TALE OF TWO DIFFERENT PARTY GOERS

James and Ricky both get invited to all kinds of different parties or lounges or clubs throughout New York and Seattle. These social gatherings range from high-class parties in a private club or nice home of one of their student's parents, to the local pub down the street where aspiring musicians are hanging out, all with the hopes and dreams to be the next Eric Clapton or Jimi Hendrix.

First, let's follow Ricky into a party at one of his top student's parents' penthouse apartment in the Upper East Side of Manhattan.

His taxi slows down to an almost complete stop in front of the bellman. Ricky jumps out and notices the two huge statues in front of the entrance of the building, right behind the bellman, who seems to stand just about as tall as one of the statues. He's gotta be at least 6'5" and about 260 lbs. "Ex-football player for sure," Ricky tells himself as he tells him that he's going up the Elsberry residence.

"Oh, that's the penthouse. Follow me," he commands, in a strong but welcoming voice.

As soon as Ricky walks into the penthouse, Mr. Elsberry sees him out of the corner of his eye and yells over at him, "Ricky, get over here—I was just talking about you! I was just telling Fred here about how incredible of a guitar player you are! Wait, let me grab this guitar over here and see if we can get Ricky to play a little solo. What do you think guys?!"

Thirty seconds later, Mr. Elsberry comes back from grabbing one of his "Clapton guitars" that he bought at a charity event auction and shoves it into Ricky's chest. Ricky really doesn't have a choice in the matter.

"Sure, why not," Ricky mutters. He gives a nonchalant response, but inside Ricky loves all the attention. The feeling he gets inside when he sees people admire his guitar-playing talents is almost indescribable. That feeling of admiration and accomplishment might be the biggest reason he started playing a guitar in the first place. (At first, it was really about picking up chicks, but I guess that really goes back to being admired, doesn't it? Ding, ding, ding, I think we have a winner!)

IS THIS OFF-TOPIC?

What does any of this have to do with Facebook ads? Patience you must have, my young Padawan. Patience.

And you might wanna pay close attention to some of the details.

Ricky grabs the guitar. Mr. Elsberry tries handing him a pick, but Ricky already has his favorite one in his pocket. He shakes his head, pulls out his favorite pick, and quickly checks the tune on the strings.

"Good enough," he says and starts ripping away.

Every single person in the entire penthouse stops their conversation dead in its tracks, and starts staring over at Ricky playing the guitar like a master. People in nearby rooms start making their way into the living room where he's playing. They are mesmerized.

Ricky makes it look like he's one with the guitar—almost like it's an extension of his arms and hands. The energy in the room is palpable.

After he finishes, the room remains silent for about five more very long seconds, while everyone stares in amazement. Then, the person who Mr. Elsberry was talking to before Ricky walked in the door, says, "Man, how in the heck did you get that good? How long have you been playing?"

"I've been playing as long as I can remember. I've definitely put my 10,000 hours in," Ricky answers.

The man continues, "So tell me, in your opinion, what is the biggest difference between an Eric Clapton, the dude down the street playing in his garage band, or the guy or gal who plays weekends at the martini lounge down the street?"

Ricky hands the guitar to Mr. Elsberry, and says, "That's a great question. It's really a combination of things. First of all, you need to get hundreds or thousands of hours of practice under your belt. I have definitely passed the famous Malcom Gladwell "10,000 hours" mark. It takes getting coached by a good teacher, playing a lot with other musicians or in a band and last, but definitely not least, it takes natural talent: coordinated hands and fingers, a great eye and ear for music and melody, and that artistic gift that's really difficult to describe."

Then, Ricky says to the man: "You know, I teach guitar lessons down in the Meatpacking District. My normal rate is $100 per hour, but I can give you a 15 percent off deal because you're a friend of Mr. Elsberry's. And we also have bulk discounts, where the hourly rate goes down even lower when you get a package!"

The man looks at him with a blank stare for a moment, pondering. Maybe he was still admiring Ricky's skills, or maybe he was doing the math in his head of 10,000 hours times $85.

He then said, "Oh man, thanks for the offer; I appreciate it! Why don't you give me your business card, and I'll check it out next week?"

Ricky knew right then that the man was never coming into his studio. He wasn't going to follow up and purchase a lesson—let alone a package of lessons. He's heard that same line a hundred times, if not more. Shoulders already starting to slump, he slowly reaches into his pocket and gives him his business card.

And Ricky was right—that guy was never going to follow through and look him up or purchase a lesson.

But, why not? He showed them how amazing he was at playing the guitar. He was even referred by a friend, Mr. Elsberry. So, what went wrong?

To truly understand what went wrong, you need to follow Ricky's twin James through a similar scenario.

JAMES GOES TO A PARTY

James, who was raised by an architect and an orchestra conductor, had a thriving music teaching business in downtown Seattle, Washington. At his 10,000 square-foot studio, he has several excellent guitar instructors who teach his methodology, as well as a few other musicians teaching piano, percussions, and other musical arts.

James spends most of his time building relationships in the community and doing performance-based teaching to larger groups of people where he mixes in music, entertainment, and audience involvement to demonstrate to them how quickly and easily you can make good music if you know some cool tricks. (Basically, a mix between a magic show and a music show).

One Friday night James got invited to a party by Mr. Smith, one of his clients, who lives in a nice home in West Seattle looking out over the Puget Sound. (The same exact type of party Ricky went to—similar crowd and vibe.)

Out of the corner of his eye, Mr. Smith caught James walking in the front door and yelled, "Hey James, we were just talking about you! I'm glad you made it—get over here!"

As James is walking over, Mr. Smith says "Man, we were literally just talking about you right as you were walking in the door. Hey, would you mind doing that cool time warp guitar thing you do? I've got an acoustic right over there you can grab."

"Sure, no prob." James says somewhat reluctantly.

James takes the guitar. He then grabs a pick out of his pocket and starts tuning the strings. Still tuning the strings of the guitar, he says to the people gathered around, looking each person in the eye as he says, "Did you know that once you know how to play the most popular four guitar chords: G major, C major, D major, and E minor, you can play almost any good song?"

He plays each chord once. Then starts playing a popular song from the '40s. Then playing a popular '50s song. Then a popular '60s song.

He stops and looks around, admiring the "aha moment" look on everyone's face, and says, "Who here has tried the guitar but gave up after two or three lessons?"

A lady and guy both raise their hand—barely above their head. James pulls the shoulder strap over his head and says, "OK great. Which one of you wants to try and experiment?" The guy volunteers.

James gives him the guitar, and in less than five minutes he has him playing all four chords. The guy now has a grin on his face, from the confidence building up. Then, James tells him to play each chord he calls out as he commands it.

Next thing you know, this guy is rifting popular songs from the 70's, 80's, 90's, and up to today, smiling ear to ear.

"That's good," James says. "How'd that feel?"

"Amazing! I can't believe how easy that was—it was like magic!"

"It's not magic at all. That was all you, my friend. All you." James says with a genuine smile. "You just had a little help learning some shortcuts."

James is truly happy. The most fulfilling thing in the world to him is when he gets to see other people get amazing value from all the hard work he put into building his teaching system and methodology.

Next James says, "And check this out—if you text "guitar master" to 555-555-play, I'll send you a cool "Five-day guitar boot camp for $20" coupon that one of my best instructors puts on every week. He shows you even more tips, tricks, and secrets to getting great at the guitar fast."

The guy doesn't even hesitate—he texts the number right then and there. Four other people who are standing around watching, do the same thing. (One lady didn't even want the lessons for herself—she texted the number so she could pass the coupon on to a friend of hers!)

WHAT WENT WRONG AND WHAT WENT RIGHT

Did you notice the differences in the party scenario between James and Ricky? They were both equally talented. They both had similar personalities. But notice the difference in parental models for each of them.

Ricky's dad was a day-trader, with a short-term outlook for making profits. His mom was a talented musician. But you need more than one great musician to have an amazing band.

James's mother was an architect, who must understand the big picture, the whole system—and have a long-term vision. She knows that one small thing at the very beginning of a process map can exponentially affect the end result. His father was a conductor of an orchestra. A great conductor must know how to fit all the pieces of the puzzle together to make amazing music.

QUICK NOTE ON THE PARENTS' CAREERS

I, as well as the other authors of this book, have absolutely nothing against being a day-trader or a talented musician. I just chose these paths to prove a point. I know some amazing, and genuine (and long-term thinking) people who are day-traders. This was just to try and prove a point.

As genius Steve Jobs once said, "I play the orchestra." He had amazing "musicians" at Apple, but in order to win big and dominate the competition he knew he needed to "play the orchestra."

ARE YOU THE STAR OF THE SHOW OR IS YOUR AUDIENCE THE STAR?

Ricky's onlookers were probably intimidated and scared to even try and get started on that 10,000-hour journey, so they gave up before they even started. And this is an example of a pretty cool guy, who is talented, still failing. Ricky was the star of the show, and he made success feel untouchable.

James, on the other hand, made everyone feel at ease. He made them feel like anyone could do it.

He wasn't the star of the show—his audience was the star.

A lot of times you will see much worse scenarios—like "that guy" at the party who is trying to sell you his business opportunity or sell you an appointment with him at his office the next week to discuss "retirement opportunities." I didn't even go there with this example.

I used a much subtler example in my fable of what not to do. The reason is because there is a very thin line between success and failure with Facebook ads. Most "great marketers" or "great copywriters" don't truly understand how to win big with Facebook ads.

This book will help you be more like James instead of Ricky. And we will teach how to clone someone like James, so your brand is showing up at cocktail parties, corporate events, community events, and coffee shops all over the world—giving people "aha moments," building relationships, and motivating people to want to consume your content, try your services, and buy your products.

Chapter 5

Two Questions
"Is Facebook for Me?" and "Which Facebook Strategy Is Right for Me?"

In the last two editions of this book, we said that not every business can benefit from advertising on Facebook. Well, we changed our minds since then. Facebook has evolved into a powerhouse that has infiltrated almost every single device on the planet. I would be willing to bet that at least 80 to 90 percent of your customers have Facebook accounts. They might not be super active, but they at least have accounts so they can log in to see what friends and family, business acquaintances, business competition, employees, potential employees, or anybody else they might know or want to know, are up to. Heck, it seems like every other new software tool out there now makes you sign up or sign in using Facebook, so you *have to* have an account!

> "*If* I had asked people what they wanted, they would have said 'faster horse's."
>
> —HENRY FORD

After seeing thousands of case studies of businesses in dozens and dozens of different industries from direct-to-consumer products to high-end business-to-business sales, transformed almost overnight in many cases, our position on the benefits of Facebook advertising has changed.

Let's say you sell the top-of-the-line customer relationship management system or solution, or an enterprise-level accounting solution, and you know a bunch of C-Level executives will be having dinner and socializing at some upcoming charity events or some other social gatherings happening in several big cities around the country. Would you want some of your top sales people at these events?

Or, maybe you have a consumer product—you sell the only bottled water that does not leak toxins into the water inside the bottle after it has been sitting in the hot sun all day. Would you want your top sales people attending local events or putting up a booth at the local "go green" event? I sure hope you would, especially if you knew that you wouldn't have to pay an upfront fee to attend these events or put up a booth. How about if the booth was free, and you only paid after an interested person comes by your booth and chats with your sales people? Or, what if you could advertise on television or do product placement ads inside movies or shows on Netflix or iTunes but your messages were only delivered to people who you knew were in your exact, ideal target audience? What if you only paid after each viewer saw your ad and called the number or visited the website URL in your message?

Well, that my friend, is essentially Facebook advertising. Once you truly understand the reach Facebook has, the amazing ability to optimize, micro-manage campaigns with automation, and track the ROI down to the individual ad creative and audience so you don't waste your precious advertising dollars, you will understand why we advise almost every single business to advertise at least at some level inside Facebook.

You can still find out where Facebook advertising should fit in with your business type by going to www.IsfbForME.com where you will get a score from 1 to 10. Even if you have taken this quiz in the past, we highly recommend taking it again, as we have changed the formula so you should get a different score this time around. If you find out that Facebook *is* for you, then we will give you a specific strategy and mind map designed and outlined for your specific business type. Understanding and implementing the specific Facebook strategy for *your* business type can be biggest difference maker when it comes to winning or losing at Facebook ads. (This is one of our key USP's over at our company.)

If you already know that Facebook is for you, then you can skip that quiz and go directly to www.FBstrategyForME.com, where you can find out what is the Facebook campaign and selling system is right for your business, updated with the most current Facebook tactics.

Later in this book, starting with Chapter 12, we take you through different selling systems for different industry types. But please be aware that Facebook changes so fast that it would be impossible to lay out a strategy in a printed book that will not evolve with time and technology. I wish that was possible!

In the next chapter, the goal is to get you some quick momentum. You do not want to get bogged down with trying to figure out the best possible strategy right out of the gate—you will get overwhelmed, frustrated, and dragged down by its complexity. This is why you want to start using Facebook's "easy button" as quickly as possible!

Chapter 6

Facebook Easy Button
Boosted Posts

Ever been excited to start a new project, knowing it's super important, only to find that weeks have gone by with no progress? Often, it's because it's overwhelming and complicated to take that small but crucial first step

Don't let that be the case with your Facebook advertising!

In this chapter, we're going to show you the simplest thing that you can do right now to get started advertising on Facebook and that is boosting a post.

Boosting a post is done directly from your business page. Just add some content on your page and click the big blue Boost Post button. Then, select your audience and assign a budget. That's it! It's Facebook's Big Easy Button (see Figure 6.1 on page 36).

> "You don't have to be great to start, but you have to start to be great."
>
> —Zig Ziglar

Now, remember boosting a post is like any other marketing activity. You won't hit it out of the park every time. My co-author for this strategy, Dennis Yu, calls a home run post a "unicorn." At the end of this book Dennis has included a bonus section where he goes in-depth on his strategy for boosting posts for clients, like the Golden State Warriors NBA team.

For boosting posts to work for your business you still need to have the right content in front of the right people, but there's no easier way than boosting a post to quickly test

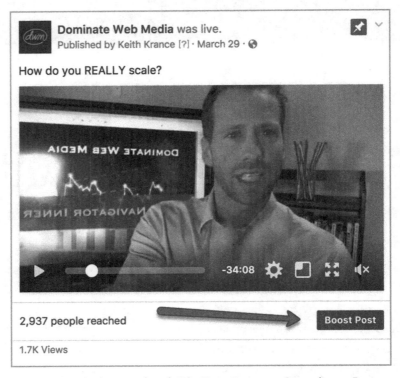

FIGURE 6.1–The Facebook Big Easy Button—Boosting a Post
from Your Business Page

different hooks. Instead of having to try and guess how your market will respond, you can let the Facebook data tell you what's good and what's bad. Dennis often recommends boosting posts for as little as $1/day for 7 days.

Another advantage of boosting posts is social proof—building likes, shares, and fans. This social proof gives you authority in your marketplace i.e., people are more likely to trust you if they see other people trust you. Boosting posts and Like Campaigns are typically some of the cheapest ways to do this.

Boosting posts is also a great strategy for local businesses. For example, if you're a restaurant, dentist, chiropractor, lawyer, cosmetic surgeon, locksmith, etc., you could boost a post that says something like, "Hey, I'm Ralph, and I'm a locksmith. I've been doing this for 20 years. I've got three vans." Then go on and tell the rest of your story or talk about how you recently solved a problem your potential customers might be experiencing. It may or may not have your phone instantly ringing off the hook but the consistency and top-of-mind awareness that a boosted post creates will have people thinking of you when the need arises.

A pizzeria owner we know boosts posts saying, "Hey, tonight, check out this lasagna." Or, "Check out what we have on Mother's Day." He'll just post pictures of food. The guy is not technical or anything like that; he doesn't even know WordPress. He'll just boost posts to several audiences, such as the audience of all the food critics who write for the local newspapers.

Boosted posts can also be very powerful when you approach them like a journalist, trying to influence the people who can influence your customers. Some examples could be people who work at magazines, radio stations, newspapers, TV shows, bloggers, conference attendees, etc.

FACEBOOK AD TIP

Create a Saved Audience for Influences inside the Audience Section in your Ads Manager to easily access when boosting posts. (See Figure 6.2.)

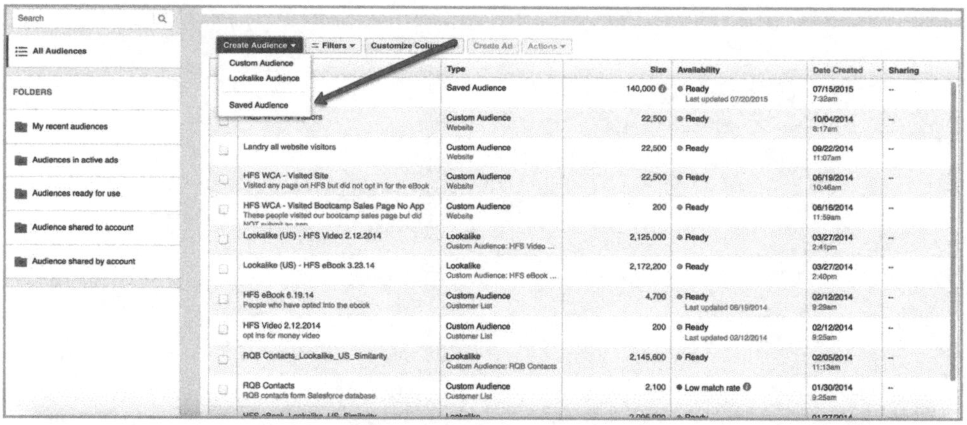

FIGURE 6.2–Saving Audiences for Easy Access When Boosting a Post

Boosting posts may or may not be your final end game plan for success on Facebook but if you don't get into the airplane and start flying, you won't make it off the ground. Boosting posts are great for testing fast, testing with small budgets, testing different hooks, audiences, building social proof, and just overall engaging more with your market and the people who influence your market.

If you want to dive in deeper on boosting posts, and see some amazing case studies (like a Golden State Warriors boosted campaign), please check out www.perrymarshall. com/fbtools as well as the appendix at the end of this book written by Dennis Yu.

Chapter 7

The Power of the Pixel

One of the most misunderstood elements of the Facebook ads platform is the "great and powerful" Facebook Pixel, but once you pull back the curtain, it really becomes much more simple and clear. Facebook describes it as: "The Facebook Pixel is an analytics tool that allows you to measure the effectiveness of your advertising by understanding the actions people take on your website. You can use the pixel data to:

> *"For my ally is the Force, and a powerful ally it is."*
>
> —YODA

- Make sure your ads are being shown to the right people.
- Build advertising audiences.
- Unlock additional Facebook advertising tools."

According to Facebook, with the Facebook Pixel you can:

1. Reach the right people (Audience Building)
2. Drive more sales (Optimization)
3. Measure the results of your ads (Tracking)

In a nutshell, the three main purposes of the Facebook Pixel are:

1. Audience Building
2. Optimization
3. Tracking and Measurement

If you thought the pixel was only used for tracking and measuring, don't worry; you're not alone. This is a very common misconception, so let's dig into each super power.

CONVERSION TRACKING

This is generally the most understood and most utilized purpose of the Facebook Pixel. You simply place the pixel on any web page you want to measure your results from your advertising. You can measure actions such as number of leads or cost per lead, purchase data, shopping cart and checkout page activity, visitor engagement, visitor events (like clicking a button on your site), and other important data that will help you measure the results of your advertising and make data-driven decisions to increase your overall ROI.

What happens after Facebook receives the data from the pixel is what is really powerful. Facebook attributes each measurable action accordingly to the appropriate ad that triggered that conversion event.

For example, let's say you have three different ad campaigns running, each with 20 different ad sets, and each ad set has two different ads inside it, all with the goal to sell the same product or offer. After running for three days, you generate a total of five new leads and one new customer. In your reporting, Facebook will show six total conversions. During the first two days, they may attribute two new leads to campaign #2 > ad set #3 > ad #1, two leads to campaign #3 > ad set #11 > ad #2, and one lead to campaign #3 > ad set #9 > ad #1. Then on day three, they may attribute a new customer to campaign #2 > ad set #15 > ad #2.

Poor old campaign #1 didn't generate any conversions. (However, this DOES NOT necessarily mean that campaign #1 didn't affect the positive outcome of those six conversions—more on this matter in later chapters—as this is one of the most-costly assumptions marketers make with their Facebook ads analysis and decision-making.)

Facebook's amazing algorithms do all the heavy lifting for you if you've setup and configured the pixel properly, which is why this is so important to take the time to do right. Without the pixel set for proper conversion tracking, you're flying blind. You won't know what's working and what's not working.

AUDIENCE BUILDING

The most misunderstood power of the Facebook Pixel is one of our favorites and is surprisingly not utilized to its potential—that is the audience building capability. Every single page of your website should have the Facebook Pixel installed on it.

When anyone visits your website's home page, blog posts or article pages, sales pages, add-to-cart pages, checkout pages, and anything in between, you should be tracking that and building custom audiences based on that activity so you can retarget or remarket to at a later time or even simultaneously.

The Facebook Pixel does this for you seamlessly.

All the data we share with Facebook by simply having the pixel installed in each page of our website is analyzed and correlated behind the scenes to create segmented audiences based on dynamic user behavior. These audiences can be based on several different user behaviors that we won't talk about in depth in this chapter, but the most common is website visitor activity. Facebook is continually adding more and more visitor engagement options every few months so you can have more options to segment your audiences. Plus, this will make it easier for you to put the right message in front of the right audience based on their level of awareness, intent, and trust.

In case you didn't already get how powerful this truly is, let's do a quick example and pretend you own a sporting goods business that sells things for two sports—tennis and basketball. In your blog, you've published two articles. Article one is titled: "Three Quick Tips to Easily Add 10 MPH to Your Tennis Serve," while article two is titled: "Try this In-Home Exercise That Can Quickly Add Up to Two Inches or More to Your Vertical Leap, in Just Five Minutes a Day."

These are free, content-rich articles or videos that don't require a visitor to purchase access, opt-in, or subscribe to your mailing list to get access to.

With the Facebook Pixel firing properly, you leverage the power of segmented audiences being automatically built behind the scenes. You can then tell Facebook to show your "Special Edition Tennis Racquet" offer to only website visitors of the serving tips article (and any other tennis related article), and your new "Vertical Leap Explosion" basketball skills program to all website visitors of the vertical leap exercise article—and any other basketball related article or video you published.

This is just the tip of the iceberg. The important thing to understand is that you are able to architect and engineer any path you would like to put in front of your engaged visitors. And if you are not already getting visitors coming to your site organically, you can always use strategic Facebook ads to get those initial visitors consuming your content!

ADS OPTIMIZATION WITH ARTIFICIAL INTELLIGENCE (AI)

Many people don't fully understand the second super power of the pixel—ads optimization.

When you create new ad sets inside the Ads Manager, you select a "campaign objective" to optimize for the goal you are trying to achieve for that campaign. It may be Brand Awareness, Engagement, Lead Generation, Video Views, Product Catalog Sales, and more. And more importantly, you can set a specific website conversion or event that you want Facebook to optimize for—aka put your ads in front of other users with similar interests and behaviors as your converting visitors.

For example, if you run a campaign using the website conversions objective and you want Facebook to specifically optimize for webinar registrations, then you're telling Facebook to show your ads to users more like the people who are registering for your webinar. What happens is that the pixel is feeding data back to the Facebook database every time that campaign objective is fulfilled. Facebook takes the data from the pixel, analyzes it, and more intelligently and accurately does more of what it has already successfully done.

Now, if a different conversion objective than the one you chose to optimize your campaign around is achieved and triggered, Facebook will still track that conversion inside the reporting tool—as long as you created a Standard Event or a Custom Conversion. (More details and instructions on this in Chapter 27.) So in essence, your targeting gets better and better after every single webinar registration you generate thanks to Artificial Intelligence.

Chapter 8

A Few Fundamentals

Guest Author Angela Ponsford, Dominate Web Media

There are a few fundamentals you, the Facebook advertiser, must know before you begin spending your hard-earned cash. These terms and definitions are so important that you really should understand them comfortably and completely before giving Facebook your credit card and telling them to go for it.

The rest of this book assumes you know this vocabulary down pat. So if you are totally new to pay-per-click or pay-per-view advertising, pay extra close attention.

> *"First master the fundamentals."*
>
> —Larry Bird

Please don't skip this chapter if online advertising is totally new to you. It is really important that you 100 percent understand everything in this chapter before you purchase your first ad. A quiz at the end of this chapter will test your knowledge and understanding.

Take the quiz. We will not grade you—the marketplace will. The penalty for failing is a hefty bill from Facebook with no $$ in your bank account to show for it.

This chapter isn't the final discussion on these topics, just the first wave.

ADS

An ad in Facebook is content displayed to Facebook users at an advertiser's specific request (see Figure 8.1).

FIGURE 8.1–A Facebook Ad Displayed in the Newsfeed

These ads are frequently seen in your Facebook newsfeed. There are several different places that ads can be seen, including the newsfeed, the right-hand column, Messenger, Instagram, and other external websites and applications.

Every time an ad is displayed, a user could potentially read the ad. Facebook calls that an impression. An impression is an opportunity for someone to see your ad. If the ad seen in Figure 8.1 had 1.4 million impressions, then the ad had 1.4 million opportunities to be seen.

However, impressions do not mean individual people have had the chance to see the ad. Your ad has not in fact been shown to 1.4 million people. The reach for this ad tells you the actual number of people that have seen the ad. In this example, the reach is reported by Facebook to be 200,000 people.

So, if this ad has had 1.4 million impressions and an estimated reach of 200,000 people, we can work out that, on average, each of those 200,000 people has had seven opportunities to see the ad.

Most people do not click on an ad on the first impression. As users browse Facebook, the same ads are displayed multiple times.

If the ad headline—the line underneath the image—is good and the ad image is compelling, the ad may eventually capture the attention of a Facebook user, who then will actually look at it and read the ad copy. (See Figure 8.2.)

FIGURE 8.2–Ad Headline, Image, and Copy

If the ad interests the user enough, then the user will click on the ad. Facebook captures and reports the number of times all users have clicked on each ad. They cleverly name this reported element clicks.

HOW WELL IS MY AD WORKING?

One of the first questions everyone asks is, "How well is my ad working?" This question is actually trickier than it first seems because there are many measures of "working":

- Does the ad encourage the users to click?
- Will users do the next step we want them to after clicking?
- Will users ever purchase from us?
- Will users stop buying stuff from the other guy?

All four of these questions may be different ways to define working. Facebook helps us track and answer the first question, "Does the ad encourage the users to click?" You will learn secrets to answering the remaining questions in later chapters.

Facebook reports how well an ad encourages a user to click in a statistic called the click-through rate (CTR). This rate identifies how many impressions it takes on average before a user clicks on the ad.

CTR is clicks divided by impressions (clicks/impressions).

(10 clicks/1,000 impressions = 1 percent.)

If your ad has had 1,000 total impressions and users have clicked on the ad 10 times, then your CTR is 1 percent.

The ad in Figure 8.3 had 376,409 impressions leading to 344 clicks. What is its CTR? Don't peek at the answer. Seriously, calculate this yourself at least once.

FIGURE 8.3–Calculate the CTR for this Ad

Did you get 0.091 percent? If not, do the math again.

The formula: 344 clicks/376,409 impressions = 0.091 percent CTR.

If you are still having trouble getting the math right, don't fret. Facebook reports the impressions and the clicks and calculates the CTR automatically.

There are actually two CTR metrics reported in Facebook, and it's important to understand the difference between them.

- CTR (All)—Measures all clicks that happen on the ad, including post reactions, comments, shares, and clicks on the profile picture.
- CTR (Link Click-Through Rate)—Measures only clicks on external links within the ad.

If you're running an ad that takes people to your website or some destination off of Facebook, then you'll want to be looking at the CTR (Link Click-Through Rate) metric and not the CTR (All) metric.

Landing Pages

When users click on an ad, where do they go? Well, that depends on the type of ad you're running.

You can send a user who clicks on an ad anywhere that does not violate Facebook's landing page policies. You may send users to your own web page or you may send users to other locations within Facebook—such as a Facebook page, Messenger, event, or group.

If you're sending people to your website, the page that is displayed after a user clicks on an ad is called a landing page. The advertiser specifies the URL of the landing page when they create the ad.

Bidding and Budgets

Facebook does not display ads out of the goodness of its heart. It wants cold, hard cash. You must provide a credit card before Facebook will even think of displaying your ad. Once they have your payment information, they let you create an ad.

When you create your first campaign and hit go, your ads will enter the Facebook Ad bidding system. This system aims to show relevant ads to the people most interested in seeing your ads.

Your ad is competing with all the other advertisers that want to show their ads to the same audience that you have chosen. And while there are many opportunities to show your ad, Facebook won't be able to deliver on all the requests.

From your perspective, the bid is a bit of a sham. Initially, the higher your bid the more likely your ad will be displayed. After a few thousand impressions, additional factors weigh in to affect the cost of your ad, including the CTR, the Relevance Score, and whether users "like" or complain about your ad.

The good news? Facebook reserves the right to "lower the price" you pay per click. You read that right! They will actually charge you less than you bid, and lucky for you, they do this all the time.

When you set up your ad campaigns, you'll have the option of choosing a daily or lifetime budget. See Figure 8.4.

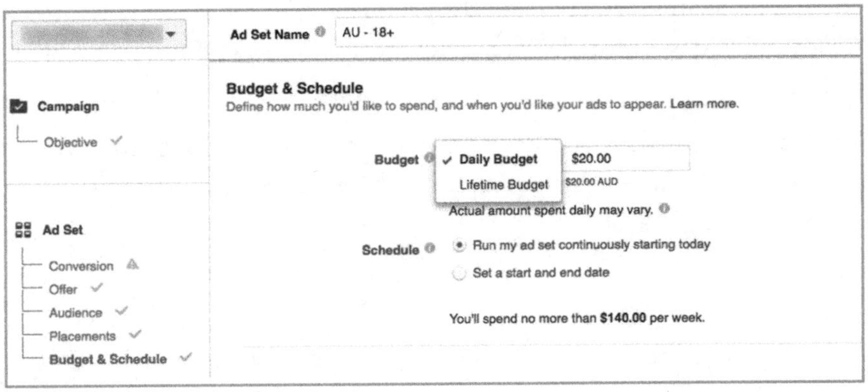

FIGURE 8.4–Daily or Lifetime Budget at the Ad Set Level

- A daily budget is the average amount you're willing to spend on an ad set every day.
- A lifetime budget is the amount you're willing to spend over the entire lifetime of your ad set.

Once you've chosen which type of budget to use, you can't switch between the two different types. You'll need to duplicate an existing ad set to change the budget type.

The budget you choose will have a direct effect on the number of people you can reach with your ad. In Ads Manager and Power Editor, Facebook will show you an estimated daily reach based on your budget. This is the estimated number of people in your chosen audience that your ad can reach per day. See Figure 8.5 on page 49.

There are different bidding types available for different types of ads, and depending on the type of bid you choose, you'll only pay for clicks or impressions. See Figure 8.6 on page 49.

If you choose to bid for clicks, you will be charged only if a user clicks on the ad. You can specify the amount you are willing to pay for a click, starting at one cent per click. If you say that you are willing to pay 17 cents for a click, then that is the most you will be charged for a click.

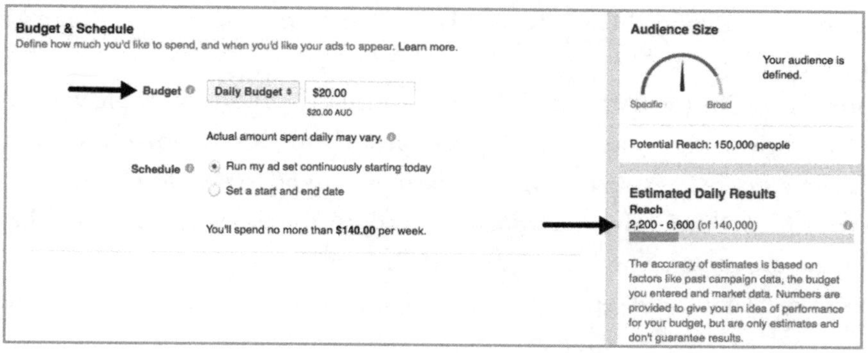

FIGURE 8.5–Estimated Daily Reach

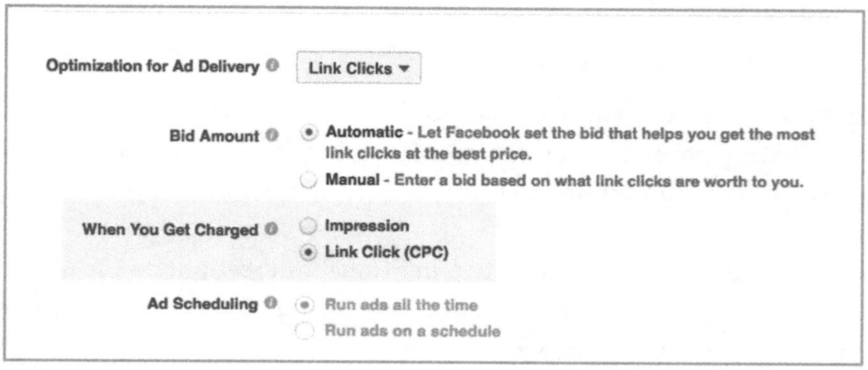

FIGURE 8.6–Pay for Link Click (CPC) Bidding Selected

CPM vs oCPM

You may also select to bid on impressions instead of clicks. You actually bid what you are willing to pay for 1,000 impressions of your ad. This is called cost per impression (CPM). The advertiser is paying for someone to view the ad whether or not the user clicks on the ad.

If you're thinking, "M? What is the M for?" Do you remember your Latin?

Mille means 1,000 in Latin.

M is 1,000 in Roman numerals.

Our word millennium means a span of 1,000 years.

CPM stands for cost per M impressions (M = 1,000). Get used to that crazy little "M." It is not going away.

CPM is frequently associated with brand advertising where the goal is only to get the user to see the brand name and not to get a click. You're basically telling Facebook that you are willing to pay simply to have it display your ad 1,000 times whether or not anyone clicks on the ad. For most advertisers, this is not the best option for bidding.

Optimized CPM (oCPM) is a bid type that shows your ad to people who are more likely to take the action you want. For example, if your advertising objective is to get more Facebook page likes, an oCPM bid will show your ad to people who are more likely to like your page. Your bid will automatically adjust to help your ads reach the people you care about, but you won't spend more than your budget.

This is the default bid type for all campaign types except for Brand Awareness and Reach.

Bidding strategy is covered in greater detail in later chapters. If we covered it all now, you might run screaming from the room and that would not help anybody!

Reach, Frequency, and Ad Fatigue

Ads display on Facebook multiple times to the same user. The number of individual people who have seen your ad during a specific period of time is reported by Facebook as reach. The average number of times each individual user has seen your ad is reported as frequency.

Facebook puts limits of how often an individual can see your ad each day in their Newsfeed, and it's different for fans of your Facebook Page and non-Fans. Currently, the daily limit is four for fans and two for non-fans.

If you continue to run your ad in the Newsfeed for long enough, your ad may eventually have a frequency of 10 or more. This means it has been displayed to each individual user an average of 10 times. Even if the ad is excellent, the users will get tired of seeing it, and then they stop clicking on it (frequency can be much higher for Right Hand Column).

This is called ad fatigue—your prospects stop clicking on an ad as the frequency gets high simply because they've grown tired of seeing it.

Have you ever watched a television commercial and really enjoyed it? Perhaps you thought it was funny, clever, or emotionally moving. Later, after seeing the same commercial over and over and over and over again, you slowly begin to hate it. If you've had that experience, then you've experienced ad fatigue firsthand! Get the free video tutorials system updates and strategies at www.perrymarshall.com/fbtools.

Chapter 9

Set Yourself Up for Success

Guest Author Angela Ponsford, Dominate Web Media

Before you start running your Facebook ad campaigns, there are certain items you need to have in place first e.g., your Facebook page, ad account, and unique selling system. In this chapter, we cover setting up the basics.

CREATE YOUR FACEBOOK BUSINESS PAGE

If you're like the two billion other people on the planet, you already have a Facebook PROFILE that you use for personal use. However, if you want to run Facebook ad campaigns you'll need to have a Facebook PAGE for your business. Want to know the easiest way to spot the difference between a profile and a page?

- PROFILES have "Friends"
- PAGES have "Likes"

To create your Page, go to https://www.facebook.com/pages/create/ and choose a Page type. Figure 9.1 on page 52 shows some of the options to choose from.

> *"We are what we repeatedly do. Success is not an action but a habit."*
>
> —ARISTOTLE

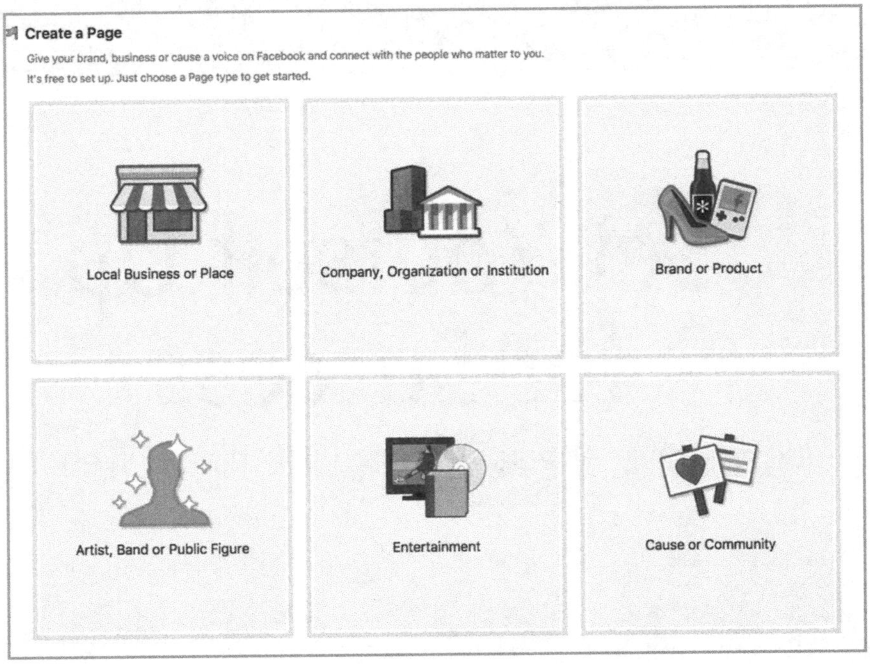

FIGURE 9.1–Types of Facebook Pages

You'll then be prompted to choose a Category. You can go back and change the type and category at a later date, so don't worry if you choose the wrong one. Then, give your page a name and click Get Started.

Before you start sharing and promoting that you have a new Page, it's best if you add a profile picture, a cover photo, and a description of what your business is about. Figure 9.2 shows the recommended dimensions of the profile picture and cover photo.

You can use a tool such as Canva (http://www.canva.com) to create your cover photo. They have pre-sized templates to make your life easier.

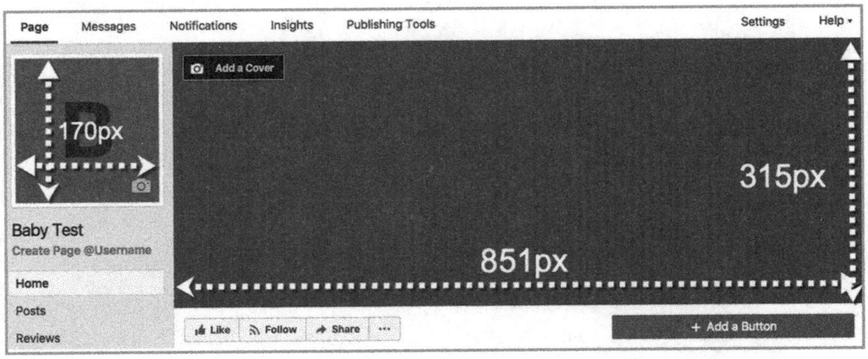

FIGURE 9.2–Profile Picture and Cover Photo Dimensions

You'll also want to create a username for your Page, which makes it easier for people to find your Page in search. Your username can't already be in use by someone else, so you may have to try a few things before you get a free one!

The final step in creating your page is to post some content to show that you're active and ready for business!

Setup Facebook Business Manager

Business Manager is Facebook's recommended platform for managing your Facebook ads. It allows you to easily give access to anyone who needs to work on your page or ads. By having all your Facebook assets linked in Business Manager, it also shows to Facebook that you're a legitimate business.

To get started, go to https://business.facebook.com/ and click on "Create Account." You'll be asked to log in with your personal Facebook details and then you can add your business name, your name, and your business email to create your Business Manager Account.

Figure 9.3 shows the initial screen you'll see once your new Business Manager account has been created.

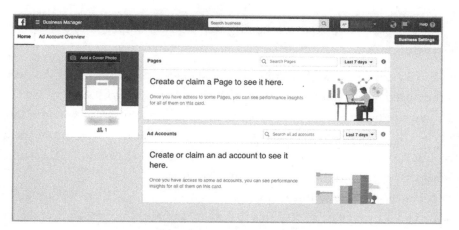

FIGURE 9.3–Business Manager Home Screen

Click on "Business Settings" to add your page and ad account to your Business Manager account.

On the left-hand side, you'll see a column of icons. If you hover your mouse over them, they'll pop out and you'll be able to select Pages first. Then, you'll click on "Add New Pages" and "Add a Page." Start typing in the name of your Facebook page and it should auto-populate into the name field. Then, click on "Add Page," and because you're already an admin on your Business Page, it will be approved automatically.

The next thing to do is to add an ad account (if you've previously created one) or create a new ad account.

Once again, hover over the icons on the left-hand side and click on "Ad Accounts," then "Add New Ad Accounts."

Figure 9.4 shows the options available to you for adding ad accounts.

FIGURE 9.4–Adding New Ad Accounts

To add an existing ad account to Business Manager, click on "Add an Ad Account." You'll then need to put in the Ad Account ID of the account you want to add. To find this ID, you need to have the ad account open in a different tab or window and then look at the URL. You'll see ACT= and then a string of numbers; those numbers are the Ad Account ID. Copy and paste the string of numbers into the account ID section back in Business Manager and then click on "Add Ad Account."

To create a new ad account in Business Manager, just click on "Create a New Ad Account." You'll then be prompted to add a name and also the time zone and currency. You can't change the time zone and currency once the account has been created, so make sure you get this right. Once you've entered all of the information, click on "Create Ad Account."

So now that you have your Page and your Ad Account added into Business Manager, you need to add People and Partners.

Add People and Partners to Business Manager

If there are other people that you want to have access to your Page and Ad Account you also need to add them into Business Manager.

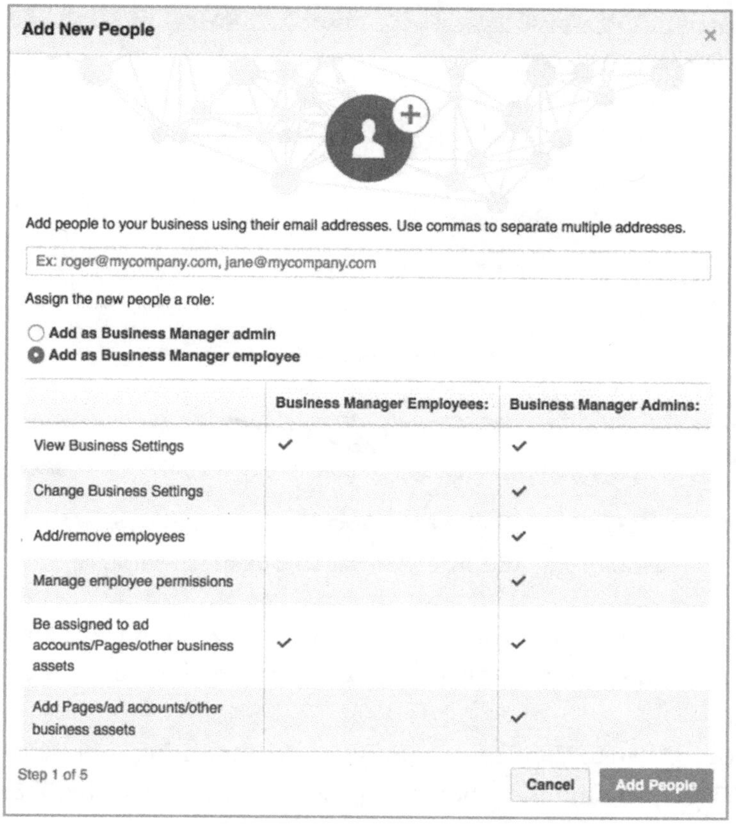

Add New People

Add people to your business using their email addresses. Use commas to separate multiple addresses.

Ex: roger@mycompany.com, jane@mycompany.com

Assign the new people a role:

○ Add as Business Manager admin
◉ Add as Business Manager employee

	Business Manager Employees:	Business Manager Admins:
View Business Settings	✓	✓
Change Business Settings		✓
Add/remove employees		✓
Manage employee permissions		✓
Be assigned to ad accounts/Pages/other business assets	✓	✓
Add Pages/ad accounts/other business assets		✓

Step 1 of 5   Cancel   Add People

FIGURE 9.5–Adding People to Business Manager

So you need to hover over the icons on the left-hand side again and choose the top one, which is People. Then click on "Add New People," and you'll see the options shown in Figure 9.5.

Put the email address of the person you are adding into the email field at the top and then select whether they will be an admin or an employee. Then, click on "Add People." You'll then see a series of options for assigning Pages and Ad Accounts to this new person. Add the relevant Pages and Ad Accounts and continue to click Next. Once you've gone through all the screens, the new person will receive a notification via email that you have invited them to join your Business Manager account. Once they accept, they'll be able to work on the Pages and Ad Accounts that you have allocated to them.

If you're going to have an agency or consultant running your ads or managing your Facebook Page, then you can add them using their Business ID. You can find the Business ID in the URL stream when in Business Manager. Similar to the ad account ID, it's the string of numbers showing after ?business_id=.

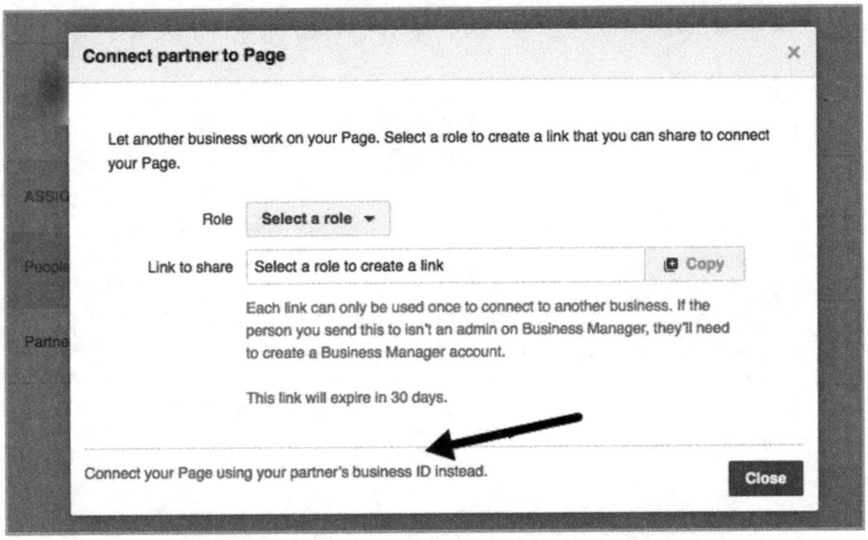

FIGURE 9.6–Adding a Partner to Business Manager

To add the agency or consultant, select your Page or Ad Account in Business Manager settings and then click on "Assign Partner." You'll then see the screen shown in Figure 9.6.

Choose the option to Connect your Page/Ad Account using your partner's business ID instead. Then, you can insert the ID they have given you, and they'll be added with whatever Role you choose.

Now that you've set up your Business Manager you're just about ready to start running some Facebook ads.

Chapter 10

Your Facebook Flight School

After I had been running Facebook ads for about three years, I came to the realization that creating, managing, and optimizing profitable Facebook advertising is not much different than flying an airplane. In fact, I believe learning how to run long-term-scalable, and profitable Facebook ads that can change your business (and your life) almost overnight in many cases, is more difficult than learning how to fly an airplane.

However, the big "aha moment" came for me when I realized how much we can learn and model from the aviation industry. Think about it—pilots and passengers' lives depend on the quality of flight training, systems, policies and procedures, checklists, SOP's, redundancy, etc.

There's a great book written by Dr. Atul Gawande, *The Checklist Manifesto: How to Get Things Right* (Picador, 2011), I read about four years ago that made a huge impact on me. This book really inspired that big "aha moment." In the book, Dr. Gawande describes a bunch of different case studies where certain hospitals started to model their procedures after the airline industry and adapted checklists into those standard operating procedures.

> "*A*nybody can land an airplane. But not everybody can land it safely."
>
> —Anonymous

He shows statistics of mistakes on the operating table of hospitals not using checklists versus hospitals using checklists, and the numbers are staggering—and scary to think about. Point being, any business—from hospitals to your online ecommerce site—has something to learn from the airline industry.

Those lessons have been evident to me throughout my own career. As mentioned previously, I went to college at the University of North Dakota (UND), one of the premier aviation schools in the world, to get my four-year degree and become an airline pilot. By the end of my second year in college, I had my Commercial Pilot Multi-Engine Certificate, Instrument Rating, and Aerobatics and Tailwheel endorsements. After three years, I also earned my Certified Multi-Engine Instrument Flight Instructor certificate. When you become an instructor, you first get your Certified Flight Instructor Instrument Certificate (CFI), then you work on getting your Certified Flight Instructor (CFII) certificate, then you get your Multi-Engine Instructor certificate. (MEI). At this point, you are now qualified to train pilots working on their private pilot certificate all the way up to their commercial pilot, multi-engine instrument ratings.

Midway through my senior year, I got hired by UND as a flight instructor. I took a semester off to go live in Aspen, Colorado and work as a baggage service handler for United Express, throwing bags from 1 P.M. to 9 P.M. each day and skiing or snowboarding (depending on the snow quality). I still graduated after four years and was quickly building my hours and experience as an instructor pilot. A year after I graduated, I was hired by Horizon Air, a subsidiary of Alaska Airlines. During my first two years at Horizon, I flew a Fokker F28 regional jet, as seen in Figure 10.1. Figure 10.2 on page 59 shows the cockpit.

FIGURE 10.1–Horizon Air Fokker F28 Jet

FIGURE 10.2–F28 Cockpit

Next, I moved to a CRJ 700 regional jet, which is a little like the sports car of airline jets. A much more advanced aircraft than the F28, as you can see by the cockpit avionics and navigation systems. (See Figures 10.3 and 10.4, which is on page 60.) But landing those F28's was so much nicer! It was pretty much like driving a classic Cadillac compared to driving a new Porsche.

FIGURE 10.3–Horizon Air CRJ 700 Regional Jet

I left Horizon Air after six years, after my entrepreneurial spirit started kicking and screaming during all those long, boring flights with the autopilot on,

FIGURE 10.4–CRJ 700 Cockpit

listening to pilot after pilot moan and complain about their contract, their schedule, management, yada, yada, yada. I felt like a flying bus driver, with my life completely controlled by my seniority number, the airline's schedule, and all the pilots with higher seniority numbers than me.

Fast forward a few years, after almost 4,000 flight hours, about 14 different certificates, ratings, and endorsements in nine to ten different airplanes, some real estate investing, owning and operating several different locations as a franchisee of two separate franchises (which included owning and operating the third and fifth ranked locations in the entire franchise)—but, during a huge business model change around 2009 that caused a ton of chaos and cash flow crises across the franchise—all while the banking industry was completely freezing up, my soul was suddenly sent down another path (somewhat forcefully haha), searching for something different.

Even though my monthly customer count was up 5 percent year over year, we were burning cash. Forced into a membership model *only*, with a 30-day free trial entry point, my best store was averaging $40k/month in sales, compared to $110k/month the previous year. (The franchisor literally locked the point of sale (POS) system down to force the new model.)

No more up-sells, no more high-end package sales, no more cash flow. Well, there was plenty of cash flow—it just wasn't positive. I was burning about $20k to $30k a month.

Through my many desperate searches for cheaper customer acquisition strategies and other ways to monetize existing customers, I ended up buying a $3,000 digital product from Mike Koenigs called "Main St. Marketing Machines," which showed you how to use video and YouTube to grow a local business. (For the business owner and for consultants looking to do it for clients.)

Looking back now, I realize that program actually played a pivotal role in the development of our current Facebook ads system, as the core principle to their video strategy was to provide value in advance. And what do you know—the foundational principle to our Facebook ad formula is to provide value, drive awareness, and build up intent.

It also sent me on the journey to become a consultant and build a Facebook ads agency. About a year into being a consultant, I started seeing these ads on the right side of Facebook—and I thought, "Dang, that's like putting up a billboard for free, and we used to spend $10,000/month for a *cheap* billboard—just for the first month. These right-side Facebook ads (there were no newsfeed ads at the time) are like putting up an electronic billboard that only displays to your exact target audience, for free! And paying $1 whenever a car pulls over and calls the number on the billboard or visits the website.

I pushed in all my chips that day. I went "all in" on Facebook ads.

That was 2011. Here we are today. The crazy thing is, I truly believe that learning how to run successful and highly-profitable Facebook advertising campaigns is more difficult than learning how to fly an airplane. It takes time, energy, great training, and quality experience. But, the reward for putting in the time, energy and focus, and investing in great training, far outweighs the work required.

So, if you want to build a true machine—an automated machine that will transform users on social media who are unaware of the problem your product solves and are unaware of your brand, into people who are aware of the problem, aware of *your* solution, and have intent to purchase your product, then treat the process of learning the system just like learning how to fly an airplane. Once you learn to fly once, it's just like riding a bike. You never forget it.

I want you to think about the rest of this book as a mini Facebook Flight School. This "ultimate guide" is filled with the most important lessons, strategies, normal procedures and checklists, abnormal procedures and checklists for troubleshooting, flight planning guides, and more to show you the way to build the most profitable campaigns possible. Execute and watch your business take off and fly to the next level and beyond.

Chapter 11

Facebook Simulator
Like Campaigns

In this chapter, we're going to explain why and how to run a Like campaign (Get more people to Like your page). We'll explain what Like campaigns do, how to build them, and—most importantly—what to put in them to produce the best results.

This chapter is all about building momentum and getting results. It's about landing quick wins and enjoying little victories so that you can start building your foundation and adding more complex strategies as you move forward.

> *"If people like you they'll listen to you, but if they trust you they'll do business with you."*
>
> —Zig Ziglar

Like campaigns are simple. You don't have to build landing pages or thank you pages. You don't need conversion pixels or conversion tracking or any of that complicated stuff. You can just get in there quickly, create a campaign right away, and start seeing results.

You'll see how your audience reacts, how different interests work compared to other interests, whether you win more likes on desktop compared to mobile, in the right column or the newsfeed, and so on. You'll start building an audience of leads, and you'll start collecting real, usable data.

You'll also be getting used to the Power Editor. You'll be in the cockpit with your hands on the yoke, but you won't be in the air with a serious risk of crashing. It's a bit like flying in a simulator.

You'll get used to the controls, feel the pressure on the yoke, steer with the rudder, even practice your communication skills. Like campaigns deliver a similar experience. There's not a lot of complexity and there are few risks, but you're going to create your campaign inside the Power Editor. That Power Editor can be overwhelming sometimes, so Like campaigns are great practice.

THREE REASONS TO RUN A LIKE CAMPAIGN

So running a Like campaign gives you a free education. It's a powerful, hands-on way to learn how to use Facebook advertising. It gives you that first burst of momentum that you'll need to move forward faster, but it also delivers three benefits with real value:

Like Campaigns Deliver Social Proof

Once you've run a Like campaign, you can do connection targeting. You can aim your ads at friends of fans and make the most of instant credibility. Your ads are no longer just a cold interruption. They appear recommended by a friend. They look popular. Viewers can see that other people, including people they know, have liked you, so they feel comfortable about liking you, too. A Facebook page that has 1,000 fans rather than 500 or 50 looks more credible.

It's like walking past two restaurants, one that's empty and one that has a line outside the door and your friends at a table inside. Which one would you want to eat at?

Fans See Your Ads More

Few people realize that Facebook shows your ads to your fans twice as often as they show them to non-fans.

That might change since Facebook frequently adjusts its rules. But Facebook has told us that currently non-fans can only see your ads in the newsfeed a maximum of twice a day, while fans may see your ads up to four times a day.

Display ads in the right column are different. They don't have frequency limitations. But Facebook doesn't want people abandoning the platform because they feel their newsfeed is being spammed by the same ads over and over again.

Since fans can see your ads in the newsfeed four times a day, you have twice the amount of space to reach fans on Facebook's most valuable real estate.

Building Warm Audiences

Targeting your fans with conversion-focused campaigns will always yield the best ROI. You're hitting a warm audience. It's like targeting people that have already joined your list or already visited your website.

Provided you have quality fans.

If you're running Like campaigns the way we teach, then you should be acquiring *quality* fans. You don't want to try and trick them into liking your page with the promise of impossible rewards or too broad of an appeal. For example, you wouldn't want to have an ad that says "Click 'Like' if you love being in shape" or "Click 'Like' if you Love Making Money." See Figure 11.1.

You want to encourage people to click "Like" because they genuinely want to hear more from you.

FIGURE 11.1–Social Proof on an Ad

The top of this ad from Sixth Division shows that Scott Rawcliffe, Justin Lofton, and 37 others like the company. Those people are friends and the viewer sees them even before they see the name of the page and the word "Sponsored." (By the way, the guys over at Sixth Division are genius when it comes to smart marketing automation.)

This is instant, subconscious social proof. People immediately drop their guard and are more likely to click the ad, opt-in, and take action. Both these ads are focused on generating leads and building customers. They are not Like campaigns, but they do show the result and the benefit of investing time and money in Like campaigns. You just get higher click-through rates, higher opt-in rates, and a better ROI.

And you also get faster growth. You get to build leads at exponential speed. Let's say that Sixth Division has 10,000 fans. Since this company helps online marketers, it might target people who like Digital Marketer and who are connected to someone who also likes Sixth Division. That's called Friends of Fans Connection Targeting.

A company with 10,000 fans might have 200,000 people who like Digital Marketer and are friends with someone who likes Sixth Division. If advertising to that group pushes the company from 10,000 fans to 12,000 fans, their friends of fans targeting audience could jump from 200,000 to 230,000. The numbers just keep growing.

Like campaigns won't take up most of your budget. We have had a client with particularly high conversions that ran them as high as 20 to 25 percent of their campaign budget but somewhere between 5 percent and 10 percent is more typical. It's a great place to start, and once it's up and running, you can set it, forget it, and leave it to run so that your audience is always growing with fresh leads.

CREATING YOUR LIKE CAMPAIGN

Like campaigns start in the Power Editor, which you can reach at https://business. facebook.com.

Once you're inside your Ads Manager, choose Power Editor from the drop-down menu shown in Figure 11.2.

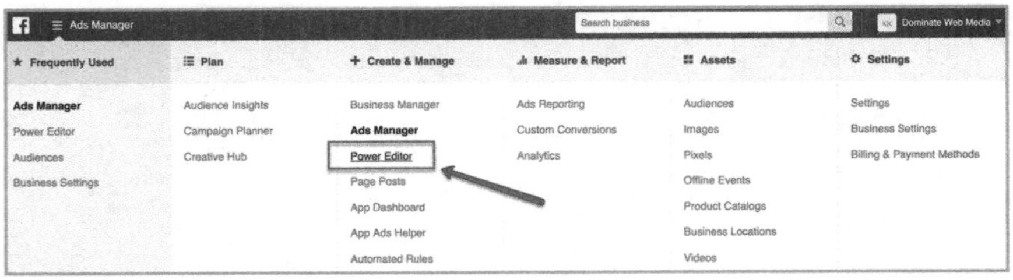

FIGURE 11.2–Selecting the Power Editor

FOUR MYTHS ABOUT LIKE CAMPAIGNS

A lot has been said and written about Facebook advertising in general and Like campaigns in particular. Not all of it is worth the blog space it's published on. Here are the four most common myths about Facebook Like campaigns, and why they're baloney:

Likes Are Worthless

Likes are worthless if you don't do anything with them. A Like is a lead. It gives your brand an audience and permission to contact that audience. It also gives you access to that audience's network, massively increasing the size of your potential reach. If all you do is run Like campaigns, you'll get little out of it. But if you use a Like campaign as the lead generation for a later marketing campaign, you'll create the first step in your conversion funnel.

You're Going to Pay for Poor Quality Leads

This isn't entirely a myth. If you target carefully, compiling an audience of poor quality leads is less likely to happen. It's the brands that appeal to anyone around the world that load up on poor quality leads—and their real Likes aren't worth much either. Choose your targeting carefully, and your poor quality Likes will be inconsequential.

There Are Cheaper Ways to Buy Likes

You can find companies off Facebook that will sell you page Likes by the bulk. None of them will be worth a dime. You don't just want to boost your page numbers. You want to build leads and gain access to new leads. It will backfire. If you have a high ration of fans who do not engage on your page, you will pay the price by not getting any organic reach.

You Won't Be Able to Reach Your Audience

Facebook limits organic access to a page's audience. If you want to communicate with a large percentage of your leads, you'll need to pay for that access. That's fair—and it pays. And today, with Facebook Live being so powerful, the more engaged fans you have, the more profitable your Facebook live sessions will be. (And remember, you can amplify these Facebook lives using advertising!)

Once you're inside the Power Editor, choose "Create Campaign" and select the campaign objective "Page Likes."

After selecting "Page Likes," you'll need to name your campaign. Choose a name that identifies your goal, such as "Like Campaign." More important is how you name the ad sets that you'll build inside the campaign.

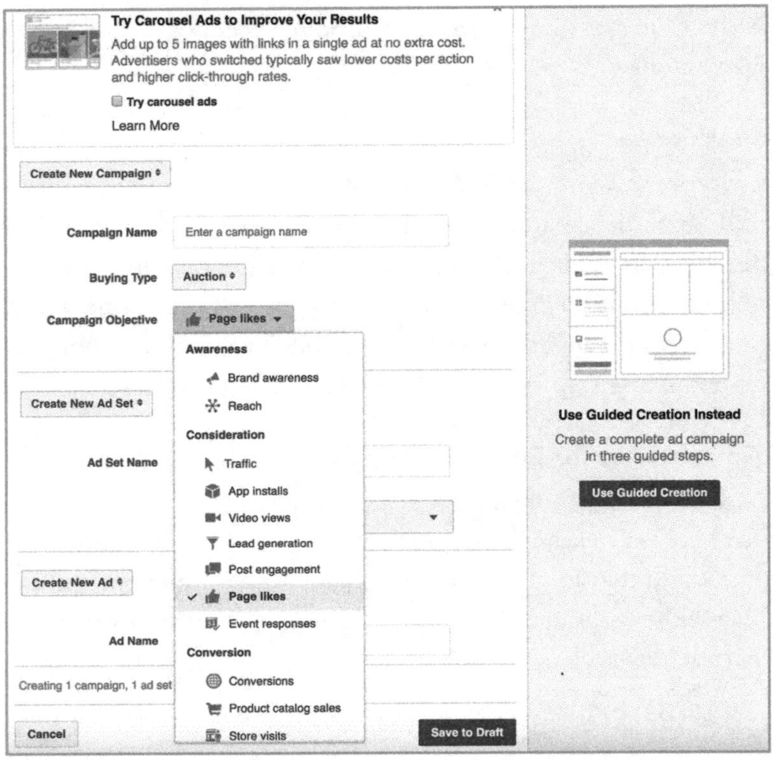

FIGURE 11.3–Create Page Like Campaign Using Power Editor

Facebook changes the design and functionality of the Ads Manager and Power Editor but the current order of tasks during ad creation is: setting the "campaign objective," (in this case, Page Likes); building the "ad set," which involves defining the audience, placements, and budget; then designing the "ad" itself, which is the creative part of the task and requires picking images and writing the copy.

CREATING AD SETS

Once you've chosen the Facebook page you want to promote, the next step is to pick an audience.

For a Like Campaign, you should focus on targeting cold audiences. If appropriate for your business, a good place to begin is the main five English-speaking countries: U.S., Canada, United Kingdom, Australia, and New Zealand. If you want to hit other countries, such as those in Europe, make sure that under languages you choose "English All" so that you're only hitting the English-speaking people in those countries.

Next up are age and gender. If you were selling women's sportswear or a cure for male pattern baldness, you could use those options to hone down your audience.

Detailed targeting lets you focus on people with particular interests. This is where your research becomes useful. For example, if you were promoting a fitness product, you might try targeting people who have expressed an interest in the Atkins Diet and the South Beach Diet.

As soon as you pick one interest, you'll start to see similar topics. Facebook has become really good at matching interests so you can add more related groups very easily, but that doesn't mean you should. Creating different ad sets for different interests will let you see how the response of each of those interests compares. For now, just choose one or two related interests to build a reach of around 1.5 million.

Beneath the Detailed Targeting are Connections. Select "Exclude people who like your page" as these people are already fans.

So you've set the objective, picked the page, and chosen the audience. Next up is Placements—where your ads will appear.

Since this is a Like campaign, all of the platform options that Facebook offers under Edit Placements—Instagram, Audience Network, and Messenger—are ineligible. You can just stick with the recommended Automatic Placements option. Facebook does allow you to restrict your campaign to mobile devices or non-mobile devices, and even choose the kinds of devices you want to run the ads on. It's unlikely you'll need to.

The final option for the ad set is the budget. A good amount to start with is $10 per day per ad set, though you can do a little less if you want. Keep the bidding automatic, and name the ad set based on your targeting and placement so that you can easily identify it. If you decide to change your targeting or placement before you go live, you can change the title, too. You might end up with an Ad Set called "U.S., CA, GB, AU, NZ, Women 25 to 45, Android." It's not catchy, but it is useful.

CREATING IMAGERY AND AD COPY PEOPLE LIKE

With the campaign chosen and ad set settings determined, the last stage is to write the copy and choose an image.

For a Like campaign, the Power Editor provides just three options. You can choose to use a single image, a single video, or a slideshow. See Figure 11.4 on page 70.

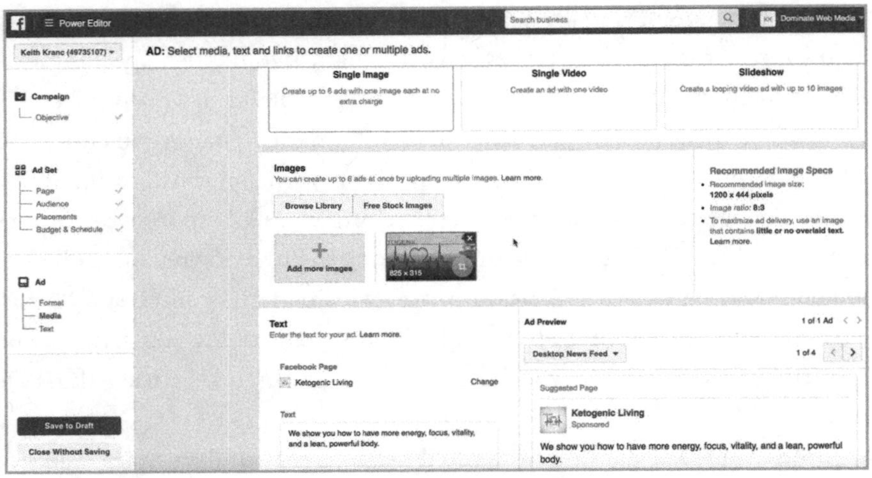

FIGURE 11.4–Selecting Images

A single image is simple and works fine. Just note that the recommended image size is unusually wide. Facebook recommends using a picture that's 1200 x 444 pixels instead of the more familiar 1200 x 628.

If you have an image of your own that you can use, complete with the rights and permissions of anyone who appears in that image, that's great. You can take it from your library or upload it. But you don't need to. Facebook will use your cover photo as a default, and it also has a partnership with, a stock photo company that gives you free access to a giant commercial image bank. Just select "Free Stock Images" to start searching for a picture that suits you.

There are no hard and fast rules about which images work best on Facebook. We've found that in general, using images that clash with Facebook's colors tend to work well. That might be a solid background that contrasts with Facebook's white and light blue color: a black background or bright backgrounds. We've also had good results with black and white images, and close-ups to the face seem to catch people's eyes too.

You'll need more than one image because you'll want to run tests. Normally, you might test two or three ads in each ad set but bear in mind that Facebook does limit the impressions. If you have more than one ad in an ad set, Facebook will start to limit the exposure on the ads it finds aren't working. That can happen very quickly, and while it's a clever bit of programming, if you're hoping to collect data, it can be frustrating. But with three ads, whose only difference is the choice of image, you will be able to collect some valuable information about your audience's preferences.

Once you've chosen your three images, you can scroll to see how each image looks in each different feed: mobile newsfeed, desktop newsfeed, desktop right column, and so on. You can crop the image and move it around.

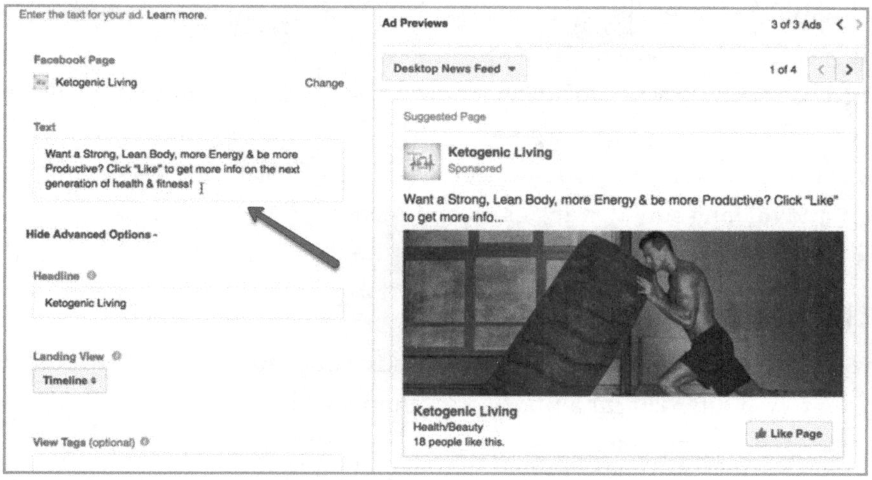

FIGURE 11.5–Like Ad Copy

In future chapters, we'll show you how you can organize your ads to put each image in its own ad set but for now you can let Facebook optimize the image for you.

You'll then have to enter the text that runs alongside each image. See Figure 11.5.

Facebook limits the copy to just 90 characters, so you have to be able to be pretty concise. You can use https://wordcounter.net to easily keep track of the number of characters in your copy. You also want to make sure that you're not making any promises you can't keep in return for the user clicking Like. You just want to let them know that clicking the button will give them great content that they'll find useful. "Click Like to join" is a simple enough call to action, and it works.

Facebook won't let you change the headlines of Like ads so this text is the only thing you can change. You can also check the mobile feed to make sure that it works on the small screen.

The Landing View indicates where the user will go if they click the headline instead of the Like button. You can choose between the timeline, likes, and photos. The timeline view is usually the best option, so make sure you have good content there as well.

At the bottom of the page, you can choose to track "All conversions from my Facebook pixel." That's worth doing because you might find that somebody clicks Like and then a week later opts in to one of your lead generation ads. Your Like campaign will show that conversion.

Sometimes, you'll see a message from Facebook saying that "Your ad's reach may be slightly lower." Facebook won't disapprove an ad at this stage if the copy is too long or if they don't like the image, but they will give a little heads-up that they might restrict the exposure of the ad if it fails to pass a review.

We've found that if you see that message, it usually pays to just submit it and see what happens. Often, it won't affect your impressions at all.

When you're ready, you can hit "Place order" and your Like campaign will be up and running.

Now you just want to double-check that everything's fine by opening the Ads Manager and making sure that it's listed and there are no errors.

DUPLICATING YOUR AD SETS

Once you've created one ad set with multiple ads, you'll also want to create at least one more ad set with different targeting. To save money, though, you can wait to see how the ads in this ad set do first.

Let these ads run for a few days, see which image performs the best, and then create a duplicate of that ad. You can then split-test two versions of the ad copy against each other with the same image and see which copy performs the best. Before you start testing your audience, you'll have the optimal image with the optimal copy.

Alternatively, you can add some more targeting groups.

Find your campaign in the Power Editor and select "Duplicate" at the top of the page. You'll want to keep the same campaign so keep the status option checked. Hit "Create," and you'll see the new campaign with the word "Copy" in the title. Don't retitle it yet; wait until you've finished with the targeting. That's the only change you're going to make in this ad set.

If you're promoting a new brand, you won't have any custom audiences yet, but you can add more interests and see who else might hit that Like button. As you add those interests, you'll see the reach change. You can repeat this process with your other ad sets, creating more sets aimed at different interests. Remember, each ad set will contain multiple ads, so you're getting a good spread and some valuable data.

When you're ready, press "Review Changes" to see what you've changed, then hit "Continue" and check the Ads Manager again to make sure that all your ad sets are listed.

That's it! Your Like campaign is up and running. You're starting to see who likes your page the most, and you're building your fan base.

Chapter 12

The Best Proven Facebook Selling Systems

There's two different but related frameworks you need to understand before designing and building your Facebook funnel. In this chapter, we'll cover one of the frameworks—Selling Systems—while in Chapters 14 and 15, we'll cover the other framework—Facebook Flight Plan.

When describing a funnel, we also call it a Selling System. This may be semantics but the phrase sales funnel conjures up the image of a process working in isolation, where it's more strategic to picture how your entire system works together to produce your desired end result.

> "*Everything at Apple can be best understood through the lens of designing. Whether it's designing the look and feel of the user experience, or the industrial design, or the system design, and even things like how the boards were laid out.*"
>
> —John Sculley

That is a major problem with the selling system most businesses are using when advertising on Facebook. It's very possible we unintentionally contributed to this problem in an earlier version of this book or perhaps in some of our earlier trainings.

If that is the case, we deeply apologize. You see, some of our initial most successful agency clients were information marketers and in our teachings, we were sharing what worked for them.

But the problem is, when it comes to interruption marketing, there's NO one-fits-all solution. Yet most businesses advertising on Facebook are trying to follow a marketing model that was created and designed specifically for information marketers.

The good news is the vast majority of businesses advertising on Facebook fall into one or more of the three following Business Categories . . .

1. Retail, Local, and Service Businesses
2. eCommerce and Physical Products
3. Digital and Information Products (*including SAAS companies*)

The importance of recognizing the three different Business Categories is because they are very different in terms of what they offer, inventory requirements, pricing strategies, profit margins, frequency of purchase, competition, and costs of business—including rent, manufacturing, shipping and handling, etc.

On top of that, the three categories typically ask prospects to take a very different action as the next step in the customer journey. For example: compare downloading a cheat-sheet Vs signing up for a free chiropractic assessment Vs purchasing supplements online.

Think about the difference level of trust required before opting-in for a cheat-sheet Vs traveling across town for an appointment vs. pulling out your credit card and purchasing a $70 bottle of powder.

In this chapter, we'll share with you the three best-selling systems for generating leads and customers on Facebook in each of the three different business categories.

ECOMMERCE AND PHYSICAL PRODUCTS

The first funnel is a Facebook ad to a lead magnet, to a product sales page to an order form (Figure 12.1 on page 75). Figure 12.2 on page 75 is a Facebook ad to a product sales page to an order form. There may not seem to be much of a difference between the two funnels—they are selling the same product. But, the second is just one step further down the sales funnel.

You might be thinking, "I will sell 150 products; I don't have a dedicated sales page for each product. This won't work for me." But in reality, it will. Remember, you want to focus your messaging on your audience's ultimate desire or biggest frustration. Find your top selling product, keep it simple, and use these funnels.

In the example, both are video ads. The first funnel brings the target to a basic squeeze page lead magnet where they can download a one-day detox. A traditional link post ad works here because the goal is to just get a lead. The purpose of the video after the lead magnet is to acknowledge their last action, give directions on how to access the

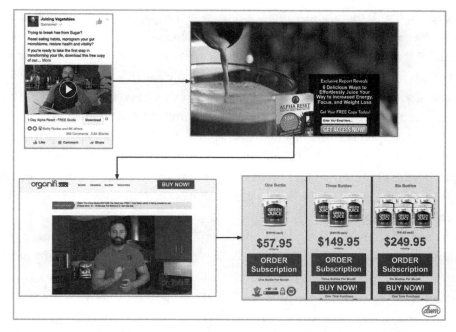
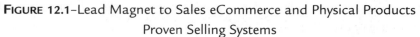

FIGURE 12.1–Lead Magnet to Sales eCommerce and Physical Products
Proven Selling Systems

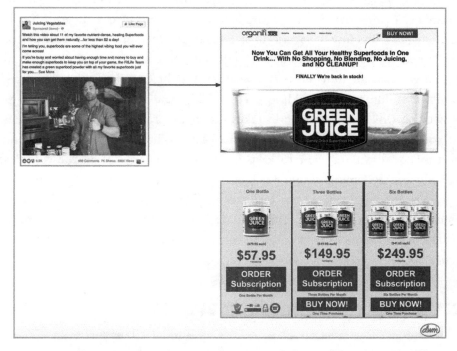
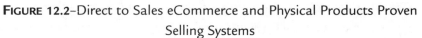

FIGURE 12.2–Direct to Sales eCommerce and Physical Products Proven
Selling Systems

lead magnet, thank them, and guide them in whatever direction they need to go to use the offer. At this point in the funnel, you want to transition into why your product is the absolute next best step. A video ad was specifically chosen because we knew we wanted quality leads in order to make the transition to the sale easier. We want people who we've built brand awareness with and who have good feelings towards us because ultimately, they are much more likely to pull out their wallet after they have opted in.

In this example, the one-day detox download hooks the target with the promise to jumpstart weight loss. The funnel then transitions into the sale by telling them to imagine having 11 amazing super foods in a great tasting, convenient, on-the-go powder that you can take every day. It does a great job of transitioning to the sale and really worked for this campaign.

The second funnel shown takes a person right from Facebook to a sales page. Most people will try to run a regular link post ad and send the user right to a catalog of all their products or a coupon without any effort to build rapport. They don't have messaging to build interest or desire in the product. It is very important to raise awareness to your audience's frustration, their challenge, and their deep desires. If you do that and get the messaging right, you can take cold audiences from Facebook directly to a sales page. That is exactly what this funnel is doing.

This sales page is a long-form sales page with information about the product, testimonials, a video that creates desire, and order form buttons. It gives much more value than just directing someone to a generic product page. The product benefits are explained concisely, testimonials provide an element of trust, and the product is presented in a way to show how it solves their weight loss challenges. This ad does a good job of building trust, building a relationship, and effectively transitioning to the offer, which is why it can successfully take potential customers directly to the sales page.

If you have several products, pick your best product and create a great message around it. For now, you want to keep it simple. You can add all the complexity of retargeting and dynamic product ads later. That's icing on the cake. Starting out, you just need to focus on one of the two proven sales funnels. The key to success is to understand the basic principles. Once you do that, you can take your specific situation and make adjustments as necessary to see what will work best for your products and audience.

DIGITAL AND INFORMATION PRODUCTS

The first funnel shows a Facebook ad, which leads to a lead magnet opt-in (Figure 12.3 on page 77). After they opt-in, they are presented with a tripwire offer, then on to the core offer, and finally an upsell (Figure 12.4 on page 77). If you are unfamiliar with

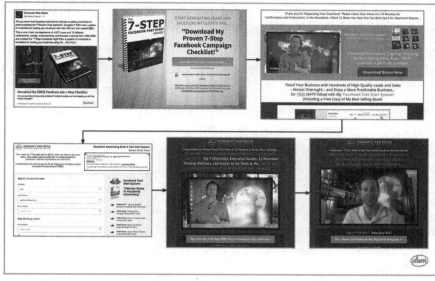

FIGURE 12.3–Lead Magnet Digital and Information Products Selling Systems

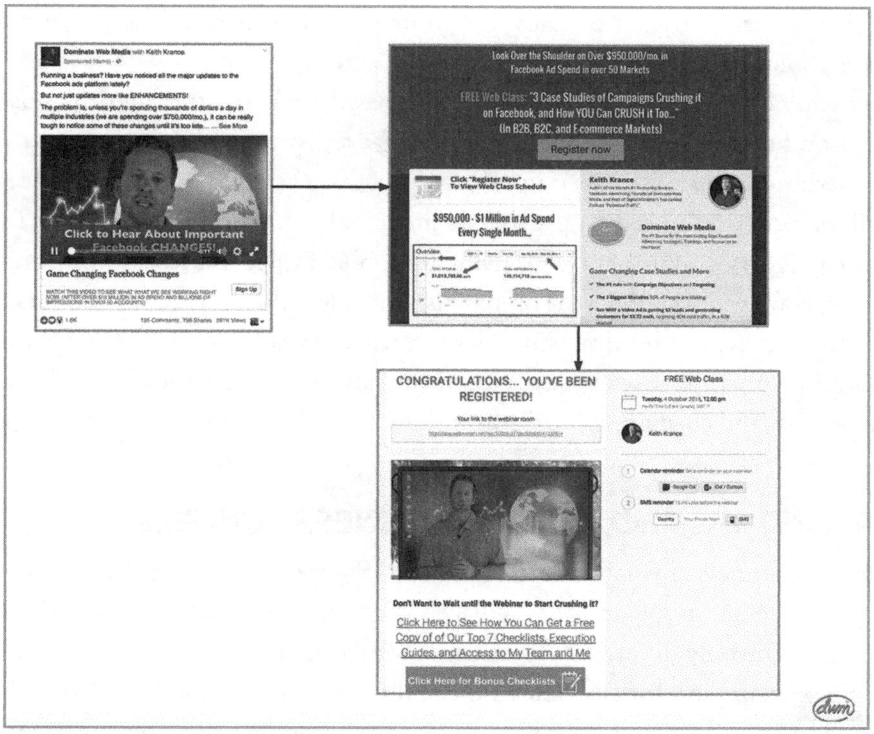

FIGURE 12.4–Webinar Proven Digital and Information Products Selling Systems

some of these marketing terms, "tripwire" was coined by Digital Marketer and refers to a low-priced (usually less than $20) impulse-buy product. The core offer is the product or service you are trying to sell.

In the example, we used a basic link post ad offering a valuable lead magnet. On the thank you page our tripwire was a free-plus-shipping offer for the previous edition of this book. After that, we offered a ten-day free trial to our continuity program, followed by an upsell offer to purchase one of our trainings.

This funnel works really well in big B2C businesses like fitness and passionate niches. It also works well for B2B like the above campaign.

The second funnel takes a potential customer from a Facebook ad, to a webinar or live event registration page, and then on to a thank you page. The thank-you page can just say, "Hey, thanks for registering," or you can give them some information to get them excited about joining the webinar. You could include a small offer like a $50 product to help offset ad costs.

Webinars are great at warming your audience up if you have a high-priced product because you have a lot more time with your potential customers. Focus on their deep desire or biggest frustration. During the webinar, you can demonstrate that you can help them and then transition into how your product can help them even more and ultimately solve their problem.

Did you notice how in the first funnel, in the ad, we used an image link post ad but in the second there's a video going to the webinar registration?

Something you want to keep in mind is if you are asking the user to do something very minor, you don't need to provide as much value in your ad, but if you're asking them for a bigger commitment, e.g., giving up some of their time to show up and attend a webinar, you need to build a lot more trust and add value in your ad and messaging.

These are two proven, successful sales funnels we've seen across the board for digital products, information based products, and education based businesses. Understand the fundamentals, and then adjust and tweak these funnels to your specific situation.

LOCAL, RETAIL, AND SERVICE BUSINESS FUNNELS

The top two funnels are really the same funnel (Figure 12.5 on page 79). They are both website conversion campaigns driving Facebook traffic to a landing page with a coupon or giveaway. The only difference is one uses a video ad and the other a link post ad.

In these examples, for the first funnels, the client already had a video and we just ran a video ad to a landing page to get a $30-off coupon. We also used an imaged-based Link Post Ad and that's what I would recommend for most people when starting—keep it simple and easy (see Figure 12.6 on page 79).

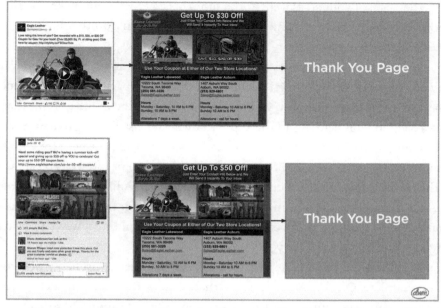

FIGURE 12.5–Discount/Incentive Proven Selling Systems for Retail, Local, and Service Businesses

FIGURE 12.6–Lead Ad Proven Selling Systems for Retail, Local, and Service Businesses

If you're a local business like a restaurant, a salon, or a gym, where people have to walk in the door, a great offer to use is a coupon or a giveaway.

You can do a lot of different offers with coupons. Offer seven days free at your gym, buy one get one free, a free consultation, etc. People like to share coupons, which broadens the reach of your ad as well. At the time this ad ran, Facebook kept it all within Facebook, so it didn't have a thank you page. Now, you can't do that anymore so you want to make sure you have a thank you page.

Let's say you have a service-based business, and you're doing a free giveaway. The majority of your leads won't be high quality, so a thank you page is extremely important. After they enter to win the giveaway, you want to have some kind of offer on the thank you page like a coupon. This helps to sift through those who are just entering to have a chance at getting something for free and those who actually have an interest or need for your service. You want to give them an incentive to pick up the phone or come into your business.

In the third funnel, we are using what is called a "Lead Ad." The advantage of using a Lead Ad is that people can opt-in without ever leaving their newsfeed; in other words, there's no need to have a web page. So if the thought of building a web site scares you, this might be the best option for you.

Even if you do have a website, with a Lead Ad, the user is probably not going to end up on your site. On the "Success" page, there is a button they can click to be taken to your thank you page, but in our experience, typically only about 20 to 25 percent of people click through.

For Local Businesses, there's a third type of campaign you should consider running, and that's a branding campaign. This campaign may or may not have a direct call to action but it is important to help establish your business as top of mind when someone in your community develops intent. We recommend allocating a small portion of your ad budget to branding.

A branding campaign can be as simple as boosting a post. For example, pretend you own a restaurant. You can post a picture of people having a great time in your restaurant and say, "Come into the restaurant, mention Facebook, and get a free appetizer." It's that easy.

If you're a real estate agent or an automotive dealership, consider doing a video ad or an article. Your goal here is to have people see you and to build trust with them. Just boost it so people see the video or article all month long. Then, when they are ready to sell their house, buy a house, or buy a car, who do you think they will think of first?

This too can help you to build your invisible targeting lists—we'll talk more about that in the Audience Chapter.

Facebook is a really inexpensive way to get your message out when you compare it to TV advertising, billboards, radio, or direct mailers. If you have 1,000 people watch at least 25 percent of your video that will probably cost you somewhere around five or ten cents for each view. Those are quality views and that is a big deal. If you can do a monthly video or article, it's an extra bonus.

Now that you are armed with proven funnels and selling systems for your specific business, it's time to put these fundamentals into practice and tweak them.

Chapter 13

Understanding Audience Awareness

The customer buying cycle is an interesting phenomena. In Figure 13.1 on page 82, you can see a diagram of the typical buying cycle. It doesn't matter what you're buying—a new car, hairspray, or attorney services—there's a specific subconscious process we all follow. It's human nature.

Think about it. What was the last significant purchase you made?

If you're like most people, when you think back, it probably started with a problem you wanted solved.

Now a problem doesn't have to be a major catastrophe; a problem can be some common everyday scenario like wanting to look good for an upcoming school reunion, generating more customers for your business, or where to take your special someone for your anniversary.

> *"The journey of a thousand miles begins with one step."*
>
> —LAO TZU

To be able to solve your problem, depending on your current level of market knowledge, you may need to do some research (e.g., you may already have a favorite romantic restaurant or maybe you haven't purchased a fashionable item of clothing in the last ten years). Research could entail visiting your local mall, performing a Google search, reading Amazon reviews, or asking your family or friends for recommendations.

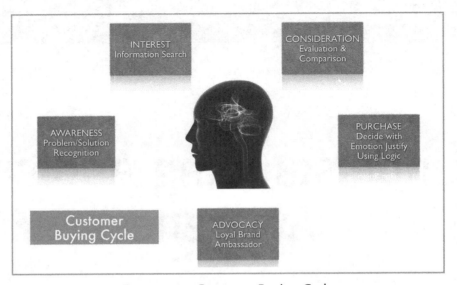

FIGURE 13.1–Customer Buying Cycle

After gathering information, the next step is to evaluate options—not necessarily from a logical perspective, but from an emotional one—such as how will this product or solution make you feel?

When a solution feels right, all that's left is finding a great logical reason to go ahead and buy, but remember "the mind will justify what the heart has already decided," as Roy H. Williams repeats over and over again in his many teachings.

After you've purchased your product or service, if you truly love it you might become a raving fan and start telling other people about it. People do this for two main reasons:

1. To help others.
2. To further justify their buying decision. If their friends buy the same solution and love it, they'll feel better about their purchasing decision.

This last level is called Brand Ambassador and where we strive for all of our customers to end up. And in a nutshell, that's basically the customer buying cycle.

HOW FACEBOOK FITS IN

Don't confuse Google AdWords with Facebook Advertising. They are two completely different animals. In fact, a lot of the skills needed to be great on Google AdWords don't really carry over to Facebook. In some ways, AdWords is actually easier than Facebook Advertising (but also more expensive).

The reason for this is because people searching on Google or YouTube are already showing intent. They're actively looking for a solution to their problem so we have an idea of the conversation that might be going on inside their head.

If we look back at the customer buying cycle, Google or YouTube Searchers are beyond the first step of the buying cycle and already into the second step: "Interest."

Think about it.

What was the last thing you Googled? Were you looking for an answer to a question or trying to solve a problem?

So when advertising on AdWords, offering a specific solution to a specific problem is a winning strategy. If your water pipe bursts in your basement, and you see an ad saying "We fix broken water pipes, we won't rip you off and can be there in 30 minutes," you're probably going to click that ad, right?

FACEBOOK IS VERY DIFFERENT

But the previous plumbing ad example would be a disaster on Facebook.

Why?

Because Facebook Advertising is interruption marketing.

NO ONE on Facebook is actively looking for a solution. In fact, chances are they're looking for the exact opposite. They're looking for an escape like catching up with family or friends or watching the latest viral video.

THAT'S WHY FACEBOOK'S SUPER POWER IS YOUR KRYPTONITE

You've probably heard Facebook collects an incredible amount of data on its users including what websites they visit, what they like, and what they click on. MIT's

FIGURE 13.2–Facebook's Super Power: Targeting

Technology Review states it's "the most extensive data set EVER assembled on human social behavior."

The mistake most people make when advertising on Facebook is thinking it's all about targeting. That leveraging this incredible wealth of data to show your ads to an extremely targeted audience will yield success and fortune.

But unfortunately, in my experience, rarely does this strategy work. Letting yourself get enamored with the potential targeting and retargeting options typically causes people to miss the big picture. And that is . . .

STRATEGY AND MESSAGING BEATS TARGETING AND NINJA OPTIMIZATION

Even if you are showing your ads to the right type of people on Facebook, you have no way of knowing what problems or concerns are at the top of their mind at that very moment or if they're even actively looking for a solution. In fact they might not even know a solution exists or worse yet not even be aware they're experiencing a specific problem.

So what do you do? How do you move someone through the Customer Buying Cycle if you don't even know where they currently are in the Buying Cycle?

BREAKTHROUGH ADVERTISING

In 1966, the late great Eugene Schwartz published the now classic marketing book called *Breakthrough Advertising* (Bottom Line Books, 2004).

Inside the book, Eugene describes five levels of product awareness. They are:

1. *Most Aware.* These people know your product well. They are brand ambassadors. They've made multiple purchases and openly endorse your product or services.
2. *Product Aware.* These people know your product but haven't purchased yet. They're familiar with what's available in the marketplace but not sure if your solution is the right one for them.
3. *Solution Aware.* They know of different solutions to their problem but don't know which solution is right for them. They don't know your specific product or service.

FIGURE 13.3–*Breakthrough Advertising*

4. *Problem Aware*. They recognize they have a problem but don't know what to do about it.

5. *Unaware*. They don't even realize they have a problem.

INTRODUCING UPSYD

To make this incredible framework easy-to-remember and Facebook friendly, I've reversed the order and come up with the acronym UPSYD (pronounced "upside").

UPSYD will change the game for you. You'll be able to diagnose why previous campaigns didn't work, how to fix them, and exactly who you should target.

As corny as it might sound, there really is a lot of UPSIDE from embracing "UPSYD."

So, what does UPSYD stand for?

U = Unaware

P = Problem Aware

S = Solution Aware

Y = Your Solution Aware

D = Deal*

(*Deal = just need a great deal to purchase)

To illustrate how to use UPSYD I'm going to share with you a behind-the-scenes peek at a campaign we ran for a brand new fictional business we created purely as a demonstration for a Facebook ads course, called Ketogenic Living (see Figure 13.4).

In just one month, we went from a concept to having over 29,000 fans and over 5,000 leads for this brand-new business (see Figure 13.5).

To give you more context, let me first give you a little background about their niche—Intermittent Fasting.

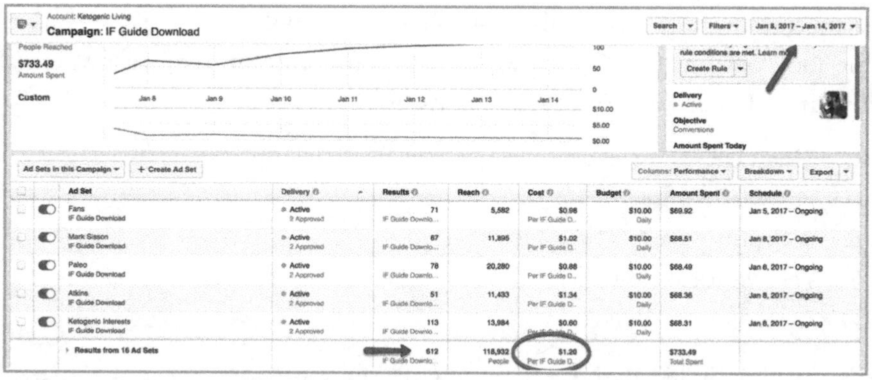

FIGURE 13.4–30-Day Keto Like Ad Campaign Results

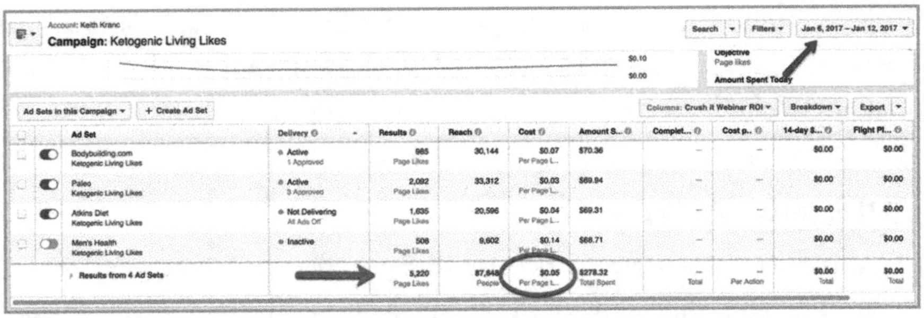

FIGURE 13.5–30-Day Website Conversion Campaign Results

Intermittent Fasting is in the Health and Wellness space. It's a different way to approach eating. It's not so much a diet but more changing the timing of when you eat, more specifically increasing the amount of time that you DON'T eat. For example, if your last meal of the day is at 8:00 P.M., your next meal might not be until noon the following day giving you a 16-hour fasting period.

The benefits of Intermittent Fasting include weight loss, reducing your caloric intake (because you're eating less), natural detoxification, normalizing blood sugar and hormone levels, plus increasing energy levels and focus.

When I first tried Intermittent Fasting, I lost almost 30 pounds, and I didn't even think I was overweight!

CREATING ADS

For a business like this, someone from a Google AdWords background might create an ad using Intermittent Fasting as the main hook, e.g., "Download your FREE Intermittent cheat sheet now!," where the cheat sheet positions their product as the next logical step. This makes a lot of sense if you're targeting someone who is googling "Intermittent Fasting."

But there's a problem with this approach on Facebook.

If we look back at UPSYD, an ad talking about Intermittent Fasting would only work if your audience was "Your Solution Aware."

U = Unaware

P = Problem Aware

S = Solution Aware

Y = Your Solution Aware

D = Deal

Let's say the circle on the left represents the entire Health and Fitness Market (See Figure 13.6 on page 87), which might include people who are interested in *Men's*

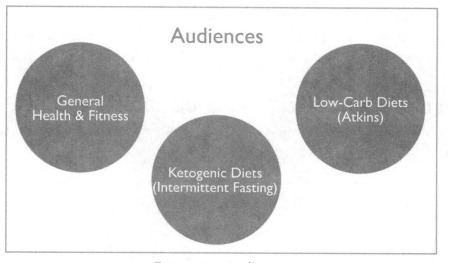

FIGURE 13.6–Audiences

Health magazine, *Women's Health* magazine, the Atkins Diet, the South Beach Diet, and different fitness celebrities.

There'll be a certain percentage of people in this audience who might be interested in the benefits of Intermittent Fasting but don't know what it is—just hearing the word "fasting" might actually turn them off thinking it's a religious ritual.

So even though a percentage of this audience might be interested in what we're offering, an ad talking about Intermittent Fasting is going to go straight over their heads. It may not even register on their radars. To be effective, these people need to be educated first to progress through the levels of awareness.

If we look deeper into the Health and Wellness Market, there's a reasonably large segment of people who are interested in dieting (circle on the right). They might have interests, such as low carb diets, the Atkins Diet, and the South Beach Diet. These people are aware that changing what you eat can cause weight loss but may not be aware that changing when you eat can also do this.

Once again, even though a percentage of this audience might be interested in what we're offering, an ad talking about Intermittent Fasting probably won't work with this crowd as they too need to be educated—perhaps not as much as the more general audience, but still, some education is needed to progress their awareness level.

Then there's a much smaller, more targeted segment of the Health and Wellness audience who already know about Ketogenic Diets and Intermittent Fasting, and perhaps are looking for a way to get started or perform better. They might have interests like Bullet Proof Coffee, Ketosis, and Dave Asprey.

This is the segment where our ad would probably be most effective, it's the low-hanging fruit so to speak, but it's also a small audience, which means it's going to be challenging to scale using this marketing message.

CRAFTING YOUR PERFECT FACEBOOK HOOK

Think about UPSYD as a staircase with giant steps, where U (Unaware) is at the bottom and D (Deal) is at the top (see Figure 13.7).

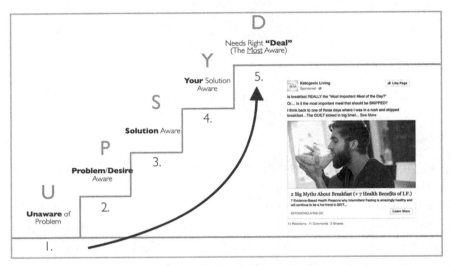

FIGURE 13.7–Staircase

Now imagine standing at the bottom and stepping up onto the first step. How challenging is that? Not too bad, right?

Now try skipping a step, go from standing at the bottom and stepping up onto the second step. This is a little harder and requires a little more effort, but it's still manageable.

Now what happens if you try to go straight to the third, fourth, or even the fifth step? Gets more and more challenging, right? In fact, it's no longer possible to step from the bottom to the top—it's more like a leap!

This is how I want you to think about your Facebook ads.

When you don't know exactly what your audience wants, use your targeting to figure out where they might be on the UPSYD staircase. Once you know where your audience's awareness level is, you can figure out what's needed in your messaging to get them up the rest of the steps.

The higher you start on the staircase, the more direct you can go for the sale, but also realize your audience will be smaller. The lower you start on the staircase, the more value you need to provide to move people up the staircase but the easier it is to scale because you can target larger audiences.

Now this might go against traditional direct marketing. You've probably heard the saying "the riches are in the niches," which is true.

Remember, you can always use the content in your ad to niche down, but I'm telling you that if you can target big and broad audiences and give the Facebook's algorithms a chance to do its magic, you'll be much better off in the long run.

Let's bring this back to our Ketogenic Living example.

So a hook that talks about Intermittent Fasting, targeting people who already know about Intermittent Fasting is like starting all the way up on Step 4 "Your Solution Aware." You will get sales and may not have to work too hard to get them, but you'll find it very challenging to find enough audiences to sustain your business long-term.

MESSAGING FOR BROAD AUDIENCES

Figure 13.8 on page 90 is an ad we used to target people who were down on Steps 2 and 3. We could have even targeted people on Step 1 and exponentially increased our potential reach. Let's look at the results. After reaching 469,000 people, this ad has 1,100 likes and 557 shares. That's a 2:1 Like-to-Share ratio, which is really good. Typically in a B2B market a 3 to 1 Like to Share Ratio is really good, so a 2:1 is doing really, really well.

You'll also notice there are a lot of comments, so people are engaged, and people are tagging their friends to check out the ad. In the real world that's called a referral.

So how did we achieve these great results?

Let's take a closer look at the Long Copy Ad we used in Figure 13.8.

AD BREAK-DOWN

In Figure 13.9 on page 90 you can see the ad breakdown. Basically, what we're trying to achieve is to give our audience a "Big Aha Moment," something that goes against conventional wisdom and grabs attention coupled with great content to add value, which makes people want to share.

We decided to use the hook "Is breakfast really the most important meal of the day, or is it the most important meal that should be skipped?"

You may have heard me talk about the six principles of why people share before, which comes from Jonah Berger's book *Contagious: Why Things Catch On* (Simon & Schuster, 2016).

Here's a quick recap. Jonah uses the acronym STEPPS to explain why things catch on where:

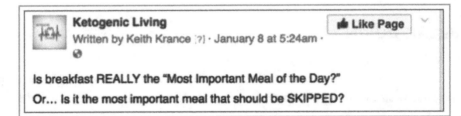

Figure 13.8–Keto Long Copy Ad

Figure 13.9–Keto Ad Breakdown, Part 1

S = Social Currency

    e.g., We share things that make us look good.

T = Triggers

    e.g., Top of mind is tip of tongue.

E = Emotions

e.g., When we care, we share.

P = Public Visibility

e.g., When something is built to show, it's built to grow.

P = Practical Value

e.g., Something that you can use.

S = Stories

e.g., Information that can be shared in an entertaining manner.

The hook, "Is Breakfast really the most important meal of the day, or the most important meal that should be skipped?" is trying to leverage as many of these principles as possible. It's a piece of useful information that makes the reader look clever if they share, provides hope of what's possible, wrapped up in a story of my own experience, and that has the potential to be retriggered daily whenever someone sits down to eat breakfast.

> The crazy thing is that the reasons behind the "breakfast is the most important meal of the day" phenomenon are mostly all MYTHS...
>
> Only backed by OBSERVATIONAL STUDIES, which can NOT demonstrate causation.
>
> Breakfast eaters tend to have healthier habits in general, so many studies have shown breakfast eaters tend to be healthier.
> **The problem is these studies only show that people who eat breakfast are MORE LIKELY to be healthier, but they CANNOT prove that breakfast itself CAUSED it.
>
> MYTH #1. Eating Breakfast Boosts Metabolism:
> > Eating breakfast does NOT boost metabolism. Studies show that there is no difference in calories burned over 24 hours between people who eat or skip breakfast. Whether we eat or skip breakfast has no effect on the amount of calories we burn throughout the day. This is a myth.
>
> MYTH #2. Skipping Breakfast Causes Weight Gain:
> > Yes it's true that skipping breakfast causes people to be hungrier and eat more lunch, but this is NOT ENOUGH to overcompensate for the breakfast that was skipped. In fact, some studies have even shown that skipping breakfast may REDUCE overall calorie intake by up to 400 calories per day...

FIGURE 13.10–Keto Ad Breakdown, Part 2

The ad also provides value by educating about the two biggest myths associated with eating breakfast, which are:

1. Breakfast kick-starts your metabolism in the A.M.

2. Skipping breakfast causes weight gain.

> Skipping breakfast is actually a common part of many Intermittent Fasting methods, and is what I do every single day. And it has been the best decision I've ever made.
>
> I dropped over 30 pounds very quickly (without even thinking I was overweight to begin with or being on a diet), my days are simpler, I have more focus & energy all day long, and my body naturally removes toxins on a daily basis, without having to take any weird supplements.

FIGURE 13.11–Keto Ad Breakdown, Part 3

You might be wondering why I used my own personal story (how I dropped 30 lbs) rather than make a promise to my audience, such as, "Want to Drop 30 lbs?"

That's because Facebook hates claims and promises.

Facebook is a young company full of young professionals with a culture of making the world a better place. They much prefer you to talk about your product or service and spend much less time talking about your audience, especially if you are calling out flaws or imperfections.

This goes against the whole "WITFM" direct marketing principle, but if you don't follow their rules, you can't play with their football.

For example, you can't write "Lose 30 lbs in 30 Days"—that will get your ad banned. But if I share how I lost 28 lbs in six weeks, it's OK because I'm sharing my own results. Testimonials work well, too, but there are certain rules in some industries, like you can't show before and after pictures in the weight loss niche.

So now that I've caught their attention and sparked their interest with the hook, it's time to introduce the solution, which is Intermittent Fasting (see Figure 13.12).

> Here's 7 Evidence-Based health reasons why Intermittent Fasting is amazingly healthy and will continue to be a hot trend in 2017:

FIGURE 13.12–Keto Ad Breakdown, Part 4

Here (Figure 13.13 on page 93), I'm providing further proof on why Intermittent Fasting is so great.

And now we start to pivot into a pitch (Figure 13.14 on page 93).

BACK TO UPSYD

The goal with your Facebook ads is to move people from awareness to intent (Figure 13.15 on page 94).

1. It helps Weight Loss Happen Fast - Since we eat fewer meals and take in less calories in a 24-hour period (even if we eat larger meals). Additionally, Intermittent Fasting keeps us at ideal hormone levels (lowers insulin levels and increases human growth hormone).

2. Reduces Oxidative Stress and Inflammation in the Body - Several studies show that intermittent fasting may enhance the body's resistance to oxidative stress. (Oxidative Stress impacts aging & chronic diseases)

3. It May Improve Cardiovascular Health (Help the Heart) - Intermittent fasting has been shown to improve numerous different risk factors, including blood pressure, total and LDL cholesterol, blood triglycerides, inflammatory markers and blood sugar levels. (However, a lot of this is based on animal studies, so we will not see official data about the effect on humans until more studies on humans can be completed & published.)

4. It May Help Prevent Cancer and Induce Cellular Repair - When we fast, the cells in the body initiate a cellular "waste removal" process called autophagy. Increased autophagy may provide protection against several diseases, including cancer and Alzheimer's disease. Fasting has also been shown to have several beneficial effects on metabolism that may lead to reduced risk of cancer. Although human studies are needed, promising evidence from animal studies indicates that intermittent fasting may help prevent cancer

5. It Improves Brain Function - Studies have shown to increase Synaptic Plasticity (Improve Learning and Memory), Enhanced performance on memory tests in the elderly. Several studies in rats have shown that intermittent fasting may increase the growth of new nerve cells, and that it also increases levels of a brain hormone called brain-derived neurotrophic factor (BDNF), a deficiency of which has been implicated in depression and various other brain problems.

6. It May Help Prevent Alzheimer's Disease - A study in rats shows that intermittent fasting may delay the onset of Alzheimer's disease or reduce its severity. In a series of case reports, a lifestyle intervention that included daily short-term fasts was able to significantly improve Alzheimer's symptoms in 9 out of 10 patients. Animal studies also suggest that fasting may protect against other neurodegenerative diseases, including Parkinson's and Huntington's disease. However, more research in humans is needed.

7. It May Extend Lifespan - Studies in rats have shown that intermittent fasting extends lifespan in a similar way as continuous calorie restriction. In some of these studies, the effects were quite dramatic. In one of them, rats that fasted every other day lived 83% longer than rats who weren't fasted. Although this is far from being proven in humans, it is still powerful information.

FIGURE 13.13–Keto Ad Breakdown, Part 5

The variety of health benefits of Intermittent Fasting (IF) is quite amazing, and no wonder it has changed my own life and so many other early adopters in such a dramatic fashion...

Which is why we've created "A Beginner's Guide to Intermittent Fasting" - a FREE guide we are giving away for a limited time to help spread the word about IF as quickly as possible!

This guide gives the step-by-step plan for the Top 3 Intermittent Fasting Methods out today, the most popular and easy to apply.

Download Now >> www.KetogenicLiving.co/Get-Lean

FIGURE 13.14–Awareness to Intent

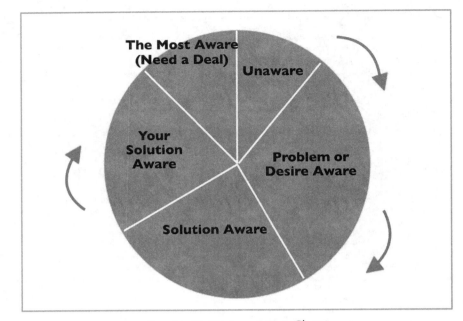

FIGURE 13.15–Awareness Chart

The purpose of this ad is to target people who are "Problem Aware." People who know they need to lose weight or would like more energy or more focus, and so on. By using the breakfast curiosity hook it's also possible we might start to attract people who are in the "Unaware" segment. Those people who are thinking they're healthy, but don't realize there might be a better way.

Now if someone is already "Solution Aware," this ad will still work. It's a good hook; plus, it's educational. If someone is "Your Solution Aware" and wants other people to not think they're crazy because they're doing Intermittent Fasting, guess what they're going to do? They're going to share this. So it's going to work well for these people as well.

Now if you're trying to target just people who are "Your Solution Aware," you may or may not use this ad. You could use a much simpler and more direct ad, such as one that goes straight to your product's sale page.

IS IT REALLY POSSIBLE TO JUMP ALL FIVE STEPS WITH JUST ONE AD?

Believe it or not we actually have several clients who target large broad audiences and sell them a physical product (taking people from the bottom of the staircase to the top) with just one ad.

Now we also use retargeting strategies with these clients to maximize ROI, but I just wanted to make it clear that it really is possible to sell directly on Facebook.

How do we do this?

By using our Three-Step Video Ad Formula and the UPSYD framework.

In other words, in this example, you could use the same hook and copy we've discussed here for the Long Copy Ad and make it into a video, and because video is such a great medium to build trust, make connections, offer value, and build your brand, it's much easier to ascend the five steps in a very small amount of time.

Plus, video ads have other advantages.

With video ads, you're building warm audiences quickly and cheaply. Just some of the new audiences you can create from a video ad include: people who have watched three seconds of your video, people who have watched ten seconds of your video, people who have watched 25 percent of your video, people who have watched 50 percent of your video, people who have watched 75 percent of your video, and people who have watched 95 percent of your video.

Since you can build these audiences fast, in our experience, these are also some of the best sources for creating look-a-like audiences, e.g., providing Facebook large amounts of data to go out and find more people who are just like your current prospects and customers.

So in conclusion, to win big on Facebook, you've got to understand UPSYD. You've got to be perpetually moving people up the staircase from Level 1 to Level 5.

The best way to do this is to start with Level 3, build some momentum, and then expand out—identifying the best messaging for each level. People think Facebook is all about targeting when really it's about getting your messaging right. It's understanding the conversations in people's minds and meeting them where they are—connecting with them, adding value, and increasing their awareness of both you and your business. When you couple the right messaging with a video ad, now you're in the position to take your business to a whole new level.

I've seen it happen over and over again. Discover how to move people from casual interest to rabid fans at www.perrymarshall.com/fbtools.

Chapter 14

First Two Stages of the Facebook Flight Plan™

When learning a new skill, success is almost always dependent on two things—a solid understanding of the basics and gaining experience with those fundamentals. You can't expect to start flying a Boeing 747 as a brand-new pilot. You have start in something small, like a single-engine Cessna 152, Piper Warrior, or something similar. And your flight instructor does most of the hard work, so you can focus on just the most important, core elements of flying the airplane. Doing so allows you to gain the needed experience or foundation to build upon in the future. Learning to run a successful Facebook campaign is the same. So many Facebook marketing rookies get caught up in all the complexities and the possibilities rather than master the fundamentals. As you begin, the best advice you can follow is to keep it simple and gain experience.

> "*All you need is the plan, the road map, and the courage to press on to your destination.*"
>
> —EARL NIGHTINGALE

FACEBOOK CAMPAIGN BLUEPRINT

Let's walk through the Facebook campaign blueprint. For those of you beginning your marketing journey on Facebook, Figure 14.1 on page 98 shows two proven campaigns to help you achieve your first zero to 100 conversions (leads, sales, etc.).

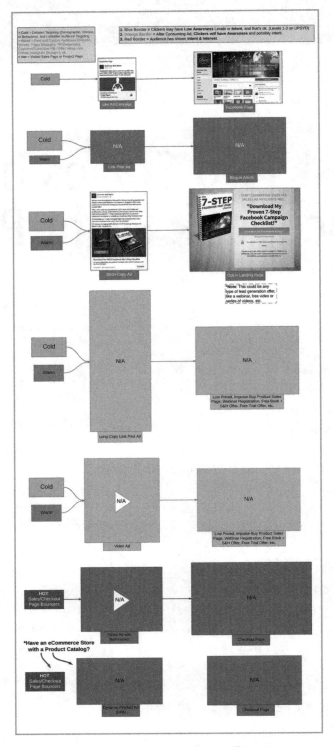

FIGURE 14.1–0–100 Conversions Selling System

The first is called a "Like" ad campaign. In this example, the call to action is to click "Like" if they want cutting-edge tips and resources about Facebook ads from someone "in the trenches." Notice that there is nothing in the destination column. This is because this ad will keep them within Facebook. Once "Like" is clicked, the user can continue scrolling through their feed rather than being taken out of Facebook to another website. The second example is called a Website Conversions Link Post Ad. Normally, you will use the Website Conversions campaign objective. However, this could even be a Boosted Post that drives traffic to a landing page, with the purpose of generating conversions. (Facebook's algorithm won't be able to optimize based on Conversions; they optimize based on Engagement, but that's OK because this gets you momentum, traffic, conversions, and most of all—DATA!) The image you see is a clickable link, which once clicked will redirect the user to another website (aka: Link Post Ad). You can also run a Facebook "Lead Ad," which is where the user fills in the form right inside the Facebook newsfeed. Facebook will pre-populate some of their contact fields, making it simpler with less friction to opt-in. (*Note*: with Lead Ads, users are not automatically redirected to your confirmation page. They remain on Facebook, with an option to click a button to visit your website after they sign up.)

The destination is a simple landing page. This ad can target both warm and/or cold audiences, depending on the situation. At this point, you most likely haven't done much to build warm audiences. You may be getting traffic from search engines and referrals and maybe even have some fans on Facebook. Don't worry about building warm audiences just yet. Remember, we're keeping it simple. These two campaigns are all you need to start gaining momentum on Facebook. That's it! It's very simple and doable for even the most novice of Facebook marketers.

Once you have anywhere from around 101 to 1,000 conversions (this is not a hard and fast rule—just a guideline for novices), you are understanding how things work a bit more and can start to layer on more ad types and strategies. In Figure 14.2 on page 100, you will see a video ad as your third ad campaign type.

However, this doesn't HAVE to be a video ad. This could be a Long Copy, value-based, or story-based ad (kind of like a mini blog post that is written as part of the post of the ad).

Congratulations! If you've generated 100 or more conversions for your new campaign, you made it through the most difficult part of the entire journey. Whether it's your first campaign ever or this is just a new campaign, getting to this point is like getting through those critical first two minutes of a space shuttle launch, before the solid rocket booster separation. (OK, maybe not quite the same, but you get the point.)

And like always, please take your unique situation and adjust accordingly.

You may be ready to add this next layer after generating 20 to 25 conversions.

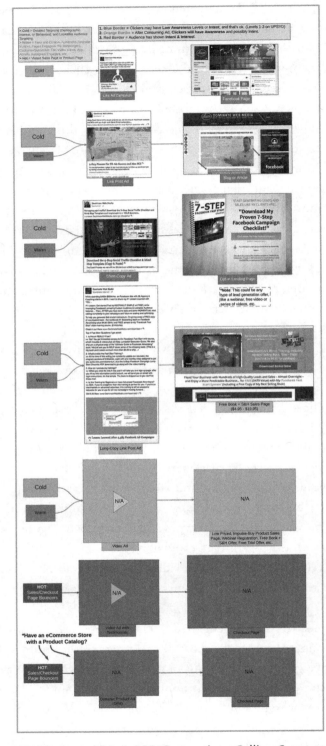

FIGURE 14.2–101–1,000 Conversions Selling System

You may not be generating leads.

You may not be generating sales conversions online at all. You may be running ads with the goal to get people to go into Home Depot and buy your baseboard heater covers (like one of our clients does), and Home Depot won't even let you track any of your ad performance. (But you know your ads are working because after they were running for two weeks, your Home Depot sales went through the roof!)

Remember, these are guidelines to give you a framework so you can go out and handle any given situation and dominate.

Now it's time to layer on another ad type so you can target more audiences, connect better with more people with different levels of awareness, levels of intent, levels of trust and rapport, and different buyer personas inside your existing audiences. You're following some people down the customer journey, and you're helping others move down the same journey.

The next ad type should be a Long Copy Link Post Ad or Content with Call-to-Action (CTA) Video Ad. This really depends on your situation, assets, style, landing page content, which ad type you started with, and how big your "ask" is.

Let's say your goal is to get webinar registrations from cold traffic and offer a product or service for $500 or more on the webinar. Webinars are great at warming your audience up if you have a high-priced product because you have a lot more time with your potential customers. Use your messaging to focus on their deep desire or big frustration. During the webinar, you can deliver tons of value, build trust, rapport, and desire for your product or service, then transition into how your product can fulfill that desire or solve their problem.

However, even if your webinar is free, your best potential customers will value their time just as much as or more than their money, so if your goal is to persuade a random Facebook user who has never seen you or your brand to not only sign up for one of your webinars but to actually show up for the webinar, then you've got a lot of work to do!

And I haven't even touched on webinar consumption, which is paying attention and actually watching and listening to the content on your webinar.

This is one of the reasons why long-copy ads and video ads are so powerful. They will usually bring in a much higher quality lead than your typical short-copy ad that you see most advertisers using.

Now, if you are the type of person who feels comfortable writing long-copy ads or making video ads, you might start out with a video ad or long-copy ad as your very first primary ad, back in the 0 to 100 takeoff phase.

Let's say you bottled water, but not just any bottled water. A scientist on your team discovered a secret formula for making the only plastic bottles in the world that do not leak toxins into the fluid inside the bottle after it sits in the sun for a few hours, like all the other bottles in your industry do. (Of course, you have all the necessary patents and trademarks.)

After reading through Chapters 16 to 19 of this book, along with using our Ad Builder tool mentioned in Chapter 18, you quickly came up with a great hook that resonates with people way down at step one or two on the UPSYD staircase—they are either completely Unaware of the problem or they are Problem aware, but not solution aware. So, you start out with a long-copy ad that makes people aware of the problem and transitions to showing them how your solution is the answer to solving that problem. The first line in your ad says, "Are your water bottles leaking cancer-causing toxins into the water you or your kids are drinking? New study reveals [really scary statistic goes here]" Your ad shows the results of the study (making them aware of the problem), then transitions into how and why you created your amazing non-cancer-causing bottles that somehow also make the water taste amazing and be more effective and healthy. Your ad also shows how your company is running a special pricing offer or promotion right now (until supplies last), because you feel like it's your mission to get these water bottles into the homes of as many people as possible, to make the biggest impact possible and to save lives. Add a line that says something like, "To try this amazing water before supplies run out, click www.AmazingWatersXYZ.com."

After that ad starts running, gathering some data, and generating some conversions, you start getting excited and want to add in another layer of ads. But this time, maybe you run a simpler, short-copy ad that resonates with people at step two or three in the UPSYD journey. Essentially, you are speaking to those people who already know about the plastic water bottle epidemic and may know there are companies out there that make toxin-free bottles.

Maybe this ad starts with something like, "Award-winning Amazing Water XYZ is saving the world one bottle at a time . . . and to celebrate, they are giving away some of their water for free! (You just have to pay a few dollars for shipping. Don't worry, you can think about those measly few bucks that you didn't spend on a Big Mac as money that went to making the world a better place.). Click here to get yours free, while supplies last. (And please share this post if you want to spread the love.) www.AmazingWaterXYZ. com/free."

That's the bulk of this simple ad. Now, you can start running this ad to cold audiences, as well as warm audiences—maybe to someone who read your other longer copy ad or video ad but didn't click through—or someone who saw your other ad or Like campaign and clicked through to your landing page but didn't buy. These two very different style of ads can be running to the same exact target audiences. Remember, there will be different people with different levels of awareness and intent in the same audiences.

Also within all these audiences, there are people of all different personality types, or "personas," or "buyer types." According to Merriam-Webster, the definition of persona is: "an individual's social façade or front." People have different innate personalities, and they also have different buying habits depending on the current situation in their lives right at that moment. Some people are impulsive and will pull the trigger on anything they see that looks like a good deal or bargain. Some people are much more analytical and need lots of time before they make any decision in their lives. These are the 9's and 10's on the "Fact Finder" scale on the Kolbe personality assessment. Some people are more emotional or humanistic. These types are also slow decision-makers, but they go with more of a "gut-feel" instead of a more structured, methodical process for decision-making. Some people just want the best. They're the competitive type who always want to win; they drive the best car, wear the best clothes, the best watch, etc.

These different levels of awareness, intent, and personality types will all live inside your target audiences, so this is why you must create many different types of messaging that will resonate with different people. And many people will need to see your ads over and over again before they ever take action—that is just their way of life.

So, you need ads running that will resonate with all these types of people and awareness levels. If you do steps one and two right, by following the process laid out for you in Chapters 16 to 20, you will have a foundation for massive scale and long-term ROI for your campaigns and your business. And the next chapter will help you take things to the next level and have a true perpetual system for generating awareness, engagement, fans, leads, sales, scooped-up abandoned sales, repeat sales, and massive goodwill for your brand along the entire way.

Chapter 15

Stage Three of the Facebook Flight Plan™

Welcome to Stage Three of the Facebook Flight Plan. By now, you've generated 1,000+ conversions at a cost that's acceptable to you. Remember, a conversion could be a lead, registration, or a sale. The point is, you've done the hard work, tested different hooks and offers, and found something that is working plus returning an acceptable ROI (*return on investment*). See Figure 15.1 on page 106.

> "*S*imple can be harder than complex: You have to work hard to get your thinking clean to make it simple. But it's worth it in the end because once you get there, you can move mountains."
>
> —STEVE JOBS

Now, it's time to start adding on to your Facebook selling system by adding even more layers to your campaigns and helping you turn cold traffic into warm audiences and warm audiences into customers.

If you followed along in Chapter 14, you should already have built something that looks like this:

- Like Campaign
- Link Post Ad
- Short-Copy Ad
- Long-Copy Ad

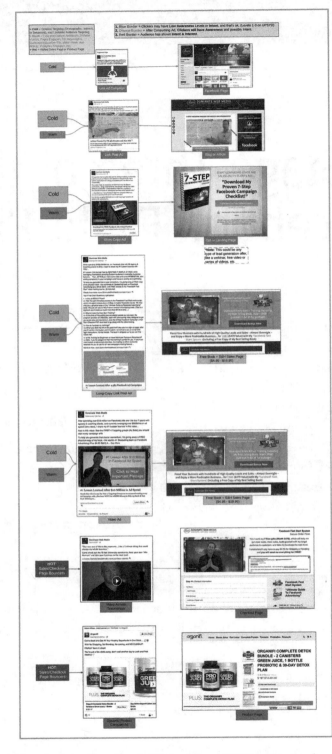

FIGURE 15.1–Facebook Flight Plan—1000+ Conversions

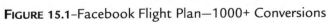

Now it's time to include:

- Video Ads
- Retargeting Strategies for Hot Prospects

Remember, this is just a model to guide you. Your specific situation may vary in some manner depending on your goals, your creative assets, your time and resources, your product, etc.

VIDEO ADS

Videos ads are incredibly important for long-term success on Facebook. That's why we've dedicated an entire chapter in this book to the topic. So, it might surprise you that video ads are not introduced until the third and final phase. This is because video, although extremely powerful, can be difficult to produce. It is resource intensive. (Not always, though!) It can take time to storyboard, script, film, and edit. In the first two phases, you're still figuring out exactly which hook and offer resonates best with your audience. During the first two phases, it's much simpler and faster to test different hooks and offers by changing your text and image rather than making a whole new video, or even a different segment of an existing video.

This is why it's more efficient to first run long-copy ads before introducing video. (Like I did with the free book funnel.) A helpful tip is to turn your best performing long copy ad into the basic script of a video. However, some people find it easier to create videos than they do writing long copy. If this is the case, then you want to start with video right out of the gate. (This is what I do in some cases, as sometimes it's faster for me to just make a video than write out the story for a great ad.)

RETARGETING TO HOT AUDIENCES

A hot audience is made up of people who started the buying process, but for some reason did not complete it. It's possible that the reason they didn't purchase was because they weren't interested in your offer. However, it's entirely possible (and common) they just got interrupted or distracted. The attention span online is about five seconds. So, if you don't have a system picking up these lost customers, you're leaving tons of easy money on the table.

The following are some proven strategies that work.

A Different Message

Remember, inside every audience, there are different people with different levels of awareness and intent, as well as different buyer personalities. There are the "I want the

---

LEVERAGING EXISTING ASSETS

Some of the best performing Facebook ad campaigns for a few of our clients are video ads made from a video they *already* had on their YouTube channel. The first thing Ralph Burns, The Agency CEO, does with new clients is watch every video on their YouTube channel if they have a channel. Some of our best success stories are campaigns using videos they already had!

---

best" people, who are competitive and sometimes egotistical, the "I'm an impulse buyer" people, and the "I am a process-driven person" people, who are methodical, slow, structured, and are logic-based decision makers. And finally, there are the "I go with my gut" or "listen to my heart" people, who are slow, unstructured, humanistic, emotion-based decision-makers. The best way to deal with these different personality types is to have different messaging and/or ad types hitting them with different angles and hooks.

A TESTIMONIAL TEMPLATE THAT DRIVES SALES

Hot Tip: Here's a list of questions to ask people if you want some testimonials that will sell the heck out of your products. Use these questions for gathering great stories for your main website and sales pages too.

1. Ask what problem, challenge, pain, or frustration they were looking to get help with before using your product/service.

2. What were they worried, concerned about, or hesitant about your product before they pulled the trigger? (This will help overcome common objections, and give you more data around objections for your sales process.)

3. What were their results? How is life or lifestyle, business, etc. better now? (Looking for transformation stories.)

4. What did they like best about [your product]?

5. Would they recommend [your product] to a friend? If so, how can it help them?

Testimonials

Testimonial videos (or image ads using screenshots) work great as an authentic way to provide more proof that your product can do what it claims. Plus, may help your prospect believe they can also achieve a similar result. Be careful not to over-produce these types of videos. Sometimes, if it's too perfect or polished, people may not trust them as much as a video that looks like it was shot on an iPhone.

Buying Incentive (Discount, Scarcity, etc.)

Perhaps your prospect just needs a little nudge to get them to take action. One of the best ways to do this is to give them an incentive —a deal. (Remember the "D" in UPSYD?!) This could be a bonus, a discount, an expiration, etc. For example, "Get a 40 percent discount if you purchase by tomorrow!" Or, "Get a free tote bag with purchase of any performance gear! (*Value $25. Hurry—offer ends soon!*)"

Cross-Sells or Bundles

Another easy strategy, especially for ecommerce stores with multiple products, is to offer a cross-sell of a similar or complimentary product. Maybe you piqued their interest, but the item they were looking at wasn't quite right. If you have other products, this may be the perfect time to make your prospects aware of them.

DYNAMIC PRODUCT ADS

Dynamic Product Ads are effective. They are definitely an important piece of the puzzle for ecommerce stores. But please understand this very important point: if you could only take ONE key thing away from this entire book, I would tell you that getting the messaging right or nailing your "offer" is the key to producing sustainable, profitable campaigns. This is why DPA's are introduced at the end of Phase 3. If you don't get the offer or messaging right, you won't be able to scale your campaigns—no matter how much of a ninja Facebook expert you are or you have on your team. And in the next chapter, we start showing you how to come up with the best offer and create the best possible message and ad type that will work well with your offer or promotion.

So, there you have it. Use this template and start your master Facebook Flight Plan™ that you can fill in as you start to gain more experience and momentum.

If you have an ecommerce store, a great way to do this is by using Dynamic Product Ads (DPAs). Dynamic Product Ads are customized ads that automatically promote the appropriate products to people who have visited those specific products or product categories. For example, if you own an online clothing retailer, you can set up automation rules to show unique ads to anyone who visits the add-to-cart page or checkout page for your "Fall Selection Boots." You can show them product ads reminding them to get the boots before they are out of stock, you can show them other similar products they may like, or you can do something different. You don't need to get it perfect. Remember: this is "low-hanging fruit." You just need to get *something* running—you can always get fancy later.

Chapter 16

Hacking the Hook

Contributing Author Ralph Burns

What the heck is "hacking the hook"? Well, first of all, what the heck is a "hook"?

Think of a hook as a tool that you use when you, the humble advertiser, are "fishing for customers." Even though I live on Cape Cod (where I'm fairly certain a lot of fishing goes on), I've never actually "fished" on Cape Cod, so I'm certainly not the most qualified person to talk about fishing, but let's give it a try anyway.

In our little analogy here, think of your customers as "the fish" and your marketing message as "the hook." The hook (yes, I know it doesn't work well without "the bait," but go with me on this one) "hooks" your customer into your sales system, turning people who don't know you into lifelong customers.

> *"There's a fine line between fishing and standing on the shore like an idiot."*
>
> —STEVEN WRIGHT

REELING IN YOUR CUSTOMERS WITH A HOOK

So what is a hook? Simply put, it's the marketing message. It's your front-facing message that your would-be customers see prior to becoming customers. It's the thing that intrigues them and reels them in. It's the primary reason why people want to take you up on your offer.

Now, a hook and an offer are two different things. Both of those key elements of customer acquisition work in tandem with each other to "reel that customer in" (back to the dang fishing analogy).

So let me give you an example. In the Ketogenic Living ad that we discussed in previous chapters, the ad title reads: "Is breakfast really the most important meal of the day?" When prospects read this they think,"Geez, I thought it was, but maybe he's saying it **isn't**?" With this hook, what we've done is create "a knowledge gap."

What's a "knowledge gap," you say? This happens when we feel a gap in our knowledge, which makes us feel an inherent pain like an itch we can't scratch. To "scratch" it, we need to fill "the knowledge gap." In the ad, we've triggered the curiosity to want to learn more, so they continue to read to do just that, while filling the knowledge gap at the same time.

And that's just one kind of a hook.

As you can see in Figure 16.1 on page 113, this ad is a perfect example of both being counter-intuitive while evoking curiosity via a "knowledge gap." In using a counter-intuitive statement like "Is breakfast REALLY the Most Important Meal of the Day?" the ad copy serves to both shatter conventional wisdom and challenge the reader's understanding of "what good nutrition looks like" while also creating a fairly hefty knowledge gap.

David Ogilvy said something along the lines of "the reason why you write your headline is so that they read your sub-headline and the reason why you write your sub-headline is so that they read your body copy." As the father of modern day advertising, he knows what he's talking about.

This concept is the exact same thing with any ad you write. That first line, that essential chunk of copy that is the prospects' first point of contact with you, has to be so knock-their-socks-off good that they feel compelled to read onwards all the way to the end. At that point, they do what you ask next in your call to action. Namely, give up their contact information (become a lead) or plunk down their credit card and buy (become a customer).

In Figure 16.1 you can see there's a lot of content on there, but the call to action at the end is constructed to take them to the next step.

The hook functions as a mental appetizer that gives them just enough of a taste of the good stuff to leave them wanting more. It's a sample that gets them on the same page with you so that you can reel them in (yes, back to the fishing analogy). All of which ultimately leads them down the path to become a buyer.

But that journey all starts with your hook.

FIGURE 16.1–Ketogenic Living Long Copy Ad

The reason why there's so much copy in that ad (and the reason why we advocate using video ads so much in Facebook ads) is because you want people to be pre-framed for the next step in your sales system. You don't want people to just opt-in and then be done with you. Sure, we can get cheap leads all day long on Facebook, but the truth is that "cheap leads" don't run businesses. Buyers run businesses. Customers run businesses. In an ideal world, you want to be able to pay more for your leads then your competition can. Not just because you want to squeeze your competition out but because often times, more expensive leads are far more qualified leads. And qualified leads become customers, which is what you need if you're going to thrive as a business.

Leads tend to be more qualified hen you write a long copy ad like we did for Ketogenic Living, as seen in Figure 16.1, that contains a good hook like, "Is breakfast really the most important meal of the day?" This is largely because your prospects have consumed a fair amount of content. In this case, nearly one thousand words of content, which means successfully pre-framing that prospect to the next step in your sales system.

In this chapter, I'll be giving you some examples of hooks in many of the markets we've worked in, and ones you're probably familiar with. So let's get into it, fishing pole and all.

A CAUTIONARY TALE: HOW TO FLIP A HOUSE WITH NO MONEY

Your prospect wants to make money in real estate investing. They know that real estate investing is a great way to create wealth and achieve a measure of financial freedom. The problem is that they have no money and no credit, so they can't even imagine themselves doing it. This probably means that they have no money, and they want to leave their job or they want a better life.

So if you're in the real estate investing niche, this by no means is all-inclusive for real estate investing, but it's an example of a hook that we've used very effectively with a lot of our real estate investing customers.

Due to the dozens of reality TV shows on this topic, you may think of "flipping houses" when the topic of real estate investing is brought up. If you were to use "how to flip houses" as your hook, that wouldn't necessarily be a great hook because so many people in the real estate investing market are already aware of this potential solution. The problem with that hook is that it's just not novel or unique enough. But it could be on the path to finding what would actually be the hook. This is because "flipping houses" may be the solution that they get after you reel them in with a more specific hook.

In this particular case, where the hook is slightly altered to be "how to flip a house with no money," "flipping houses" may or may not have something to do with the offer they purchase after you pull them in with your initial hook.

For example, we have a "house flipping" agency customer who actually had a downloadable ebook that we used as a lead magnet that used "how to flip houses in five simple steps" as the hook. The "offer" in this case, was the eBook that taught them how to flip houses. It is a great hook for a great lead magnet, and it did really well in getting thousands of very cheap leads.

The problem is that the customer's ultimate solution (their core product) was a paid eight-module training program on "how to flip houses."

Let's be clear, I don't think "how to flip houses," is a bad hook. In fact, my customer ran plenty of traffic with that hook and did extremely well. The problem we ran into was that nobody was buying their core offer because we gave all of it away in the lead magnet!

So, it's important that when you craft a hook as well as an offer, don't give them the whole darn thing in your lead magnet. Out of the thousands of names and email addresses we got in that campaign, nobody would buy the eight-module training program because the lead magnet was so good. Why would they buy another training program when we've already taught them how to do it for free?

So when crafting your hook and your offer for a lead magnet type of campaign, the "incompleteness" of the offer is vital to the success of your campaign. Remember that your goal when generating a lead isn't just to get a lead. Instead, it is to eventually get a buyer.

Now, let's take a step back. If this customer's solution was a complete portfolio of real estate investing courses where you learn wholesaling, how to buy long-term real estate, and how to invest in mobile homes, then the hook "how to flip houses in five simple steps" would have been far more effective. If they had a dozen different products in their library, and they're pulling out "house flipping" as one of them and using that as a hook, that might have been a better way of going about it.

UNDERSTANDING AWARENESS LEVEL TO HOOK THEM IN WITH SOMETHING GOOD

In the last section, I mentioned that "how to flip houses" may or may not be a good hook. The UPSYD framework can help explain why. Looking at the UPSYD framework that we discussed in Chapter 13, a good prospect for "how to flip houses" would fall into the "solution aware" step, the low hanging fruit as shown in Figure 16.2. This means that they already are up on Step 3 in your continuum of adoption.

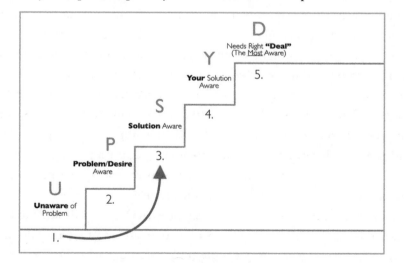

FIGURE 16.2–The UPSYD Framework

If your solution was a "flipping houses" related program and you were targeting an audience that is "solution aware," then your hook could be "how to flip a house with no money down." This would in fact be an excellent hook for this "solution aware" market.

But the problem is that this is a fairly small sub segment of a larger overall market. You'd eventually run into scalability problems because your message is simply not resonating with a large enough chunk of the broader real estate investing market. In order for your hook and offer to be super effective on a wider scale, you may need to change them.

If the hook is just "how to flip a house," then the audience must be very targeted. We know they are into house flipping, so they are solution aware as shown in Figure 16.2.

This is the case unless, for example, you have a video ad where you are showing your prospect how you flip houses with borrowed money—no cash of your own—and make an average of $50,000 per deal. In this case, the hook is "how to make money very quickly in real estate without using any of your own money."

Another way to think about the right hook is answering the question: "why house flipping?" Because it is the biggest opportunity that people don't know about. Because how can you invest in house flipping without having your own cash? If you answered that question, then you would've found your hook. In this case, the hook now becomes: "How to invest without any of your own cash."

USING "TRANSFORMATION" AS A HOOK

Clayton Morris, one of our coaching customers who teaches people how to flip houses, has a video ad where he shows you the actual process of flipping a house. It's a video where the hook is of the prospect being able to see the transformation of a house that Clayton paid a mere $40,000 dollars for and then quickly sold it for $90,000. In so doing, he's taking the prospect on a transformative journey with him through the entire video ad itself, so the embedded hook is "how to invest in flipping houses."

The reason why this works as a great hook is because in order to flip houses like Clayton does, you actually need the money to acquire them. And surprise surprise, that's where his product solution comes into play. In the video, Clayton gives the prospect useful and practical information, builds credibility, and establishes rapport with the video ad. In so doing, he has pre-framed the prospect to take the next step, which if you're going to do what he did, you need some money!

In Clayton's business, the goal is to get prospects on a call and talk them into investing with them. They're looking for people to invest, and then they do the work for them. They're not actually teaching people the same thing that they're showing in the video. Now granted, they could do just that.

With "house flipping," you might be educating your prospects on the process of how to flip houses in the ad itself, but then your solution is to do it in an easier way. In this example, the easier way could be investing money to have it done for you—where Clayton's team takes care of everything—or it could also be to have it done with you—where you get access to the team and all the resources you need to make it happen. You have to understand and think about what the end goal is, and then work your way backwards from the offer and eventually back to the beginning, to the hook.

If "buy a house with no money" was your hook, your actual offer may be a checklist or a cheat sheet of "15 things that you must do in order to flip your first house." And, oh by the way, one of them is you need money to fund that flip. We've got a customer that does exactly that where they present the idea of flipping houses with their hook. In this case, that hook is actually fairly good because it's part of their business as a solution to help prospects get to whatever that initial goal is.

Part of the reason why "flipping houses" as a hook would work in some cases is because bigger brands have commercialized to the mass market the idea of flipping houses as a way to invest money and make a good return. Because of this TV exposure, people subconsciously associate flipping houses as a known way to make money and achieve freedom. If this sense of awareness wasn't present, then it would be far more difficult to use "flipping houses" as a hook.

In essence, "flipping houses" has gone mainstream so much so that if you ask anybody on the street what flipping houses actually is, they'd probably know. But if you were to do the same with intermittent fasting, you'd get some interesting reactions to say the least, with most answers sparking intense confusion.

Some of you probably already get it. You understand, or at least you think you understand, what a hook is and perhaps have even written some hooks for your product or service. Hooks are the trickiest thing you'll do in advertising and it's a subtle science and art to get good at, so the more examples, the better you'll understand.

DRIVE 10 YARDS FURTHER

This one is fairly straightforward. What's the one thing that a golfer really wants? If you asked a hundred golfers what they want most (notice how I didn't say *need* most), the chances are pretty good that more than one in five will answer to drive the ball farther. Especially for male golfers, they want to be able to earn the bragging rights. They want to be the big dog who drives the ball off the TV 300 yards, leaving the other players in his foursome shocked in astonishment.

Sure, many high-level golfers might say "how to one putt every green" or "stay more consistent" or even "cure my slice" (all pretty good hooks by the way), but none looms larger than being large off the tee. What "driving the ball farther" has over the other hooks mentioned here is that there is an emotional attachment to driving the ball further. It taps into the male ego, making it emotionally charged as well as an intense desire. If you were to brag about being able to one putt every single hole to your friends, what kind of reaction do you think you would get? Perhaps an "atta boy" or a "good for you," but the reaction would be pretty lukewarm. Now, if you were to drive 10 yards farther than your buddy, THAT gives you immediate bragging rights. It's simply far more emotionally charged. What's even better is that when the hook is paired with a specific end result like "ten yards farther," we've now injected a promise of a specific outcome alongside the emotionally charged desire. When you can combine a hook that speaks to a specific desire that has a defined and measurable outcome, you probably have a pretty darn good hook.

If my hook is "drive the ball ten yards farther," then my offer could be a video where I show you step by step how to do this using, perhaps, "One simple trick." Maybe in the video, I show you how to place your hands like this, and then do this. Maybe it's how to transfer your weight from one side to the other, while still maintaining solid contact. The video is the offer and the hook is how to drive the ball ten yards farther.

Making sure we don't make the how-to-flip-houses mistake our customer made, the logical next step after showing the prospect how to drive the ball ten yards farther is to sell them a paid program on how to improve your golf game. Perhaps the hook of that paid program is "How to take 10 strokes off your golf game in less then 30 days." The hook and the offer lead directly into the next logical step, namely to purchase a paid program that delivers on not necessarily what they want, but on what they need.

SELL FROM THE STAGE

In the coaching niche, one of the very important things to learn how to do, especially if you do a lot of life speaking, is to learn how to sell your product from the stage. If you're not as successful as you want to be in doing this, learning this skill will definitely make you more effective as a coach. One of our agency customers, Ted McGrath, has a product that helps coaches do that better than anybody I know.

If you really think about it, what a coach needs, it is to learn how to be a better coach. The urgent want is "how am I going to pay the mortgage this month if I don't sell at least a few new coaching customers in the seminar I have scheduled for next week?" This is a highly specific outcome that your prospects want right now.

The end result might be to create a six-figure coaching practice, reach as many people as you possibly can with your message, increase your influence, become a sought-out motivational speaker, and so forth. Those all could be hooks in this space but not nearly as effective as a hook that is super specific and delivers an immediate result. Specificity and immediacy are two very important ingredients in the crafting of a solid hook. When you're crafting a hook, think about that one tiny, little thing that will actually trigger—or better yet, compel—your prospect to click on the ad to take the next step.

"How to sell from the stage" is a hook that has done well because of its specificity and its immediacy. It's not "how to be a better coach" or "how to create a six-figure income as a coach." That's all well and good, but those wouldn't work on Facebook as well (we've tried, by the way). Also, the latter hook may run you into trouble with policy as it's making a subjective income claim. Any hook that gives the expectation or promise that your prospect can make a specific amount of income, and even worse if you specify in a specific amount of time (e.g., "make $30,000 in 30 days"), chances are very good that you'll have some trouble with Facebook policy.

If "how to sell from the stage" is your hook, then a logical offer could be a checklist of "The 15 things to do on your next presentation," when you're actually up there on stage. In the offer checklist, your tips would all be very specific things and laid out in order from one through 15. All easily consumable information that gives immediate and specific results, but more importantly, it's incomplete to the entire solution. The logical next step after this initial offer is perhaps a course on "how to sell new clients into your coaching practice" or "how to create a profitable coaching system."

The offer is highly specific, easily consumable, provides immediate results when implemented, speaks to a known desire, and most importantly, is incomplete with relation to the end product goal. In this case, the paid program offered immediately after the initial offer serves to satisfy that incompleteness.

LEARN TO PLAY FIVE ROCK LICKS

Now we're talking hooks. This example is even more relevant to explaining what a hook is because any popular rock song, or any popular song in any genre for that matter, has a great "hook." The "hook" in a popular song is the part of the song that raises the hair on the back of your neck, gives you goose bumps, or just compels you to sing along. A hook in a song is the reason why you listen to it in the first place.

Starting to sound familiar?

According to our friends at Wikipedia, a hook in a song is defined as "a musical idea, often a short riff, passage, or phrase that is used in popular music to make a **song** appealing and to 'catch the ear of the listener.' The term generally applies to popular music, especially rock, R&B, hip hop, dance, and pop." This example makes our hook for this niche far more relevant.

So let's say, for example, you are selling digital guitar training. Selling a new lead for training is the ultimate goal of your advertising. To hook a new lead in, we don't want to use the "learn how to play the guitar better" as your hook. Yes, that is what they ultimately need, but to hook them in, let's talk about what they really want. When someone first starts playing the guitar, the biggest thing they want to learn how to do is play their favorite song or at least a part of their favorite song.

This gets us into a discussion on what's known as "splintering" your offer. We've been dancing around this one for a bit here, but it's important for you to understand the basic principles of the hook before this particular concept.

So let's say you sell ten different guitar lesson courses. One of those digital products is "How to learn how to play rock guitar." In that course, you have seven different lessons, the most popular of which is your lesson on how to play hundreds of some of the most popular rock guitar riffs in rock history. Inside that lesson there are five really killer rock guitar licks that all your students love. Those licks are: *Iron Man* by Black Sabbath, *Whole Lotta Love* by Led Zeppelin, *Bad Moon Rising* by Credence Clearwater Revival, *Day Tripper* by the Beatles, and *Enter Sandman* by Metallica.

When you are trying to figure out an offer to put in front of cold traffic, the idea behind "splintering" is that you find an easily consumable, highly actionable, highly valuable, and popular chunk or piece of your main product, then "splinter" that chunk off to use as your offer to entice people to engage with you. And I'm willing to bet that you already have something like this in your product portfolio right now.

Marketers are somewhat reluctant to do this because they think they are giving away their best stuff and then people will be disappointed when they actually buy. Don't fall into that trap. The idea is to give away your best stuff, but just make it incomplete so they want more.

You could argue that "learn to play guitar" is a hook, as it is specific to a group of people interested in playing an instrument. It actually could be used as a hook. It's just not specific enough to be a great hook. If you use that as your hook, you might fall into the trap that we fell into in the how-to-flip-houses-in-five-simple-steps example we used above.

For one of our customers, we had them make a video where they taught the prospect to play three repeatable riffs that can be played in any rock guitar solo. The video is long, clocking in at over ten minutes, but he gives highly actionable advice on how to play a specific type of guitar ref. The hook at the end of the video simply tells them to take the next step, which is to purchase the entire course on how to solo like a rock star. In this case, our "lead magnet" is actually an "ungated" piece of content (meaning you don't have to give your name or email address to get the content), which to some marketers is extremely contrarian. However, because the call to action at the end of the video is to purchase the course as the logical next step, this ad does extremely well. The video in the ad simply demonstrates that they can help the prospect by actually helping them and then simply leads them down the path to the logical next step, namely purchasing more of what they just showed them how to do.

BUILD YOUR FIRST DIGITAL PRODUCT

This is one that probably appeals to people in both the digital product business as well as the information product business. The end result of this hook is the building of a digital product, but in a broader sense, this hook is targeted to people who want to start their own business. The reasons for starting your own business are varied, the biggest of which is the desire to leave a job or "escape the 9 to 5," as it were.

In that vein, the hook could potentially be "start your own business and leave your dead end job," which is a good basic hook that's been used thousands of times for thousands of products. But for our purposes it falls short because it lacks super specificity. When it comes to creating a hook, as we've said before, the more specific you are, the more you will effectively attract your ideal customers.

In this case, a "build your first digital product" hook is far more effective because it triggers curiosity, creates awareness that in order to start a business one does not need to build physical products, and even makes your prospect curious of the possibility. They all of a sudden go from "I can't start my own business because I can't think of a physical product to sell" to "I can build a digital product and go into business for myself? What is that exactly?" This hook creates an awareness that building a digital product is in fact a way that they can leave their job and start a new business. When you have both curiosity and education all wrapped up together, chances are you probably have a pretty effective hook.

"Build your first digital product" works well targeting people who are solution aware, which is what we would consider the "low hanging fruit audiences." The types of audiences you would advertise this to include people who are familiar with online marketing, digital marketing tools, and specific authority figures in the digital marketing space. In fact, this is one of the hooks that we're running traffic to right now, and not surprisingly, it's working extremely well.

But if you want to go after the unaware audiences you have to have a slightly different hook. The offer could be a live training where you show your prospects exactly how to create their first digital product. In that live training you would tie the building of the product back to the deeper desire of achieving personal freedom or so that they can reach other specific benefits that are lifestyle or monetarily related. This kind of hook can of course target a much larger market and one that would provide a tremendous amount of scale for a business like this.

HOW TO FIND THE RIGHT HOOK

By now, you probably have a fairly good understanding of what a hook is, and you may be starting to formulate ideas for improved hooks or initial hooks for your product or service. If you are, you're on the right track. Knowing what a hook is, is important, but it is far more important to know how to find the right hook. Even if you've identified what you think is a good hook for your product or service, you can always refine it just a little bit more by getting clear on the following points in the section.

IDENTIFY YOUR AVATAR

First and foremost, to write a good hook for your product or service, you must first identify your avatar. For established businesses, this is fairly straightforward and can be answered in one question: Who are my customers?

Once you've answered that question, your next job is to figure out what they want the most. What are their pain points, what are their fears? Write all of them down. Then identify an easy-to-implement solution that you provide in your product portfolio that will immediately solve that problem or fulfill that desire.

Ask yourself this question: What is the solution my products or services can create for them? Remember, if your initial offer to cold traffic is going to be a lead magnet or a low-priced offer that leads them ultimately to your full-priced product, the solution for a front-end hook shouldn't be your entire product (remember our house flipping example in the first section of this chapter). Sounds simple, but how do you do it?

We also ask ourselves an alternate question, which is: "who is our most valuable customer?" Your most valuable customer is your ideal customer, and in most cases, it's your best customer. If you've been in business for any length of time, you know that not all customers are the same. For some of our agency customers we've had to change and edit our hooks over time to target the ideal avatar, not just "the avatar." Both the customer and we realized that the best customers are people that we actually pay more to acquire. They become the best customers because they spend far more as buyers as well as generate the most amount of referrals.

In one case, one of our agency customers at our company did a huge meta-analysis of all their leads and customers to determine customer service requirements based on the lifetime value of each customer respectively. They found out that their leads who had not become customers were occupying so much time from their customer service staff that we decided to change our entire acquisition strategy. They decided to no longer give away any free information in the form of video tutorials for lead magnets but instead to focus on just producing buyers. They subsequently scaled their business back by nearly threefold in revenue while decreasing customer service requests nearly two-thirds. In fact, the drop-off in customer service requests was so much that they actually had to lay off staff as a result.

Is that an avatar? Yes, in my opinion, it is because it's a qualified buyer and not just merely "a lead." Their avatar became the one who buys vs. the one who just wants freebies.

That sounds straightforward enough but perhaps in your business there are sub-avatars within your ideal customer. There can be so many different ways to sub-segment your avatars, and if you've got solutions for each one of those segments you probably need different hooks to pull them in.

For example, in the "learn how to play the guitar" niche, "how to play guitar" only speaks to the broader guitar niche, which is the reason why that hook probably isn't a tremendously great one. But if your avatar is males who play guitar between the ages of 25 and 65, chances are pretty good that you've got guys who do solos, guys who play blues, guys who play slide guitar, acoustic guitar players, and on and on and on. As you can see, there are multiple sub avatars within your overall avatar. This one is fairly complex with potentially hundreds of different variations.

The reason why this is so important is that a hook has to be highly specific. The more specific your hook is to your audience, the better. You're going to have a very hard time selling your "Learn to play like Eddie Van Halen" guitar product to someone who wants to learn how to play classical guitar. But put a "Learn to play Eddie Van Halen's Top 10 Guitar Licks" hook in front of guitarist who loves to play hard rock guitar, then you probably have a pretty good hook.

MOVE TOWARDS DESIRE

As you may recall from an earlier section, I've shared with you my somewhat painful experience of the "how to flip houses in five simple steps" eBook lead magnet. Yes, it was a great lead magnet and generated a ton of leads. As a 70-page book that taught you everything you needed to know about flipping houses, it definitely helped a lot of people. The problem was that because we gave them everything in that one eBook, it didn't help my customer's business very much.

The problem was that we didn't splinter out one little part of the paid product.

The problem was clear ("I don't know how to flip houses"), and the solution helped them get closer to their goal, but the whole thing wasn't in line with our business objectives. So we went back to the drawing board and did some research on our customer's avatar. We then asked ourselves these three questions:

1. What are our prospect's desires?
2. What does our prospect want more than anything else?

3. What do we have as a part of our product that will move our prospect towards achieving the one thing they want more than anything else?

In the guitar niche, this is fairly straightforward. For our hard rock guitar players who want to play like Eddie Van Halen, it's simple. They want to learn how to play his most famous guitar songs like *Eruption, Spanish Fly, Jump, Running with the Devil,* or *Somebody Get Me a Doctor.*

Some of our ad copy for that avatar is along the lines of:

1. Want to play those Van Halen songs you've always wanted to play ever since you were in high school?
2. Learn how to play like Eddie Van Halen!
3. Struggling to play *Eruption* and can't get the fingering down?

With your hook, you must get super specific with your prospect on one particular thing. All these do just that.

To get even deeper into the mind of your prospect, ask a follow-up question on why they really want this. Write it down. Then ask it again: why do they want this? Write it down. Then ask as many times necessary, why do they want this? Ask enough times until you get to the desire behind the desire.

When you've identified that specific desire behind the desire, think about the end benefit that fulfilling that desire brings. From our rough ad copy above, this now becomes: "Learn how to play like Eddie Van Halen so you can impress your friends" or "Learn how to play like Eddie Van Halen so you can steal the show at the next family reunion."

In short:

- "What they want more than anything else" is their specific desire.
- "Why do they want this" is the benefit they get from fulfilling that specific desire.

Whether you know it or not, you're now starting to craft your actual ad copy you'll be using in your ads.

The formula looks like this:

They want [specific desire] so that they can [benefit].

Write out about a dozen of these and keep writing—even if they're really bad at first. With enough brainstorming, you'll find the perfect match of a specific desire and benefit you can then use to hack the hook.

MOVE AWAY FROM PAIN POINTS

What is your target market's greatest problems? Or more specifically: what keeps your prospect up at night? As Tony Robbins once said, "people will do more to avoid pain then they will do to gain pleasure." Keep this in mind when you're researching and writing your hook. In economics and decision theory, loss aversion refers to people's tendency to prefer avoiding losses to acquiring equivalent gains: it's better to not lose $5 than to find $5. Some studies have suggested that losses are twice as powerful, psychologically, as gains. Loss aversion was first demonstrated by Amos Tversky and Daniel Kahneman.

Going back to the solo guitar player avatar, one of the simplest problems could be: "I don't know where to go next on the fret board after the A note." This is a problem because maybe Fred, the solo guitar player, wants to play the *Bob the Builder* theme song to his kids, but he doesn't know what to do after the A note and because of this, both he and his kids are frustrated.

This brings us to the second question, "What are they most afraid of?" In this case, Fred might feel afraid that he won't live up to be the father he wants to be for his kids if he doesn't learn this part of the song. He's afraid that when his kids are older they won't remember how he used to rock the guitar to *Bob the Builder* and his legacy as a great dad will be tarnished.

I'm being somewhat obviously melodramatic, but you should always ask this question with regard to your avatar's biggest pain: why do they want to change? Fred wants to master this song because he knows how rabid his kids are about *Bob the Builder*. He wants to create an indelible memory of his kids laughing and dancing around to the song when he plays it. At the end of all this, he wants to be able to play the song because that would make him and his kids happy. At a very deep level, yes, he would then feel like he's being the father he always wanted to be—and perhaps the father his kids can maybe brag about to their buds in preschool.

Here's what to ask for your reference:

- What are your target market's greatest problems?
- What are they most afraid of?
- Why do they want to change?

When you find the reason behind the problem, behind what they are most afraid of, and behind why they want to change, you can then embed your solution inside the hook and cure it with your offer.

FIND A SOLUTION

Remember my customer's lead magnet how-to-flip-houses-in-five-simple-steps?" You may be eager to know the solution we came to as I have left you hanging a couple times on that. Again, the problem was that we were giving away a 70-page downloadable eBook on "how to flip houses in five simple steps" in exchange for a name and an email address. The problem was our ultimate solution was to sell them an 8-module program that would in essence do the same thing as the lead magnet itself, namely teach them how to flip houses. We got lots of leads, but very few customers—not ideal.

Using the series of questions outlined above, we eventually figured out the biggest problem that faced our market was, namely: I don't know how to raise money. We also know that we had a solution for this problem. So with this in mind, we came up with the hook for our new lead magnet: "17 words you need to say to an investor to fund your next deal." The offer was a three-page checklist that fulfilled the promise of the hook.

Was the content "as good" as the previous lead magnet? Was it "as complete" as the previous lead magnet? No, on both counts. But it worked way better towards fulfilling our ultimate objective, namely getting more people to purchase our product.

Go back and review your notes on your market's desires and pain points. When crafting a solid hook, this is the most logical starting point. Then, force-rank those pain points and desires. Next, start coming up with solutions that your hook will promise and your offer will fulfill. Be careful to separate out wants from needs. They are not the same.

Remember that when you think about a solution that fulfills your avatar's desires or pain points, your end goal is for the offer to fulfill the promise of the hook, but in order for it to work for your business, it must be incomplete, so the bigger solution your paid product delivers.

HACKING THE HOOK

> *"At 60 miles the loudest noise in this new Rolls-Royce comes*
> *from the electric clock."*
> —OGILVY

Perhaps you've seen this ad copy before?

This one line is considered to be one of the, if not the most, famous headlines in the history of advertising by David Ogilvy, whom many consider to be the father of modern advertising. This ad was first published in March 1959 as shown in Figure 16.3 on page 127.

> *"Good artists copy; great artists steal."*
> —PICASSO

You might think he actually wrote this himself, which he did. But the little known secret is that he may not have come up with it all on his own. After doing a little research, it turns out he likely stole it. Almost 30 years earlier, the people at Pierce Arrow published an ad with a strikingly similar hook for their vehicle, namely: "the only sound one can hear in the new Pierce-Arrows is the ticking of the electric clock" as you can see in Figure 16.4 on page 127.

FIGURE 16.3–Rolls-Royce Newspaper Ad Published in March 1959

FIGURE 16.4–Pierce Arrows Newspaper Ad Published in 1933

Ogilvy sure did his research. Research is a key element to a great hook. I'm surely not saying that you should just go out and find your competition's ads and simply copy them. Absolutely not. However, you're depriving yourself of a tremendous source of ideas if you completely ignore what your competition is doing. Some of the greatest and most effective hooks we've ever created in the agency have come from ideas sparked by our customer's competition.

In Ogilvy's case, he pretty much outright copied the folks at Pierce Arrow, slightly altering the copy for his own application. But that's not all he did. If the fulfillment of the promise falls short of the promise itself in the hook, the ad and hook are no longer effective.

The backstory is that when Ogilvy and Mather won the Rolls-Royce account, in addition to his research studying ad copy from the competition, Ogilvy also spent three weeks poring over the Rolls-Royce product manual, meticulously searching for a competitive advantage that he could then exploit in his advertising. One of the hooks he found was the silence of the engine sounds and the metronomic quality of the ticking clock.

The lesson in all this is not to outright copy the competition. Once again, this is not recommended. But what's important is when you are searching for a good hook, you've got to be resourceful. The more you study, the more you analyze your competition, and the more time you spend on the desires and fears of your target market's avatar, the better your hook will be.

Get ideas from other people. Get ideas from bad ideas. In fact, good ideas often come from bad ideas. Collaborate. And do your research.

In later years, when Ogilvy and Mather secured the Mercedes-Benz account, he and his staff flew to Stuttgart, Germany, the home of Mercedes-Benz, for three weeks. There, he and his staff met with engineers, toured the production facilities, pored over Mercedes-Benz owner's manuals, talked to actual Mercedes customers, dissected every aspect of the brand in the hopes of acquiring knowledge to create a great advertising hook.

Like with Rolls-Royce, he again wanted to figure out "what is it about Mercedes that makes it so good?" He found it eventually, increasing Mercedes-Benz sales 400 percent in just one year, an increase from 10,000 to 40,000 cars at a time when Mercedes wasn't very popular in the United States. According to Ogilvy, the research was a critical element in that success.

So how do you get a good hook? You do your research and become like Ogilvy. If the greatest ad man in the world takes three weeks to do research, don't you think you can do at least a few hours on your own product? The bottom line is that hooks don't come easy; you have to put in the work. If you're a consultant, if you work for an agency, or if you work for our agency, you've got to put in the time to research the product, the market, and the competition because chances are, it's not going to come to you immediately.

As a side note, the reason the guitar hooks come far more easily to me, is because I'm a guitar player. I am the avatar so I understand exactly what it is the avatar is thinking. But for the majority of our other customers, I don't know a thing about their products, so the research is essential. You've got to be resourceful. You've got to do the research.

RESEARCHING THE HOOK

In this section, I'm going to share with you the most practical ways we've effectively found the perfect hook for our own and our customer's Facebook ad campaigns. Yes, it's time-consuming and no it's not glamorous, but if you're not doing this for your own or for a customer's business, it's going to be very challenging for you to find a great hook without it.

There are four basic ways to do research in order to "hack the hook." They are as follows:

1. Google
2. Surveys

3. Interviews

4. Facebook

GOOGLE THE HOOK

As previously discussed, when it came for David Ogilvy to do the research to eventually create what is known to be the greatest advertising hook of all time, namely: "At 60 miles the loudest noise in this new Rolls-Royce comes from the electric clock," Ogilvy did his research, starting with the owner's manual. Next time you get into your car, look in glove box and see if the car manual is still in there. You'll soon realize that the owner's manual for any make or model is pretty thick and incredibly boring. But dull research is oftentimes just what's needed to discover a great hook.

For Ogilvy, that research paid off handsomely. Ogilvy and Mather were able to keep the Mercedes-Benz advertising account for over 20 years, filling his agency's covers with millions of dollars in revenue. And it all started because he did his research. An example of one of his ads is shown in Figure 16.5, with the hook "You give up things when you buy the Mercedes-Benz 230S. Things like rattles, rust, and shabby workmanship."

If you haven't gotten the point by now, it's clear that Ogilvy didn't skimp out on his research, which means there's no reason why you should either. Unlike Ogilvy, you don't have to go to the local library or fly to Stuttgart, Germany to figure out your hook. That's because now you have Google. Your research starts with a simple Google search although I wouldn't mind flying to Germany on Mercedes-Benz's dime.

For our brand Ketogenic Living, our hook started with a simple Google search, as well. To be fair, we had some experience with intermittent fasting so we weren't going into this completely naïve. If you're a consultant for an agency, you may need to start this with an even simpler Google search like the primary keyword for the customer's product. If you're doing this research for your own business, our Google search behavior will probably more closely mimic yours.

To start, we typed in "intermittent fasting questions" like you can see on Figure 16.6. on page 130, and Google pulled up about 500,000

FIGURE 16.5–Mercedes Benz 230S Newspaper Ad Campaign

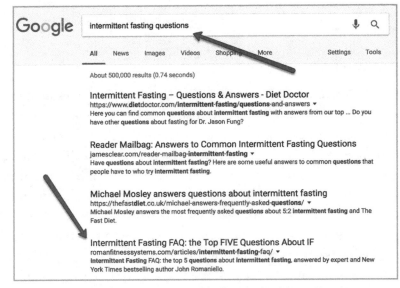

FIGURE 16.6–Google Search for Intermittent Fasting

results in 0.74 seconds. Immediately, all with the number of searches for this keyword phrase, there seemed to be some interest in the topic, which is always a good sign.

We then clicked on the FAQ article by expert and *The New York Times* best-selling author John Romaniello. Within that article, we discovered the first question: "Fasting for 16/24/36 Hours Seems Hard; Like, *Weawwy* Hard—Will I Die?" as shown in Figure 16.7. It seems that there's some contrarian thought on the topic, with the perception that fasting doesn't seem like it's all that healthy.

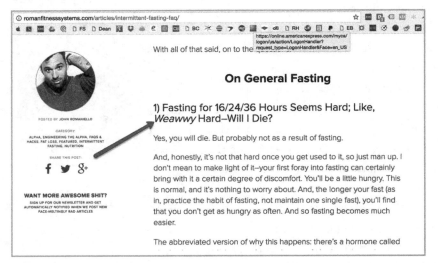

FIGURE 16.7–First Question Inside the Article "Intermittent Fasting FAQ—the Top FIVE Questions About IF" by John Romaniello

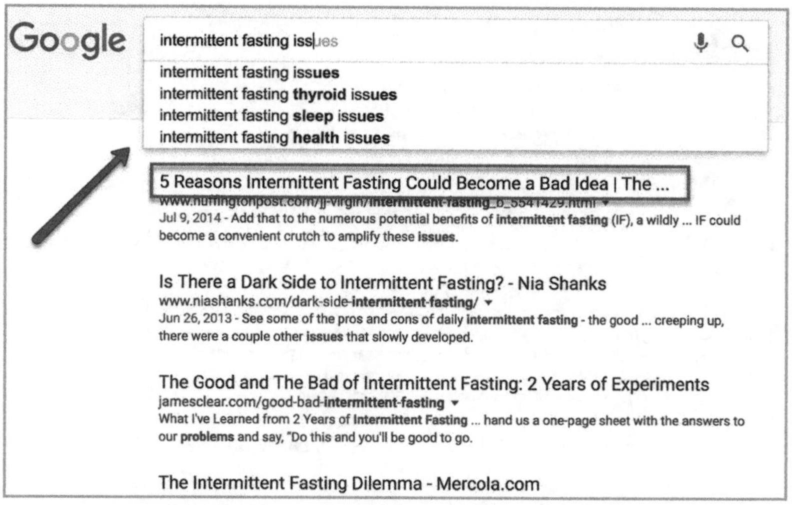

FIGURE 16.8–Google Search for Intermittent Fasting Issues

Sensing that we might be onto something, we went back to Google, but this time we typed "intermittent fasting issues" and it was almost like Google knew through its suggestion tool. The Google suggestion tool is a *great* way to find the most popular keyword searches—search results that could become the root of a great hook as seen in Figure 16.8.

The top hit was "5 Reasons Intermittent Fasting Could Become a Bad Idea," an article by celebrity nutritionist and fitness expert JJ Virgin as seen in Figure 16.8. Extremely promising. In that article, we found this little hook: "Is breakfast really the most important meal of the day?" as seen in Figure 16.9.

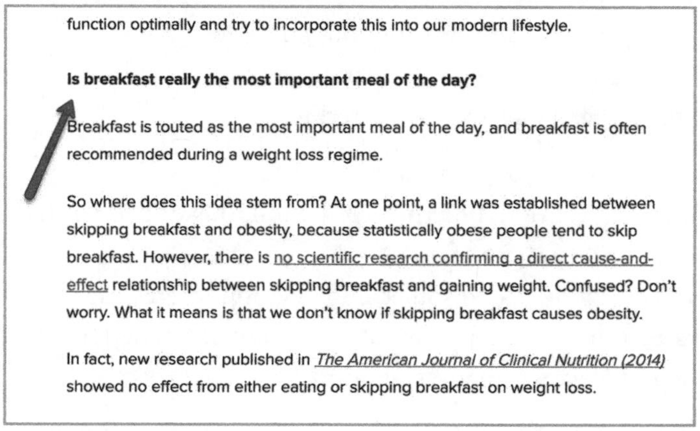
function optimally and try to incorporate this into our modern lifestyle.

Is breakfast really the most important meal of the day?

Breakfast is touted as the most important meal of the day, and breakfast is often recommended during a weight loss regime.

So where does this idea stem from? At one point, a link was established between skipping breakfast and obesity, because statistically obese people tend to skip breakfast. However, there is no scientific research confirming a direct cause-and-effect relationship between skipping breakfast and gaining weight. Confused? Don't worry. What it means is that we don't know if skipping breakfast causes obesity.

In fact, new research published in *The American Journal of Clinical Nutrition (2014)* showed no effect from either eating or skipping breakfast on weight loss.

FIGURE 16.9–Where We Found the Hook—"Is Breakfast Really the Most Important Meal of the Day?"—J.J. Virgin's Article "5 Reasons Intermittent Fasting Could Become a Bad Idea"

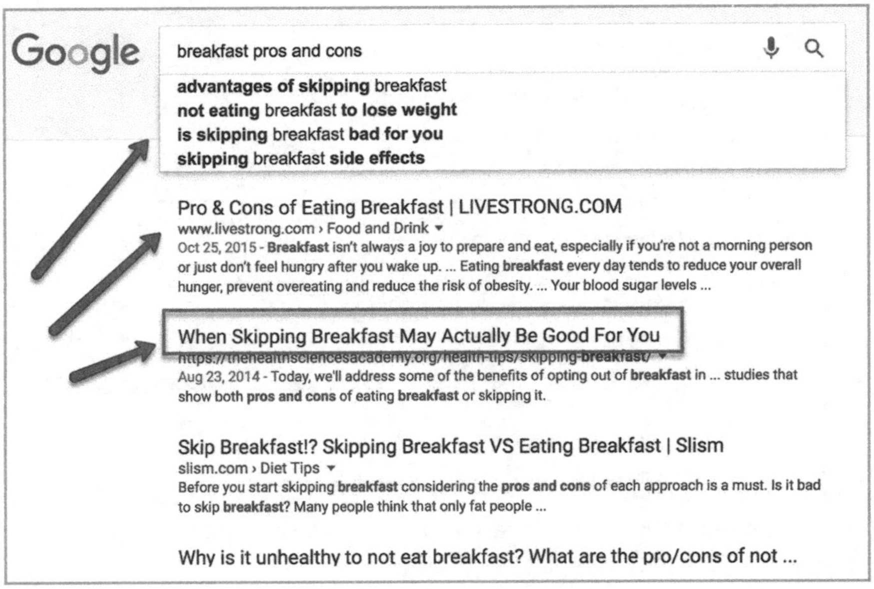

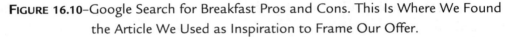

FIGURE 16.10–Google Search for Breakfast Pros and Cons. This Is Where We Found the Article We Used as Inspiration to Frame Our Offer.

Getting more excited, we went back to the bar, and this time we typed in "breakfast pros and cons" as shown in Figure 16.10. Once again, Google suggestions assisted us in our search direction. The second hit was an article published by The Health Sciences Academy and titled "When Skipping Breakfast May Actually Be Good for You." Out of this article we pulled much of the research for what we used for our lead magnet.

We didn't plagiarize. We didn't copy. We just simply borrowed the hook much like Ogilvy borrowed from Pierce Arrow for Rolls Royce. But once we figured out that skipping breakfast may actually be good for you, and had some solid research to back up that claim, we immediately knew we had stumbled on a great hook. How did we know?

The hook for Ketogenic Living works because:

- It's curiosity-based and contrarian.
- It shatters a conventional myth "held by millions of people that breakfast is the most important meal of the day.
- It educates and informs on something new and interesting
- It speaks to our avatar's potential pain point that they never have time to eat breakfast and always feel guilty about it.

If you have a new customer or you're not particularly familiar with a market or an avatar for your product or service, a Google search to determine your hook isn't optional—it's essential. And if you know the market really well, going through the same steps we went through for Ketogenic Living will help you uncover pain points and desires you probably never would've thought of on your own. In fact, you're going to be surprised at how much you find.

SURVEYING THE HOOK

A friend, whom I'll call Bob, ran a Filipino mail-order bride service targeted at single men. Bob ran advertisements in "obvious" places, like *USA Today*.

Marketing legend Dan Kennedy asked Bob: "Are there any idiosyncrasies that your customers have in common? Where they hang out? Hobbies? The type of work they do?

Bob didn't know. So he took a survey and discovered that 40 percent of his buyers were truckers! Bob had never noticed this before, but in hindsight it made sense. The road is a hard and lonely job. Bob could now put ads in trucking magazines and fliers and signs at truck stops. Bob could write new ads in the language of trucking, making his prospects feel immediately at home. His business skyrocketed and his ad cost plummeted.

We had the same experience when we surveyed our Facebook training customers. Almost 40 percent of them were consultants or agencies! It's amazing what you can discover by simply asking a few questions.

There are about a dozen or more solutions you can use to build and host surveys. For us, we use Survey Monkey, which is free. We have the paid version because it correlates

FIGURE 16.11–A Survey Showed Us That Once a Third of Our
Customers Were Consultants

the data a little bit better, but regardless of whether you have a free or paid version of any survey solution software, there's no doubt about the power of surveying your audience. If you have a list, you should be surveying your audience so you can figure out what their big concerns are, what their big desires are, and what their big pains are.

Here are some of the questions we used in our survey:

- "What's your number one single biggest challenge or frustration with using Facebook to drive traffic and sales right now? (Please be as specific as possible. Please go beyond saying "too confusing" or "too expensive." The more specific and detailed you are, the more likely I'll be able to cover your topic :-)"
- "Why do you want to grow your business using Facebook ads or any online channel? What is the biggest reason why you want to master this or have someone master it for you?"

By collecting survey data like this you can discover the super specific pain points and the super specific desires of your target market. For us, we certainly could run ads with the hook: "how to run Facebook ads." That's a pretty good hook, but it's kind of a weak hook as it lacks specificity. But armed with our survey data, we can now frame our hooks far more effectively, all backed by actual data. Here are some of the actual answers from real people who we surveyed as shown in Figure 16.12.

For our own advertising, we pull hooks from this data all the time. After we got all the answers, we analyzed, correlated, and identified patterns in the survey data in Figure 16.13 on page 135. We then used this customer-generated information to not only create hooks for our ads but to also create entirely new products. The Austin, Texas certification program was just one of those products.

FIGURE 16.12–This Is Some of the Survey Data that Created a New Business that Had Been Invisible to Us Before

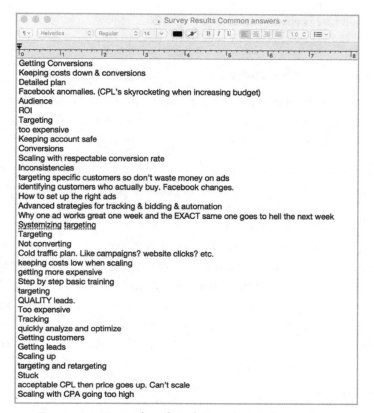

FIGURE 16.13–Analyzed and Correlated Survey Data

The point is this: surveying your list will not only help you to dial in your hook, but if you're observant, you may find that there are some million-dollar product ideas contained in those answers. Once we analyzed our data, it was clear to us that we had a huge opportunity on our hands, and it's fair to say that those outcomes changed our business forever.

INTERVIEWING THE HOOK

This is one we somewhat stumbled upon. After the great success we had using surveys for our own business, we quickly realized that for some of our agency customers, we were overlooking one important part to the hook puzzle: we weren't getting them to do surveys on their own.

We were doing our regular onboarding questionnaire for one of our new agency customers who sell a data analytics solution. On that call, the line of questioning went something like this:

Q: Who is your customer?

A: Business owners and consultants. Those are my two big avatars.

Q: But which one is your best customer?

A: Well, businesses . . .

Q: Why are they your best customer?

A: Now that I think of it a little bit more, consultants are actually better. They buy more of the higher end products, and they don't bug customer service as much, plus they give us referrals. So really they're way better.

Q: Alright then, let's focus on them. Do you think it would be a good idea for us to ask then what their biggest frustrations and/or desires are?

A: Yeah, for sure!

It just so happened that one of our Facebook Account Managers was part of a Facebook group of consultants. Instead of us relying upon the customer to provide us with consultants of theirs, we went ahead and found them on our own. Our strategy was simple: go into the group and simply ask them a couple questions about what their fears, desires, concerns, and potential solutions are.

Lo and behold, they came up with some very useful answers. Here are some answers they produced that revealed their greatest fears:

Question: What are you most afraid of?
Answers:

1. "With ecommerce customers, I just can't see the ROI I thought you could, and you end up with customers thinking that you don't know what you're doing because you can't even tell them how well the ads are doing."
2. "I've had ecommerce customers and Facebook has been showing me one thing and their GA (Google Analytics) is not attributing the sales to Facebook. So it makes me look like I'm fabricating results to make my efforts look better."
3. "It puts me off taking on certain customers because I can't be sure that I can properly attribute sales to my efforts."

All we did was ask them what their fears were, which yielded some seriously good potential hooks, such as "customers thinking that you don't know what you're doing." That's a pretty big fear if you're a consultant. I'm actually having a panic attack just thinking about it.

It was clear to us that with regard to data and analytics for this customer avatar, there is a clear need and a clear fear that could potentially be used as a hook. It was also very clear to us that for this customer avatar, there is a need to be able to convince a customer that your efforts are worthwhile. The big fear is that if this doesn't happen, you'll lose the account. What's worse is if your customers are thinking that you're "fabricating results to make your efforts look better," this is a real problem that needs a real solution.

We also asked the same group about their greatest desires. Here are some answers they produced:

Question: What do you want more than anything else?
Answers:

1. "I'm so paranoid about my reputation that I want everyone who works with me to be very happy."
2. "I'd like easy customer facing reporting (looking for charts or graphics) that would allow me to pull a report that I could show to a customer who doesn't care about the details and only wants a high-level report."

This is pure gold. In fact, I can already see the headline for that first one—"Want to keep your customers happy? Click here to learn more."

Now it doesn't get any clearer than this. "I want easy customer-facing reporting that allows me to pull a report that I could show to a customer." With this answer, the prospect is expressing a specific desire and suggesting a specific solution, namely: looking for charts or graphics.

Remember this formula?

They want [specific desire] so that they can [benefit].

They want to be able to see easy customer-facing reporting with graphics or charts that show the process they're making with Facebook ads so that their customers know they know what they're doing.

In this case, the solution is embedded into this statement. Check it out:

- Specific desire— they want to be able to see the process they're making with Facebook ads
- Benefit—so that their customers know they know what they're doing
- Solution—easy customer-facing reporting with graphics or charts

Here are some suggested solutions they came up with while expressing their fears and desires (their problems) by asking some more simple questions:

Question: If there was a solution to this problem, what would it look like?
Answers:

1. "I'd love if there was something that would really simplify all the setup and analysis. It would actually allow me to take on more customers if I had a reliable system."
2. "...seeing a graphic or a diagram that shows the progress we are making with ads and also multi-channel attribution."

Can you see the hooks starting to form using our tactics here? How about this one: "If only there was a reliable system out there that would simplify all the setup and analysis, then that would allow me to take on more customers."

This is the If and Then statement:

If only [solution]

If only there was a reliable system out there that would simplify all the setup and analysis.

Then [benefit]

Then that would allow me to take on more customers.

The "if" statement is the solution while the "then" statement is the benefit. In this case, the "if" statement reveals the solution, but it can also reveal the desire or pain. The benefit in this case comes from a fulfilled desire, but keep in mind that it could also come from a pain.

What if I told you there is a way to simplify all the setup and analysis so that you can effortlessly help new customers get on board? Now we just so happen to have a solution for them that can do exactly that, and a hook could be something along the lines of "how to reliably track leads, sales, and ROI for your customers."

It's time to spill the beans. Up until till now I purposely didn't reveal who the customer was or the solutions they offered because I wanted you to think of this market's desires and pain points, then think of solutions to satisfy them. The customer that provides the solution is Wicked Reports. They intuitively correlate multi-channel data, then display it to the user using a graphical interface that then attributes all of the traffic back to the correct channel.

Notice our hook is not "how to get results with Facebook." Yes, that is a hook, but it's not a great hook because it's simply not specific enough. If we wanted to get even more specific with this hook, our hook could be something along these lines: "how to reliably track your Facebook leads, sales, and ROI for your customers." In this case, our hook is only speaking to consultants and agencies that offer Facebook ads in their service portfolio. This is a very specific hook that speaks to a very specific problem, and then embedded in the problem is the solution offered by our customer. This is a very important point once again; you need to make sure that the solution to the problem you're agitating is embedded in your own solution. This could be a solution offered by your downloadable cheat sheet or if you're going directly to your offer, in your offer itself.

Just like any other research method, simply asking your customers what their biggest problems are and what their biggest desires are is by no means a guarantee that you'll figure out the killer hook to your next winning campaign. But it is certainly a powerful tool you should strongly consider leveraging. Whether or not the hooks produced by these efforts are great instead of merely good varies per situation. But I do you know this, it's very simple to do. So why not try it with your customers?

"FACEBOOKING" THE HOOK

If there was ever a doubt in your mind that Facebook's sole intent is to take over the world, then maybe this will persuade you otherwise. When we take a new customer onboard inside the agency, one of the first things we do is have them fill out a questionnaire, which then leads to a discussion on a live call. On that call, we discuss many of the things included in this chapter on hooks. But our research doesn't stop there. Typically, once our new customer goes through our onboarding questionnaire they come out with a very different perspective as to who their customer avatars are. But the honest truth is that prior to that exercise, a lot of them can't give us a quick answer to a lot of the questions we ask them. So it's our job to dig deeper.

This is where we delve into their Facebook ad data. Now, in your case, you may not have prior Facebook data, which is fine. Even if you don't, though, make sure you pay attention to this section. Our agency customer Wicked Reports had been running Facebook ads for quite a while before they came on as a customer. So we had a pretty good hunch that there would be a treasure trove of ideas in there. I mean, if you or your customers have any amount of Facebook data, you ought to be using it all the time because, well, why wouldn't you?

Once we more or less figured out the naming conventions for their campaigns, ad sets, and ads, we quickly determined that they had been boosting their posts from their blog. Knowing that results from boosted content is much ignored, but tremendously helpful way in which to discover a hidden hook, we immediately zeroed in on this data.

Inside the Ads Manager we did a campaign search to sort for the words "post" and "blog" while setting the time filter to "Lifetime." See Figure 16.14 on page 140. We immediately identified two campaigns that stood out, which used "link clicks" as a driving metric named: Ungated Blog Post—Best Time to Send Email and Facebook Conversion Blog Post. See Figure 16.15 on page 140.

We then took a closer look at those campaigns. It should be noted that the reason we performed this particular search was because we discovered during our onboarding call that a large portion of their ad spend in the past year was from "boosted posts" to blog content. The easiest way to view this data is to sort your reporting columns by "Performance and Clicks." We then used link clicks as our driving metric as you can also see in Figure 16.15. The reason we use the link clicks as our driving metrics is that we

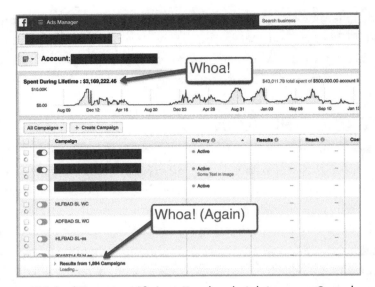

FIGURE 16.14–Wicked Reports Lifetime Facebook Ad Account Spend and Results

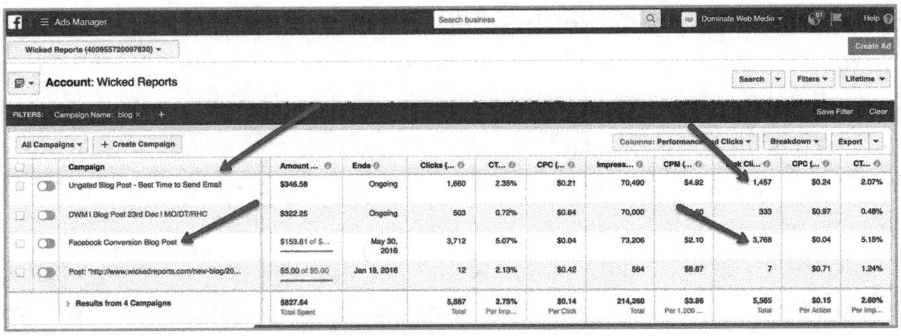

FIGURE 16.15–Wicked Reports Campaign Name Search for "Blog"
and Sorted by Link Clicks

figured if people like the subject matter of a post, then they are probably going to click on the link to read the post itself. As you can see, this is by no means rocket science.

Since they had boosted quite a few posts over the course of the last year, our goal was not only to simply look for the best performing blog posts using link clicks but also using secondary performance metrics, such as a click-through rate (CTR), cost per click (CPC), and Relevance Score.

And lo and behold, we started to see the same blog post pop up over and over again named: "When Is the Best Time to Send Email"

So here are the steps we took below. For your reference, see Figure 16.16 on page 141.

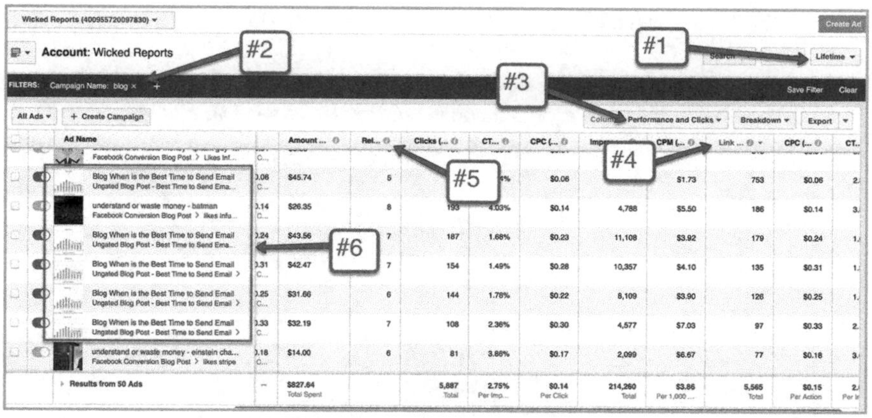

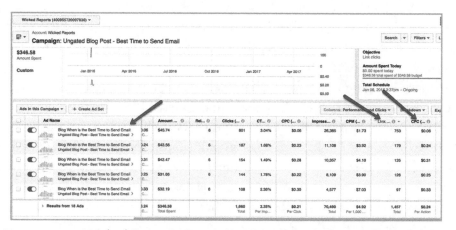

FIGURE 16.16–Research Steps for Wicked Reports Facebook Ad Account

1. Set lifetime filter
2. Search campaign name: blog
3. Sort columns by performance and clicks
4. Sort link clicks from highest to lowest
5. Pay attention to CTR, CPC, and Relevance Score
6. Analyze your data!

The results of this post looked really promising, so we dug deeper. We then went inside the campaign named "When Is the Best Time to Send Your Emails" and looked at link clicks and CPC as you can see in Figure 16.17.

We immediately observed that in comparison to other ads and campaigns, the cost per click for this one post was incredibly low. This is a big deal. The data is practically

FIGURE 16.17–Wicked Reports Campaign Search for "When Is the Best Time to Send Your Emails?"

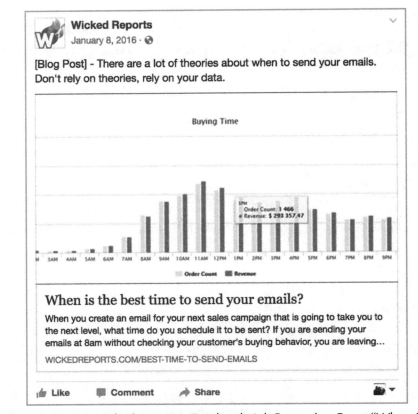

FIGURE 16.18–Wicked Reports Facebook Ad Campaign Post, "When Is the Best Time to Send Your Emails?"

screaming at us that our target market is thirsty for this kind of content. We did a pretty good job during their onboarding, but this hook never even came up in any discussions we ever had with them. But inside their Ads Manager, the message was loud and clear. We then dug a little bit deeper to find the exact Facebook post and immediately copied the ad copy (see Figure 16.18).

As shown in Figure 16.18, the headline reads "[Blog Post]—There are a lot of theories about when to send your emails. Don't rely on theories, rely on data." It's kind of a weak looking image if you ask me, but the data speaks for itself.

When you stop to think about it, as an online business owner, wouldn't you want to know when the best time to send your email is? Yes, you would like to know that and the masses have made it very clear by so positively responding to this blog content. Our customer had their best hook embedded in their data and had it within their reach. All we had to do was go in and mine it.

Now because our customer is Wicked Reports, they just so happen to have Wicked Reports tracking on everything so we went and took a look at their data. We found out

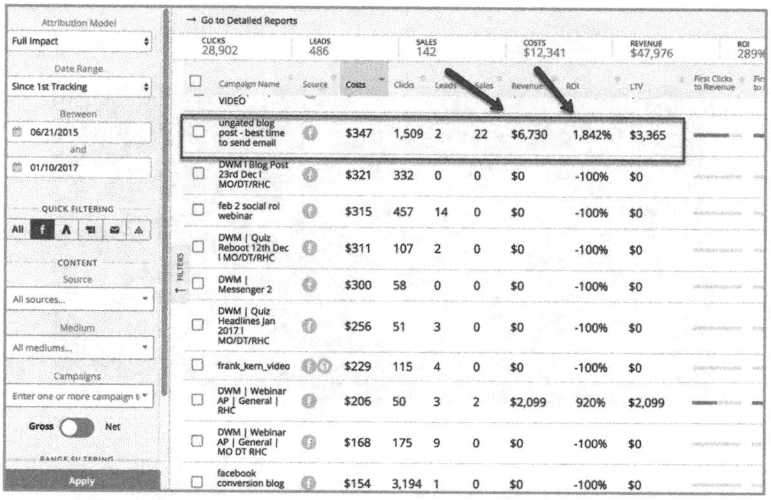

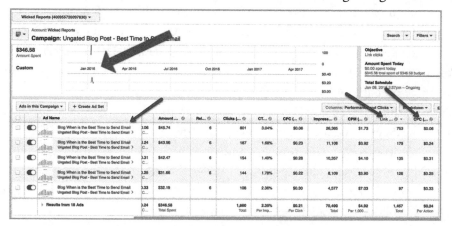

FIGURE 16.19–Wicked Reports Campaign Results from "When Is the Best
Time to Send Your Emails?"

that campaign, "When Is the Best Time to Send Your Emails?" had generated $6,730
in revenue on a mere $347 ad spend. As you can see in Figure 16.19, that represented a
1,842 percent ROI (return on investment).

The obvious next step was to use this hook as one of our front-facing hooks and
then tie it back into their offer.

The next logical step is to create an ad next using this same hook, "When Is the Best
Time to Send Your Emails?" We then created the ad here in Figure 16.21 on page 144:

Then we took a quick look at their landing page from their previous Facebook
ad with this same hook and quickly realized that their landing page was not entirely
congruent with the hook in our ad. The headline was something along the lines of "3x

FIGURE 16.20–Wicked Reports Campaign Life Span of "When Is the Best
Time to Send Your Emails?"

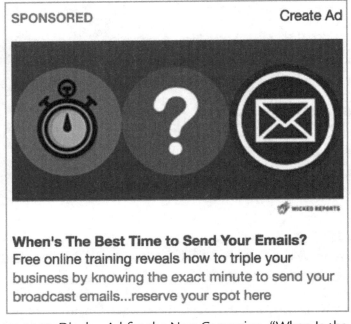

FIGURE 16.21–Display Ad for the New Campaign, "When Is the Best
Time to Send Your Emails?"

Your Ad Spend and Increase Your ROI While Getting a Handle On Your Metrics." So
we changed the headline and some of the copy on the page to be more in line with the
"ad scent" of our ad, namely: "When Is the Best Time to Send Your Emails?" as shown
in Figure 16.21.

Notice that the ad copy and the landing page headline match. This is not by accident
as congruency from ad to landing page is essential for good conversions. Even the color
schemes match to assist in the congruency as you see in Figure 16.22 on page 145.

When we pulled the data a week later, we came to find out that the ad with the hook
"When Is the Best Time to Send Your Emails?" had generated 23,119 percent ROI. All of
this on an ad spend of $53.87, yielding a whopping $12,508 in revenue as you can see in
Figure 16.23 on page 145.

Insane results for sure, but I wasn't 100 percent convinced. It seemed too good to be true
so I did some digging and found out that even though the ad was very profitable on its own,
the vast majority of sales came from an agency who had clicked the ad and then bought 14
accounts all at once. Even taking out those 14 sales, the ad still absolutely crushed.

One of our other ads didn't do too badly either, racking up a 3,807percent ROI, with an
$85.47 ad spend that generated $3,339 in revenue..

These kinds of results are not average and if your first ad doesn't produce results
like this, don't get frustrated. This is not going to happen all the time for you, and it

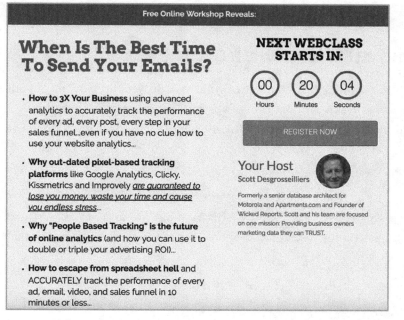

FIGURE 16.22–Old Landing Page with a New Title for the Campaign, "When Is the Best Time to Send Your Emails?"

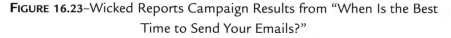

FIGURE 16.23–Wicked Reports Campaign Results from "When Is the Best Time to Send Your Emails?"

certainly doesn't always work like this for us either. But still, even if it's five times less than that—100, 200, or even 300 percent ROI—it's still good. Just keep refining your hooks with all the techniques mentioned in this chapter, and sooner or later as long as you keep swinging for the fences, you will hit a homerun.

THE 95/5 RULE IN GOOGLE AND FACEBOOK ADS

The 80/20 rule says 20 percent of what you do gets 80 percent of your results. But on the Internet, most things are even more extreme than that— 95/5 not 80/20. In Google AdWords, 5 percent of your keywords get 95 percent of your traffic. And if you test LOTS of ads, you'll also find that 5 percent of your ads get 95 percent of the traffic.

This is just as true on Facebook, if not more so. In fact, on Facebook it's probably closer to 97/3 or 98/2. Why? Because of Likes and Shares. Once an ad has accumulated a lot of Likes and Shares, what was previously a slight advantage becomes a huge advantage.

So these are the rules: If you write 100 ads . . .

- Ad number one will get 18 percent of all traffic

- Your top ten ads will get 55 percent of all traffic

- The other 90 ads will share the remaining 44 percent of traffic

And that's being conservative. Odds are, your results will be even more unequal than that.

If you write ten ads, the best one will probably get three times the CTR of the worst one. If you write 100 ads, the best will get ten times the CTR of the worst one. And the traffic your ads get will be hugely out of proportion. Even a slight increase in CTR brings enormously more traffic.

—Perry Marshall, author of *80/20 Sales and Marketing*

Remember that a great ad on Facebook all starts with a great hook. If you're not doing any of the steps mentioned in this chapter, you're leaving a lot of money on the table. So before launching your next campaign, do your homework. You've got to be willing to put in the work, do the research, ask questions, and look at your data because with the right hook, you can catch a lot of fish.

Chapter 17

Proven Facebook-Friendly Offers

After $27.7 million worth of ad spend, and a lot more by the time you might be reading this, we've identified six proven Facebook appropriate offers that have worked across the board in multiple industries for our agency clients.

In this chapter we'll be sharing with you these six proven Facebook offers in reverse order of commitment:

1. Coupon, Sweepstakes, or Blog
2. Checklist, Swipe File, or Cheat Sheet Download
3. Quiz/Survey Funnel
4. Webinar or Event
5. Free + Shipping for Physical Products
6. Product Sales Page

Before I get into these respectively, I want to again clarify that they are listed in reverse order of commitment. This means that number one takes the least commitment while number six takes the most commitment.

> "*I'll make him an offer he can't refuse.*"
>
> —Mario Puzo, *The Godfather*

FOUR MOST-USED AD TYPES FOR GETTING CONVERSIONS

There are four proven Facebook ad types I'll be sharing with you. These are also listed in reverse order of commitment.

1. Short copy ad to a blog post.
2. Short copy ad to a simple lead magnet.
3. Long copy ad to a complex lead magnet, webinar, or product.
4. Video ad to lead magnet, webinar, or product.

If you're a beginner and are just starting off with Facebook ads and are launching your very first campaign for yourself or your clients, don't get overwhelmed by all of this. Once you understand every offer and what ad type match works best with each respectively, and specifically for your business, you're going to start with just one offer to get that initial momentum and results.

If you're at an intermediate to advanced level right now, and you're looking to scale your business or that of your clients, then you might not just pick one. But it totally depends on the situation. If you're in a situation where you need to get momentum and results, then you still want to pick the best one. But you always want to be thinking about matching the right offer with the right ad type, and I'm sure this chapter will help you do just that.

PROVEN OFFER #1: COUPON, SWEEPSTAKES, OR BLOG

Video Ad to Coupon

This offer is the one with the least commitment. The offer could be a coupon for a product or service, and it works wonders with local businesses. This is an ad that I ran quite a while back for one of my first local clients in the early days. It is a 30-second video that they had created for a local 30-second TV ad spot. You can see a screenshot of it in Figure 17.1 on page 149.

Because they already had this asset, I proposed to repurpose it for a Facebook ad and so that's what I did. This video ad goes to this landing page, as shown in Figure 17.2 on page 149, and it just absolutely crushed it.

Short Copy Ad to Coupon

The next logical question is—does it have to be a video ad to a coupon offer for it to work? The answer is no, it does not. We did the same thing here with just a creative ad, as shown in Figure 17.3 on page 150. This one went to a slightly different coupon offer, and it worked just as well.

FIGURE 17.1–Eagle Leather 30-Second Video Ad to Coupon

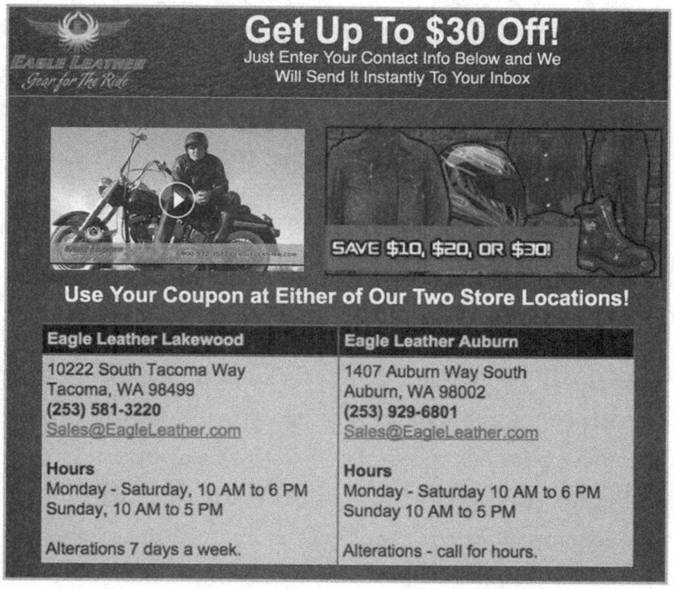

FIGURE 17.2–Eagle Leather Landing Page for a Coupon of Up to $30 Off

What's also happening is that they are getting massive organic brand exposure because people are engaging with this ad content. They're not just getting customers from those who see the ad and come into the store to redeem their offer, but these

FIGURE 17.3–Eagle Leather Short Copy Ad to Coupon

prospects and customers are also sharing it with their friends. At the time I took the screenshot of the ad it had generated 793 likes, 79 comments, and 58 shares.

One of the hidden benefits of this is that because of all this brand awareness in the local market from these ads maybe people visit the local business or just the landing page, as shown in Figure 17.4 on page 151, but they are not ready to buy just yet.

Now they subconsciously know that there is a solution for their problem in their local market. When this problem aggravates or becomes more relevant in the future, then their minds will subconsciously associate their problem to the solution your business provides.

Short-Copy Ad to Blog Post

This is not a blog post to promote a coupon or sweepstakes. Instead, this is an ad to "ungated" free blog content as shown in Figure 17.5 on page 151. Ungated just means

FIGURE 17.4–Eagle Leather Landing Page for a Coupon of Up to $50 Off

that the visitor is not required to give anything in exchange for consuming the content, like their email address, their money, etc.

With this one it's very important that you have proper tracking in place with a software like Wicked Reports because you want to be able to accurately track your

FIGURE 17.5–Short Copy Ad to Blog Post: The Purpose of this Was to
Bring Cold Traffic into a Remarketing Campaign

best performing blog content so that you can spend more time promoting it and subsequently make more money, as we shared with you in Chapter 16.

This is a long-term goodwill strategy in a lot of cases, but it also works very well in the short-term if executed properly. It's all about coming up with the right hook, so that a prospect clicks on your ad, reads your blog content, and gets indoctrinated with your brand, as shown in Figure 17.6.

If properly done, this can easily lead to a sale either directly or indirectly. This is powerful, trust me. It is one of my favorite ad type campaigns to run.

Perry Marshall
Published by Emily Caporuscio Brookins [?] · June 27, 2016 · 🌐

Business insights form Archimedes. 80% of your "levers" will only spin your wheels and kick up dirt, but 20% will give you the traction you need to accelerate out of any ditch. Discover 4 simple 80/20 gears to scale your business fast...

80/20, Adwords, & Archimedes – 4 Tips To Grow Your Business |
Archimedes said "Give me a lever & a place to stand & I will move the world." 80 percent of your levers get you nowhere & 20 percent will get you what you want.
PERRYMARSHALL.COM

FIGURE 17.6–A Facebook Post to a Pure-Content Blog Post
Supports the Sale without Being Pitchy

PROVEN OFFER #2: CHECKLIST, SWIPE FILE, OR CHEAT SHEET DOWNLOAD

As you can see in Figure 17.7 on page 153, this one has slightly more copy than other short copy ads, but it's still considered short. The offer is a tool that will allow your prospects to scale their businesses with maximum ROI and minimum money wasted. This ad goes to a simple landing page where they opt-in to download, as shown in Figure 17.7 as well.

This is a downloadable PDF checklist for a lead magnet, but then there's a webinar registration page right after so that's why the copy is a little bit longer, and hits on some desires and pains. But the first step, which is a simple opt-in to get a free download, is still a simple ask, hence why the ad and landing page copy are not very long.

FIGURE 17.7–Short Copy to a Checklist Lead Generation Campaign for
"The 7-Step Facebook Campaign Checklist"

One of the longest running lead generation campaigns from Digital Marketer is this social media swipe file, as shown in Figure 17.8. Notice that this is a display ad and not a newsfeed ad, but they do run both placements, and it does incredibly well in both.

FIGURE 17.8–Short Copy Display Ad to Swipe File for
"The Ultimate Social Media Swipe File"

FIGURE 17.9–Landing Page for Michael Smart PR Promises an Immediate 24-Hour Boost for People Who Pitch Reporters

Michael Smart teaches public relations skills to corporate PR managers. They need to get their companies mentioned in news outlets.

Figure 17.9 shows how he taps into the exact moves their career success most depends on. The use of three hooks, and three headlines and three videos instead of one is clever.

Video Ad to Lead Magnet

Normally, we don't recommend doing a video to a simple lead magnet because the level of commitment is so low, you don't need to in order to have great results. But our agency client Drew Canole loves videos, and he does a great job at producing them for his company Organifi.

This is a four-minute video ad he created that takes prospects to download his free ebook *Alpha Reset*, as shown in Figure 17.10 on page 155.

He's got about 20 million video views at the time I'm writing this, and a lot more by the time you read this so it works. There's a lot of different ways he could have chosen to bring people into this lead magnet, but he chose this for a very specific purpose—because of what happens next after they get the free download on the landing page as you can see in Figure 17.11 on page 155.

FIGURE 17.10–Drew Canole's Video Ad to Lead Magnet for His Alpha Reset ebook

FIGURE 17.11–Drew Canole's Landing Page for His ebook,*Alpha Reset*

The key here is that a video on the first point of contact with the prospect builds rapport and credibility. Then they get the Alpha Reset for free, so there's value upfront being received, but more importantly, they have subconsciously committed to the Organifi green juice Drew is going to sell them on the thank you page. So this video ad does a great job at pre-framing prospects and warming them up for the sale on the thank you page—where the magic happens.

PROVEN OFFER #3: QUIZ/SURVEY FUNNEL

When it comes to using a quiz or a survey funnel, the key is really to have a great hook, and they are almost always curiosity-driven hooks. Like we talked about in Chapter 16, a hook reels your prospects in, but with a quiz or survey funnel, you go one step forward because you are immediately engaging them. There's a quiz campaign that we launched and manage for one of our agency clients, and in Figure 17.12 you'll see a link post ad that takes you to the quiz landing page.

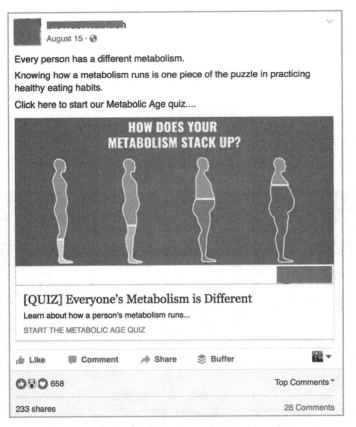

FIGURE 17.12–Quiz Funnel Link Post Ad

FIGURE 17.13–Survey Landing Page for the Campaign—"How Old Is Your Metabolism?"

This campaign has worked incredibly well because the hook itself leaves people wanting more so they fill out the survey to find out, as you can see in Figure 17.13.

You have to think of quizzes and survey funnels like a doctor's prescription because it functions with branch logic, it is tailored specifically to a particular person, and at the end produces an answer-based solution. Through a series of strategic questions you take your prospect down a path where they are telling you, based on their answers, what their problem is and then you can prescribe a solution to solve that problem, which in this case, is a free downloadable report. People have to opt-in to be able to get their results, and the prescription can be a free or paid product. Even if they don't buy, you have an incredible amount of data that you can use to discover your customer avatar's greatest fears and desires to come up with hooks like we talked about in Chapter 16.

PROVEN OFFER #4: WEBINAR OR EVENT

Many people value their time much more than their money, but it does go both ways. Because the level of commitment is higher and you're essentially asking people to spend at least 90 to 120 minutes with you on a webinar, you have to pre-commit your prospects with your long copy. One way that I've successfully done this for our company is by using a short 30-second clip with a text overlay highlighting the hook, and then elaborating a lot more in the long copy, as shown in 17.14 on page 158.

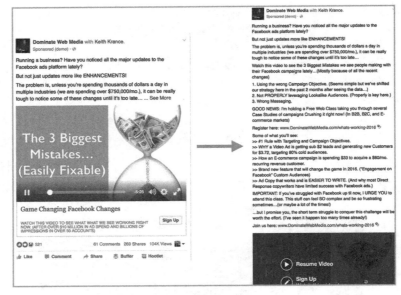

FIGURE 17.14–Our Company's Video Ad to Webinar Campaign for
"Game Changing Facebook Changes"

What I'm doing here in the copy is restating the hook from the video and making prospects aware of a problem that they either may or may not know that they have, as you can see in Figure 17.14. I then deliver the promise of the hook by revealing the three biggest mistakes, and then invite them to register for my free web class, as shown in Figure 17.15, where I'm promising to teach them the solution.

FIGURE 17.15–Webinar Registration Landing Page for the Campaign,
"Game Changing Facebook Changes"

What's important to know here is that each step is seeding the next. Once they read my copy, I want them to register and then show up to the webinar, but I'm delivering value every step of the way to where I want them to be. And as long as you're doing that, you don't need to use a video ad, but I recommend you do.

PROVEN OFFER #5: FREE PLUS SHIPPING FOR PHYSICAL PRODUCTS

For this particular offer, there's a very clear distinction from the level of commitment of offers 1 through 4. Now you're asking people to pull out their credit cards so the upfront value needs to be that much more. I had a successful and long-running campaign promoting a free plus the cost of shipping offer for the second edition of this book as you can see in Figure 17.16.

FIGURE 17.16–Video Ad to Product for the Campaign, "#1 Lesson Learned After $10 Million in Ad Spend"

To pre-frame prospects into buying my book on the next step, I made a video where I taught them the number one lesson learned after spending an average of $600k a month on ad spend. Now our agency, manages an average of three million dollars a month so we've gone a long way since this campaign ran. But what's important here is that in this video, I deliver on the promise of the hook and teach them the four targeting groups (ad sets) that they should start every campaign with.

The length of the video is not as important as the content and how it delivers on the promise of the hook while leading them to the next step. But I know you want to know, so to keep your mind at ease, this video was about ten minutes long or so.

Once I've educated my prospects and subsequently elevated their status because now they are smarter and more informed because of what I just shared with them, I invite them to buy my book so that they can learn even more. By delivering value in the form of content that speaks to their desires and pain points, I am also creating a greater desire within them to meet those desires and pain points, and find a solution for them. I then offer my solution—to get a free book so they can learn more, as shown in Figure 17.17.

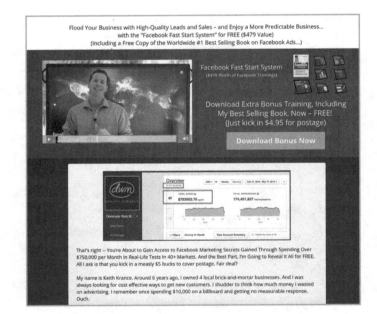

FIGURE 17.17–Landing Page for a Free Plus Shipping Offer of the Book, *Ultimate Guide to Facebook Advertising*, Second Edition

The hook on the top of the fold is a known desire of my customer avatar to flood your business with high-quality leads and sales, and enjoy a more predictable business so it does a great job of reeling them in to watch the video where I make the offer, as shown in Figure 17.17. This works very well with cold audiences because it lowers the barrier of entry at a very minimum in order to convert your prospects to qualified buyers. In order for me to give out my book for free and just ask for a minimal cover for shipping, we actually had to pay for those leads because this book is not self-published so we have to incur the cost of buying it from the publisher. Now the reason this works for us is because I know that although we deliver an incredible amount of value in this book, we also know there's a lot more value that we offer in every step of the funnel when our prospects ascend our value ladder. It is because of this that it makes business sense for us to pay more up front to qualified buyers.

PROVEN OFFER #6: PRODUCT SALES PAGE

There's no doubt video ads are the most powerful ad type, which is why I'm explaining them that much more here and even more so in Chapter 22 where I go over the three-step video ad formula. At our company, we also encourage all of our agency clients to do more videos, and so should you. If you're running a video ad to cold traffic, there's value that needs to be given to your prospect up front. Drew Canole does this very well with this video ad on "11 superfoods," as shown in Figure 17.18.

FIGURE 17.18–Drew Canole's Video Ad to Sales Page for the Campaign "11 Superfoods"

When you're running traffic to people who are unaware of who you are or the solution you provide, a great way to build authority, credibility, and rapport is to educate them. If you're thinking about just putting up a video with a straight call to action to buy your product, don't do it because it won't work. There has to be a whole lot more to it than just a CTA. In this video, Drew educates his prospects on the "11 superfoods," but after all that upfront value there's a pivot at the end on how they can take the next step. After he teaches them about what these superfoods are and why they need them, he tells them how they can get all these superfoods at mostly specialty stores, but then he offers a much easier solution—his product Organifi. Instead of having to buy 11-plus different bottles of supplements to yield all the benefits that eating these 11 superfoods give you, there's an easier way—and that is Organifi, a simple and tasty green juice supplement that will give you all the vital nutrients you need in an all-in-one drink. Prospects will naturally want to learn more because you've educated them so well, and have elevated their status in the process, and now they want more so they are taken to the product sales page, as shown in Figure 17.19.

FIGURE 17.19–Product Sales Page for Organifi's Green Juice Supplement

The hook at the top of the fold restates the benefits of the product, and the rest of the long-form sales page restates a lot of what Drew shared in the video. The reason this campaign works is because the video scripts are written in a specific way, and that is to present juicing with the Organifi product as the next logical solution to yield the benefits that come from these nutritious superfoods. After the video ad, they've been taken from a state of unawareness all the way up the UPSYD ladder as we talked about in Chapter 13 and as shown in Figure 17.20 on page 163.

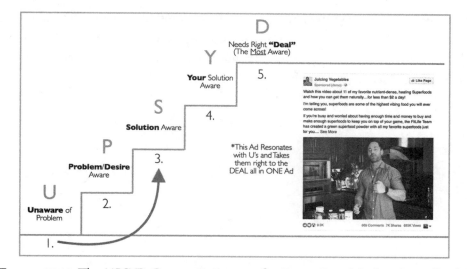

FIGURE 17.20–The UPSYD Customer Journey for Drew Canole's "11 Superfoods"
Video Ad to Sales Page Campaign

I'm assuming your next logical question is—how long is the video? This is one of
the longest running video ads we have for this particular client, and we have several
different versions of the same one. The length of the different versions range from 6
to 12 minutes, and they mostly all run to cold traffic and work incredibly well. The
question here really needs to be—am I efficiently implementing the three-step video ad
formula? We'll dig deep into this in Chapter 22.

Now before I move on to the next chapter, I want to briefly answer your
question—how much of this video is going to cold traffic vs. warm or hot traffic?
About 90 percent of the audiences are cold, which leaves only about 10 percent or so
for retargeting, and the average order is about $100. Some of you have blank stares
in your face right now, but this is what actually happens. We always tell people not
to get caught up on retargeting because in the greater scale of things what matters
the most is your hook and offer. Get that right, and then retargeting really just
becomes icing on top.

CLOSING THOUGHTS

Now it's your turn to create your own proven Facebook appropriate friendly offers and
start producing some winning campaigns. The next time you're crafting either your own
or your clients' campaigns, come back to this chapter and refresh your memory so that
you can make sure you're implementing a proven winning strategy. Also, remember to
always see a Facebook ad account as a valuable asset to your business. The Facebook
advertising platform is the greatest and most powerful tool for businesses of all sizes to

reach their customers, so be smart and wise when using it, and you will yield incredible results. More importantly, make sure you thoroughly read Facebook ad policies and abide by them at all times so that you can guarantee the health and longevity of your ad account and ultimately of your business.

Chapter 18

The Facebook Ad Builder

Seven Building Blocks for Fast (and Profitable) Ad Creation

After reading the last two chapters, you should now have a solid plan in place for what kind of hook (or hooks) you will be testing, and what "offer" you will be sending your Facebook traffic to or what changes, if any, are needed to improve your existing hook or offer. Now, it's time to start putting it all together and writing some killer ads.

In this chapter, we take you through a framework we use to make sure we get at least some of the most impactful blocks of content into the ad copy. This will help you quickly create winning ads, multiple ad variations for testing, optimizing, and reducing ad fatigue.

> "*It is not the beauty of a building you should look at; it's the construction of the foundation that will stand the test of time.*"
>
> —DAVID ALLAN COE

This framework is so effective, we created a tool to help automate the process described in this chapter! Go to www.PerryMarshall.com/fbtools and check it out and see if it helps you create more profitable ads, faster than before.

HOW THE AD BUILDING BLOCKS WORK

As you will see in the coming examples, you can mix and match the different ad blocks any way you want. Think of it a little like getting into a Lego mini-figure building contest, where each person starts with a tray of Legos with seven different small compartments—like in one of those plastic desk tray organizers in Figure 18.1. One compartment has five to ten different heads, one has five to ten different hats and helmets, one has five to ten different bodies, one has legs, one has weapons, and one has capes and similar gear. Some of your Lego guys may have a helmet and a cape, some may have a helmet but not a cape. Some may have a weapon and a hat, but no cape. Some may have two weapons—one for each hand.

FIGURE 18.1–Desk Tray Organizer

Your ad building should be just like building these Lego guys—some ads will have all seven building blocks and some ads may only have two or three. Some of your ads will have the building blocks in the same sequential order as I list them out in this chapter. And some ads will have building block #3 as the start of your ad copy, and building block #1 as the Link Description below the video or image in a newsfeed ad.

AD BUILDING BLOCKS INSIDE REAL ADS

In the following examples, you will see each building block pointed out. As you will see, some ads have almost all of the building blocks and some ads have just a few. This is where you get to get creative and mix and match and test whatever you want in any order you want. In Figure 18.2 starting on page 167, you will see a list of different ads pointing out the individual building blocks.

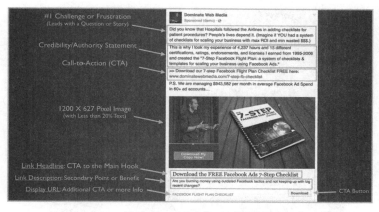

FIGURE 18.2–Link Post Ad for a PDF Download

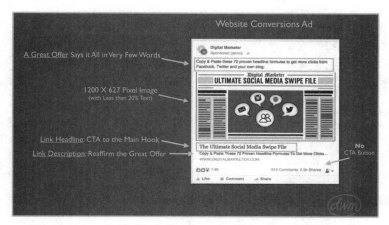

FIGURE 18.2–A Great Offer Says It All in Very Few Words

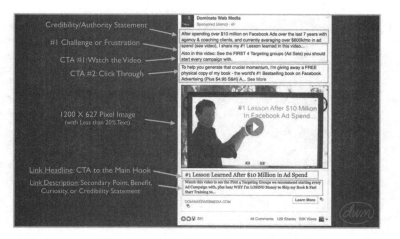

FIGURE 18.2–Video Ad to a Free Book + S&H Offer—Part 1

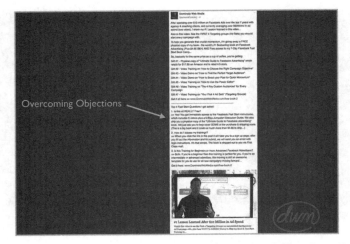

FIGURE 18.2–Video Ad to a Free Book + S&H Offer—Part 2

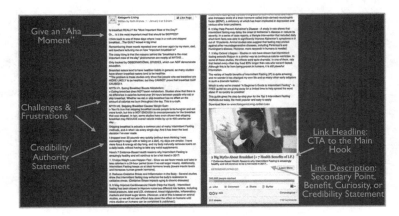

FIGURE 18.2–Long Copy Link Post Ad

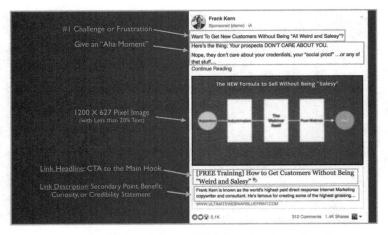

FIGURE 18.2–Video Ad to a Webinar Registration Page

TIME TO BUILD SOME AD BLOCKS

The purpose of the Ad Builder is to pull from the work you have already done. Refer to any notes from the previous chapters to spark ideas for each of these different building blocks. The best way to use the online Ad Builder is just to do it as an exercise on a notepad or whiteboard and write out as many different options for each building block as you can. Some you may never even use. Some you may only use once or twice. And you may use a couple of your phrases in almost every ad you create.

BUILDING BLOCK #1: CURIOSITY

Curiosity-based hooks are some of the most battle-tested and proven strategies for grabbing someone's attention and getting them to read on, watch on, or listen on. You can ask a thought-provoking question, use shocking statements, make a statement that goes against conventional wisdom, and many more. Figure 18.3 shows an example.

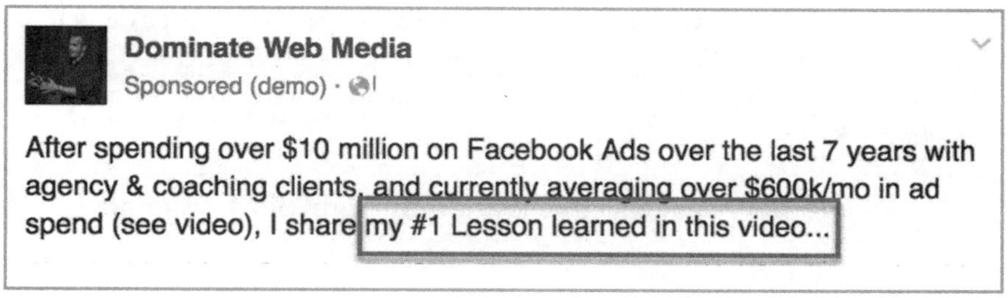

Dominate Web Media
Sponsored (demo) · 🌐

After spending over $10 million on Facebook Ads over the last 7 years with agency & coaching clients, and currently averaging over $600k/mo in ad spend (see video), I share my #1 Lesson learned in this video...

FIGURE 18.3–Curiosity Ad Block Example

BUILDING BLOCK #2: CHALLENGE, FRUSTRATION, PAIN, OR DESIRE

The best and easiest way to get these ad blocks written for you is to survey your audience. Dr. Glen Livingston and Ryan Levesque have some of the most amazing material on using surveys and quizzes to take your business to the next level. Be sure to check out Ryan's book, *Ask: The Counterintuitive Online Formula to Discover Exactly What Your Customers Want to Buy . . . Create a Mass of Raving Fans . . . and Take Any Business to the Next Level* (RL & Associates, 2015).

Read Chapter 13 in Ryan's book to remind yourself of what you need to run a deep-dive survey. I have two questions regarding challenges and desires that I use in my deep-dive survey to hundreds of potential ad building blocks:

1. *Frustration or Challenge.* "What's your number-one single biggest challenge or frustration with using Facebook to drive traffic and sales right now? (Please be

as detailed and specific as possible. Go beyond saying "too confusing" or "too expensive." The more specific and detailed you are, the more likely I'll be able to cover your topic.)"

2. *Desire.* "Why do you want to grow your business using Facebook ads or any online channel? What is the biggest reason why you want to master this or have someone master it for you?"

In the ad in Figure 18.4 I highlighted the frustration for many Facebook advertisers that I called out on the opening line of copy, "scaling your business with max ROI and minimum wasted money." I pulled this phrase right out of my deep-dive survey responses. We had several responses almost exactly like this one, with just a slight variation.

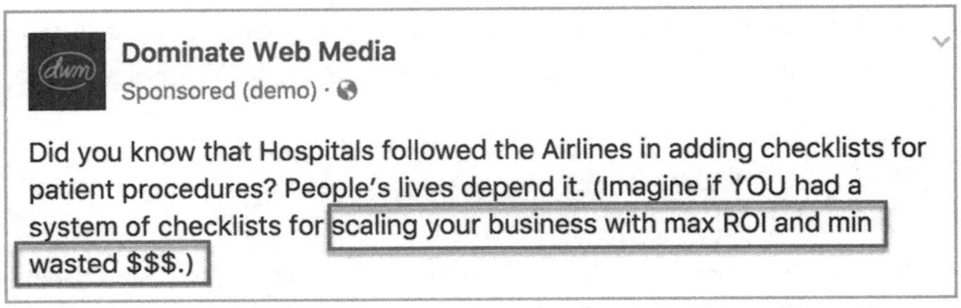

Dominate Web Media
Sponsored (demo) · 🌐

Did you know that Hospitals followed the Airlines in adding checklists for patient procedures? People's lives depend it. (Imagine if YOU had a system of checklists for scaling your business with max ROI and min wasted $$$.)

FIGURE 18.4–Challenge Frustration Building Block Example

BUILDING BLOCK #3: BENEFITS AND DESIRES

What is the desire or benefit that the reader will achieve? What is the true, deep down, desire they are looking to achieve? To see if you can get deeper with your audience, you just need to add the three words "so you can" or "so that" to the end of any benefit you already have. Try it—it's kind of fun! Just be aware that with Facebook's stringent ad policy, sometimes using benefit-driven statements can violate ad policies and get your ads disapproved. Please carefully read through the Ad Policy section online at Facebook.com.

In Figure 18.5 on page 171, notice the benefit statement. The guys over at Samcart are always making great ads. They have a checkout page-building software that makes it super easy to create high-converting checkout pages, upsells, etc. without dealing with all the tech issues. And notice the benefit they focus on with this ad—it says nothing about checkout pages. They're talking about doubling your sales, as they know that this is the conversation going on in the mind of their prospects. Figure 18.5 shows an example of a benefit statement.

FIGURE 18.5–Benefit Statement Ad Block

BUILDING BLOCK #4: CREDIBILITY OR AUTHORITY STATEMENT

Why should people listen to you? What credibility or authority do you have in the marketplace to make people want to pay attention to you, trust you, and do what you ask them to do? This is one of those ad blocks you want to be strategic with. If you're not careful, you can come across as boastful. However, you will get better and better as you get more experience.

In Figure 18.6 on page 172 you will see a few examples of this, even one with kind of an inherited credibility where I use my airline experience as the credibility to speak on the "airlines using checklists" metaphor.

BUILDING BLOCK #5: GIVE AN "AHA MOMENT"

What information can you reveal or story can you tell that can give someone a sudden insight or realization? How can you expose a common belief as being a myth, inaccurate, or recently changed in some way? How can you give someone a revelation, and make

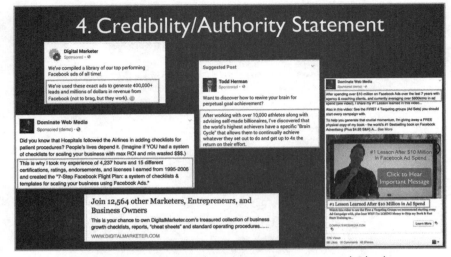

FIGURE 18.6–Credibility Authority Statement Ad Block

them aware of something they didn't know existed, didn't know was available, didn't know was possible, or something else that will give them an "aha moment?"

You won't be able to do this in all your ads, but when it's appropriate, either within your ad copy or within a video, it is powerful on many levels. It makes people immediately trust you and want to learn more. And it makes your ad much more shareable. This is HUGE in terms of Facebook's algorithm—the more shareable your ad is, the more Facebook rewards you with cheaper clicks, cheaper impressions, cheaper views, more impressions, and higher ROI.

In Figure 18.7 on page 173, you will see a very popular common belief exposed.

BUILDING BLOCK #6: CALL-TO-ACTION (CTA)

What action do you want the viewer to take next? How can you have natural CTAs woven into your ad copy or into a video? If you don't make it crystal clear what you want the reader or viewer to do, then they won't do it. Remember, people are very distracted and are probably just skimming your ads.

Note: With longer video ads, around three minutes long and up, we always try to get at least a soft CTA within the first 60-90 seconds. In Figure 18.8 on page 173, you see an example.

BUILDING BLOCK #7: OVERCOMING OBJECTIONS

We have run many experiments where the conversions increase even after we added an overcoming objections section in the ad copy. Even if it makes the ad copy much longer,

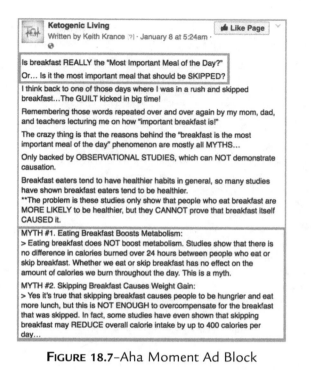

Ketogenic Living
Written by Keith Krance [?] · January 8 at 5:24am ·

👍 Like Page

Is breakfast REALLY the "Most Important Meal of the Day?"
Or… Is it the most important meal that should be SKIPPED?

I think back to one of those days where I was in a rush and skipped breakfast…The GUILT kicked in big time!

Remembering those words repeated over and over again by my mom, dad, and teachers lecturing me on how "important breakfast is!"

The crazy thing is that the reasons behind the "breakfast is the most important meal of the day" phenomenon are mostly all MYTHS…

Only backed by OBSERVATIONAL STUDIES, which can NOT demonstrate causation.

Breakfast eaters tend to have healthier habits in general, so many studies have shown breakfast eaters tend to be healthier.
**The problem is these studies only show that people who eat breakfast are MORE LIKELY to be healthier, but they CANNOT prove that breakfast itself CAUSED it.

MYTH #1. Eating Breakfast Boosts Metabolism:
> Eating breakfast does NOT boost metabolism. Studies show that there is no difference in calories burned over 24 hours between people who eat or skip breakfast. Whether we eat or skip breakfast has no effect on the amount of calories we burn throughout the day. This is a myth.

MYTH #2. Skipping Breakfast Causes Weight Gain:
> Yes it's true that skipping breakfast causes people to be hungrier and eat more lunch, but this is NOT ENOUGH to overcompensate for the breakfast that was skipped. In fact, some studies have even shown that skipping breakfast may REDUCE overall calorie intake by up to 400 calories per day…

FIGURE 18.7–Aha Moment Ad Block

Juicing Vegetables
November 11, 2016 ·

Looking for an easy way to get more superfoods?

Organifi Green Juice is an organic, greens powder, with all your healthy superfoods in one drink.

On it's own or added to your smoothie, Organifi is a delicious way to get your superfoods everyday!

Check it out here >> http://fitlife.tv/organifi-green-juice-h1/

Detox
Replenish
organifi
GREEN JUICE

Get All Your Healthy Superfoods In One Drink
-->

GET ORGANIFI GREEN JUICE   Learn More

280K Views

FIGURE 18.8–Call-to-Action (CTA) Ad Block

it ends up building trust and giving you higher relevance scores and higher conversions. At the end of the ad in Figure 18.9, after the first CTA, you will see a mini FAQ that is used to overcome objections and build trust. And it flat out works.

Gift #7 - Video Training on "Your First 4 Ad Sets" (Targeting Groups)

Get if all here >> www.DominateWebMedia.com/free-book-2

Top 3 Fast Start Questions I get asked:

1. Is this all REALLY Free?
>> Yes! You get immediate access to the Facebook Fast Start mini-course, which includes 6 videos plus a 5-Step Jumpstart Execution Guide. We also ship you a physical copy of the "Ultimate Guide to Facebook Advertising" book. We just ask you to help cover SOME of the purchase & shipping costs. (This is a big book and it costs us much more than $4.95 to ship...)

2. How do I access my trainings?
>> When you click the link in this post it will take you to a sign-up page; after you fill out the information and hit submit, we will send you an email with login instructions. It's that simple. The book is shipped out to you via First Class mail.

3. Is this Training for Beginners or more Advanced Facebook Advertisers?
>> Both. If you're a beginner then this training is perfect for you. If you're an intermediate or advanced advertiser, this training is still an awesome template for you to use for all new campaigns moving forward...

Get it here: www.DominateWebMedia.com/free-book-2

1.00

▶ **Resume Video**

🌐 **Learn More**
DOMINATEWEBMEDIA.COM

FIGURE 18.9–Overcoming Objections Ad Block

Those are the seven ad building blocks! Now it's time to start making your blocks so you can build killer ads. But guess what? In the next two chapters, Ryan Deiss and Ralph Burns give you some priceless tips and elements to fill your metaphorical Lego-building tray up with even more parts and options.

Chapter 19

The 13 Elements of Persuasive Ad Copy

Guest Author Ralph Burns of Dominate Web Media

For dinner tonight, you decided it will be charbroiled steak on the grill. You poured yourself a glass of your favorite velvety Cabernet, your hand-cut slabs of deliciously marbled rib eye sit greedily on your kitchen counter cutting board while your outside charcoals have reached their perfect grey-red ambient glowering perfection. The grill is scrubbed, oiled, and ready. All you need to do is to season those deep crimson and cream-marbled beauties with your favorite seasoning, but which one should you use?

The truth is that when you're grilling a delicious steak there's almost an infinite number of ways in which to season it. No matter the spice, whether it's the tried and true salt and pepper or it's some exotic Hawaiian steak spice rub you discovered by accident on vacation, chances are that no matter the spice, it'll be a delicious steak no matter what. In fact, unless you overcook the thing to resemble old shoe leather from your grandpa's World War I duffers, there's really no way you can screw this one up regardless of the spice.

Writing ad copy for Facebook ads is really not much different. Unless you break every rule in the book and completely forget everything you've learned thus far in this book,

> *"Nobody who bought a drill wanted a drill. They wanted a hole. Therefore you should advertise information about making holes, not drills."*
>
> —PERRY MARSHALL

you're on the right track to writing good ad copy in your ads. I mean, even a rib eye with no spice rub is still a pretty darn good steak.

The point is that there's no one singular way to "spice up" ad copy, which is why we have so many different "seasonings" here in this chapter on how to do it. The 14 elements of persuasive ad copy are simple tips taken from actual ads that are currently converting and doing well from a CPA and ROI perspective.

Do they all fall inside the framework for all the ad blocks? Some of them do, but some of them don't. The point is that when you're writing good Facebook ads, you need both a framework to start from and also some simple suggestions that can "spice up" that ad copy while at the same time will inject your own individuality in where it's needed.

Remember that Facebook at its core is a social network, where being authentic to your company's mission is a big key to your success. And since your business is like nobody else's, your ads should reflect its (and perhaps even your) own personality. So use all of these 14 elements sparingly, and please don't think that you necessarily have to have all of them in every one of your ads. But rather, the idea here is to spark some creative ideas that will make your ads stand out, be genuine to you and your brand while reinforcing the hooks and offers you've worked so hard on—all in order to achieve the business result you most desire.

13 ELEMENTS OF PERSUASIVE AD COPY

The image in Figure 19.1 on page 177 is based on a podcast episode of *Perpetual Traffic* on iTunes that we did on the 14 elements of persuasive ad copy. Like all things on Facebook they have changed over time as Facebook changes like a constantly moving shoreline, so these 14 may be somewhat different than the ones you may have listened to in the past. For this chapter, we have reduced it to 13 elements, as one of the elements (Curiosity) was covered in Chapter 18. Since we run a very high volume of ongoing Facebook advertising, we constantly change and edit these elements for the pursuit of "the perfect Facebook ad." We may never get quite THERE, but we do use these elements because they flat-out work in doing what people pay us to do every day, namely helping to convert cold traffic into leads and sales. In Figure 19.1 you will see all 14 elements listed out.

In each one of the examples, I'll call out an individual element of persuasive ad copy, then give you an example of exactly what each looks like in an actual ad that is working to create actual conversions many of which have millions and millions of impressions and hundreds of thousands of conversions. BEWARE: all of the ads shown in this list are all REAL ads that have produced REAL results. No theory here, just **real** ads that work **real** well.

Now, on to the ads.

14 Elements of Persuasive Facebook Ad Copy

1. Be Authentic
2. Simplify
3. Write For Homer
4. Show Proof
5. Use Questions
6. Answer Immediately
7. Use Revealing Words
8. "You" Rules:
9. Use "Non-Standard" Callouts
10. Capitalize
11. Embrace The Ellipsis
12. Mix It Up
13. Be Counter-Intuitive
14. Employ Emojis

FIGURE 19.1–14 Elements of Persuasive Facebook Ad Copy

Element 1: Be Authentic

It may sound clichéd, but remember when you write ad copy, you need to write in your own voice. "Well, who's voice would I write in?" you may say. If you've done any level of ad copywriting training, chances are you probably know what I mean. For me, my biggest ad copywriting influences (in no particular order) are: Jon Carlton, Gary Halbert, Claude Hopkins, Frank Kern, Perry Belcher, Brian Clark, John Morrow, Ryan Deiss, and Robert Cialdini. Throw in *Cosmopolitan* magazine for some of the best eye-catching headlines in the history of copywriting, but I digress. My point is this: don't try to write like any of your copywriting heroes and just copy their stuff; instead, steal their stuff and make it your own, which is what I've done in this list here. Yes, if you know any of the characters in the list above, you may recognize some of the patterns in these 14 elements. Of course, I've added "my own take" into all of it, so it's not theirs any more—its mine and now . . . I give it to you. After all, as the great Pablo Picasso was once quoted as saying:

> "Good artists copy . . . great artists steal."

If you're a solo entrepreneur, or work for a company's marketing department, chances are that nobody can write exactly like you can when it comes to writing about your business. And if you're an agency or a consultant writing on behalf of a customer, it's essential for you to do deep and profound research up front before you even think about how to write like your customer.

The image in Figure 19.2 on page 178 is an ad that we're currently running as of this writing. I'll be using this customer a lot in some of the case senarios and will refer back to them on occasion. We call on this one not because their ads are so effective (they are), but

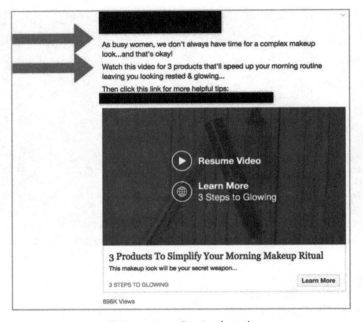

FIGURE 19.2–Be Authentic

rather because they are so genuine. They're in a mass market niche, which can potentially apply to so many types of businesses, perhaps even yours.

Authenticity is easy to tell people to do, but in actuality it's difficult to execute and still make sales. As I said in the previous section, it's best to not steal copy, but if you're short on time and need to get some ads going, copying what other people are doing is the quick fix.

Quick, yes. Effective, no. Ad copy takes time to get right as there are so many elements that go into a great ad. So, if you have little time to write good ad copy, sometimes it's best to just set it aside and do it when you do have time, because that's when the best copy comes. Being authentic should be your guidepost at all times, because the authentic and effective ads are better than just effective alone.

Case in point: we actually wrote this ad above in our customer's voice: "As busy women, we don't always have time for a complex makeup look—and that's OK!"

There's nothing in this ad that complies with our ad blocks per se but, because it's written in a personal, casual tone that simultaneously calls out its primary avatar. Even though the ad copy is short, this ad is an ideal one to demonstrate the power of "being authentic" as it uses imperfect English grammar with some unconventional language not typically seen in ad copy. Words like "morning makeup ritual" say what we all know we do every day, but they do it in a slightly different way that's authentic and unique.

What really makes this ad work is that the customer is actually in the video as the voice of the business, so the ad copy reflects that personal, "just us women," feel in the content of the video as well as the copy. What makes this ad copy work so well is the combination of actually calling out our avatar, calling out a pain point (fully compliant with Facebook Policy by the way) while at the same time expressing the customer's individuality in the ad copy, reinforced by the video itself. This is the exact formula that we use for nearly all our videos that we're going to talk about a little bit later.

The copy doesn't necessarily pose a question, but it does get the prospect thinking about a problem she may share and then simply instructs the reader on what to do next, which is namely, watch the video, then once you do that, click on the link for more helpful tips.

The good thing about Facebook ads is that you don't have to be a professional copywriter, but you do need to write your ad copy as genuine as possible and as clearly as possible. Simply put: write in your own voice, be authentic and always remember that Facebook is a social network. Your competition for attention in the newsfeed is squirrels waterskiing and pictures of grandkids, so in order to get your share of that attention, don't write ad copy that makes you come across like you look like an ad. Just be authentic.

Element 2: Simplify

Simplify. Simple to say, much harder to do, especially with Facebook ad copy. This is why it's so critical to (as much as humanly possible) use one word in the place of two or three in your copy.

Consider the average Facebook user for a moment. Chances are very good it's a perfect demographic cross-section of the country you're advertising in. For example, if your business is in the United States, according to the Literacy Project Foundation, 50 percent of adults cannot read a book written at an eighth-grade level. So, when you write your ad copy, keep things simple. No big twenty-five cent words, and don't even break it up into five nickel-sized words, just choose a single five-cent word instead.

Also, wherever possible, use words that have one syllable instead of those with two or three syllables. One of the big findings about the presidential election of 2016 was that Donald Trump spoke at a fifth-grade reading and communication level and that strategy (whether it was intentional or not) helped him win a historic Presidential race unlike any other race that this country has ever seen. Using big words only makes you think you look smarter, but trust me, it will hurt your conversions and your scale. And that might make you look pretty dumb for trying to look very smart.

There are a few key resources we recommend for simplifying your copywriting. Believe it or not, reading simple poetry will help you simplify your writing. Some of my personal favorites are anything written by Robert Frost or Mary Oliver. Many people, such as Tim Ferriss, recommend a classic book on simplification called *The Elements of Style* by William Strunk and E.B. White (Pearson, 1999). It's all about simplification and using short and very clear sentences. Stephen King's book, *On Writing* (Pocket Books, 2001) is also an excellent resource. The beginning of the book is more of a memoir, but he really talks about the style of writing about two-thirds in. If you read that portion of the book along with *The Elements of Style,* plus you read really good fiction and poetry classics, I guarantee you'll have a better understanding of how to simplify your own personal writing style.

As with all "rules" there will always be some cases where you can write a more flowery style, especially if your niche is highly technical and jargon is unavoidable. But in general, we've found simplifying to be the most effective way to communicate with a given audience.

In most cases, considerable simplification of your ad copy is the best way to go. A perfect example is Digital Marketer's ad in the image below. It doesn't get much simpler than this. There's only one line in this ad. I confirmed that they were still running this ad, and they were in fact still using it because it has been very effective in selling one-dollar access to their "DM Lab."

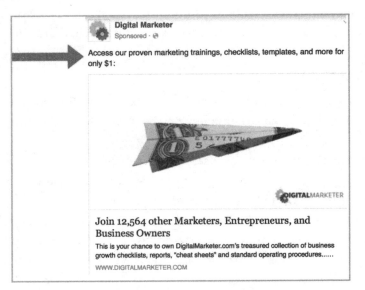

FIGURE 19.3–Simplify—$1 Digital Marketer Lab Access

The ad in Figure 19.3 includes a fair amount of social proof at the bottom as well, indicating that when you join, you'll be in good company with 12,564 other smart marketers like you. The headline is a bit more of an untraditional one for us, but because the offer is so good, not many words are needed. If your offer is a killer one like this one is, than more is less in your ad copy. In a word: simplify. It works.

Element 3: Write for Homer

Yes, if you are teaching writing in the United States it's now passé to say "write at a fifth grade reading level." I get it, I really do. But what the heck does that mean?

What that really means is that you should write for a Homer (Simpson) and not Hawking (the astrophysicist). This rule kind of goes back to our treatise on simplifying above, but if you really stop and think for a moment about your avatar and all the distractions you have to get him or her to set aside in order to click on your ad, you may see what I'm saying.

Picture your avatar, the yellow-skinned, cue-ball-eyed cartoon character with his three strands of hair furiously thumbing through his news feed, hungrily searching for content that is humorous, meaningful, or eye-catching. He really doesn't want to click on an ad—no way. He wants an escape from his humdrum life at the power plant and he ain't gonna pay attention to anything that looks like work.

The more you can write in clear and concise words and cut to the chase in your ad copy, the more likely that avatar is to "stop the thumb scroll" largely because it's easy to understand and to grasp with his fifth-grade reading level. If your ad copy is too long, with no breaks, cannot come up for air from drowning in its own punctuation (or lack thereof), then Homer (Simpson) is simply not going to stop his thumb on that ad. Hawking might, but unfortunately, there aren't many people at his intelligence level (IQ of 160) on Facebook these days. Homer will only interact with an ad with super simple ad copy that cuts to the chase, just like the ad in Figure 19.4.

When you read that ad copy, Homer immediately knows a few things as soon as he glances at it. He doesn't have to think much to know you get a military grade flashlight just like the image tells you. That's because all this ad is doing is simply telling them what you're going to get. He also knows that it's "valued at $14.95, for just a $0.01." A good deal, plain and simple. Of course, the offer in this ad is really good, nearly irresistible in fact, which doesn't hurt either.

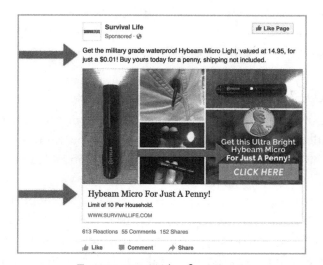

FIGURE 19.4–Write for Homer

The hook is to just show how cool the thing is (pure emotion) and then to simply offer it with a killer $0.01 deal. These two factors combined simultaneously hit the dual emotional and rational triggers that tell the prospect, "OK, OK, this is cool AND I can afford it!" This ad is comparable to a local business coupon as it's essentially a pure impulse buy that for the cost of a measly penny, all of which (provided it is actually true) doesn't require a whole lot of thought to rationalize. The result: Homer is in and it only took a few seconds to convince him.

Element 4: Show Proof

When you're targeting cold audiences and no one knows who you are, trying to establish a level of authority and credibility is a challenge. After all, who buys form someone they don't know and trust?

Well, the first thing to do to overcome this challenge is to show proof that what you're saying is true. This element is typically used in longer copy, which we used in the ad in Figure 19.5 on page 183, and to this day, it continues to do well at a 2:1 return on ad spend.

One of the primary reasons it does so well is because it inserts credibility statements throughout the ad copy, which are then all neatly tied into pain points. In this case, the pain point of our primary avatar is: "not knowing which four target groups you should use for your ads." By making a credibility statement (after spending $10 million on Facebook ads—instead it's closer to $100 million now—and then showing a screenshot in the video of the $10 million spent), the reader can't help but want to listen. Why? Because you know that the guy appearing in your newsfeed knows what he's talking about because he's spent a lot of money on this platform.

As you view this ad, you probably think something like, "If he's spending that kind of money then he's probably getting a return from it, so I should probably listen!" And you do. Then you buy because the incredible has become credible, giving you a good feeling about taking the next step. Figure 19.5 on page 183 shows an example.

Element 5: Ask Questions

One of the time-tested elements that we tend to use on nearly every one of our ads is inserting a question in the first line of our post copy. We then restate that question as a statement in the headline, so in essence we're hitting on the same theme but in two different ways in two different places.

In my opinion, the most important line of copy in a Facebook ad is your first line in your post copy because it's the first words your prospect sees in an ad that appears in their newsfeed. When you use a question to start your post copy, the headline should reinforce that question for consistency. And if you've crafted a good hook, then just

FIGURE 19.5–Long Ad Copy to Show Proof

simply ask a question that addresses that hook, then simply restate it as a benefit in your headline.

The ad in Figure 19.6 is a perfect example of asking a question and reinforcing that question in a different way in the headline. "Looking for an easy way to get more superfoods?" is the question, while "Get all your healthy superfoods in one drink" is the restatement/pitch to the next step. It's really a pretty simple ad that's targeting cold traffic, but we also use it for retargeting, image ads, and even a slideshow ad. The

FIGURE 19.6–Ask Questions

important thing to remember with this ad is that the question in the first line works well to grab attention and reinforce your hook, while the solution is then encased in the product itself.

Element 6: Answer Immediately

Working in concert with Element #5, when you ask a question in your ad copy, try to give the answer to that question immediately on the next line, or at the very least, tell them what to do next in order to discover the answer. The ad in Figure 19.7 is a good example of one where we ask a question and then we immediately say what to do next. Borrowing a technique from the sales world that "great salespeople lead sales discussions, mediocre salespeople follow them," the world of advertising in direct response is really no different.

People want to be led; it's far easier than doing the leading. And ultimately people want to be led to reach the logical solution for their problems. If you do in fact have the solution to their problems, then lead them to your solution in your ad copy.

To be an effective direct response copywriter, it's perfectly fine to tell people what to do inside your ad. This is very different from manipulation. If your product or service genuinely provides value, then **you owe it to your prospects to lead them to buying it.** If your initial question is compelling enough, they're going to want to do the next thing you tell them anyway.

FIGURE 19.7–Answer Immediately

In the case of this ad here, the next thing we want them to do is watch the video to get the solution to the question we ask in the first line. What's even better is when they watch the video, the video itself will show them exactly how to solve their problem. To get even more help, they can then click to the next page to take things to the next level.

Whenever you use video to sell an information-based product service or lead opt-in, always try to show people you can help them by actually helping them. You'll hear us say that a lot and although it's a really basic concept, it works as the greatest "selling tool" there is. What's even better is that typically those kinds of helpful videos are the ones that get shared the most—largely because they create some sort of "aha moment," inducing the viewer to discover something they never knew before, something that's both helpful and useful. Figure 19.7 is an example.

Element 7: Use Revealing Words

Revealing words have been a little bit overdone in recent years in online marketing, so I caution you on their usage in Facebook ads. Prior to starting the agency, I spent hundreds of thousands of dollars of my own money on advertising as an affiliate on display networks, PPC, and banner buys to sell all kinds of crazy products in the business, health, and consumer product niches. There are some shady companies out there that only want to separate you from the contents of your wallet. And the last thing in the world they care about is value. Yes, its true!

Suffice to say, words can indeed be powerful, so whatever you do, don't overstate or exaggerate. It will do nothing but repel more customers than it will attract them, so beware of creating ads that are more hyperbole than helpful.

One way to avoid this hyperbole issue is to simply try to keep adjectives in your ad copy to a minimum if at all possible. A good rule of thumb to use when you're writing your ad copy is to use more action verbs than adjectives in at least a 2:1 ratio. No, you don't have to count them all up and do the math, just eyeball your ad copy for too many adjectives, especially those that denote best, finest, and outstanding.

In that vein, some of the worst ads I've seen are the ones that are guilty of breaking the rules stated above. Such flagrantly offensive (and ineffectual) ad copy such as: "Best digital marketing training EVER. Click here to learn more!"

You just don't need to put a lot of adjectives in there to TELL people how awesome your stuff is. What you do need to do is SHOW people by using more action verbs and by showing them how great your product is in a video or in a longer copy ad that underscores your credibility or authority. Let's be clear: revealing words are not overblown or exaggerated; rather, they are simply words that imply new discovery or novelty, like we use in Figure 19.8 on page 186: "Discover the seven hidden iPhone camera features."

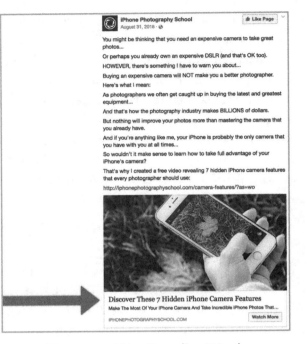

FIGURE 19.8–Use Revealing Words

In other ads for this customer, we use similar ad copy using revealing words, such as *astonishing*, like: "Shoot astonishing photos with your iPhone" and "Want to shoot astonishing photos with your iPhone?" *Astonishing* is kind of a 50-cent word, but for whatever reason, that word tends to work really well to explain a breakthrough solution—as it says that something is "new" in a whole new way. Keep in mind that if you do use ad copy like this in your ads—just make sure your product or solution is, in fact, "astonishing."

Element 8: "You" Rules

"You" is a very powerful word in advertising, but in Facebook advertising it has to be used correctly so you don't get on the wrong side of policy. Although we do use first person oftentimes with words such as "I" and "we" (especially in video scripts), second person usage of "you" is a very effective way to capture attention and immediately create possession and implied ownership.

As stated previously, when using "you" in your ad copy, you do have to be careful, especially if your product or service is in the health and fitness space. This is especially true when using "you" in relation to a personal attribute. Such lines as "Do you want to lose weight?" or "Do you have diabetes?" or "Do you want to have a thicker fuller beard?" all use "you" in tandem with a personal attribute. This, unfortunately, is a big Facebook Policy no-no.

The point is that you can use "you," but you just cannot use it with relation to a personal attribute, especially if you're in any of those niches where personal attributes play a large role in the advertising message.

The ad copy in Figure 19.9 is completely compliant, as well as highly effective because it's both genuine, conversational, and it uses the word "you" to capture attention. It says, "I'm telling you, superfoods are some of the highest vibing food you will ever come across!" The "you" in the next sentence is more direct (as well as implied) in calling out the avatar side-by-side with one of the many challenges they may face in daily life. This line: "If you're busy and worried about having to buy superfoods," immediately makes the connection with the avatar and their daily struggles. The ad makes use of the word "you" multiple times in the extended version of the ad as well.

A word of caution, however. Like the guy you meet at a cocktail party who purposely overuses your first name "to build rapport" throughout your initial small talk chinwag, if you overdo your use of "you" in your ad copy, you end up coming across as creepy and manipulative.

As long as you don't do that, definitely deploy them for the simple fact that people really don't care about you, the advertiser; they only really care about themselves. Unless you're using first person with relation to Element #4, err on the side of the second person as it's a highly effective way for people to identify with and then engage with your ads.

Using credibility statements like: "This is the result of running $14 million in Facebook ads since I started" or "When I was an airline pilot" are highly effective in

FIGURE 19.9–"You" Rules

establishing credibility but challenging to pull off without sounding well, arrogant. So in most cases default back to "you" because "you" works.

Element 9: "Non-Standard" Callouts

When you announce something novel, try framing it with non-standard callouts like brackets or parentheses. We tend to use this callout either at the beginning of a sentence or at the very start of a headline. In some rare cases, we may even use it in the middle of a sentence in the post copy or even in the headline. Since these punctuation marks look different and don't conform to the normal shape and form of the regular 26 letters, brackets and parentheses are great to use to accentuate a specific thing you want them to take action on. You can see an example of this in the retargeting ad in Figure 19.10.

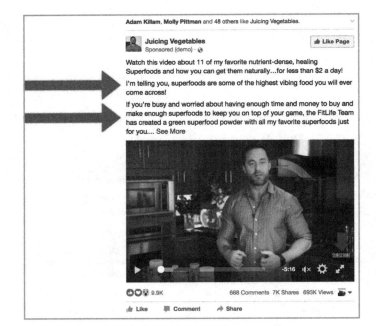

FIGURE 19.10–"Non-Standard" Callouts

The words framed in brackets, "[Special Discount]," allows us to remind the retargeting audience that after they've watched the webinar, we now want them to buy now using a special discount. In using brackets, we are highlighting the most important point we want to call out in the ad. In some of our other retargeting ads in this campaign, we have ads that say: "Don't miss your opportunity" in brackets as well.

Simply put, people's eyes are drawn to words framed in brackets because it's a non-standard punctuation mark in advertising and it's not something that we see routinely.

Element 10: Capitalize

Just like brackets, capitalizing words is another non-standard callout, which works well to highlight the most important point in your ad. You can capitalize the words (or words) that you want to emphasize but, as with any of the 14 elements, just don't overdo it.

Keep in mind that if you have all caps in too much of your ad copy, you'll probably get Facebook policy starting to notice because it looks scammy. Instead of DOING EVERY WORD IN YOUR ADS IN CAPs (so annoying), just use caps to highlight the ONE thing you want your audience to really remember.

In Figure 19.11, the "free training" that SamCart is offering is the most important part of the ad. It's reiterated in the post copy but it's especially highlighted in the headline just below the ad image, which serves to make the ad more effective and eye-catching.

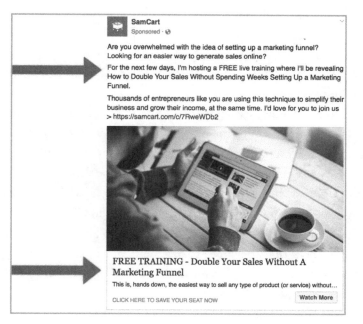

FIGURE 19.11–Capitalize

Like Homer, remember that the audiences you are targeting in your ads are "thumbing through" their newsfeed looking for something that catches their attention. Keeping this in mind, it's important to immediately get to the point of what you're trying to say. In the example image above, Samcart could have added brackets to the "free training" part of their ad if they'd wanted to, but in that particular case, capitalization works well as it does a good job highlighting the most important chunk of the ad.

Element 11: Embrace the Ellipsis

This is probably my favorite element to use in ad copy . . . ☺

Think of it this way. At a basic Advertising 101 level of understanding, the purpose of each line in your ad copy is to lead them to the next step. So, the first line in your ad copy's purpose is to get the reader to read the second line, the second line's purpose is to get them to read the third line and so on.

The ellipsis' job is to lead the reader from one thought to the next, creating a broken thought that needs resolution on the next line. Oftentimes, we use it in concert with the natural break in the Facebook ad in the post copy, but this is more challenging to do regularly.

We love the ellipsis so much that undoubtedly, you'll see the ellipsis in just about all of our ads, so much so that whenever I quality check ad copy in the agency, typically the only thing I'll edit in the ad copy written by our copywriters and account managers is the insertion of an ellipsis or multiple ellipses.

We use the ellipsis all over our ad copy in different places as demonstrated in the ad in Figure 19.12 on page 191. This ad is more of a "future pacing" kind of ad copy where we're trying to get people to imagine where they'd be in the future after they bought the book we are selling them.

At the end of the "imagine" sentence, the ellipsis acts to continue the thought. By using the ellipsis, it subtly takes them to the next logical step. The "If you have no idea how to take your life to the next level. YOU ARE NOT ALONE!" shocks them back to reality before the clear call to action tells them what to do to actualize the thought continued in the first line of copy, stating "Just click here to get your FREE copy . . . while they last."

Like in Figure 19.12 on page 191, you can also use an ellipsis between your call to action as a subtle reminder that they need to act quickly. The ellipsis in this ad does just that by reminding them that they need to get their copy of the book now, but the time scarcity is separated by an ellipsis to remind the reader that they should buy now before the 10,000 copies run out. In this ad, we want to make certain that people don't miss out and the ellipsis almost calls out that scarcity in a subtle way. That's why we typically use it when we not only want to highlight a continuation of a thought but when we also want to underscore the importance of the next line.

Element 12: Mix It Up

When writing Facebook ads, it's good to test all kinds of different copy types. We often split test a number of different ad copy lengths, be it ultra-short, short, long, or long-ass copy to see which works best. The ad in the image below is a good example of one that's a video ad with long ad copy.

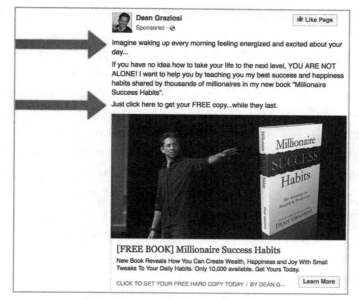

FIGURE 19.12–Embrace the Ellipsis

Ultra-short ad copy may only have one or maybe two lines of copy, whereas short copy will have upwards of three to five, long copy is five-plus, and long-ass copy is just plain long . . . upward of a thousand words, if not more. Figure 19.13 is more along the lines of "long copy" with lots of individual link callouts and emojis.

We added more live links in the ad copy than we typically do, but based on the offer, it just seemed to make sense. As a rule, we'll typically test three or four versions of the ad

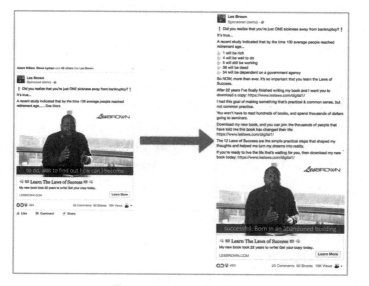

FIGURE 19.13–Mix It Up

copy (depending on what the ask is) and this one was the winner by far with all the copy taken directly from the video in the ad.

In this case, long copy works because the next step is a fairly big ask for cold traffic, so we felt that we needed a little bit more persuasion. We do use short copy with many of our video ads, so it's good to mix it up and test all four types if your budget permits.

If you have a really solid video that convincingly sells your audience to take the next step, then you may find that a tremendous amount of ad copy just isn't needed. In that case, you could use shorter copy since the video does "all the selling for you."

However, if you're using an image ad to sell a core product offering or an appointment for a consult call, then you'll want to test longer ad copy. In most cases, using short copy with an image ad may not do the job to convince them to take the next step.

Element 13: Employ Emojis

The usage of emojis are a recent discovery of ours, but man, do they work well. As of this writing, emojis are still somewhat of a novelty, which may be one of the reasons why they work so well when deployed, but more importantly, they instantly insert familiarity and appear non-threatening. They are also great to reinforce the messages you are relaying in your ad copy. To use emojis, simply insert them where appropriate to punctuate the benefits and main message, but don't over do it. You'll see that some of our ads have emojis and some of them simply don't, but most of our recent ads have them, largely because we split tested it and found that ad copy that has emojis, have higher click through rates, higher Relevance Scores, lower cost per click, and most importantly, lower cost per acquisition.

The ad in Figure 19.14 on page 193 is a really good one because it uses just enough emojis that are actually in relation to the message being portrayed. First, there's a clear call out to the avatar using horns, speakers, and stars around it, not so subtly reinforcing the message of the copy. Then there's a dollar bag and clapping hands, which is obviously related to that line, helping to tie the whole ad together.

Also notice at the bottom of the ad in Figure 19.14 they use the word "I" to help tell his story, saying, "I used this map to make $672,000 in sales in one weekend." In most cases, this kind of copy will get disapproved but since it's written in the first person, it works. Plus, it's a really good way to use a credibility statement as well.

BRING IT ALL TOGETHER

Suffice to say, you don't have to use all 13 elements in your ads, but if you can do it, while also making the ad appear natural and real, do it. If you can't use all 13, then just

FIGURE 19.14–Employ Emojis

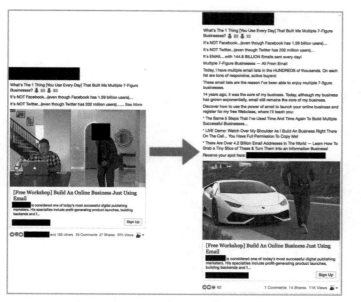

FIGURE 19.15–Bring It All Together

adding a few elements in to lightly season your ads may make the difference between a winner and a loser.

The ad in Figure 19.15 is an example of an ad where all 13 elements are used in the ad copy. It's a funny educational video ad that did well on its own as an organic post on the customer's page, but when we redid the ad copy using the elements contained here in this chapter, it quickly became the most consistently highest performing ads in a series of conversion campaigns. We did a number of variations of this same ad—some using short and long copy, but this one here was the clear winner. Was that because it just so happens to have all of the 13 elements contained in it? Could be. But the caveat is that a great video will do well regardless of the ad copy as ad copy really does play a supporting role to a great video ad. Having said that, employing many of the 13 elements we discuss here in this chapter can turn a good ad into a great ad, which this one clearly was.

Chapter 20

How I Know When My Copy Is Ready—Power Questions

Guest Author Ryan Deiss

This chapter is really a summary of episode 84 of our podcast, *Perpetual Traffic*. The podcast is hosted by DigitalMarketer at www.DigitalMarketer.com—and on episode 84, Ryan Deiss, the founder of Digital Marketer, came on the show to reveal the seven things he thinks about before writing any piece of ad copy.

> "*A* well-framed question will burn a hole in peoples' brains for months . . . even years."
>
> —PERRY MARSHALL

The theme that keeps coming up again and again is the idea of how to keep the focused attention of your prospect. As marketers, so often when we're writing copy and marketing pieces, we just start with the assumption that people are going to see what we're creating and just automatically consume it.

"He's going to read this," or, "Of course they're going to watch this video."

Nothing in life is as important as you think it is as it is while you're thinking about it yourself. As humans, we are taught to believe that what is in front of us, that which is focal, that which is salient, that which is top of mind, is really important.

Even if it isn't.

It's one of the reasons there is so much focus on retargeting ads in Facebook. When you run retargeting ads and people keep seeing those same ads over and over and over again—even if the ad is only being shown to them and a small group of people—they're thinking, "Wow, this brand is a really big deal. It's really important."

How do we do this as marketers? How do we draw focused attention from our prospects? In my research about this, I came up with a list of seven questions that I ask myself before I finish any piece of ad copy. The most ideal situation would be to have a good answer to all seven questions, but if at least one or two of them are effectively answered, the end result will be a much more powerful piece of marketing, a much more powerful piece of copy, and a much more powerful ad.

Why? Because it's actually going to get viewed. And that's the biggest thing of all.

How do we make sure that our brand and our message become focal? How is this done so that the brand and message become so obvious they begin to permeate the prospect's mind? In researching this for myself, I created these seven questions that I ask myself before releasing any type of ad copy to ensure that the brand and message have a prospect's focused attention. Here they are:

1. NOVEL, UNIQUE, AND DISTINCTIVE

The first focusing question when writing ad copy is, "How do we make our offer appear novel, unique, and distinctive?" This is really, really easy if the offer happens to be novel, unique, distinctive, or brand new—something that the market has never seen before. It's more challenging if it is a commodity or something that has been on the market for a while.

One of the best open rates for an email subject line is something like: "Major announcement." In using a subject line like "Major announcement," people are going to open it even if they don't really care what the announcement is. Cable news has figured this out, "Breaking News . . ." At the bottom or top of the screen are the words "Breaking news."

Everyone wants to know what's new, what's novel, what's unique. Looking at human biology and why humans react this way, it is because "the new" is something that might try to kill us. Humans are taught to pay attention to something new for their own survival. If it's unfamiliar, it's going to capture our gaze. It's going to draw that focused attention. And that's the same type of attention that marketers seek to attract.

If your offer is something new, that's great. But if your offer is not new— if it is something people are used to seeing—here are some questions to ask in order to attract the prospect's focused attention:

1. What's a way to make the offer feel new and noteworthy?
2. What's a way to make the offer new?
3. What's a different angle?

4. Are there any current news stories that can be used to help attract attention to the offer?

2. SIMPLE AND EASY

Question number two: how can you make your offer simple and easy to understand?

This is **SO** important, and it's something easily overlooked. The challenge is that what seems simple to us is not simple to our customers. What seems like such an obvious and compelling idea to us isn't that obvious to them.

The challenge is to make it simple and easy to understand. This is critical because when people grasp something quickly and effortlessly, they not only like it more but they tend to ascribe more validity and worth to it. In other words, when people grasp the idea, when they understand it, they don't just like it, they believe that it's worthier. That's how arrogant human beings are.

It's like this: "Well, if I understand it, then it must be true." And it's the reason why things like rhythm and rhyme can make messages more consumable. Going back to the OJ Simpson trial, "If the glove doesn't fit, you must acquit!" People could get that concept and easily understand it. That's why it was so effective.

Making ideas simple and easy is really hard to do because sometimes, it means pulling back on claims in your ad. It means not explaining every little nuance and detail of the product. For some people, this is really, really hard to do, especially if the offer is for your own business. Most potential customers just don't care about the details.

You must be wondering, "How can I make my offer seem simple and easy to understand?" Think back to every major hit song—go back and listen to them. Google the top 100 most popular songs of all time, and then listen to the chorus. They're made up of single-syllable words. As humans, we don't just like things that are simple, we ascribe more worth and validity to them. As a bare minimum, try to be simple when writing ad copy.

3. TRIGGERING A DESIRE

In the ad copy, what will trigger a desire for consistency that will drive a sale or action? As you can see, this question is a little bit complicated and requires some explaining. Robert Cialdini talked about this concept in his book, *Pre-Suasion: A Revolutionary Way to Influence and Persuade* (Simon & Schuster, 2016). He illustrated this with an example about a survey company—a company that big brands pay to send people out to the street with clipboards and say, "Hey, would you mind taking a survey?" Most people when approached by these survey people usually say something like, "No, I really don't want to," or "No thanks." Either way, it's a little bit awkward for both the person asking the question and the person saying no.

To overcome this awkwardness, they changed the question to, "Pardon me—do you consider yourself to be a helpful person?" It was a question that when was asked, people had a hard time saying no to. When asked, they were likely thinking, "Yes, I am a helpful person."

Once people answered that question, the surveyor could say something like, "Great! If so, I can really use your help. I'm trying to get answers to this survey, and it would really mean a lot to me if you could help out." When the survey company made this change, their survey completion percentage went up 70 percent.

This type of questioning triggers this need for commitment and consistency. "Yes, I'm a helpful person, and because I'm helpful, I'm going to remain consistent to that, and I'm going to help you with your survey." Here's an example from a recent promotion for a workshop that used this same technique. The start of the sales letter read:

"Let me ask you a question. Is your product or service good? Does it work? If you put it in their hands, if you put it in front of the right person, will they get a good response? If you answered yes to that question, then I want to show you how to sell a whole lot more of it."

The triggering of desire for consistency by using the question, "Is your product or service good?" means that everyone who reads this question should be like, "Yeah, it's good." Then the subsequent line in the copy of, "I want to show you how to sell a whole lot more of it" is the push toward driving the sale.

Questions are compelling. Questions in and of themselves will draw some attention. For instance, by asking a general question it engages the mind. But it doesn't engage heart. And it doesn't engage identity. When asking someone, "Are you brave? Are you helpful? Is what you're doing good?" the person is saying something about themself. Whatever it is they're saying about themselves, if that informs the next action that you would like for them to take, then all the better.

For some of you, this may seem manipulative. And you're right; it can be taken too far. For instance, the surveyor in the example above walks up to folks and says, "Do you consider yourself to be a helpful person?" For me, I wouldn't want to do that. There are better ways to get the same outcome. That example is an instructive example, but to say to somebody, "Hey, is what you're doing good? Yes or no?" If they're sitting there really questioning themselves and ultimately answer, "I don't know," then they are someone that I won't be able to help.

By asking someone, "Do you consider yourself to be brave?"

And they answer "Yeah, I do." Then you can move them toward the desired action like this, "Cool. Then are you brave enough to end one of the biggest schisms that has been in business between sales and marketing?" "Yeah, I think I am." Prior to that, they weren't really considering it as much, but by engaging not just their mind but their heart and their identity, now they want to take action. Now they want to do something to show that they really, really mean it.

4. PRE-EXPOSURE

Question four is, "How can marketers pre-expose their audience to a concept linked to the desired emotional stimulus?" When thinking about how to pre-expose the audience to a concept linked to a desired emotional stimulus, the first thing is to uncover the desired emotional stimulus. In other words, how do we want our audience to feel so that they will want to make a purchase? What does their emotional state need to be if they're going to make that final purchase decision?

Here's an example that Robert Cialdini gave in his book, *Pre-Suasion*. Cialdini wrote about this experiment that was run basically by taking advantage of machismo middle-aged men. What the experimenter would do is have a young, attractive girl walk up to a middle-aged guy on the street and say, "Hey, these ruffians over here (pointing to a group of guys) just took my cellphone. Will you help me get it back from them?"

In most cases, the guy listened to the girl, then looked at the group of guys and went, "Yeah, no. You seem cute, you seem nice, but those guys will kill me. Sorry you lost your phone. You might want to call the cops."

That was the "control" scenario in the experiment. They then wanted to test to see how they could change the outcome. In other words, how could they increase the odds that these guys will say yes and actually help out; meaning that they'll go against their natural tendencies? So in the next scenario, the experimenters had a woman approach the guy and say, "Excuse me, can I get directions to Valentine Street?" Now Valentine Street was simply a street in the area. She didn't say anything about Valentine's Day or anything like that. She just said, "Can I get directions to Valentine Street?"

The mention of Valentine was intentional. Valentine was an exposed concept. It exposed the concept that exists in western culture, the idea of Valentine's Day representing romance, representing sex, representing "man help woman, man get sex from woman," that kind of thing. Simply put, very carnal things.

Immediately afterward, a second woman approached them and asked the question in the control scenario: "Hey, can you help me get my phone back from these ruffians?" Instantly, the number of guys that were willing to throw themselves into harm's way on behalf of a strange woman who walked up to them and asked for help went up dramatically.

Was it maybe that just two women approached them? Testing again, the first woman went up and said, "Hey, can you give me directions to Main Street?" which was a concept unlinked to Valentine's Day. When the second woman walked up asking for help to get her phone back, the result was similar to the control group—very few men offered to assist to get the woman's phone back. The mere mention of Valentine Street pre-exposed those men to a concept linked to the desire to emotional stimulus, which in this case was romance. This is why in every single perfume ad, they're basically selling sex because that's why people buy perfume and cologne. That's the desire to emotional stimulus.

Figure 20.1 is the same concept in a Facebook Ad by Digital Marketer. The ad was for an early bird sale that was about end. The ad image was of the low battery warning on the iPhone. If you've ever pulled your phone out of your pocket, and it's at 10 percent battery life, the image is just a little sliver of red. If you own an iPhone, you've seen that low battery warning icon, and the emotion that you feel in that is this sense of urgency like, "OMG. I've got to plug it in."

What does your phone running out of juice have to do with the fact that this event is nearly sold out? They have nothing to do with one another, just like Valentine Street has nothing to do with protecting a woman. The low battery image exposes people to the idea, to the emotional stimulus, which in this case is nervous energy, urgency, and

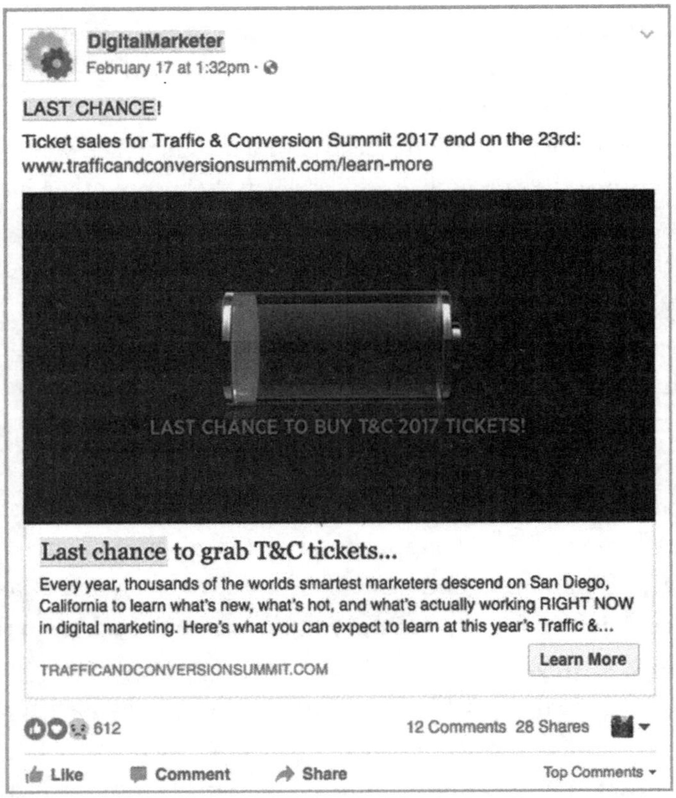

FIGURE 20.1–Pre-Exposing the Audience to a Concept by Using a Well-Known Metaphor in the Image

the need to act now. In using this commonly known image, it exposes the desire to emotional stimulus, which causes the action to take place.

5. MENTAL LINKS AND ASSOCIATIONS

The fifth question is along the same lines as question four. With number four, the focus was on how to pre-expose the audience to the desire to emotional stimulus. With number five, the focus is on identifying mental links and associations. In other words, what kind of nostalgia can be tapped into and positively associated to the offer? In question five, it's not just tapping into emotions but into memories. It's a much deeper feeling. If you've ever listened to a song that almost made you cry, it wasn't because of the sadness of the song. It was because the song brought you back to a moment in your life when you were feeling sad. That's what nostalgia is all about.

The reason that happens is because we as human beings create thought through associations. That is how thought occurs. It is by associating one thing with another thing. It's, "I know to fear this because it kind of reminds me of this other thing that hurt me at one point in time, so I'm going to fear it, too." This idea of association is big. How can you associate your product, your service, with a known common experience? That's really what is being asked in question number five. What mental links and associations can be tapped into and positively associated to the offer?

Great ads do this all the time. They tap into the memories and the feelings of an entire group of people and then associate a product to that. That's basically the way that Coke has been selling brown sugar water for decades. They've been associating this product to people's lives, whether it's family or friends or good times. Even if you never had that exact experience, it brings you back. To accomplish associating a product with a memory, it's necessary to know the positive associations the audience has experienced and finding a way to take them back there.

A good way to do this is through metaphors. When creating a metaphor, it is associating one thing to another thing that appears to be irrelevant. One way to do this is through imagery. An image, even if it's just there subtly in the background, can harken back to a memory, to something that happens every day, or to somewhere memorable. By mentally associating a product with this positive experience, either a past experience or desired future experience, this is the idea in question five.

Again, what mental links and associations need to be tapped into and positively associated to the offer? Ones that are just beyond emotion. Emotion is so powerful. In associating the offer to a real lasting memory or to a deep-seated future desire, this is where the power lies. With positive mental associations, whether the person experiences it, whether they know someone who experienced it, or if they could imagine themselves experiencing it, it's those same positive feelings that are transferred to the product and it becomes instantly understood, like what was discussed in question number two. The concept is grasped more easily. And, therefore, it's trusted more rapidly.

6. OPEN LOOPS

How can open loops be used to hold attention and leverage through the close? How can the idea of an open loop or a cliffhanger be introduced? Introducing mystery is another way to capture attention. What's a compelling mystery that can be leveraged at the beginning of a message to hold the audience's attention? This is something that has been used extensively on TV. Soap operas are famous for this. Right before the big thing happens, it fades to black to a commercial or that episode ends.

This idea that humans need closure was developed by a psychologist named Zeigarnik. She actually was eating lunch with a group of other colleagues one day, and they noticed that there was this waiter that had this almost uncanny ability to remember everyone's order. We've all been to restaurants where everybody at the table is throwing different combinations of their order to the waiter, they're not writing anything down, and yet they manage to remember it all. Well, the story goes that they had this waiter, and they were wondering what it was about this person that allowed them to memorize everybody's order? They were going to ask the waiter about it. But what they realized a short time later was that the waiter didn't actually remember their order anymore. Once the waiter delivered their meal, and came back around, they asked him, "Hey, by the way, how did you remember that I wanted this and this and this without writing it down?" The waiter was like, "Honestly, I don't remember even what you ordered."

What Zeigarnik realized is before you have closure, the brain keeps it open. The brain is hyperactive, and it can hold attention on a subject, even a fairly complex one, really well. The waiter was able to keep in his mind this multiple-person, complex order but the second that the plate hit the table, Boom!, cognitive closure. Job done. Erase. Clear. No more keeping that info in random access memory. Clear it. Let's move onto the next thing.

In leveraging a story in marketing, don't tell the story and then go into the sales or marketing message. Tell the story and then weave in the message. If you close the story too early, the audience is done. Brain off. They're no longer paying attention. Cognitive closure to the story needs to occur at the point of sale or when the sale close happens.

7. PORTALS

This is the last and possibly the creepiest technique of all. How do you create a visual or mental portal for the prospect to pass through that will make them more open to new opportunities? This may seem a little bit weird, but the reality is you probably have experienced it yourself. You're sitting on the couch, and you get up because you need to go into another room to get something. You get up, and you walk into the new room, and when you get there you're like, "Why the heck did I come here? What was I looking for? I don't remember."

There is something fascinating in how our brains work when moving from one room to another, passing through a door. It really does change the way that we think. It is an attention reset. This has been proven and studied in dogs. Robert Cialdini, in *Pre-Suasion*, talked about the infamous Pavlov's dog experiment where Pavlov was able to associate a ringing bell to get dogs to salivate. What most people don't realize, however, is that there was another conclusion to this experiment.

Anytime Pavlov would take his dogs into a different room to show another researcher, "Look at this thing that I figured out. I've trained these dogs because I would ring a bell and then feed them meat. Now anytime I just ring a bell, look, they salivate because they've associated bell ringing with meat eating." Pavlov would take the dogs into a new room to show this behavior to one of his colleagues, but the dogs wouldn't salivate at the ringing bell. The ringing bell no longer had the same effect. What Pavlov realized is that when the environment changes, there is a mental reset.

This is very useful to know as marketers who are trying to get people to take action. Sales people realize this. People who are actively dating and pickup artists realize this and use it for super uncool ways, but this is something that folks have realized for a long, long, long time. By getting someone to move from one place to another, they're more likely to make a decision. And this is the notion of portals—this idea of passing from one place to another. You've probably seen this if you've watched a product launch or something like that. You've seen the marketer driving in his car, and there you are in the car, and he's explaining some stuff. You're riding with him. You're passing from one place to another visually. The image of riding in a car while you're talking to your prospects is a type of portal.

Dating experts teach that a good way to increase intimacy with a member of the opposite sex is just to move from one point to another throughout a particular bar or club. They'll say, "Let's go over here. I want to introduce my friend. Now let's walk over here to the bar. Let's go outside and get some fresh air for a little bit. Now let's go on the dance floor and dance." Moving around, even within the same four walls, increases intimacy because you're passing through portals together.

The best film and video directors in the world get this. They get the idea of portals. One of the most obvious examples of this came from the movie, *Wizard of Oz*. When Dorothy is transported from Kansas to Oz in the tornado, her house lands, and she goes to the door. Now you're seeing the world through her eyes, it's worth going back and watching, as the door swings open, and instantly everything changes from black and white to color as she passes from Kansas, the real world, into Oz. That passage through the doorway is a portal.

Portals can also be created with sound, too. For instance, changing the background music just slightly as a transition occurs. For example, in the *Wizard of Oz* example, there's no background music as Dorothy is walking through her house, but as soon as she opens the door, music begins. That's a visual-auditory portal.

To help illustrate this further, here's an example you could use for a local plumbing business. The video starts outside of the building. The plumber says, "Hi, I'm Fred, the plumber. We're really excited. We're doing some great stuff, but come inside. I want you to meet some people." Now the camera follows Fred, the plumber, as he opens the door and goes into the store. That's a portal.

We as human beings tend to make decisions after we have moved from one place to another. We are trained to do that.

The ceremony of walking down the aisle when getting married is a portal. The portal is of friends and family. The bride starts at the back of the crowd behind everyone and walks through this narrow portal. When the couple leaves, they exit back through that same portal. The bride and groom arrive separately, but they leave as husband and wife.

All these little subtleties denote that, "Hey, something has changed. What was before is not the same anymore. That it's OK to act and to pursue a new path." In not giving a visual or auditory portal the audience is less likely to make a change. Just think about it. A visual portal could be really, really subtle like a background color change. Whether subtle or more obvious, there needs to be some type of mental cue that, "Hey, we're passing into something new together. It's time to make a change."

THE SEVEN QUESTIONS SUMMARY

1. *How do I make the offer appear novel, unique, and distinctive?* Basically how do you make the offer appear new? That's the first thing. Remember, the goal is focused attention. It doesn't matter how great the product is. It doesn't matter how compelling the message is. If people don't focus on it, if they don't hear it, if they don't pay attention to it, it's not going to convert them.

2. *How do I make the offer simple and easy to understand.* Humans love simple. We love easy to understand. If we understand it quickly and effortlessly, we like it more, and we ascribe it more validity. How can things like rhythm and rhyme be leveraged? Children learn the alphabet by simple and easy songs. It's a simplifying mechanism, and people like it because of that.

3. *What's an opening question that, when answered, will trigger a desire for consistency and drive a sale or action?* What's an opening question that, when answered, will make the prospect say, "Yeah, this is who I am and this is how I'm going to answer." It's questions like, "Do you consider yourself a helpful person? Do you consider yourself to be brave? Is your product or service good?" Good opening questions draw attention, but the questions that when answered drive consistent action and, specifically, consistent action that's consistent with the desired action, that's even better.

4. *How do I pre-expose the audience to a concept linked to a desired emotional stimulus.* In other words, how to pre-expose the audience to make them feel a certain way? How can a link be established to a product or service and then to the desired emotion? This is best illustrated by the ad that had the iPhone battery almost dead to denote that tickets were about to be sold out. The emotional stimulus there was urgency. The battery image denotes urgency even though it's unrelated to the early bird sale. How about the, "Can you tell me how to get to Valentine Street?" example. Remember that example? The mention of Valentine made middle-aged men feel more romantic, which made them willing to throw themselves into harm's way for a woman they did not know.

5. *What mental links and associations can be tapped into and positively associated to the offer?* Question four looked at emotional links. With question five, the focus is mental links. It's all about memory. It's all about identity. Mental associations like the metaphors, memories, common shared experiences, and nostalgia that become associated with a product in a positive way—that's the focus of question number five.

6. *How can open loops be created to hold attention and leverage the close to create that cognitive closure that the customer's brain so desperately desires?* Here it's about things like mystery. It's about a story, but a story where the ending isn't offered until the message about the product or service is complete. To capture and hold attention, that's how to truly leverage a story. Don't just tell a story. Tell a story; talk about the product, close the story, and then the close of the story draws them to the action.

7. *How do I create a visual or mental portal for the prospect to pass through that, when they do, makes them open to new opportunities.* Is it a visual thing, such as walking with the prospect? Are they passing through a door? Is it a change in background, tone, and music? What is the signal that will make people say, "Now it's time to make a change."

By using these seven questions before you finish writing a piece of copy and before you finish crafting an ad, you're going to have much more powerful messaging. You're going to find hooks that you had previously missed or ignored or not capitalized on. If your product or service is good, then you're going to make a lot more people happy. If you can get one or two of these questions answered, you're going to be doing a heck of a lot better than your competitors.

Chapter 21

Creating Killer Ad Creatives That Reflect Your Hook

Guest Author Molly Pittman

Creativity isn't something you can teach step by step. However, by walking through how we do this at Digital Marketer and sharing a lot of examples, good and bad, you can learn the thought process and get helpful tips to use while you are developing your own creatives.

The creative, other than targeting, is probably one the most overlooked aspects of the campaign. People outsource a lot of their images or videos, which is fine. Companies like Design Pickle do a good job, and you can get unlimited designs from them. Tools like that can be a little expensive, but it's nice if you don't have a designer on your team. That being said, probably the best thing that ever happened to our ads was hiring a designer that just creates our ads. Even if you're managing multiple brands, having one person that you can communicate with and that understands how advertising works is super important. Keep in mind that you can't rely on the designer, whether it's an outsource or someone on your team, to come up with good ads. That may sound counterintuitive, but it's true. Designers are not marketers; instead, they

> "*A creative life is an amplified life. It's a bigger life, a happier life, an expanded life, and a hell of a lot more interesting life. Living in this manner—continually and stubbornly bringing forth the jewels that are hidden within you—is a fine art, in and of itself.*"
>
> —ELIZABETH GILBERT, *BIG MAGIC: CREATIVE LIVING BEYOND FEAR*

like to create pretty pictures. However, that doesn't always mean that the pretty picture is going to be a high-converting ad creative. The designer is there to produce the image or the video, but they need a lot of instruction. This isn't because they're bad at designing, they just don't understand marketing. Realizing your role in this whole system is very important. A lot of thought goes into the creatives that we produce at Digital Marketer and our different sister properties.

A great book I read about this process that I highly recommend is called *Big Magic: Creative Magic Beyond Fear* by Elizabeth Gilbert (Riverhead Books, 2015). It taught me a lot about how to think about being creative, because whether you know it or not, you actually are creative. You just

FIGURE 21.1–*Big Magic*

need to understand how creativity comes to you. It has helped me understand how our designer thinks, how I should be thinking, and how ideas come to play.

SIX IMPORTANT ASPECTS YOUR CREATIVE SHOULD HAVE

An important thing to remember is that the creative doesn't necessarily need to be all about the offer. Make sure that your creative reflects the marketing message or hook, the message you're using to sell or to get someone to take action on, that's in your copy. A lot of people mess up on this aspect of the creative by setting up an ad campaign and telling their designer that they need an image of the product or something that just looks good. While using an image of the product may work in some cases, that's not always what's needed for a high-converting campaign. You want to start getting into the mindset that the image and video creatives are just the visual elements that should be supporting the rest of your campaign as a whole.

There is a lot of thought that goes into this process, and there are six important things to think about whenever you are working on your creatives. All of them don't have to exist in every creative, but number one definitely does.

1. Your Creative Should Be Reflective of Your Hook

Your hook is not your offer. Whatever you're trying to get your customer to do whether it's download a lead magnet or buy a product, that is the offer. The hook is the way you sell and market your offer. One offer could have ten hooks if you're testing ten different marketing messages to get someone to take action. Your creative should always convey the marketing message or the hook.

If your image isn't doing that, you're just using your image to catch eyeballs. Using a puppy or a pretty woman might get a bunch of clicks, but they will likely be from people who do not care about what's on the other side. Five to seven years ago, that might have worked because it was the Wild Wild West of the internet, but now it's not. Do not use an image simply to try to draw attention or clicks. It's just not going to work because the ad scent will be terrible once they get to your page or wherever you're sending traffic.

2. Tell a Story

In your ad, try to tell a story about how your offer can change or affect their life. Carousel ads are a great way to tell a story using your creatives.

3. Display the Product

If you are selling physical products or something you can literally demonstrate it is acceptable to show the product. Those are the easiest images to create because, for example, if you sell makeup brushes, you can demonstrate what your makeup brush does. This won't work for all business types, however, if you can show your product and it's further down the funnel, a simple demonstration or image of the product can work.

4. Stand Out in the Newsfeed

Although you don't want to use creatives that stand out for the sole purpose of standing out, there are some ways to stand out in the newsfeed. Our designer uses contrasting colors, so whenever she's creating an ad she makes sure that whatever colors she uses contrasts one another because that catches people's attention. Little video ads or gifs can also be used to catch people's attention because they move. If you convey the marketing message while making it a little bit flashy, but still on brand for whatever company you're running ads for, that's great. If you're running an image in the newsfeed, and it doesn't stand out you're probably going to have trouble because it's going to blend in with everything else.

5. Be on Brand

A lot of big companies are talking about this now, but what does that really mean? We have a really simple style guide at Digital Marketer with the fonts and different colors we use. We don't always stay on our brand colors and images, but when you're working with a client or for your company, make sure that you know what being on brand means. The more campaigns that you run, the more people are going to start recognizing your brand, so if you can make sure your images have something that really stands out and it's something that's across all of the images, that's really helpful. You'll notice that we use a flat cartoon style at Digital Marketer. The ads and colors may be a little bit different, but when you see the ad, you know "that's Digital Marketer." I have brand recognition there. Make sure you establish that because if you start running completely different ads across different campaigns that look different that's not good for brand lift. People aren't going to recognize your brand and as much as that's sort of a vanity metric it is important.

6. Play Off of Emotions Already Associated with an Image

This is something we've really found to work over the past year, and it's done by figuring out what associations people already have in common that we can play off of. What icons or images do people already have a relationship with?

For example in Figure 21.2, we ran an ad with an iPhone battery that was low. If you have an iPhone, which most people do, you have an emotion associated to that battery being low. You know that you need to plug it in. If you can use these different icons or images that we're all familiar with and use every day, it's really helpful because people already have an emotion associated with that. For example, if you want to portray scarcity,

FIGURE 21.2–iPhone Battery Ad

find something that has already done that in our culture like a low iPhone battery or a low bank account. You have found something that already creates scarcity in people's lives and are using that to convey your own hook.

WHAT NOT TO DO

We have a room in Slack where we're putting ads that we do and do not like every day to educate our designers. These two ads are examples where the creative failed.

FIGURE 21.3–Cat Hook for MLM: Fail

Figure 21.3 with the cat is pretty obvious. A lot of people will set up a great campaign, but then get lazy on the creative and just pull a stock image. This is the biggest part of your ad, and definitely not where you want to be getting lazy.

The reason why this one failed is because the cat has nothing to do with their hook or offer. What they are going for is playing off of something warm and cuddly that people love, but that cat has nothing to do with network marketing even if it's sitting in front of the keyboard. This mistake is costly and will end up being terrible for your brand because you will get a lot of unqualified clicks.

The next ad example (Figure 21.4 on page 212) that failed is equally as terrible but for different reasons. There's really no hook in their ad. They say "here's how we help our clients generate a strong ROI with Facebook Ads, SEO, and more," which is fine, but why do people care? Then you look at the image, and it doesn't coincide with the ad copy at all. It's a very bland image. The "digital marketing that actually

FIGURE 21.4–No Hook

works" and their logo is fine, but the graph has no meaning. This ad will blend into the newsfeed, and it simply has no meaning. This is an example that shows even if you or your designer are creating your images, it can still be as bad as pulling a stock photo of a cat if you're not going through the thought process of how you can convey your marketing message in the image.

GRADES AND REPORT CARDS

In Figure 21.5 on page 213, we had a lead magnet for social media managers you can use to audit your social media profiles. There were a lot of different hooks and avatars at play with this one because the social media manager could use it, the supervisor of the social media manager could audit the social media manager, or an agency could use it. The offer was a lead magnet for a social media audit, but one hook we came up with was "get a grade." Everyone has an association with grades in some form from school. This is a good example of a hook because we didn't literally say, "this is a social media audit; go do it." Instead, we said, "this is a social media audit that you can use to grade your accounts, your social media manager, or clients before they hire you for an agency." To convey our hook in the creative, we simply created an image that shows a report card. Instead of showing the lead magnet, it just says social media and an F.

Whenever we create these hooks, we pull the biggest keywords. In this example, it's "grade." Then, you think about what people associate with grades—report

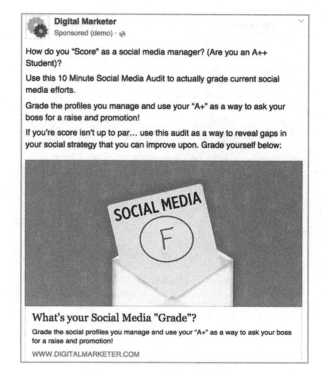

FIGURE 21.5–Get a Grade

cards. We'll then type "grade" or "report card" into Google or Dreamstime and see what images are coming up first. Google works great for this because the images coming up first are the ones that people have clicked on the most in regards to that keyword. Since Google has so much data, you can see the images that already have association with your keyword. Instead of making assumptions, let Google tell you what people are clicking on in relation to that word.

When we Googled "grade" and "report card," we got the idea for the grade F. It's a simple image that absolutely portrays the marketing message of a grade. It's not just a bland image showing a mockup of the lead magnet; instead, we took it a step further by pulling a key word out of the hook and made sure the image reflected that. We have tested this image with an A as well, but F works the best because people have a more emotional association with the F grade.

This image can be used multiple ways across all of our different avatars as well. If you want to flip this and run to bosses of social media managers instead, your first line of copy can change to, "how does your social media manager score?" The same image can be used no matter who you're targeting, and it still portrays the hook of getting a grade.

Figure 21.6 on page 214 was a "create a report" hook. We took the audit and positioned it as a report that you can actually give to someone else. We used the same

FIGURE 21.6–Create a Report

concept, but changed it slightly to portray someone actually handing over a report. This seems very simple, but remember that someone scrolling through is going to look at your image for only two to three seconds. Your goal is to make this simple and make sure it really portrays what you're trying to say. The copy is, "you should receive a weekly report from your social media manager to ensure their strategy is not only working but actually improving over time. Send this ten-minute audit to your social media manager today and ask them to report back weekly." The image conveys that simply by showing a social media manager handing over the report.

We were able to come up with multiple hooks for the same offer. This one was a little bit more fun. The hook in Figure 21.7 on page 215 was about grading your competition. The copy says "take the audit and go and grade your competition's social media profiles to see how you stack up against them." We pulled the keyword of "stack" or "stack up," and the image that came to mind from that was stacks of pancakes. This all sounds really silly, but this is exactly how we come up with our images. For our creative, we had stacks of pancakes, and this one converted really well because it's visually appealing. People understand when they read it, and it's kind of funny.

Finally, in Figure 21.8 on page 215, the hook was knowing your goals. This was targeted for a corporate type audience, asking "Is your social media strategy actually in line with the goals you set for your business?" The image we used with "are you hitting your social goals and showing progress week to week" really conveyed the marketing message.

FIGURE 21.7–Stack Up

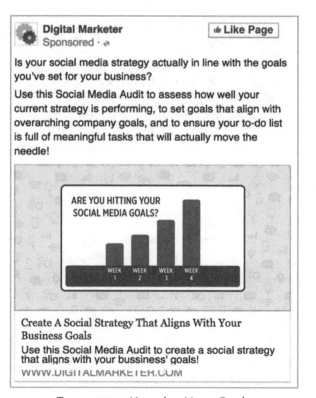

FIGURE 21.8–Knowing Your Goals

ANALYZING CREATIVES THAT WORK

Here are examples from other companies I really love. All of these portray the marketing message so well. Figure 21.9 is from Hired, and they're saying, "if you're counting down the hours until you get to leave the office, it might be time for a change." The hook in this ad is to get more out of your work/life balance. How they decided to portray the marketing message was to put work on one side of a gauge and life on the other. It's so simple, yet effective, which is why I love it. One way to enhance this creative even more is to make it a GIF where the gauge is actually moving because it would really catch someone's attention. However, this still works because instead of just putting a stock photo of people in an office counting down the hours until they leave, they took it a step further.

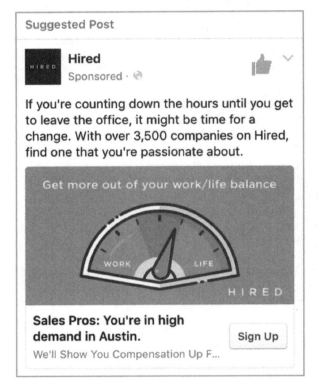

FIGURE 21.9–Hired Ads

The ad example in Figure 21.10 on page 217 also did a great job on that same thing. Their hook was, "don't bottle up your emotions." The keyword they pulled from that hook was bottle, and they have portrayed the bottles as sad to fit their marketing message. You can see that these companies are using very similar strategies.

This is also true with Figure 21.11 on page 217. The hook is "not all wounds are visible." A common image that's associated with wounds is bandages. This is really simple, and it's also on a background that really stands out.

FIGURE 21.10–Bottle Emotion

FIGURE 21.11–Bandages

Figure 21.12 on page 218 is an example from a wine delivery company. I love this image because it shows the product and it's a pattern interrupt because of the way they have the wine arranged in a pattern that makes you stop and wonder what it is. Your brain is just curious. A way they could have taken this a step further is showing someone actually delivering the wine, but I love the pattern interrupt aspect of that image.

Figure 21.13 on page 218 is an example from us at Digital Marketer, and this shows how literal we get while creating our images. The copy is "you can create a blog

FIGURE 21.12–Wine Delivery

FIGURE 21.13–60-Second Blog

content plan in 60 seconds or less by filling in these five simple blanks." We were targeting bloggers. We took it a step further and thought about what platform most bloggers use—

Wordpress. We decided to make the image look like Wordpress because it's something they're familiar with. We then added in the clock because it speaks to the 60 seconds. This is one of our highest converting ads of all time, and it's really simple. It took our designer about 20 minutes to make, but it was effective because we were playing off of psychology by using something that these people already knew because they're probably in Wordpress every day. By recreating it we can easily catch their attention.

The example in Figure 21.14 is great. The copy reads, "we can't build Rome in a day, but in less than 24 hours, we can find someone to build it for you." In this example, they took the word build and ran with it. They have little ninjas coming down and building the app. It's a very simple idea that's very literal to the hook.

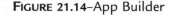

FIGURE 21.14–App Builder

Figure 21.15 on page 220 is one of Ralph Burn's ads that I think is awesome. This example circles back to the stacking keyword with "how does your metabolism stack up." In this case, it's showing progression with different colors. The image really stands out against the background and is great.

In Figure 21.16 on page 220, you can see we were really being literal with the "rock star" keyword by having a band playing. There are also marketing icons up in the music notes to really speak to the marketing message and our target audience.

FIGURE 21.15–Metabolism

FIGURE 21.16–Rock Star

Figure 21.17 on page 221 is an example from SamCart. They are saying, "are you trying to sell your stuff online, but overwhelmed by the idea of setting up a sales funnel?" In this

FIGURE 21.17–SamCart

example, they're playing off of the fact that this market is overwhelmed by sales funnels. The image portrays what we're told it's like vs. what it's really like. This is imagery that people know because you may have seen it used in different markets, but they're applying it to funnels. Brian, the founder of SamCart, has told us that this ad has done really well. This ad also has great shareability because their target audience can relate to it.

While the ad copy in Figure 21.18 on page 222 could be better, the image fits their hook perfectly. This is a financial app, and this sort of graph is familiar in culture. They're playing off of what most people do when it comes to their finances. The first of the month you stick to your budget, in the middle of the month you're terrible, and then at the end you try to get back on budget. They chose a very literal way to depict their marketing message.

This Wag example in Figure 21.19 on page 222 is very simple, but I love it. This is a retargeting ad after I visited their site. Here is an example of where you should use dogs in your creative because this company is a dog walking app. There's nothing wrong with using dogs if it actually relates to what you're doing. For this ad, they decided to use an image of dogs, but they still incorporated the offer of 50 percent off your first walk in the image as well. It's very simple, but portrays the marketing message.

Figure 21.20 on page 223 is actually a video from our sister company over at Survival Life. There's rain coming down and the lighter is still going, because the hook is that the

FIGURE 21.18–Financial App

FIGURE 21.19–Wag

lighter is waterproof. This is so simple because they're just displaying what the lighter does. They've added the penny because you can get the lighter for a penny, and then, there's just a call to action. This ad has done really well for them.

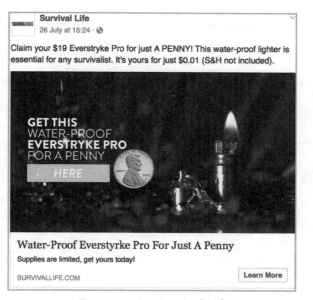

FIGURE 21.20–Survival Life

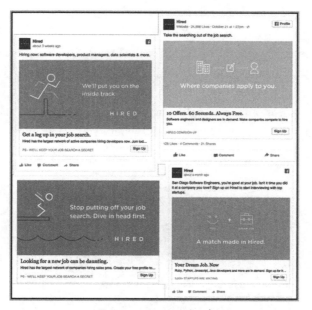

FIGURE 21.21–Hired

Hired (Figure 21.21) has some great examples of ads that are reflective of the hook in a simple way. Each of these portray the marketing hook in a literal way that's very simple yet extremely effective.

FIGURE 21.22–Library

Figure 21.22 is a great example of being really literal. This was a Facebook ad template library, so we made the image look like a library. It's very simple and literal, but it works very well.

Figure 21.23 is for an offer called a Customer Avatar Worksheet. One of the hooks we came up with was, "Can you guess where your customers are hiding?" so we

FIGURE 21.23–Guess Who

FIGURE 21.24–Brady Bunch

pulled out the word "guess." Something a lot of people associate with that word is the game *Guess Who*. Our designer didn't pull an image of the game directly from Dreamstime, but she simply mocked it up with different customers.

Another example for this offer is Figure 21.24, which is an image playing off of the image from the television show, *Brady Bunch*, and it fits right into the hook. The colors are great, and people become curious wondering, "Who are these people?"

Figure 21.25 on page 226 is a great example of how to display a physical product without being boring. Instead of just showing the makeup brush, it has pink blush coming off of it, which makes it really eye catching. This is a market that requires really good design, and they are drawn to good-looking, high-quality images. This ad absolutely speaks to that audience.

This Jimmy Buffet ad (Figure 21.26 on page 226) is another great example of successfully showing the product. This ad is being run to his fans. It's simple with the item they're getting and the sizes on the bottom. The engagement on this ad was insane because many of his fans had to stop on it.

Something to keep in mind, which this ad is a good example of, is when you're using people in your imagery, make sure they are looking at you or at your CTA. In this ad, Jimmy is directly looking at you, so when you are scrolling through the newsfeed, his eyes catch your attention when they're looking right at you. Whenever you are using people in your ads make sure they're either looking at you, the CTA, or whatever you want people to actually click on. If they're looking in a different direction you're going to look at what they're looking at, so you just want to make sure they're looking at whatever you want the customer to look at.

FIGURE 21.25–Makeup Brush

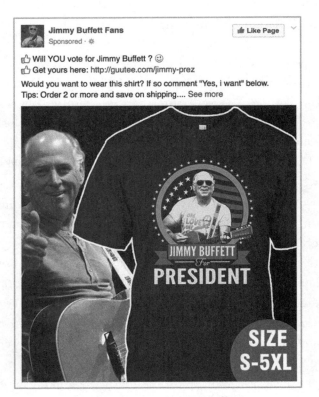

FIGURE 21.26–Jimmy Buffet

WORKING WITH A DESIGNER

Giving our designer projects takes a lot of work from me, but it's worth it. As previously mentioned, you can't just tell the designer that you need ads for your product; there should be a system in place for this. What I start with is Google. In this example I was Googling things like "social media for your brand," and I found an image that I thought was really cool. I take screenshots of whatever I like inside of Google and then I put them in a document like Figure 21.27. I do my own drawings of what I'm envisioning because I don't want the designer to knock off the image I found, on top of the fact that I don't always want exactly what they were doing. I'm just taking the concepts from what Google was telling me works and then applying it to our ads. For this ad I thought of something that shows the brand with social media icons coming out of it, because this lead magnet was a ten-minute social media audit. I wanted to take that concept, but tweak it to fit our marketing message by putting the 10 minute clock in the middle, because I knew that it worked with the blog plan ad before. I took what works, put that in the middle, and then had her add the icons around.

The process we use to come up with our concepts is the Ad Grid. We talked about this in depth in episode 33 of the *Perpetual Traffic* podcast. With this process, I figure out the different avatars and hooks and then, using Google and my own creativity, I think about each of the hooks and how they can speak to different people. I spend a lot of time brainstorming what these creatives should be and then write them out.

In hook one, I have all the different images that I want. I usually have about three to five depending on the campaign. Then I always have our designer come up with a

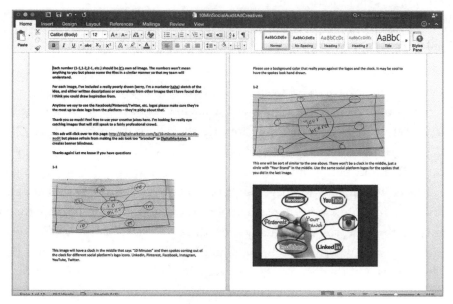

FIGURE 21.27–Designer Example

wildcard on her own because after she's gone through my suggestions, she knows where things are headed with the concept. The more she does, the better she gets, and some of the ones she comes up with now beat mine. This takes a lot of time because I'm doing research for every single hook and coming up with three to five ideas of creatives that could portray that message. While you may not need more than one or two ideas in your business, it's important to always be taking whatever you're trying to sell, coming up with the hooks, and then using this process through Google or Dreamstime to figure out what images really portray what you're trying to say.

Once I have completed the document, I send it to our designer, and she follows up with the first draft of the ads. Sometimes, they're not what I was looking for at all, and it's usually because I didn't explain it well. These documents have become really detailed to try and avoid situations like that. I will not only write it out, but I also sit down with her or get on a call to go back through everything and make sure she understands exactly what I'm envisioning for each of these images. If you don't explain your concept well enough, your designer might run with it on their own, which is not usually the best idea. They might be able to create a pretty picture but not necessarily a high converting ad. Sometimes, we go through three to five revisions, and sometimes, they're perfect right off the bat. We put a lot of time into this process, and it's not something you should just create in Snagit or outsource on Fiverr anymore. I really believe this is a super important step in your campaigns and a big investment that that you should make in your business.

Something that's important to keep in mind is to always test your creatives. Sometimes, the winner is the one I liked the least, but it doesn't matter what I like as long as it portrays that message.

TELLING A STORY WITH YOUR CREATIVES

A powerful thing to do while creating your ads is to create a story that your viewer can put themself in. You have to be careful while doing this so you don't make your copy too direct at your audience. Using the word "you" in your ads may have a negative effect because it may scare people that you are directly calling them out. Figure 21.28 on page 229 is a great example of talking about a person without using the word you. You can create a fictitious person instead, so in this example, it says "Jeff wants to grow his business. He downloads the Kabbage App to get a line of credit up to 100 grand." Even though the pictures are kind of like stock photos this is a great ad because the images tell a story. In this case, you can actually show this app in action. "He applies first thing in the morning right." Even though you're talking about "Jeff," the person is thinking about themselves. On the next image, you have Jeff withdrawing funds on his way to work, so it has an image of a guy walking to work. It then finishes with a nice call to action. This is kind of silly, but it's telling a story.

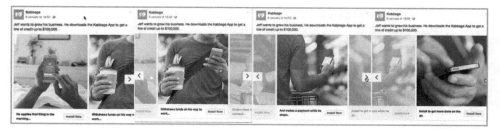

FIGURE 21.28–Kabbage App

If I were them, I probably would have done a little bit more with the images. I think stock photo images become hidden in the newsfeed because most of what your family, friends, and people that you actually care about on Facebook are doing is sharing pictures that look similar. When you use imagery that is a photo, it can get buried in the newsfeed because it's blending in with actual photos from your friends and family. I do think they did a great job here telling a story, and carousel ads are an effective way of telling a story in your ads because you can document whatever the before and after is of your product, hook, or service.

We would do something like Figure 21.29 because it's true to our brand. It's the same concept as the Kabbage App, but it fits our cartoon style, and it's a little more marketed. Since we put a little bit more thought into it, it stands out more in the newsfeed and catches people's eye. This is for our Digital Marketer HQ products, which is for larger companies who want to train their marketing team. This is also a story-based ad, and each of the images takes them through the multiple steps you need to take. If you are the avatar for this ad, you can see yourself taking each of these steps yourselves. I actually got the idea from the Kabbage ad, but I wanted to spice it up a little bit. Adding text onto the actual image for the carousel really helps because it stands out more, so that's what I would do in terms of the carousel ads.

When creating carousel ads, you are given an option to show the best performing image first. In the story-based ads like this one, we wanted to make sure that wasn't checked because it was designed in a way that it went in a specific order. However, ads like the one in Figure 21.30 on page 230 was more featured-based, so we did have that option selected.

This was for a software that we just launched called *TruConversion*, which is kind of like Hot Jar. It's an optimization software that allows you to really see what people are

FIGURE 21.29–DM Carousel

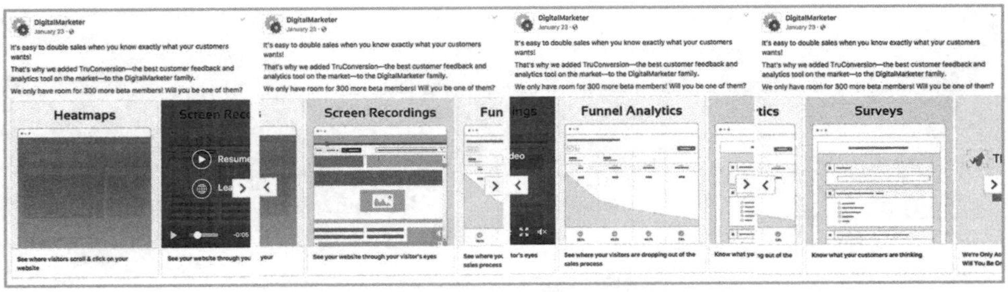

FIGURE 21.30–TruConversion

doing on your website. With this carousel ad, I wanted to show the different benefits of the software. The hook is, "it's easy to double your sales when you know exactly what your customers want." We then used the carousel to show the different benefits. This worked really well because of the colors and curiosity that it instills in people who want to see where people are clicking on their website. This example isn't necessarily story-based, but the images are showing you what the software actually does.

AD CREATIVE CHECKLIST

Our designer created a checklist for Facebook ads that walks through the thought process behind each creative.

1. Create a Powerful Message and Conceptualize Images

This is the step where you take the hook, do your research, and make sure the image portrays that hook. This is where you search Google and your competitors to see what they are doing. You also want to figure out what benefits your offer provides, who you want to target, who your audience is, what the end result is that your customer can receive, and what emotions/feelings you want to convey.

We have a perfect example of playing off of people's emotions in Figures 21.31 and 21.32 on page 231.

The first ad was run to people who visited our website for our Traffic and Conversion Summit event but didn't buy tickets. As we were getting close to increasing the price of tickets, I started running this ad that reads, "we're excited you visited the site, we're sad you didn't purchase, but there's still time. Batteries don't last forever, and neither will our 50 percent off deal." Silly, but it works. At this point in the campaign, the battery is green, so they know that it's going away soon but there's not a lot of scarcity yet.

A week before the price actually increased, the same people started seeing the second version of this ad where we had the battery about to die because it was getting really close to the end of our sale. We needed something that portrayed the marketing message of scarcity, and this worked really well because it's something people are familiar with.

FIGURE 21.31–Battery Ad

FIGURE 21.32–Battery Ad

Figure 21.33 on page 232 is another example of taking something that people can relate to or are familiar with. This was a messenger ad, and what we were trying to convey is

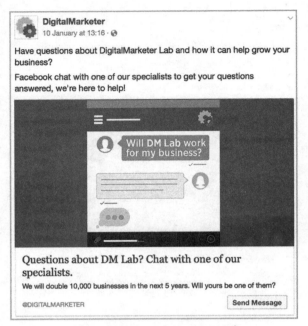

FIGURE 21.33–Messenger Ad

that if you click on this ad, you can actually chat with someone. When we thought about how to show that our designer mocked up an image to look like a message, of course you don't want it to look exactly like Facebook, but you see right away that it's some sort of message conversation that's happening. An extra aspect we added to catch people's attention even more is that we made the image move to look like you're having a conversation in real time. When you see the text bubble come up, we all associate that with someone who is talking to us. It's something that everyone's familiar with, and it's a very effective nine-second video ad that portrays the message of "Do you want to have a conversation?"

2. Sketch Out Ideas Before Laying Out any Design Elements

This is the step in the process where we use the document with all of my ideas and sketches. At this stage, you don't want to worry about colors or font choices yet. I never really tell our designer what color or font choice to use because that is where she really is good. My job in the process is to make sure all the elements are in the image that I'm looking for from a marketing perspective.

3. Use Complementary or Contrasting Colors

Facebook ads have to pop, and using only a few complementary color choices will help obtain this goal. You don't have to add ten different colors to your ads, and you don't want to because it can get very busy.

4. Choose Your Fonts

It's important to only use one or two different font families for your image. Figure 21.34 is an example of why it can be bad to use too many fonts in one image.

In this example, there are so many different fonts that it's hard to read. It's kind of cute and it's definitely on brand for her, but you can't really read it. In this case, it's not because of the black background, it's because of the use of multiple fonts. Using only one to two fonts is really important for readability if you're putting text on your ad.

FIGURE 21.34–Amy Porterfield

5. A Text and Call-to-Action (CTA) to Your Image

Almost all of our images have a text or call to action on them because we've found that that works best. A lot of people actually aren't reading your ad copy; instead, they're going right to the image. If you can take a few words of your hook that are the most important and put them onto the image it's going to work really well. We either put a little line of copy or a button with a CTA. This will engage those people that prefer to look at images more than read the copy.

6. Make Sure Your Image Is Congruent with Your Brand

You really want to make sure you are consistent overall with your designs. When someone clicks on the image and they go over to your landing page, or wherever you're sending traffic, the design elements should be similar. At Digital Marketer, we are able to maintain a certain brand because our ads are similar to the featured images on our blog. Everything is congruent so when someone sees it, they instantly have a connection and know it's Digital Marketer.

ANALYZING CREATIVES THAT DON'T WORK

Figures 21.35 and 21.36 are examples of something you shouldn't do and how you can fix it. The offer is a social media swipe file, and the hook is that it's a headline swipe file. In the updated version, we played off of newspapers because that's what people commonly associate headlines with. We made the image look like a newspaper, and the headline is "Ultimate Social Media Swipe File." We tested it in multiple colors, but

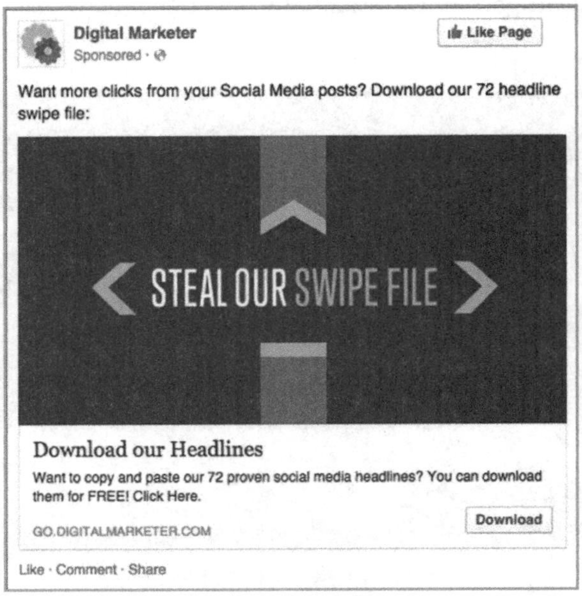

FIGURE 21.35–Outdated

FIGURE 21.36–Updated

FIGURE 21.37–Otter

the black and white did the best. It definitely stands out in the newsfeed. This was an upgrade from the original because the first one doesn't help convey the hook or have anything to do with the actual offer.

The ad creative in Figure 21.37 failed because it had nothing to do with content marketing or a crash course. Sometimes people will choose something, like the otter in this example, because they think it's cute and that people will click because of that. While the colors are great because they grab your attention, the concept is lacking.

Figure 21.38 also goes for the example talking about video ads. Having a female with a brightly colored background may grab your attention, but it doesn't correlate

FIGURE 21.38–Girl

with the hook at all. This ad will probably get a lot of clicks using imagery like this, but most will not be qualified clicks because it doesn't portray the marketing message properly. Instead, they could have used a video ad to promote the video ad hook.

GETTING INSPIRED

While learning about what works with creatives, you have to realize that this is not a process or a system; it's something you have to continuously study. AdEspresso has a great library of Facebook ads you can use to study, which is something I do almost every day. I'm constantly in Facebook taking screenshots of ads. Ryan, Britney, and everyone on the team sends me ads. We are always circulating what we think is good and bad, and this takes constant attention and practice to learn what's working.

The creative comes down to being a good marketer. It's pretty simple once you start to get in the right mindset. Just remember to always ask, "How can I convey a marketing message that will get someone to do what I want them to do?"

Chapter 22

Three-Step Video Ad Formula

ONE VIDEO CAN CHANGE YOUR LIFE

This chapter really should be titled: "How to Scale Fast," or "How to Create 'Set It and Forget It' Campaigns." Because once you get it right once and make a good video ad, it can be game over. (And this does NOT necessarily mean high production value.)

Game over for your competition. Definitely not for you. Without even searching, I can think of about a dozen different client videos that have been running for one to two years now and in some cases, longer. Just including internal Dominate Web Media Business Manager ad accounts, we have over 600 million paid video views of data we get to analyze—and time and time again, the three-step video ad strategy described in this chapter produces the best ROI.

If you want to download our most up-to-date video ad guide PDF, which includes live video ad examples inside Facebook, go to www.perrymarshall.com/fbtools.

> "*In marketing you must choose between boredom, shouting, and seduction. Which do you want?*"
>
> — ROY H. WILLIAMS

PRINCIPLES AND PRACTICE OF LONG-TERM EFFECTIVE FACEBOOK ADVERTISING

That quote from Roy H. WIlliams, the author of the bestselling marketing book *The Wizard of Ads: Turning Words into Magic and Dreamers into Millionaires* (Bard Press, 1998) explains the big benefit that a Facebook advertising campaign delivers over any other marketing channel. It takes Facebook's advantage even beyond the platform's amazing targeting and goes straight to the heart of what makes its advertising campaigns successful not just in the short term but in the long term.

That should always be the goal of a Facebook marketing campaign: the ability to create a campaign that keeps bringing in new customers for months on end and at an incredibly low price. It's what we're going to explore in this short guide: the principles that underlie every successful long-term Facebook marketing campaign.

LONG-TERM FACEBOOK CAMPAIGNS BEAT SHORT-TERM MARKETING CAMPAIGNS

Creating an advertising campaign on any platform takes effort. You need to identify a message that will resonate; brainstorm the copy; create the content; target the audience; track the results; rinse and repeat. It takes time, and it takes money. So when you've done it, you want that campaign to last. You want ads that work continually—ads that you can just run and leave.

You want ads whose effectiveness doesn't die out after just a week or two.

You've probably had that experience. You put up an ad, you track the results, and for the first few days everything's great. The call to action works. You get clicks to your landing page. The ROI is high, everything's working. And then the graph starts to go down and by the end of the week or after ten days, you're starting to think about what you have to do next.

Usually, it means you have to start all over again.

That's short-term advertising. It's a sprint, and it has to be followed by another sprint, then another one, and so on. It's exhausting and while you'll move quickly, it won't take you far. Roy H. Williams has called it a race for fools.

Direct response newspaper advertising is a sprint. It works in the short term. When a furniture store takes out a full-page ad in a local newspaper and tells readers that everything in stock is 20 percent off for the next week, it will get sales. People who happen to be thinking of buying furniture at that time will go and check it out. But what happens at the end of the week? What happens to people who aren't considering buying right now, but who will need a new sofa one day?

As soon as the ad is out of date, the store passes out of people's minds. The brand has to come up with a whole new ad. It has to start each short campaign from scratch.

Advertising in the *Yellow Pages* is the same. It's a job. You're appealing to a smaller audience, and most importantly, you need the audience to already have intent. Short-term advertising only works on audiences that are already primed to buy.

Those ads are like Facebook image ads. They're effective for some people. They're effective for now. But they aren't effective for everyone, and they aren't effective for long.

FACEBOOK VIDEO ADS DELIVER LONG-TERM ADVERTISING SUCCESS

Before the launch of every campaign we create, whether it's for ourselves or for a client, we always think, "How is that person coming into our sales funnel? Is he coming in with his virtual guard up? Did he see the word 'Sponsored' above the ad and is now expecting to be sold something he doesn't want? Is his first reaction going to be to say no to everything we offer because he's suspicious and on guard?

"Or will he be coming in with his guard down? Will he reach the sales funnel actually wanting to watch our videos, instead of sitting in front of the screen with his arms folded, his mind closed to the message. Will he want to show up for our webinars? Will he want to buy the products we offer?"

The difference between the ways a lead enters the sales funnel lies in what they do before they come in. If you're using short-term advertising, they'll have their guard up. If all they know about the brand is what they saw on an image ad, that sales funnel will still have a lot of persuading to do.

But if they've seen a video before opting in for your lead magnet, they're going to be open. They'll be more knowledgeable. They'll understand more about your brand, including what you have to offer and why they need it.

Facebook video ads are like radio and television commercials. They're the steps that make up the marathon. They produce a long-term response not short time numbers that last for 24 hours or seven days. They can keep going for six months or more. There's so much science behind this. One study by Nielsen (refer to Figure 22.1 on page 240) has shown that ad recall improves by 74 percent after just 15 seconds of a video ad. Purchase intent increases 72 percent after 10 seconds. Video works.

But here's the thing: what happens on the screen is not the most important part of a video ad. Even more important is the audio.

What comes in through our ears stays in our minds for a full five seconds before it begins to fade. What enters the eyes is gone in less than a second. You know that line about pictures being worth a thousand words? Forget it. It's not true—not unless that picture is accompanied by a memorable sound.

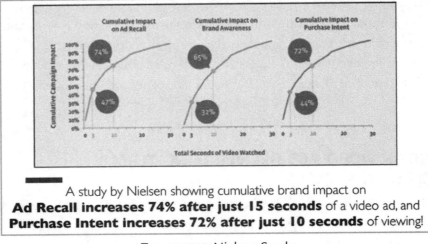

A study by Nielsen showing cumulative brand impact on
Ad Recall increases 74% after just 15 seconds of a video ad, and
Purchase Intent increases 72% after just 10 seconds of viewing!

FIGURE 22.1–Nielsen Study

You know this. Think about how radio advertising works. At the end of each ad, there's always a jingle, and that jingle will remain in your head long after the ad has ended.

You can do an experiment. The next time there's a commercial break in a television show, wait until the break ends and then ask the person next to you what product the first commercial was advertising. They won't remember. It will be literally three minutes since they saw that ad, and they'll have no idea what they just saw. But play them the first couple of chords of their favorite song, even if they haven't heard it for months, and they'll be off singing the chorus. If someone asked you to name the songs of your workout playlist in order, you'd probably struggle unless you played them first in your head. As soon as one song on a playlist ends, your mind is already playing the next one before it even begins. (That's why the shuffle feature was such a smart move; by breaking up those expectations, we get to be surprised by a favorite song instead of expecting it.)

That's the power that sound has. It's when you combine sound with an image that the image becomes worth a thousand words. You remember the sound. It stays in your head, and the sound helps you to recall the image and the message that the image broadcasts.

It works. We ran a campaign for a client for one day using a video ad. The client was selling multiple small-priced products and had an advertising budget of $1,600. He generated $6,000 in sales. That was an extreme case, but it wasn't unusual for a video ad on Facebook.

And video ads aren't just more effective than short-term image ads. They're also much cheaper. When you're running video ads, Facebook gives you what we call "quality custom audiences." The platform builds up audiences who watch three seconds of your video, ten seconds of it, a quarter, a half, three-quarters, and almost all of your video. In effect, it gives you access to invisible lists that are much cheaper than a click on a website. You end up using a list that's ten times better and sometimes two to three times cheaper. The gains grow exponentially in the long term as the audience builds and Facebook's algorithms gain a clearer understanding of the type of people who watch and serve you more of the same.

The result is that when those audiences click your call to action, they already have your brand in their hearts and minds before they're ready to buy. They're coming into your sales funnel with their guards down and their minds open. They want to know what you have to say. They want to take part in your webinars and read your ebooks.

And there's never been a better time to use those ads. In February 2017, Facebook announced that the videos on its streams would play automatically with the sound on. The company had been experimenting since the previous fall and was ready to start rolling out the change slowly around the world. As long as the sound on the phone is turned on, a user scrolling through their timeline will hear sound fade in as they reach a video and hear it fade out as they scroll away. Right from the moment a follower opens their Facebook app, you have an opportunity to grab their attention in the easiest, most direct, and most memorable way possible.

In the earnings call that announced the change, Mark Zuckerberg was clear about the goal:

> *The goal that we have for the product experience is to make it so that when people want to watch videos or want to keep up-to-date with what's going on with their favorite show, or what's going on with a public figure that they want to follow, that they can come to Facebook and go to a place knowing that that's going to show them all the content that they're interested in. The experience is designed to deliver on that promise —[that] you want to watch videos, you want to keep up with the content that you watch episodically week over week. This is going to be the place where you go to do that.*

Facebook, in other words, is maneuvering to compete directly with YouTube, which is great news for brands. The friendlier Facebook becomes to video content, the better brands will be able to engage customers with video ads. You'll be able to build a long-term marketing strategy for Facebook. You won't have to keep coming up with new ideas. You won't have to constantly change your content. You'll be able to create video ads that keep your audiences flowing into your sales funnel ready to buy.

What they do when they reach that sales funnel, though, and the number of people who reach it, will depend on how you use those video ads and how you create them.

THE PRINCIPLES OF VIDEO SHARING

What does video sharing matter when we are talking about paying for the video views anyway?

One reason: the more shareable your video is (or any other type of ad), the cheaper your impressions, views, and clicks cost. Yes, you get free impressions—but more importantly, it sends a signal to Facebook's algorithm that your ad is engaging, and they reward you with cheaper views and more impressions. (It also has a positive effect on the frame of mind visitors who click through to your landing pages)

In his book *Contagious: Why Things Catch On*, Jonah Berger, a marketing professor at Wharton, describes the success of a new bar in New York City. The bar isn't advertised. The founder, Brian Shebairo, didn't spend a dime on advertising. There isn't even a sign above the door, and yet, the place has been packed since it opened.

To reach the bar, patrons have to walk through a restaurant that specializes in fancy hot dogs. At the end of the restaurant, they'll find a telephone box similar to the type that Clark Kent used to use as a changing room. Patrons pick up the phone and dial 1. They'll be asked if they have a reservation. If they do, the back of the phone box swings open and gives them access to a secret bar called "Please Don't Tell."

In theory, that secrecy should be the kiss of death for a business. If no one knows the bar exists or where it is, how can it win customers? But what happens when you give someone a secret? They share it. They tell someone else. They pass on that secret because letting someone know that they have a secret shows that they're in the know. They're part of a special group with access to special knowledge. Sharing the secret makes them look good. And people want to hear secrets. Listening to a secret gives them possession of it and makes them part of that special group. They might not want to use the information, but they certainly want to be part of the group that has it, so they'll listen and pass it on to their own friends.

That principle, which has turned "Please Don't Tell" into one of the most successful bars in one of the most competitive cities in the world, is the first of six principles that Jonah Berger says underpins viral marketing. He calls this principle "social currency:"

> *Just as people use money to buy products or services, they use social currency to achieve desired positive impressions among their families, friends, and colleagues.*

The other five principles that make up his STEPPS guide to viral marketing are:

1. *Triggers*—Sights, sounds, and other stimuli that remind us of related products and ideas.

2. *Emotion*—Content that inspires positive emotions like *awe* or negative emotions like *anger* or *anxiety* are more likely to go viral says Berger in a 2012 paper in the *Journal of Marketing Research*.

3. *Public*—Content should be produced with the intention of being shared and enjoyed by everyone rather than exclusive to the recipient.

4. *Practical Value*—Content that is relevant and that can improve the lives of the people who see it is more likely to be shared and spread.

5. *Stories*—Content with a beginning, middle, and end matches the way we like to receive and remember information and makes it more shareable.

Those principles aren't laws. Berger stresses that there's no guarantee those elements in a piece of content will spread that content to millions of people, but they will increase the chances that the content will be shared, and they will increase the number of shares that a piece of content can receive.

Most importantly, Berger's principles show that virality and a big audience isn't down to luck. It's down to science. It requires understanding, knowledge, and hard work. Julius Dein, for example, is a British prankster who went from no followers at all on Facebook to more than six million followers within a year by uploading viral videos. He realized that his magic tricks weren't spreading so he created new content that won views and shares. He made content that was funny and emotional.

He also created content that did more than make people laugh. He uploaded videos that made the people sharing it look like they were part of a secret club of people who knew about these funny pranks. They weren't just entertaining; they also had social currency. People who hit the Share button got to say to their friends: "Look at me, I'm clued into the latest, cutting-edge humor. I know where to find the funniest stuff on the Internet." Dein made sharers look good. In return, they made him look good.

He also linked up with other content creators and shared their content. By tracking his results and marketing hard, he was able to build a large presence online and create a whole new career. It wasn't down to luck. It was down to science, and it was down to following the principles of viral content.

And it was down to using videos.

No other format has the same viral quality. No other format can deliver cheaper views and cheaper clicks on Facebook the more it's seen in the way that videos can. And no other format can bring people into your sales funnel with their guard down in the way that videos can. That's why our formula, the strategy that we use to build audiences on Facebook is to use content-rich video ads—and it's why they work so well.

THE THREE-STEP FORMULA FOR SUCCESSFUL LONG-TERM VIDEO ADS

Jonah Berger described the principles that underlie viral marketing. He didn't give a formula. He looked at the content that spread the widest and tried to identify the factors that made them so successful.

That was smart because formulas are always tough. They have to be flexible. A formula —even a proven formula with a great track record—is not always your formula. There are plenty of experts who will tell you that a video has to be 30 seconds long or five minutes long or whatever it may be. They'll recommend that length because they've seen success with videos of that length. And whatever that length happens to be, they can find a reason for its success: short videos put across the message fast and take viewers straight to the call of action at the end; longer videos allow time for more explanation and might produce more shares.

But we've found that some of our best performing videos have been as short as 20 seconds. We've also found that others have been as long as 18 minutes. For some formulas, the best rule is that the content has to match your brand and your product. Everything else is fluid.

Having said that, when we create Facebook video ads for clients, we follow three steps:

STEP 1: STOP THE SCROLL

This goal is clear. Facebook autoplaying the audio as well as the video when a user opens their news feed provides a huge opportunity, but it's only an opportunity. It's not a guarantee of anything because while you can easily grab a viewer's attention, they can just as easily snatch it back. Facebook keeps users in control and gives them the ability to find more interesting content easily. Facebook doesn't care whether an audience watches your video on the platform as long as it watches a video on the platform—and it always has more videos to serve. One flick of the thumb, and your audio starts to fade. You pass out of view. Those first three to ten seconds are vital, then, especially when the video appears as an ad in a news feed. There are some pretty simple things that you can do to stop that quick thumb-swipe and halt the scroll.

One strategy that we use is blatant hand motions, which is what I am doing during the first three seconds of Figure 22.2 on page 245. It's a direct appeal, and it can be a bit annoying, but it does still work. Give the viewer a wave. Pull them towards you in the same way that a good store demonstrator will pull passers-by into their display. Attract attention before the crowd scrolls past. It's not subtle but sometimes, simple and bold are enough to do the job.

FIGURE 22.2–Stop the Scroll

Another strategy that we've found to be very effective is text overlay. Facebook now allows advertisers to automatically add subtitles to their video ads. It's in the Power Editor, under Ads. When you select the Video Captions option, you'll be given a choice between generating the captions automatically, uploading an SRT file (the kind of file used for video subtitles), or not using captions at all.

Facebook marks the caption option as recommended for a reason: it works. If people have turned the sound off on their phone, they'll still be able to see your message. As soon as they see the text, they'll start to read it. It pulls them in and draws their attention. We can read faster than we speak so when you've got just a few seconds to grab someone and stop them scrolling, that text will help to get your message across much faster than waiting for someone to finish speaking. You'll be able to prove that you've got something they should see before their thumb starts to move. In Figure 22.3 on page 246, I am using a text overlay to tell the same story as I am saying verbally.

You can try using Facebook's automatic caption generator, but don't depend on it. If you've got a strong regional accent, it can make mistakes, and if you create the text yourself, you get to play with the size of the text and color of the background. You can really make it stand out.

The third thing we try to do to stop the scroll is use a "pattern-interrupt." That just means we try to break up the visuals. It's the same principle that makes warning signs red and pedestrian crossings black and white. If you can break up the picture so that it looks unusual, it will always attract attention.

You don't have to do anything outrageous here. We're not going back to the old days of flashing banner ads. Movement can be enough to keep eyeballs on that part of the

FIGURE 22.3–Text Overlay

screen. A very close close-up can be unusual enough to break the routine and make the video stand out against the background of other content. Video ads that look like selfies can create pattern interrupt, too, and they look authentic and real.

Those aren't the only methods that you can use, but they've all proven to be effective.

Once you get moving, you'll find that the creativity will start coming. The idea that you come up with right away might not be the one that does the job. It might be the idea that leads to the big idea. The more video ads you create, the more ideas you'll come up with—and the better those ideas will be.

Anything you can do to create some sort of pattern-interrupt is the key. The Squatty-Potty video of a pooping unicorn in Figure 22.4 is an extreme example.

FIGURE 22.4–Pattern Interrupt

STEP 2: USE THE EDIE FORMULA

Once we've settled on a way to grab attention in the opening seconds, we apply our EDIE formula. This is essentially a simple way of ensuring that at least one of Jonah Berger's principles for virality are present in every video ad we create.

EDIE stands for Educate, Demonstrate, Inform, or Entertain.

Educate

The Educate approach is something we show to all new clients. And don't even have to be on camera to educate, you can do a Power Point or Keynote presentation while recording your computer screen, and you have a great video. You don't have to stand in front of the lens and give audiences a webinar, not in a Facebook video ad. It's enough to give people tips. If you want them to register for the webinar you can tell them they'll find more there once they complete your call to action. If you give them value, they'll share it. If you give them at least one "Aha!" moment, one nugget of advice that makes them realize the value of what you're offering, they'll obey that call to action.

Figure 22.5 is a video over nine minutes long, driving cold traffic to a sales page for a free-book-plus-shipping-and-handling offer. This ad was generating customers for $5 per book purchase when we had to turn it off because the book was outdated and the

FIGURE 22.5–Video Ad Educating

FIGURE 22.6–Video Ad to an Automated Webinar

products we were selling on the confirmation page needed to be redone, thanks to all of Facebook's constant changes.

Figure 22.6 is a six-minute long video driving traffic to an automated webinar selling a product for an average price of $1,200 and was also a very profitable ad.

Demonstrate

Demonstrate works great for technology brands. Figure 22.7 on page 249 is just a 30-second video showing a blog post instantly be transformed into a PDF ebook. We all love to see gadgets, and we love to see them work. Video ads for drones and software and other tech items are always eye-catching. You only need to show the product in action to make the viewer want to see more and want to get their own hands on the product.

Inform

Inform goes further than Educate. Instead of delivering a skill to the viewer, it gives them information that they didn't know before. It's particularly useful when the product requires little education to use but has a variety of features that people should know about.

FIGURE 22.7–Demonstrate

For example, we work with a fitness brand that sells an organic, natural, plant-based, power food. We took a video (in Figure 22.8 on page 250) they already had on YouTube that informs you about 11 amazing super foods and what they do for your body—then transitions into how their product has all eleven superfoods in the ingredients. The video directly to a sales pitch, and it worked great—and it continued to work great. It ran for eighteen months and the advertiser's returns were so impressive that they ramped up spending.

Entertain

There are all sorts of levels of "entertaining" videos. To make a video as entertaining as Figure 22.9 on page 250, which is one of Dollar Beard Club's videos, is probably the most difficult. Those ads from *The Dollar Beard Club (DBC)*, for example, pitched the simplest product in the simplest possible way. DBS's first big hit was just the company's founder Chris Stoikos, a good friend of mine, basically doing a parody of a Dollar Shave Club video.

This video cost them just over $700 to produce but has generated millions of dollars in sales. They put all their initial energy and investments into the creativity—and it paid off in a big way. That's the power that an entertaining video ad can have.

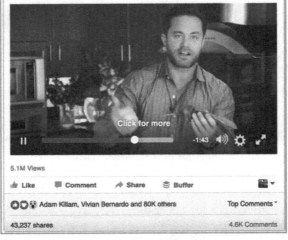

FIGURE 22.8–Inform

FIGURE 22.9–Entertain

The EDIE formula is pretty rich and offers a broad range of options. We won't try to put all of those options into a single video ad, but we will try to include at least one of them so that the video isn't just seen but also watched, enjoyed, remembered, and shared.

STEP 3: CALL TO ACTION

We find that many clients forget about the call to action. They might have heard that social media is all about branding and engagement, and that they shouldn't tell audiences what to do. Eventually, they believe, the greater familiarity that a branding campaign will generate will translate into higher sales.

It's true that social media will help with branding, and it should have engagement that generates a greater connection to the brand, but it should also tell viewers what to do next. Once you've built up that interest, not to use it to generate action would be a waste of a great opportunity.

Like the use of any formula, it's important to learn from the models, but it's vital to go with your authentic self. Whether your call to action is loud or subtle, urgent or calm, it should suit your brand. It should suit your product, and it should suit the action you want the viewer to take.

But it should be there—and it might even need to be there several times.

Sometimes brands will make a video ad that lasts five or six minutes, but they won't give a call to action until the very end. It's as though they're embarrassed to take control— to guide viewers in the direction they want them to go. They're afraid that if they include a call to action earlier, they'll put people off watching.

But only a portion of the audience will watch a video all the way through. So only a portion of the audience will see a call to action that comes at the end of a long video.

So a brand that shies away from using calls to action is going to lose people. If people don't know what they should do next and if brands leave it to audiences to try to figure it out for themselves, then one of the paths those audiences will take will be to shrug and say, "Hmm, interesting," then scroll down. They'll lose them.

In a nine-minute video I might give my first call to action about ninety seconds in. Altogether, I might make about four calls to action throughout a video that length. They won't necessarily be hard sales. A Facebook video ad isn't a late-night infomercial that demands audiences buy now while stocks last. That's the benefit of the marathon instead of the sprint. The calls to action will be natural and authentic. But we'll always be seeding the next thing so that viewers know exactly what they should do next. The clearer you can lay out the path, the more likely people are to follow it. You don't have to push them down that path. You just have to make the trail interesting enough for them to want to want to walk down it themselves and admire the view.

And it works. We once created a quick video as part of a test. The video was about two minutes longer than it should have been; viewers ended up watching it for about nine minutes instead of a more comfortable seven minutes. The lighting was wrong; by the end, it looked like we were presenting with a silhouette. We didn't have time to fix it and make it perfect as we usually would. But we didn't need to. It worked! The call to action drew people in, and we ended up creating new customers—not leads, customers—for about $5 each. We've even seen a student rack up an ROI of 2,882 percent using a smart call to action in a Facebook video ad.

START NOW, IMPROVE LATER

Whenever we create a Facebook video ad for a client, we start with some basic principles. We have a formula and a plan that we can start to apply and then play with and adapt to suit the brand. We know what works, and we can adjust to make the content work for that product.

But remember, the most vital thing that everyone needs to do to make the most of the massive opportunity that Facebook video ads offer is—they have to make a video.

Don't worry if your first efforts don't knock it out of the park. First efforts never do. But every time you film a video, you'll get better. In particular, your ideas will get better. You'll get a greater feel for how to apply those viral formulae and adjust the principles that make people stop scrolling, watch, and share so that they match your brand.

And it's the ideas that matter the most. The technical stuff—the video making and the targeting—they're simple in comparison. The iPhone's microphone is now good enough for video ad broadcast quality. You really don't need anything more than that. What really matters is the idea and the principles on which you build that idea.

FROM THE EARS AND EYES TO THE MIND AND HEART

We started this guide by pointing out the value of audio in Facebook video ads. It might be our eyes that see content, but it's our ears that hold onto it and keep it. It's the sound that reminds of what we saw and the message we were told.

When the message is right, it doesn't just stay in our heads; it moves quickly to the heart, and when it reaches there, all sorts of magic happens. The mind will justify what the heart has already decided.

We find that we can't wait to share the video with friends so that they can have an emotional reaction of their own. We want to see more, so we're willing to watch more content from that brand and to see the videos all the way through. And when we click through to a sales funnel, we arrive with our guard down, open to learn more, see more, and hear more.

Chapter 23

How to Find Your Perfect Audience

Guest Author Sasha Sibree

In earlier chapters, we stressed the importance of creating a great hook and offer and how strategy and messaging beats targeting and ninja optimization. This is something that we cannot stress the importance of enough. For the best results, though, you need to place your awesome hook and offer in front of the right audience—it's like a powerful one-two punch, and finding that perfect audience is exactly what we'll be focusing on in this chapter.

> "*S*elling to the RIGHT PERSON is more important than all the sales methods, copywriting techniques, and negotiation tactics in the world. Because the wrong person doesn't have the money. Or the wrong person doesn't care. The wrong person won't be persuaded by anything."
>
> —PERRY MARSHALL, FROM *80/20 SALES AND MARKETING*

Before we get into creating your audience game plan, I want to share with you a client story to help further illustrate the importance of having a great hook and offer—plus how the right targeting can super-charge your results.

This client was in the survival niche. Their funnel included a free-plus-shipping offer that would upsell into a continuity program. The free-plus-shipping offer was for shooting target silhouettes that would release a fluorescent chalk when hit so you could see it from far away.

Figure 23.1 on page 254 is a screenshot just before we took over their account.

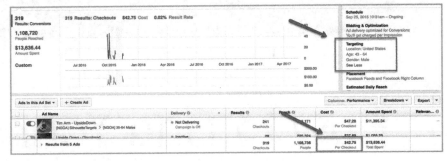

FIGURE 23.1

As you can see, their CPA was just under $43 per check-out, but look at their targeting—"United States, Male, 43 to 64." That's it! In other words, they were basically targeting all males in the U.S. between the ages of 43 to 64 and the crazy thing was their hook and offer was so good it didn't matter.

FINDING INTERESTS WITH INTENT

Our plan with this client was to tighten up their targeting to just include people who were already interested in guns. This was a no-brainer slam dunk!

We started with larger general gun-related interests like guns and NRA, but what we found worked even better was when we targeted interests a little higher in the UPSYD ladder, like Solution Aware. In other words, interests that indicated they already had guns, were probably shooting at something, but may not have been aware that they could be shooting at our client's solution. These types of interests included specific gun brands and gun types.

Luckily for this client, moving up the UPSYD ladder still provided large enough audiences, which is not always the case. By identifying the right audiences, we were able to massively scale their campaigns while simultaneously halving their CPA.

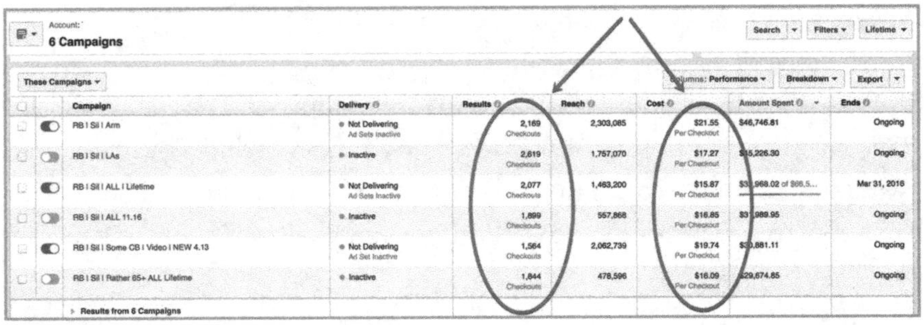

FIGURE 23.2

YOUR AUDIENCE GAME PLAN

The end game plan for your targeting on Facebook is to develop large warm audiences and get Facebook to help locate your best cold audiences. By warm audiences, we mean people who are already familiar with your brand, for example, your fans, website custom audiences, engagement audiences, and video view audiences.

By cold audiences, we are referring to fresh new leads. The reason large warm audiences are important is because the more data we provide Facebook, the better they are at finding people who are just like our leads and customers. They do this through lookalike audiences.

The exact number of people needed in a warm audience to be able to create a powerful lookalike audience can vary. We've seen lookalike audiences produce good results based off of warms audiences of around 1,000, but I've also sat in on calls where Facebook has said you need more like 60,000 to 100,000 data points before your lookalike audience is really dialed in. Now, don't freak out—that doesn't mean you need 100,000 customers. One of the many reasons we like video ads so much is because they build large video view audiences very quickly and inexpensively. The bottom line is that for lookalike audiences to work optimally, you need to provide Facebook with data . . . and the more data the better.

In order to provide Facebook with lots of data from your warm audiences, you need to start somewhere and the best place to start is by interest and behavior targeting.

THE AUDIENCE TARGETING RESEARCH PROCESS

For ecommerce, digital, and information products the audience research process is the same. We call it BCOP. For Local Businesses, the process is very different. We'll cover targeting for local businesses later in this chapter.

INTRODUCING BCOP (LOUSY NAME BUT EFFECTIVE PROCESS)

The process we use in the agency to take all the possible targeting options and quickly and easily shift through them to find the best possible starting points contains four steps. We call it BCOP. It's an acronym for:

> Step One: Brainstorm
> Step Two: Confirm
> Step Three: Organize
> Step Four: Prioritize

The end goal of this process is to identify a handful of interests that are most likely to perform well right out of the gate and give us the highest probability of success. With success, we can use the data to determine which audiences we should target next.

For campaigns with larger budgets, we recommend starting with around 20 interests, but for small budget campaigns, you might start closer to five.

User Tip: For smaller budgets, establish your daily ad spend budget, divide by 10 to estimate how many ad sets, and therefore how many interests, you will need.

STEP ONE: BRAINSTORM

Step one contains some of the same essentials we've already covered in the book. For example: you need to know your avatar, you need a great hook and offer, and you need to know what segment of UPSYD you are targeting, e.g., most likely people Unaware, Problem Aware, or Solution Aware.

Introducing the Interest Research Template

To help brainstorm potential audiences in an organized manner, we use a spreadsheet we call the Interest Research Template. To grab a copy of the Interest Research Template please go to www.perrymarshall.com/fbtools.

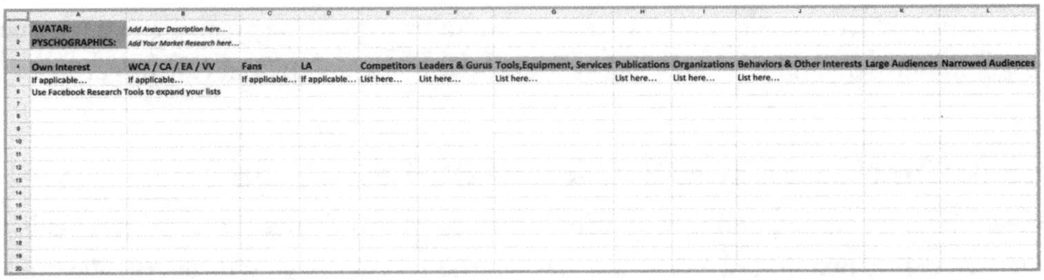

FIGURE 23.3

Let me take you on a quick tour of the spreadsheet (see Figure 23.3).

AVATAR: Describe your avatar

PYSCHOGRAPHICS: Who are these people? What are their struggles, desires, and concerns?

OWN INTEREST: Are you or your client a targetable interest on Facebook?

WCA/CA/EA/VV: Audience assets—website custom audiences, custom audiences, engagement audiences, video view audiences, etc.

FANS: How many fans do you or your client have?

LA: Based on your Audience Assets, are there any lookalike audiences that should be created?

THE SIX BRAINSTORMING TRIGGERS

The next six columns are present to help stimulate ideas for potential interests. The six triggers include:

- Competitors
- Leaders and gurus in your market
- Tools/Equipment/Services
- Publications (could include blogs, TV shows, books, magazines, or podcasts)
- Organizations your avatar might belong to
- Other Behavior—basically other ideas that don't fit into any of the other categories.

In each column, list any ideas that come to mind. Keep in mind, during the Brainstorming phase, there's no right or wrong answers. We're just trying to capture as many ideas as possible into our spreadsheet. We will use the remaining steps to sort through this list and figure out the best of the best.

The last two columns are for Larger Audiences and Narrowed Audiences. Larger audiences are defined as three million+. We'll cover how to use these last two columns later in Step Three.

AUDIENCE RESEARCH TOOLS

Facebook's Audience Research Tools have gotten so good that now you only need a limited number of brainstormed ideas in order to come up with a lengthy list of potential targeting options.

The two tools we recommend are:

1. Power Editor Suggestion Tool
2. Audience Insights

Power Editor Suggestion Tool

The Power Editor Suggestion Tool is currently our number-one recommendation for looking for targetable interests. The reason I recommend it as number one is because if you find an appropriate interest using the Power Editor's Suggestion Tool, you know it's an actual interest you can target; this is not always the case when you use Audience Insights.

Here's how you use it:

1. Create a Test Campaign using the Power Editor.
2. At the Ad Set Level, enter the interest from your spreadsheet and click "Suggestions."

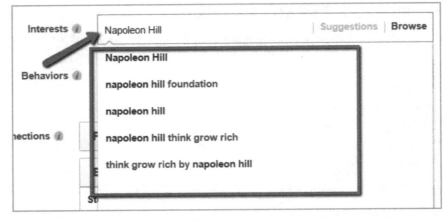

FIGURE 23.4

A list of interests that Facebook feels is related to your root interest will be displayed (see Figure 23.4). Hover over the new potential interests to see the potential reach. If it's more than 100,000, record in your spreadsheet.

Repeat the process by entering another interest from your spreadsheet until you feel that you've exhausted the options and you're starting to see the same interests over and over again.

User Tip: Try and record the actual potential reach in your spreadsheet during this Step. This will save you time in Step Two.

Audience Insights

Audience Insights is a free Facebook tool located in your Facebook Ads Manager (Figure 23.5).

FIGURE 23.5

Select "Everyone on Facebook," as well as avatar specific demographics, such as age, gender, and location. See Figure 23.6.

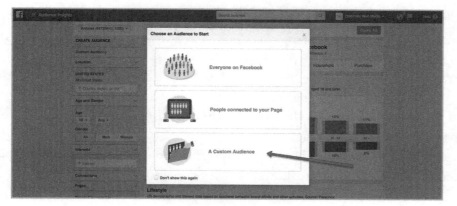

FIGURE 23.6

FIGURE 23.7

From your initial brainstorming, enter one of your interests from your spreadsheet.

Click over to the "Page Likes," and look through this list for appropriate interests to record onto your spreadsheet. See Figure 23.8 on page 260.

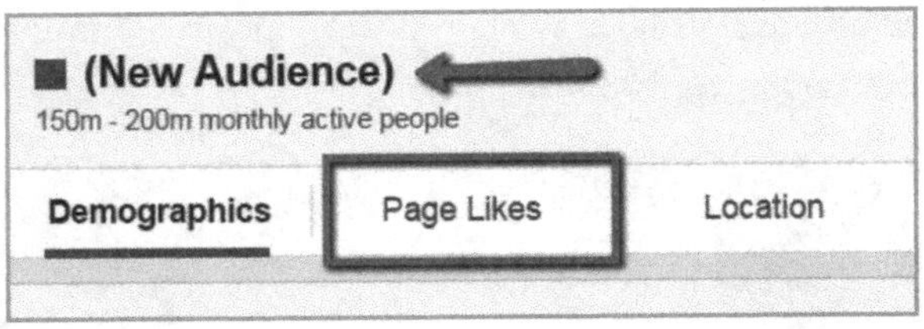

(New Audience)
150m - 200m monthly active people
Demographics
Page Likes
Location

FIGURE 23.8

If you're not familiar with the interest, you can either Google it or click on the links to open up their Facebook page.

User Tip: If you can't think of any ideas using the Audience Research Template, search for authority figures in your market on Google or on Amazon.

Data Guru

And if you're really stuck, Facebook now has a "request help" option inside audience insight. See Figure 23.9.

(New Audience)
People on Facebook
Demographics
Page Likes
Location
Activity
Household
Purchase
Age and Gender
54% Women
46% Men
Lifestyle
Selected Audience
Compare

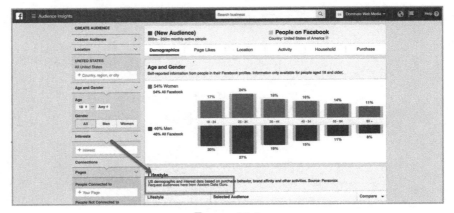

FIGURE 23.9

By clicking here and filling out a form, you can get a Facebook strategists to provide recommendations in as little as 24 to 48 hours. In our experience, we have had mixed results with these recommendations, but it can be a last resort if you're really struggling.

If you're lucky enough to have a Facebook Partner Manager, they can also provide target suggestions as well as provide targeting options that are not available to the general public. (Unfortunately, Partner Manager support is not available to everyone and is granted on an invitation only basis.)

ANALYZING YOUR ASSETS

Another great way to generate ideas is to let Facebook analyze your Warm Audiences. Since Facebook likes data, the larger the audience the better. The best and largest warm audiences to start with for most people include:

- Fans
- Website Custom Audience—All sites in the last 180 days
- Custom Audience—All leads
- Custom Audience—All customers
- Video View Audiences—10 seconds or 25 percent—you will only have this if you've been running Video Ads.

Load these audiences inside Audience Insights.

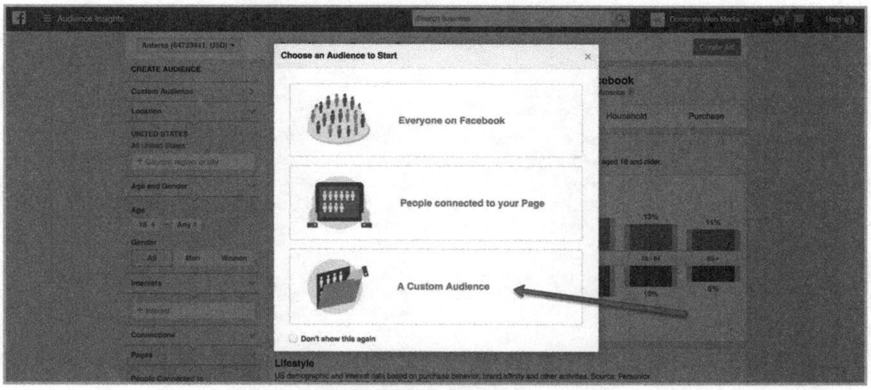

FIGURE 23.10

To get demographic information, you need at least an audience size of 1,000.

To see Page Likes, you need at least 100,000. You may need to combine several relevant audiences to have a large enough sample size (see Figure 23.10).

One thing to point out is when you're looking at demographics; the numbers listed above and below the bar graphs are the percentages of that gender not the percentage of the overall market. For example, in Figure 23.11 on page 262, "Female 45 to 54" does not make up 37 percent of the entire market, it's 37 percent of 39 percent (14.43 percent of the overall market).

Click over on Page Likes and record appropriate interests into your Audience Research Template spreadsheet. See Figure 23.12 on page 262.

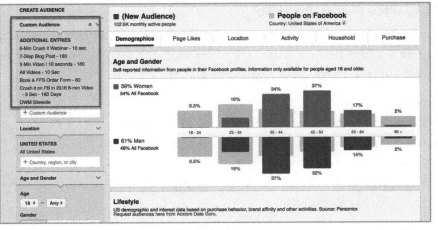

FIGURE 23.11

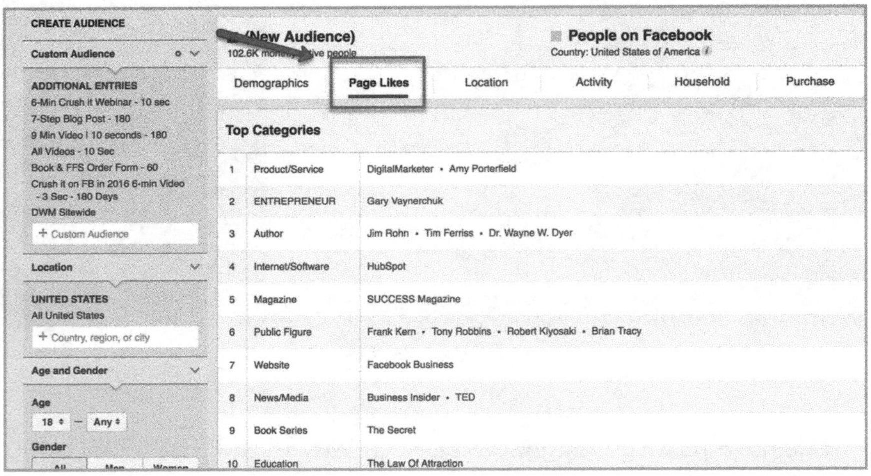

FIGURE 23.12

STEP TWO: CONFIRM

If you've used the Power Editor Suggestion Tool and already entered all the potential reaches into your spreadsheet, you may be able to skip this step.

If you've found an interest in Audience Insights, you still need to confirm it's an actual targetable interest in the Power Editor. It can be frustrating but sometimes, an insight will show up in Audience Insights but won't show up in the Power Editor.

When confirming an interest, make sure to also record the potential reach for that audience.

Potential Audience Reach Recommendations

Our recommendation for potential reach is to use a large audience. We define large audiences as 400,000 to two million if including the U.S. in your targeting.

In our experience, we've found that campaigns work better when using larger audiences. We believe this to be the case because we're leveraging the power of the Facebook algorithm to help choose who, within our potential reach, might be most suited to see our ad, rather than us trying to do this manually by separating audiences and testing them individually.

Targeting Outside the U.S.

The 400,000 to two million potential reach is appropriate if the U.S. is part of your targeting audience. For smaller population countries, we recommend 100,000 to 500,000.

STEP THREE: ORGANIZE

The next step is to organize the interests in your spreadsheet into categories. Start with the categories already listed in the spreadsheet, but also look for similar themed interests that you can further sub-categorize. Then, order your interests from largest potential reach to smallest.

By organizing interests into subcategories, this will allow you to combine relevant interests that don't match the potential reach requirements with other smaller potential reach audiences, giving a larger overall potential reach.

If a relevant interest has a potential reach of greater than three million, enter it into your "Large Audiences" column. For these large audiences, go back into your Power

A	B	C	D	E	F
AVATAR:	USA, Canada, UK, Australia 35+ M & F				
PYSCHOGRAPHICS:	Add Your Market Research here...				
Authors	**Bloggers**	**Internet Marketers**	**Agencies**	**Email Marketers**	**Narrow Large Audiences**
Writer (2.7m)	blogger (service) (2.9m)	Amy Porterfield (790k)	Asana/ Asana (software) (460k)	Digital marketing (960k)	Blog & Publishing (2.7m)
Hay House (1.4m)	online advertising (1.6m)	Gary Vaynerchuk (380k)	HubSpot (370k)	Email Marketing (410k)	Social Media & Publishing (2.2m)
Printer (publishing) (630k)	Digital marketing (960k)				Writing & Publishing (1.6m)
Print on demand (460k)	Copyblogger (805k)	**IM GURUS (1.1m)**	**SM & Marketing Tools (510k)**	**ESP & Email Mx (1m)**	Facebook Page Admins & Writing (1.1m)
The Writer's Circle (450k)	Web design (730k)	Frank Kern (260k)	Hootsuite (280k)	Mailchimp (260k)	
Creative writing (440k)	wix / wix.com (710k)	Lewis Howes (220k)	Moz (marketing software) (83k)	Email management (210k)	
	Social Media marketing (610k)	Ryan Deiss (180k)	Buffer (application) (61k)	GetResponse (120k)	
Self Publishing & Tools (810k)	Wordpress (400k)	James Wedmore (170k)	Marketo (53k)	Aweber (49k)	
Self-publishing (220k)		Mike Filsaime (160k)	SpyFu (33k)	Constant Contact (33k)	
blurb / blurb, inc. / blurb books (170k)	**Blog Platforms (660k)**	Life on Fire (150k)	Sprout Social (22k)	Opt-in email (27k)	
Smashwords (120k)	Weebly (220k)	Perry Marshall (120k)	Yoast (11k)	iContact (23k)	
Amazon Kindle Direct Publishing (110k)	WordPress.com (180k)	Eben Pagen (116k)	webtrends (9.7k)	Autoresponder (21k)	
Electronic publishing (97k)	Magento (130k)	Mari Smith (110k)	SEMRush (7.1k)	Campaign Monitor (4.5k)	
Scrivener / Scrivener (software) (43k)	Joomla (100k)	Russell Brunson (110k)	skyword (5.8k)	Email tracking (110k)	
createspace (29k)	Content management system (93k)	Mike Dillard (100k)	Kissmetrics (4.3k)	Infusionsoft (210k)	
alibris (16k)	Drupal (21k)		Studiopress (4.3k)	Kajabi (100k)	
AuthorHouse (15k)	Elegant Themes (14k)	**PPC (420k)**	Unbounce (3.6k)		
lulu (company) (69k)		Adwords (140k)	Wordtracker (2.7k)		
		Keyword Research (12k)	ahrefs (2.6k)		
		Pay Per Click (97k)	Optimizely (2.5k)		
		Facebook for Business (190k)			
			Communication Tools (410k)		
			GoToMeeting (250k)		
			Skype for Business (12k)		
			Join Me (37k)		
			Zoom Video Communications (27k)		

FIGURE 23.13

Editor and use the "Narrow" feature to see if you can find good combinations that give you a potential reach within the recommended guidelines. Enter those combinations into the "Combined Interests" column.

STEP FOUR: PRIORITIZE

The fourth and final step is to prioritize. Now, you want to look through your list and look for best possible matches to your avatar, your hook, and the potential reach you're looking for. Two questions that can help determine the best matches include:

1. Does this interest sound like my customer avatar, including where they are on the UPSYD framework?
2. Does a large percentage of this interest sound like my avatar?

Local Business Targeting

The good news is targeting for Local Businesses is typically easier than targeting for eCommerce and Digital/Information Businesses. For a local business, your targeting is primarily geographical with perhaps some demographic targeting. It is rare to use interest targeting.

GEOGRAPHIC TARGETING

There are basically two ways to geographical target. The first way is to type in a city. By choosing a city, you have the option of creating a radius around that city, anywhere from 10 miles to 50 miles. See Figure 23.14.

FIGURE 23.14

The second way is to "drop a pin." The advantage of dropping a pin is that it can create a radius around that pin—anywhere from one mile to 50 miles. See Figure 23.15.

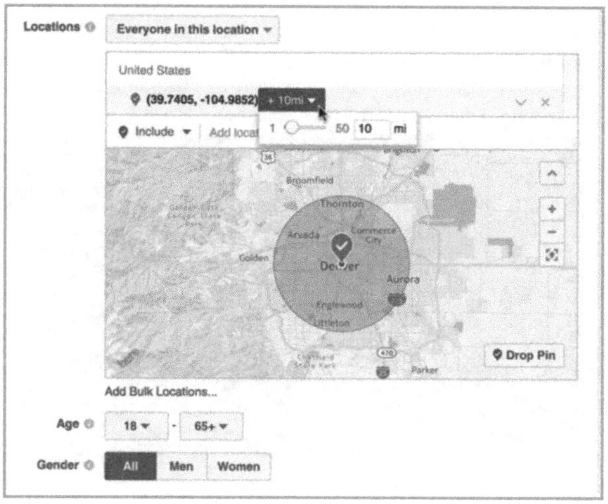

FIGURE 23.15

The challenge typically for local businesses is that their potential reach is smaller than our recommended guidelines unless of course you're located in a large metropolitan area. We'll talk about how to handle smaller audiences shortly.

How to Increase Your Radius

One way to increase your potential reach is to increase the size of your targeting radius, but this has to coincide with positioning your business so that people would be willing to travel to do business with you. The two best ways to do this are to become an authority/expert and use social proof.

The best way to create authority/expert status is to regularly post useful content to your market. That is why we recommend all Local Businesses should allocate some of their ad spend to a branding campaign.

What do we mean by social proof? You've probably seen this on ads in your newsfeed (see Figure 23.16 on page 266).

If Facebook shows you an ad, and one of your Facebook friends has liked the ad or the page, Facebook will display your friends on the ad.

HOW DOES AUTHORITY AND SOCIAL PROOF HELP MY LOCAL BUSINESS?

Let's use an example of a chiropractic practice.

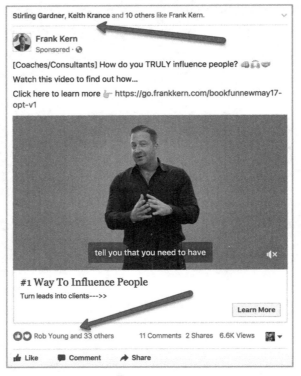

FIGURE 23.16

Chiropractic practices aren't uncommon so chances are, there are probably a couple of them within a few miles of your house. If I need chiropractic services and your office is located on the other side of town and there's a chiropractor a few blocks from me and I don't know anything about either of you, how likely is it that I'm going to travel all the way across town to come see you? Not likely, right?

But what if I've seen your name several times in my newsfeed over the last few months and I've seen you publish information about treatment for concussion in high school football players, and I see the parent of one of my son's friends has liked your page?

What if my son now happens to suffer a football related concussion—how much more likely is that that I would travel across town to come see you? A lot more likely, right?

TARGETING LARGE METROPOLITAN AREAS

If you're targeting a large metropolitan area, another targeting option is to create a 10 percent lookalike audience from your best custom audience and overlay that with your geographical and demographic targeting. Please note: you need a larger populated area for this strategy to work and give you enough potential reach.

TARGETING SMALLER AUDIENCES

So what do you do if you've found an audience that appears very relevant but is less than 400,000? This could also include warm audiences, which because they've already interacted with you and your brand, definitely should be marketed to.

The challenge with smaller audiences is that there's less inventory for your ads and more competition for those spots, so your ads will fatigue sooner, and you're not leveraging the power of the Facebook algorithm so it's challenging to scale.

Here's our recommendation for how to overcome this, but I have to warn you: this can be a lot more work.

1. Have several different ads in each ad set. Still only have one ad live at a time but have multiple ads in rotation so you can turn one off when it fatigues, such as your CPA (cost per acquisition) increases, and turn another ad on in its place.
2. Keep your budgets small.
3. You may need to change your bidding to impressions rather than conversions.

So now you know the process for finding your perfect audience on Facebook. Don't forget to download the Audience Research Template. You can find it at www. perrymarshall.com/fbtools.

Chapter 24

Audiences

One of the big attractions for advertising on Facebook is the potential option for targeting. *MIT Technology Review* once stated, "Facebook has collected the most extensive data set ever assembled on human social behavior" (Tom Simonite, June 2013, *MIT Technology Review* www.technologyreview.com/s/428150/what-facebook-knows/). As a business owner, having access to this incredible wealth of data and the ability to pinpoint your ads to a highly-targeted audience is truly a marketer's dream.

> "*There is your audience.*
> *There is the language.*
> *These are the words that they use.*"
>
> —Eugene Schwartz

But there's also a challenge from having so many options. It's kind of being like a kid in a candy store. You're so busy looking around it's hard to know where to start. It can quickly become overwhelming.

In this chapter, we're going to provide you with a powerful yet simple framework for thinking about your Facebook audiences and show you how and where to start. Then in the next chapter, provide a simple process for performing your interest research.

WARM AND COLD AUDIENCES

The easiest way to visualize targeting on Facebook is to think about warm and cold audiences. Warm audiences can be defined as people who have already had contact with your business. Examples include your fans, website visitors, people who have engaged with your ads, or people who have engaged with your Facebook page.

Warm audiences are audiences unique to your business and are based on the data your business collects. That collection can be via your CRM (customer relationship management system, such as Infusionsoft, aWeber, Salesforce, etc.), hits on your Facebook pixel, views to your videos, and visits to your fan page.

Cold audiences can be defined as people who are not familiar with or haven't interacted with your business. In reality, that's the vast majority of people on Facebook. To be successful on Facebook you need to target both warm and cold audiences.

You've probably heard the old business advice that "it's cheaper to keep an existing customer than attract a new one." Warm audiences follow this advice. Warm audiences can be your existing customer base or people moving through your customer buying cycle. On Facebook, warm audiences also serve a significant secondary role. They can be leveraged to help you find targeted cold audiences. We'll talk more about lookalike audiences later in this chapter.

Cold audiences are vital for scaling your business. A business can't grow unless it attracts new customers, but don't just show your marketing message to anyone; get your message in front of people who are most likely to be interested in your offer. See Figure 24.1.

To find highly targetable colds audiences on Facebook you have two options. The first is to leverage Facebook's incredible collection of user data. This includes, but is not limited to: location, demographics, interests, behaviors, and offline spending activity gathered from partnerships with third data companies. In the next chapter, we'll go into detail on how to perform interest research.

The second and perhaps the most powerful source for cold audiences is combining your data with Facebook's to create lookalike audiences. In other words, allowing

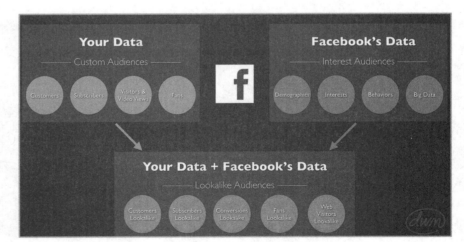

FIGURE 24.1–Facebook Targeting Options

Facebook's powerful algorithms to analyze your fans and custom audiences in order to find more people who are just like your best leads and customers.

There's a synergy between warm and cold audiences on Facebook. You need warm audiences to get better at targeting cold audiences, but you also need cold audiences to build your warm audiences. This is why it's so important to start collecting your own data inside Facebook ASAP. Let's show you how to do that.

WARM AUDIENCES

Warm audiences on Facebook can come from two different sources—fans and custom audiences. These two types of warm audiences are unique to your business as they consist of only people who have interacted with your business. Fans are automatically stored as a targetable audience in Facebook, so there's nothing additional you need to do. For custom audiences, there are four different types defined by the source they're created from. The four include:

1. Your Contact Lists—Leads and Customers
2. Engagement on Facebook
3. Website Visitors
4. Mobile App Engagement

You can make up to 500 different custom audiences per single ad account.

CUSTOM AUDIENCE—CONTACTS

Facebook allows you to upload your leads or customer information to Facebook. Facebook then tries to match these people to a Facebook user. Data that can be uploaded includes email addresses, phone numbers, first name, last name, city, state/province, country, date of birth, year of birth, age, zip/postal code, gender, mobile advertiser ID, or Facebook ID.

User Tip: Always make sure you have permission to collect information before uploading to Facebook. It's a violation of Facebook Policy to scrape data.

How to Create a Custom Audience from a Contact List

Step One: In a spreadsheet with one contact per row, add unique contact data to each column. Save as a **CSV file.**

Step Two: In Facebook's Ads Manager—Go to **Audiences** (see Figure 24.2 on page 272).

Step Three: Click **Create Audience** and from the drop-down, select **Custom Audience.**

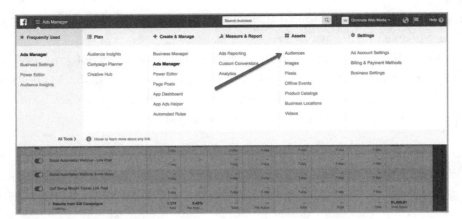

FIGURE 24.2–How to Find Audiences in Your Ads Manager

Step Four: Click **Customer File** (see Figure 24.3).

Step Five: Click **Add From Your Own File,** and Select the appropriate file.

Step Six: Edit **Data Mapping**—matching the spreadsheet column with data type.

Step Seven: **Upload** and **Create**

FIGURE 24.3–Custom Audience Options

User Tip: The more data types you provide, the better Facebook is at matching your contact to a user's Facebook profile. So, it's much better to submit first name, last name, email, phone number, city, and zip code than just an email.

Update: At the time of this writing, Facebook just released a new feature that allows you to upload your customer's lifetime value as an additional data field. So now you can create lookalike audiences based off your highest value customers!

CUSTOM AUDIENCE—ENGAGEMENT

An engagement custom audience is a collection of people who have engaged with your business on Facebook. This can include watching a video ad, opening a lead form, visiting your canvas, or interacting with your Facebook page. See Figure 24.4 below.

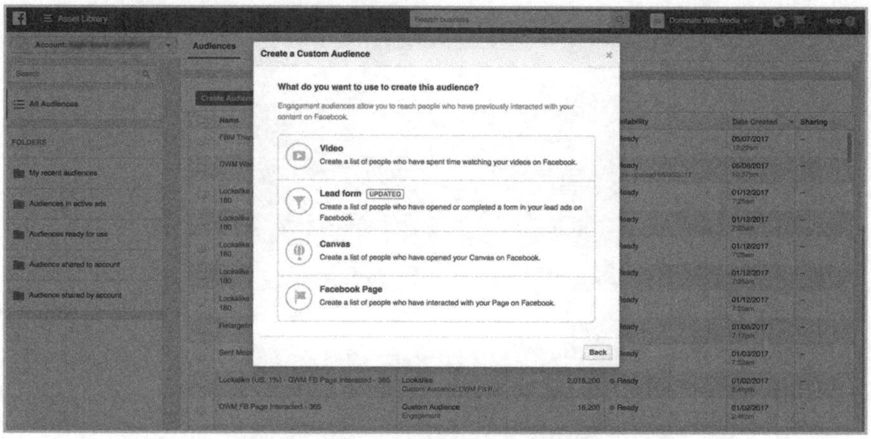

FIGURE 24.4–Engagement Custom Audience Options

When you create an engagement custom audience, you must specify a timeframe that the engagement occurred in. These audiences are dynamic, meaning new people are added as they engage with your business on Facebook while other people are removed from the audience as the engagement passes the specified time window.

How to Create a Custom Audience from a Video View

Step One: In Facebook's Ads Manager—Go to **Audiences**

Step Two: Click **Create Audience**, and from the drop-down, select **Custom Audience**

Step Three: Click **Engagement**

Step Four: Click **Video**

Step Five: In **Engagement** field—choose amount of viewing time, e.g., 3 sec, 10 sec, 25 percent, 50 percent, 75 percent, 95 percent, etc.

Step Six: Click **Choose Video**

Step Seven: Choose **Campaign**, **Page** or **Instagram Business Profile**

Step Eight: Enter **Number of Days** to go back and collect video views (Up to 365 days)

Step Nine: Add **Name** and **Description**

Step Ten: Click **Save**

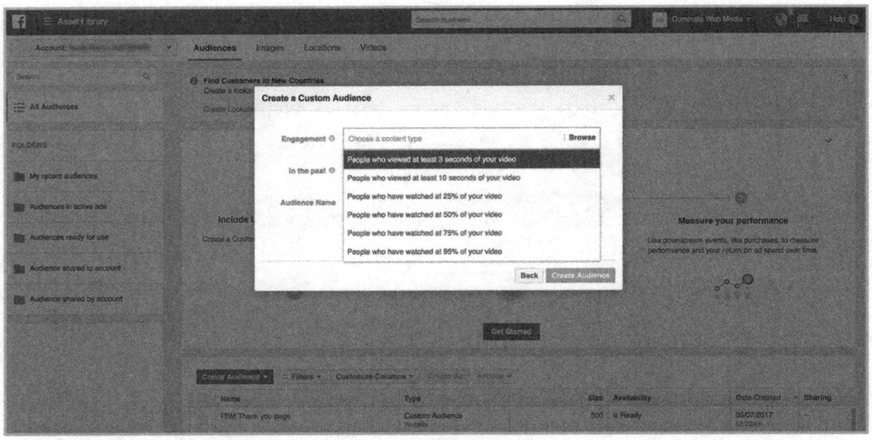

FIGURE 24.5–Video View Engagement Audience

How to Create a Custom Audience from Lead Forms

Step One: In Facebook's Ads Manager—Go to **Audiences**

Step Two: Click **Create Audience**, and from the drop-down, select **Custom Audience**

Step Three: Click **Engagement**

Step Four: Click **Lead Ad**

Step Five: Select the **Form**

Step Six: Select the type of **Engagement**

Step Seven: Enter **Number of Days** to go back and collect (up to 90 days)

Step Eight: Add **Name** and **Description**

Step Nine: Click **Save**

FIGURE 24.6–Lead Form Engagement Audience

How to Create a Custom Audience from Canvas Engagement

Step One: In Facebook's Ads Manager—Go to **Audiences**

Step Two: Click **Create Audience**, and from the drop-down, select **Custom Audience**

Step Three: Click **Engagement**

Step Four: Click **Canvas**

Step Five: Select the **Canvas**

Step Six: Select the type of **Engagement**

Step Seven: Enter **Number of Days** to go back and collect (up to 365 days)

Step Eight: Add **Name** and **Description**

Step Nine: Click **Save**

FIGURE 24.7–Canvas Engagement Audience

How to Create a Custom Audience from Page Engagement

Step One: In Facebook's Ads Manager—Go to **Audiences**

Step Two: Click **Create Audience**, and from the drop-down, select **Custom Audience**

Step Three: Click **Engagement**

Step Four: Click **Page**

Step Five: Select the **Page**

Step Six: Select the type of **Engagement**

Step Seven: Enter **Number of Days** to go back and collect (up to 365 days)

Step Eight: Add **Name** and **Description**

Step Nine: Click **Save**

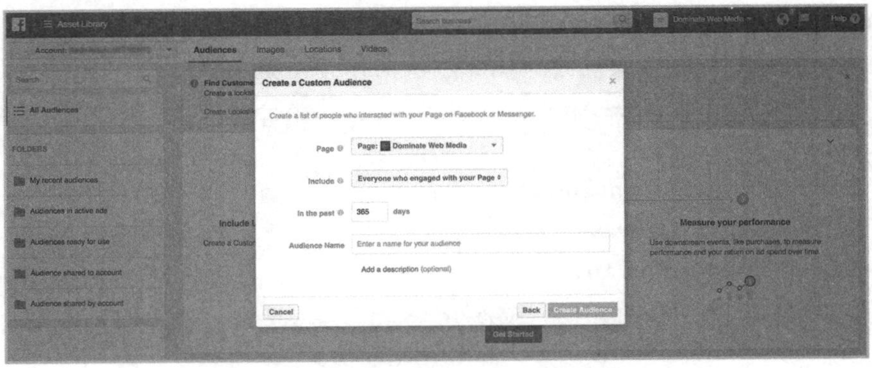

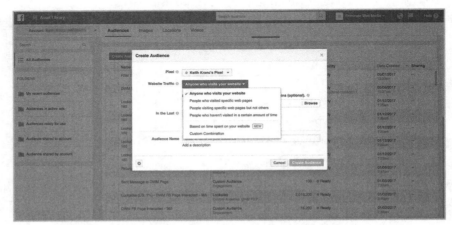

FIGURE 24.8–Page Engagement Audience

WEBSITE CUSTOM AUDIENCES

Website custom audiences contains people who have visited your website while being logged into their Facebook account. Please note you can only create a website custom audience if you have the Facebook Pixel installed on your website/web pages.

When you create a website custom audience, you must specify a timeframe that the visit has occurred in, e.g., any time within the last 180 days. These audiences are dynamic meaning new people are added as they visit your website while other people are removed from the audience as their visit passes the specified time window.

How to Create a Website Custom Audience

Step One: In Facebook's Ads Manager—Go to **Audiences**

Step Two: Click **Create Audience**, and from the drop-down, select **Custom Audience**

Step Three: Choose a **Pixel**

FIGURE 24.9–Website Custom Audience Options

Step Four: Set a **Rule Selection** (Start with an Inclusive Rule—you can add up to four more Inclusive or Exclusive Rules per audience for a total of five)

Step Five: Enter **Number of Days** to go back and collect (up to 180 days)

Step Six: Add **Name** and **Description**

Step Seven: Click **Create Audience**

Rule Selection–Standard Rules

All Website Visitors: Everyone who has visited your website in the last 180 days or less.

URL Contains: Anyone who has visited a URL containing the following values

URL Doesn't Contain: Anyone who has visited a URL that doesn't contain the following values

URL Equals: Anyone who has visited a specific URL (please note: must be an exact URL)

Frequency: Anyone who has visited a particular number of times

Device: Anyone who has visited using a specific device

Visitors by Time Spent: Visitors who've spent the most time on your website

Rule Selection–Pixel Event

URL: Anyone who has visited a specific URL

Frequency: Anyone who has visited a specified number of times

Device: Anyone who has visited using a specific device

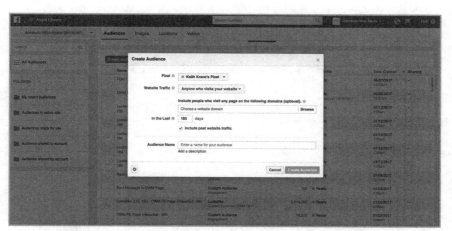

FIGURE 24.10–Website Custom Audience Selection Rules

APP ENGAGEMENT CUSTOM AUDIENCES

App engagement custom audiences allow you to create an audience from people who have engaged with your app. An app can be an Apple App, Android App, or Facebook App.

To create an app engagement custom audience, you need to provide Facebook with your mobile advertising IDs so Facebook can identify who is using your mobile app. There are the three types of mobile advertiser IDs that Facebook supports:

- Apple's Advertising Identifier (IDFA)
- Android's Advertising ID
- Facebook App User IDs

Setting Up App Events

Before you can create an app engagement custom audience, you need to register your app and set up trackable events. Setting up trackable events is done by sending app event information to Facebook via Facebook' s SDK. Events can be one of the 14 pre-defined events such as "added to cart" in an eCommerce app or "level achieved" in a game. Events can also be customized to be unique to your app.

For more information about setting up app events, we recommend visiting Facebook's developer site:

> *IOS*—https://developers.facebook.com/docs/app-events/ios
>
> *Andriod*—https://developers.facebook.com/docs/app-events/android

How to Create an App Engagement Custom Audience

Step One: In Facebook's Ads Manager—Go to **Audiences**

FIGURE 24.11–App Engagement Custom Audience Options

Step Two: Click **Create Audience**, and from the drop-down, select **Custom Audience**

Step Three: Select **App Activity**

Step Four: Add **Name** and **Description**

Step Five: Click **Action Taken** (will display events your app is currently measuring)

Step Six: Enter **Number of Days** to go back and collect (up to 180 days)

Step Seven: Click **Create Audience**

LOOKALIKE AUDIENCES

Lookalike audiences are a great way to scale your campaigns and reach new people who might be interested in your business. Lookalike audiences are created by Facebook but are based, off of your best existing audiences. So, before you can create a lookalike audience, you need to have either fans or have created a custom audience, i.e., your source audience.

Basically, Facebook has an algorithm that can analyze your source audience and quickly and efficiently search its member base and find more people who are similar, e.g., demographics, location, interests, and behaviors.

Obviously the larger the source audience is and the more like your ideal customer the source audiences is, the better quality the lookalike audience will be. Facebook generally recommends a source audience between 1,000 to 50,000 people.

User Tip: If you don't have 1,000 customers yet, you might need to use a higher step in your sales funnel. For example, if you only have 200 customers but have 4,000 leads, the leads might be a better source audience. Keep in mind a lead is not the same as a customer, so sometimes, it's a trade-off between providing more data vs. quality of data. There's not always a definite answer here; you need to test different targeting options to see which performs best.

Other important items to know about lookalike audiences:

- Lookalike audiences are country-specific. You must identify the country or countries when creating a lookalike audience.
- Your source audience must contain a minimum of 100 people from the same country, but the 100 people don't have to be from the country you want to target. So you can have a source audience of 1,000 people in the U.S. and create a lookalike audience of similar people in the United Kingdom.
- You can select the size of your lookalike audience by selecting the percentage of that country's population, e.g., 1 to 10 percent.
- You can create up to 500 lookalike audiences from a single source audience.
- People in your source audience will be excluded from your lookalike audience unless you use a pixel as your source audience.

How to Create a Lookalike Audience

Step One: In Facebook's Ads Manager—Go to **Audiences**

Step Two: Click **Create Audience**, and from the drop-down, select **Lookalike Audience**

Step Three: Choose your **Source**

Step Four: Select **Country/Countries**

Step Five: Select desired **Audience Size** (1 to 10 percent of population)

Step Six: Click **Create Audience**

FIGURE 24.12–Creating Lookalike Audiences

More important things to know about lookalike audiences:

■ Please allow 6 to 24 hours for Facebook to create your lookalike audience.

■ Lookalike audiences will automatically update as long as your source audience is updating and you're using the lookalike audience in your ad targeting.

■ If something doesn't look right, e.g., not updating or incorrect size, try recreating your lookalike audience.

Update: At the time of this writing, Facebook just released a new feature, which allows you to include the field of Customer Lifetime Value in your custom audiences. Facebook can use this information to create lookalike audiences that are just like your most valuable customers.

TARGETING GAME PLAN—THE FOUR AD SET GROUPS

So now that you know how to set up your custom and lookalike audiences, in the next chapter, we'll discuss how to further leverage Facebook's data to create more cold audiences by performing interest research, but for now let's look at how to put these different targeting options together to come up with a Targeting Game Plan.

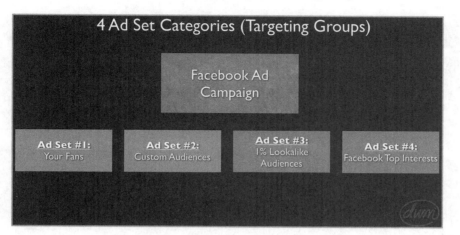

FIGURE 24.13–The Four Ad Set Groups

Think of your targeting as four main categories (see Figure 24.13). Orange represents warm audiences and the blue represents cold audiences. Ideally, you want to be targeting audiences in all four of these categories—basically having your campaigns firing on all four cylinders. But if you're just starting off, you may have to rely on just Ad Set Group #4 until you build up your numbers to make the other three work. You may have to initially use Interest Targeting while building up your fans and custom audiences, which in turn, will be great source audiences for your lookalike audiences.

The four ad set categories include:

1. *Ad Set Category #1—Your Fans*. Fans are typically a great source, not only for ROI but also to generate positive comments, shares, and likes (social proof) on your ads, but only if you've generated fans the right way (as discussed previously in this book). The reason it's listed as number one is because we often launch campaigns to our fans first to get some social love.

2. *Ad Set Category #2—Your Custom Audiences*. Custom audiences generally generate better ROI than cold audiences. This is because these are people who are already familiar with your brand. Similar to fans, the power of these audiences increase as their size grows.

3. *Ad Set Category #3—1 Percent Lookalike Audiences*. Lookalike audiences are a great source for new prospects. These audiences will too become more powerful as the source audience grows.

4. *Ad Set Category #4—Interests and Behaviors*. This is often where most campaigns start. This is where you tell Facebook which audiences sound most like your pros-

pects. We usually recommend starting with 5 to 20 interests. Even in successful campaigns we take over at the agency, we still use interest targeting.

YOUR FACEBOOK TARGETING GAME PLAN

Figure 24.14 shows a simple yet powerful game plan for your targeting on Facebook. This is what to aim for, so don't worry if you don't have all of these assets yet. Here's what to do:

Step One: Start with Ad Set #4—Interest Targeting.

Step Two: As you build your Audiences, start including Ad Set Categories #1 and #2.

Step Three: As you start to see conversions from Ad Set Categories #1 and #2, add lookalike audiences from Ad Set Group #3.

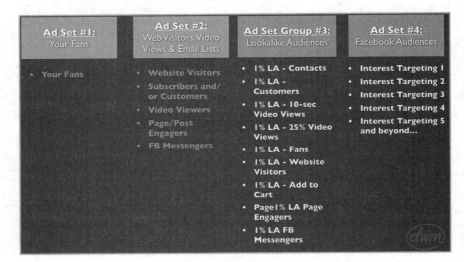

FIGURE 24.14–Your Targeting Game Plan

This game plan may need to be customized to fit your specific business, but as a general rule, this is a great reference and the best place to start for most businesses advertising on Facebook.

Chapter 25

One Pixel to Rule Them All

Guest Author Andrew Tweito

In Chapter 7, we learned about the three main functions of the Facebook Pixel and how they will help you improve your Facebook advertising performance:

1. Reach the right people (Audience Building)
2. Drive more sales (Optimization)
3. Measure your results (Tracking and Analytics)

In this chapter, our goal is to help you understand HOW to implement the Facebook Pixel for your business so that you can fully leverage the Facebook Pixel's incredible technology to drive the strongest results for your ads.

> *"Never be guided in any way by ads that are untracked."*
>
> —CLAUDE HOPKINS, *SCIENTIFIC ADVERTISING*

In order to accomplish that goal, we're going to go through the details of the Facebook Pixel in a sequential way so that, even if you're not a "techie," you can understand why you're going to set up the Facebook Pixel a certain way for your business, what the Pixel's features and limitations are, and you can understand some of the nuances that cause many advertisers headaches down-the-road.

To begin, we first need to understand how the Facebook Pixel actually works and what "Standard Events" and parameters are.

HOW THE FACEBOOK PIXEL WORKS: THE "BASE PIXEL"

When we say "Facebook Pixel," we're actually referring to a piece of javascript code that's placed on your website. This block of javascript code is essentially the same for all advertisers, where the only unique part of this code is the "Facebook Pixel ID" that tells Facebook that any activity sent from your pixel should align with your ad account.

This common block of javascript is commonly referred to as the "Base Pixel" or "Base Pixel Code." Think of this code as the foundation of any data that you'll send Facebook.

You can get your "Facebook Base Pixel Code" by going to your Facebook Business Manager → opening the main menu in the top-left of the screen, and going to "Pixels" under the "Assets" submenu column, as seen in Figure 25.1.

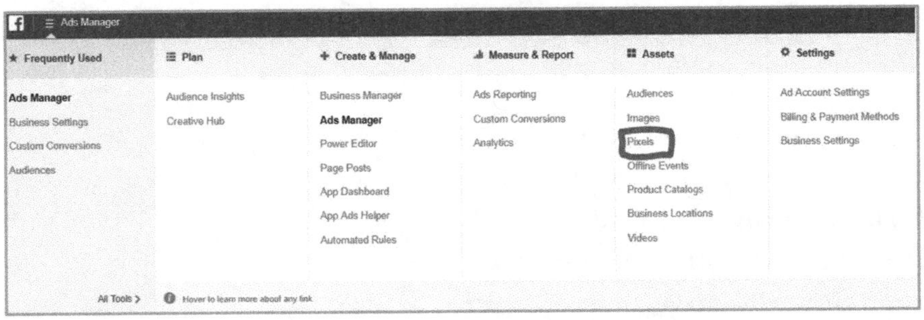

FIGURE 25.1–Pixels Navigation

If you have a new Facebook Ad Account, you'll be prompted to set up your pixel on this screen. You should do this ASAP after creating your ad account. The process to set up your pixel is straightforward, just follow the prompts, and then, you'll be given your "Base Pixel Code" at the conclusion of the setup wizard.

If you have an existing Facebook Ad Account, you can view your code by going to the Pixels screen and then click "Actions" → "View Pixel Code", as seen in Figure 25.2.

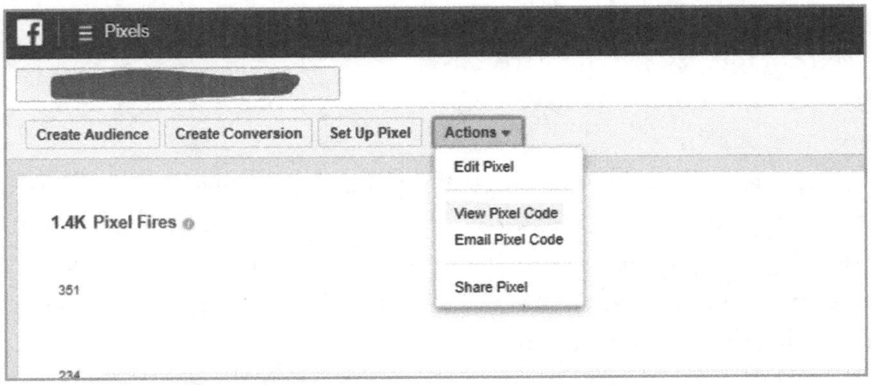

FIGURE 25.2–View Pixel Code

On the subsequent pop-up, you'll see "1 Install Pixel Base Code," and inside this section, you'll find your Base Pixel Code, which will look like this:

```
<!-- Facebook Pixel Code -->
<script>
!function(f,b,e,v,n,t,s){if(f.fbq)return;n=f.fbq=function(){n.callMethod?
n.callMethod.apply(n,arguments):n.queue.push(arguments)};if(!f._fbq)f._
fbq=n;
n.push=n;n.loaded=!0;n.version='2.0';n.queue=[];t=b.createElement(e);t.
async=!0;
t.src=v;s=b.getElementsByTagName(e)[0];s.parentNode.insertBefore(t,s)}
(window,
document,'script','https://connect.facebook.net/en_US/fbevents.js');
fbq('init', '{{YourFBPIXELID}}'); // Insert your pixel ID here.
fbq('track', 'PageView');
</script>
<noscript><img height="1" width="1" style="display:none"
src="https://www.facebook.com/tr?id={{YourFBPIXELID}}&ev=PageView&nos
cript=1"
/></noscript>
<!-- DO NOT MODIFY -->
<!-- End Facebook Pixel Code -->
```

In the code above, the {{YourFBPIXELID}} parts will be replaced by your actual Facebook Pixel ID, which is just a number that is unique to your ad account.

In the next section, we'll talk about how to install this Base Pixel Code on your website, but for now, let's review what this code actually DOES.

Let me issue a strong warning here: do NOT be intimidated by the "code" we're about to walk through. By understanding what's actually happening with your Facebook Pixel as a result of this code being run, it will enable you to grasp more advanced concepts in the following sections and ultimately **understand how to leverage this technology to its fullest-extent to improve the results of your advertising.**

The Facebook Base Pixel Code should be set up to fire on all pages of your website when the page loads.

Essentially, the Base Pixel Code does the following:

- Notifies Facebook's Ad Tracking servers that there is an active visitor on your site and asks for Facebook to send back some "functions" that will help you send data properly to their servers.

- Facebook's servers respond by confirming the "notification" and passing back to your site a set of "functions" (many of which do things behind the scenes), including the most important function: fbq. This fbq function is used to send specific data to the Facebook Ad Tracking servers in a language that Facebook's servers understand.

- In lines 8–9 of your Base Pixel Code, we see the first use of this fbq function. First, the fbq ('init', {{YourFBPIXELDI}}); function "initializes" your pixel. This is basically saying: "Hey Facebook, any data or activity sent from this page should be associated with this Pixel ID." This ensures that your site visitor's behavior is correctly attributed to your ad account.

- In line 9, we see the first "event" that we will track for our site visitors. Fbq ('track', 'PageView'); tells Facebook's servers to register a "PageView" EVENT. What you don't see in this line of code is what's going on behind the scenes that makes everything work. Not only are we telling Facebook to register a PageView event associated with your pixel/ad account, but the event data that actually goes out to Facebook's servers includes:
  - The URL (address) of the current page
  - The visitor's unique Facebook User ID
  - Timestamp of the event
  - Other "helper" data that's less important for our purposes

- So, after the Base Pixel Code fires and all of these things occur, Facebook now knows the following about the actions occurring on your site:
  - Who is on your site (based on the Facebook User ID)
  - What page they're viewing (based on the page URL)
  - The Facebook Pixel ID that corresponds to this action
  - The Ad Account(s) that are related to the Facebook Pixel ID

- Further, since we now have the fbq function available on our page, we're now ready to send other EVENTS based on what actually happens on this page, if we would like.

WHAT ARE EVENTS AND "STANDARD EVENTS"?
WHY ARE THEY IMPORTANT?

In the world of the Facebook Pixel, an "Event" is an action that occurs on your site that you'd like Facebook to know about so that you can later use this data to build audiences, track conversions, and help Facebook understand WHO is taking the desired actions as a result of your advertising (so that Facebook can target your ads more precisely to people who are similar to the "converters").

We've already seen an example of an "Event" —the "PageView" event that fires as part of the Facebook Base Pixel Code. The Facebook Pixel typically works with a predefined set of events that correspond to the key actions that advertisers tend to want to track. This predefined set of events is called "Standard Events."

In Facebook's Advertising Help section you can see the full list of Standard Events, but some of the most common Standard Events that are used are:

1. *Lead*: typically used when someone opts-in to your email list or other follow-up channels.
2. *Purchase*: fired when a purchase occurs.
3. *Complete Registration*: sometimes used for Webinar Registrations, Event Registrations, etc.
4. *Add To Cart*: when the visitor adds a product to their shopping cart
5. *Initiate Checkout*: when the visitor goes to the checkout form before purchasing

The actual events that you will use in your Facebook Pixel implementation depends on your business/funnel setup. Further, it's important to note that, aside from the Purchase event, Facebook doesn't actually know or care when/how you fire these events. The names of the events themselves don't carry any special meaning.

For example, if you decide that anytime someone visits your "Contact Us" page, you'd like to fire the "AddToCart" event, Facebook would not care that the way you're using the event is not contextually accurate.

Of course, the best practice is to try and fire the Standard Event with the right contextual meaning in the right circumstances so as to avoid confusion when you or your team are reviewing your ad performance results.

OK, so now that we know what Standard Events are, let's look at a very basic example of the code that sends Facebook the Standard Event data:

```
<script>
fbq('track', 'Lead');
</script>
```

Pretty simple right? It looks almost exactly like the PageView event we sent earlier.

You might be wondering: OK, but where would I add this code? We'll talk through implementation options in the next section, but for now, let's just say that this code can fire **almost** anywhere in the page source.

One common misconception is that this code needs to be included as part of the "Base Pixel Code" block of code. This is not true, and in many cases, it will make your implementation harder to setup.

I said "almost anywhere" earlier because there is one limitation: the event code should be present on your page AFTER the "Base Pixel Code" (in terms of where the code is placed in the page code, from top-to-bottom) to ensure the event will fire and work properly.

Typically, you'll place your Base Pixel Code in the <head> . . . </head> of your site's pages and the event code somewhere in the <body>. . . </body> to help avoid the situation where the event code is called before the Base Pixel Code has had time to run completely.

Further, there are times when you might want to fire your event code on the click of a button or on the submission of a form. This is also possible, and we'll cover that in the more advanced implementation scenarios.

How will you use these Standard Events? Many ways:

1. *Tracking and Measurement.* You'll notice that Standard Events align with the "columns"/metrics that you can use in Ads Manager for reporting on results
2. *Audience Construction.* When you go to the "Audiences" section of your Business Manager account and create a new "Custom Audience" based on "Website Traffic," you can choose the "Custom Combination" option and then change the dropdown from "URL" to "Event," and then specify which events should be used to include and exclude people from your audience.

For example, let's say you want to create an audience of people who have added a product to their cart but not purchased. You can do this like you see in Figure 25.3.

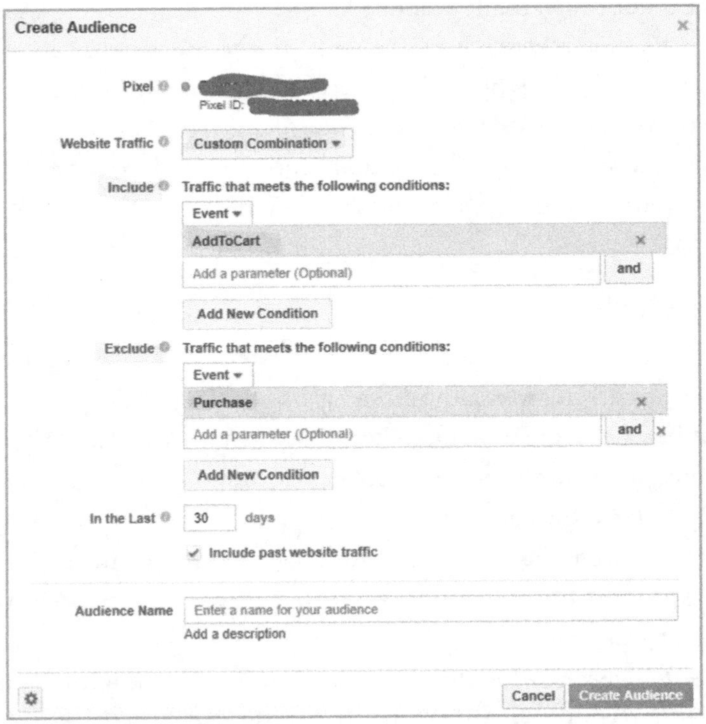

FIGURE 25.3–Custom Combination

3. *Optimization*. When you set up a new website conversion campaign at the ad set level, you designate an "Optimization Event." From this dropdown, you can select the event (usually a Standard Event) for which you'd like Facebook to optimize your ad delivery.

   Basically, you're telling Facebook: "look for people who do this certain event, and then find more people similar to them to prioritize my ad's delivery." Facebook's Machine Learning then handles the heavy lifting of determining who these "similar" people are and then taking appropriate actions to increase the odds that your ad will be shown to them.

Remember that we stated that the "Purchase" event is somewhat unique? The reason is, when we fire a purchase event, Facebook wants more information than just stating that a purchase occurred. They want to know the same thing you do: how much was the purchase worth exactly? And now we get into our last topic regarding the Facebook pixel components: parameters.

WHAT ARE PARAMETERS? WHY AND HOW ARE THEY USED?

In order to send the value associated with a purchase event, we need a way to add a "descriptor" to the event. The way we do this is through parameters. Parameters are a third section of the fbq function that contains a "payload" of descriptors that help Facebook understand more about the event that occurred. Using our purchase standard event, here's how this might look:

```
<script>
fbq('track', 'Purchase', {
value: 54.00,
currency: 'USD'
});
</script>
```

So, the first part of this event code looks familiar: fbq ('track', 'Purchase' . . .)

Then, instead of closing off our function call with:); like normal, we instead pass a third "argument" to the function, which is our payload of parameters (actually called an "object" in javascript).

So, we've added a comma after 'Purchase' to signal to Facebook that we have more information to provide, and then we add an opening curly-bracket: { to signify the start of the object (parameter payload).

Going into nitty-gritty detail on how javascript objects work is a bit beyond the scope of this book, but in short, they follow a pattern like:

1. Open Bracket {
2. Parameter Name followed by a colon value:
3. Parameter Value followed by a comma 54.00,
4. (Repeat two and three for all parameters in the object)
5. Closed Bracket }

And then, we have to close off our function call with the closing parenthesis and add our trailing semicolon to conclude the javascript statement:);

SOME FINAL THOUGHTS ON PARAMETERS

A few very important points about parameters as we wrap up this chapter:

- In the world of the Facebook Pixel, parameters are only mandatory on purchase standard events (where currency and value are mandatory parameters). They are optional for all other events. In Facebook's Advertising Help section you can see the full list of standard events and commonly used parameters and mandatory parameters for each.
- Parameters are completely open-ended. This means you can add as many parameters/descriptors to your standard events as you would like and "name" them whatever you like.
- Parameters can be used in Facebook Business Manager to configure highly-granular custom audiences or "Custom Conversions." For example, from our custom audience example earlier, we might say: include people who have performed an "AddToCart" event where the product_name parameter contained "Shoes." Note: only parameters that have had traffic/activity on your site will be available in the pre-populated dropdown menus in the Custom Audience and Custom Conversion screens.

Chapter 26

Choosing Your Campaign Objective

This is one area that seems to still be utterly mysterious to many people. In this chapter, we'll cover the different types of Facebook campaign objectives, along with how and why you would want to choose them.

It's important that you take some time to consider what type of objective you want for your campaign before you start to build it because changing campaign objectives of a live campaign is not possible with Facebook ads. You would have to start from scratch and rebuild your campaign with the proper objective so make sure you pick the objective that works for you!

> "*Lucky is the one who clearly defines its objectives and moves to achieve them, in spite of any external effects.*"
>
> —NAPOLEON HILL

ADVERTISING OBJECTIVES MADE SIMPLE

Your advertising objective is simply what you want people to do when they see your ad. Do you want them to watch a video? Do you want them to click through to a website? Do you want them to like and follow your Facebook fan page? It's a matter of stopping to think about what your overall campaign is designed for the end user to do.

Facebook has broken down advertising campaign objectives into three main areas:

1. Awareness
2. Consideration
3. Conversions

Awareness objectives are ads that are designed to generate interest or awareness in your business, your product, or your service. Consideration objectives are ads that get people to start thinking more about your business. They get people to look for more information about your business and are designed for a greater level of interaction than awareness ads. Conversion objectives are ads with the purpose of encouraging people with an interest in your business, your offer, or your products to purchase, to use, or to make a higher level of engagement and ultimately commitment to your business.

Often, people automatically assume that a conversion campaign is the obvious choice for their ads. We tend to take a direct-response style approach to our campaigns, so it would make sense that we would be running campaigns to convert leads and sales. However, there are times and situations where you need to choose other campaign objectives that fit into your overall Facebook ads strategy.

The first step in choosing your campaign objective is deciding which one of these three categories you want your ads to accomplish. Understand that the Facebook algorithm is designed to put your ad in front of people who are most likely to achieve the objective you've set for that campaign. Once you know that, then you can begin to dig a little deeper to get the right campaign objective.

Each category has specific ad formats that are available to use in your ads as well as specific Facebook platforms they will run on.

Let's start to dive into each of the three categories, awareness, consideration, and conversions.

TYPES OF AWARENESS CAMPAIGN OBJECTIVES

There are two types of awareness campaigns to choose from: brand awareness and reach. Brand awareness objectives are designed to show your ads to people who are more likely to pay attention to them, and reach objective ads are for when you want to reach the maximum number of people in your target audience and control how often they see your ads.

Both of these campaigns run on Facebook and Instagram, and if you're running a video campaign, the Audience Network is also a choice. Ad formats for both campaign objectives include single image, single video, carousel, and slideshow. The brand awareness objective also has the option to run Canvas ads.

Even though both of these campaign objectives are designed more for exposure, they both have the option to include call-to-action buttons. Keep in mind that the ads in these campaigns will not be optimized to run to people likely to click the CTA button, but it is a nice feature to include.

The brand awareness objective campaigns allow you to use the "Apply Now," "Book Now," "Contact Us," "Download," "Learn More," "Request Time," "See Menu," "Shop Now," "Sign Up," and "Watch More" buttons. The reach objective campaigns have a few additional CTA buttons, including "Save," "Sell Now," "Get Directions," "Call Now," and "Message Now."

The reach objective allows you to maximize the reach of your ads over the duration of your campaign and control how often people see your ads with frequency capping, and it allows you to use location targeting. See Figure 26.1.

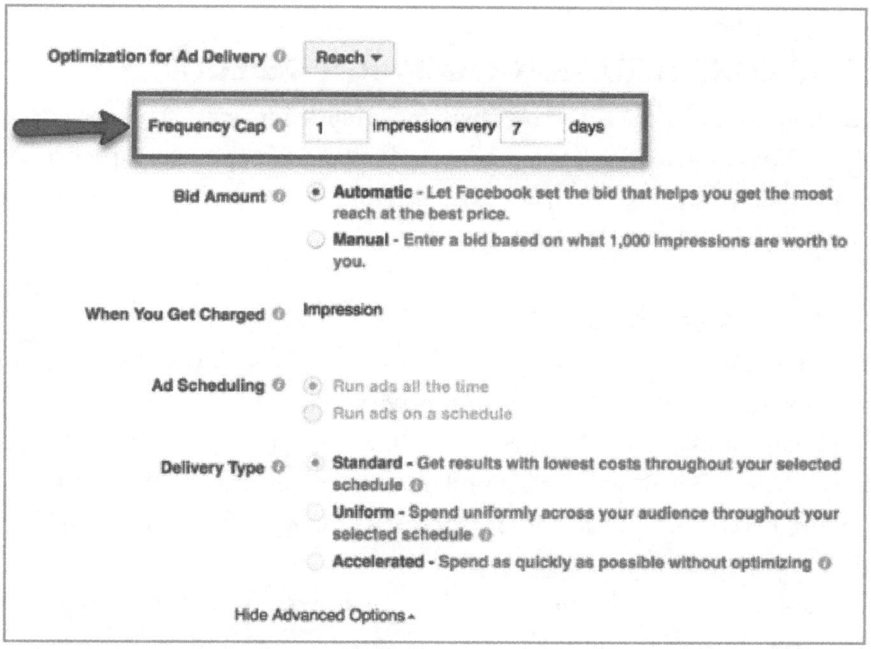

FIGURE 26.1–Frequency Capping with Reach Campaign Objective

If you have a local business with a physical location, the reach objective can help you drive more engagement in a geographically targeted area. By using the "Everyone in this location" selection in your audience targeting, you can target your ad to only people traveling nearby your location. See Figure 26.2 on page 294.

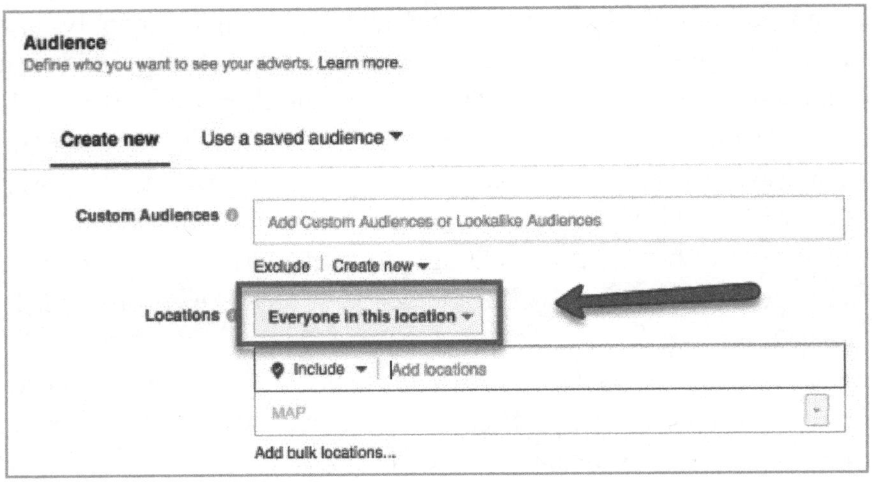

FIGURE 26.2–Location Targeting

TYPES OF CONSIDERATION CAMPAIGN OBJECTIVES

Consideration campaigns seem to be where most marketers start. This may or may not be the best choice. Again, it all goes back to what you want your prospect to do when they see your ad! There are five types of consideration campaigns: traffic, app installs, engagement, video views, and lead generation.

Traffic Campaign Objective

The traffic objective is designed to get more people to your visit your website or increase engagement with your app. This is one of the most commonly used campaigns by newer advertisers. The mindset is, "if I just get enough traffic to my site, I'll be likely to convert something!" The problem with that mindset is when you choose the traffic objective, you're telling Facebook, "put my ad in front of as many people who are likely to click through to my website as possible!"

And just like the genie in the bottle, Facebook says, "your wish is my command!" And when you are getting tons of cheap clicks to your site and no leads or sales, you think "something is wrong—this isn't working!" when in truth, the ad performed exactly like you asked it to! You asked for traffic, not leads or sales, and that's exactly what you got.

The traffic objective can work great when you're using a content amplification strategy where you've created some great content like a blog post and you just want to get more people consuming it. You may have great calls to action on your blog post or site, but don't expect to measure the success of that campaign on the number of conversions you get.

If you have a Facebook app that you want to get more engagement with, then the traffic objective is a great fit.

All of the advertising platforms, Facebook, Instagram, Audience Network, and Messenger support traffic campaign objectives. And you can use images, video, carousel, slideshow, canvas, and collection ad formats.

App Installs Campaign Objective

The app installs objective is almost identical to the traffic objective instead of sending the clicks to a URL, you're sending them to an app store so they can download your app. You can use all the same ad formats as the traffic objective and run your campaigns on Facebook, Instagram, and the Audience Network.

If you've got a killer mobile app, you'll want to optimize your campaign for mobile traffic so your traffic will go straight to the app store and download your app to their device (see Figure 26.3).

Engagement Campaign Objective

You would choose the engagement campaign objective when you want to get more people engaged with your page or your posts. There are three things the engagement campaign objective options allow you to do:

FIGURE 26.3–Mobile Optimization for App Downloads

1. Boost your posts (post engagement)
2. Promote your page (page likes)
3. Raise attendance at an event on your page (event responses)

Page post engagement ads can be extremely effective to use in a couple of scenarios. First, you can use page post engagement ads to test content you want to use in conversion campaigns. Facebook will put your page post engagement ad in front of people who are highly likely to engage with that post. It will help you determine if a piece of content resonates with your target audience, and then, you can later turn that post into another ad for conversions.

Another scenario to use page post engagement ads for is during a pre-launch phase of a new product, offer, or even company. The idea is to create some buzz and excitement before your cart opens, your product becomes available, or people can take the desired action you want them to.

We ran a campaign for a large arts and craft company that was launching a version of their product that would only be available on one day and could only be purchased on a TV shopping channel. For a week prior to the launch, we ran page post engagement ads hinting about this one-day-only event. We ran three different ads, and you can see by Figure 26.4 below and Figure 26.5 on page 297, the ad did its job! We had TONS of engagement leading up to the big day.

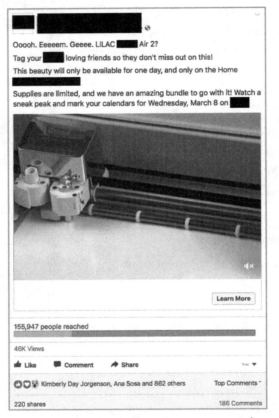

FIGURE 26.4–Page Post Engagement Ad

The day of the launch, we then ran a campaign targeting everyone who had engaged with those posts (more on audience targeting in Chapter 24) with the details of how to buy. The client sold out of inventory in less than 24 hours!

The next type of engagement campaign objective is promoting your Facebook Page, otherwise known as a "Like" campaign. There are some advertisers out there that think this type of campaign is a waste of advertising dollars, but we disagree. We actually

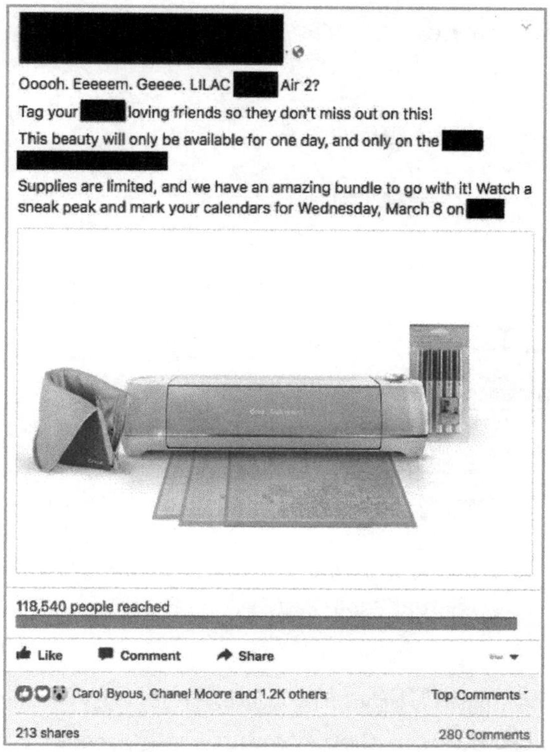

Ooooh. Eeeeem. Geeee. LILAC ███ Air 2?

Tag your ███ loving friends so they don't miss out on this!

This beauty will only be available for one day, and only on the ███

Supplies are limited, and we have an amazing bundle to go with it! Watch a sneak peak and mark your calendars for Wednesday, March 8 on ███

118,540 people reached

👍 Like   💬 Comment   ➤ Share

😊😊😊 Carol Byous, Chanel Moore and 1.2K others   Top Comments ˅

213 shares   280 Comments

FIGURE 26.5–Page Post Engagement Ad

recommend setting aside 5 to 10 percent of your advertising budget and putting that towards this type of campaign.

There are four main reasons why you want to be running a Facebook Like campaign:

1. *Twice the frequency in the newsfeed.* You can serve ads in the newsfeed to fans up to four times a day from the same Facebook page, unlike nonfans, which is only two times per day from the same page. This can be multiple ads; it doesn't matter. If you have multiple ads running, then your fans are more likely to see those ads.

2. *Social proof.* Have you seen any of those ads in your newsfeed that say so-and-so and 20 other of your fans like this page? Don't you feel like you're missing out? Nobody likes going into the empty restaurant. Social proof works, and the more fans you have, the more social proof you have.

3. *Facebook Connection Targeting* lets you run ads to friends of your fans, which is great. But, with connection targeting "Advanced Combinations," you can target an interest audience such as "Tony Robbins" who are "friends of people who are connected" to your Facebook page (see Figure 26.6 on page 298). When you select to do this, you are making sure that whoever sees your ad will have a friend who also likes your page. Instant credibility, baby.

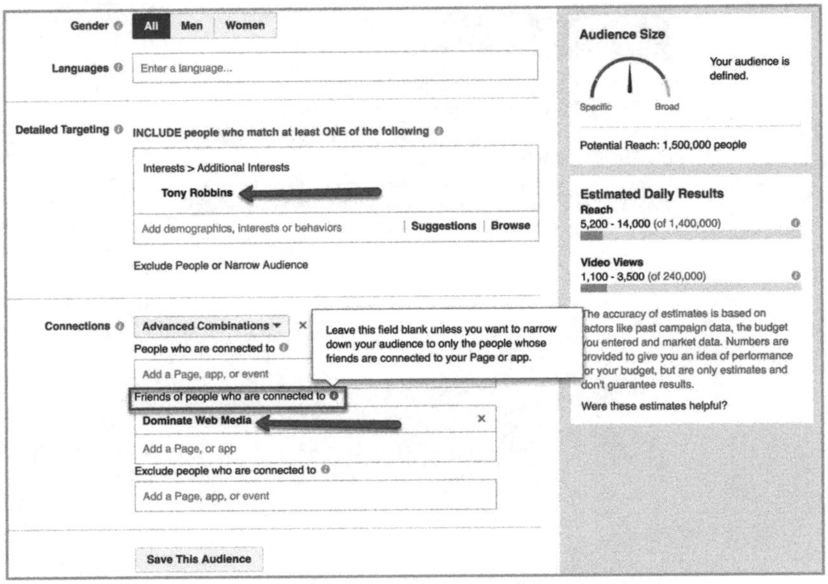

FIGURE 26.6–Page Like Campaign

4. *Facebook fans tend to have the highest return on an investment.* Provided you didn't buy Facebook likes from someone in another country on fiverr.com, odds are your Facebook fans actually are interested in what you do. At some point, they'll say they are interested in what you're doing. They'll respond to a Facebook Like campaign. They'll raise their hand and say they want to be a part of your community. Your fans are what I would call a warm market, and a warm market always has a higher ROI.

The event responses campaign objective is terrific if you are hosting an event and you want to target people who are likely to join your event. You're able to target an audience that you ideally want to attend, and when they join your event (that is hosted on your Facebook page), it will automatically be added to their calendar on Facebook.

This type of campaign objective allows you to boost awareness of your event, direct people where to sign up or join, and track how many people are going.

This is type of objective is fantastic if you have a local event, a grand opening, a festival, or something where you are promoting to the general public. If you are running a campaign for a paid event, we recommend using conversion campaigns instead of event response objective campaigns.

Video Views Campaign Objective

Video is hot. At the start of 2016, over 100 million hours of video were watched daily on Facebook, and that number is growing, especially with the introduction of Facebook

Live. People are watching videos, and with the video views campaign objective, you can get your message in front of the people who are most likely to actually watch it as well as people who watch videos tend to buy more. A lot more.

One of the major benefits of running a video views campaign is to get the most possible eyeballs on your videos and to create audiences of people who watch your video. If you're trying to build up an engaged audience to move them along the customer journey from being unaware of your business to doing business with you, video views are a great way to do it.

Think about it—you've got a five-minute video, and you run a campaign telling Facebook to put it in front of the part of your target audience most likely to watch it. A few days go by, and you have a few thousand views—pretty sweet, right? Well, imagine that half of that audience watched half of your video—that's about 1,000 people who spent two-and-a-half minutes focused on your brand. That's a lot more than if they just saw a post about your business while scrolling through the news feed.

Now, you have a much higher engaged audience of people who you can later retarget in future ads. Choosing the video views campaign objective can be a powerful way to launch a campaign introducing your product, offer, or service to a cold audience, which set them up to move along the customer journey later in the process and getting them one step closer to becoming a customer.

If the sole purpose of your video is to get someone to generate a conversion, like register for a webinar or purchase a product, then we usually recommend starting with a Conversion objective. This is because Facebook optimizes your campaign to show your ads to more people who are more likely to convert, based on the data it accumulates off your conversions. However, in some cases, such as when you hit the jackpot with a video and have one that is super engaging and also generates conversions. Videos that have has some virality to them will sometimes perform better in terms of ROI and CPA when using the video views objective, the page post engagement objective, or just by boosting the post.

There is no hard and fast rule here. (I'm sorry to disappoint all you data geeks!) This is something you just have to test. Keith's theory is that if you do have a video that's super engaging, when using an Engagement or Video Views objective, Facebook will show your ad to a larger portion of your target audience but also charge you much less per impression than with a Conversion objective. It should have a very high "Like to Share Ratio," maybe 1:1 or better. So, for every 10 likes or reactions it gets, it also gets shared at least 10 times, e.g., 1,248 reactions and 1,276 shares. In essence, you're getting a larger, broader audience, but your CPM's and CPC's are so much lower than the Conversion objective campaign that the higher volume and cheaper clicks make up for the more precise, higher quality visitors you get from the conversion campaign.

For example, let's say you sell a product called the "S3 Sauce," an amazing "Super-Secret Special Sauce" that turns almost any bland food or meal into a delicious, mouth-watering piece of heaven when you use it as a dipping sauce or pour it over your chicken, your beef, your rice, your noodles, your vegetables, just about anything! And you make a hysterical video showing an exaggerated reaction of some guy eating a horrible tasting meal, causing a scene, then sending him off into a horrible series of events, eventually ending up in jail or something like that all, initially caused by that one bad meal, played out in fast speed, of course. Then, the video does the quick rewind to do the same situation all over again, but this time after he takes the first bad bite, his friend sitting next to him quickly whips out a bottle of your S3 sauce from her $5k hand bag and pours some of the special sauce over his meal. He takes another bite, and as soon as he puts his fork into his mouth, the *Hallelujah* song (fast tempo version) blares while he is experiencing absolute satisfaction and total bliss. Pure utopia. This experience of course sends his day in a completely different direction, and he ends up hitting the jackpot and landing the super model.

If you make a video like this and get it right, where people love it and share the heck out of it, you may end up with lower conversion costs using the Video Views objective than a Conversion objective. So, in this hypothetical situation, let's say your Conversion objective campaign gets a conversion rate of 1.58 percent on your sales page, gives you an average cost per purchase (CPA) of $19.45, and generates 153,468 video views. Your Video View campaign with the same exact video, ad copy, target audiences, budget, etc., gets a conversion rate of .95 percent conversion rate on your sales page, but the average cost per purchase in this campaign ends up coming in at $17.68. This campaign generates 223,458 video views and thousands of more impressions with the same budget. In essence, the Video View campaign hit a bigger, broader audience, but the CPM's were low enough to offset the lower conversion rate. So you not only hit a lower CPA target, but you also had more brand impact, which will pay off in the future, taking more people from unaware to aware to having intent.

Lead Generation Campaign Objective

Lead generation campaign objectives have made it easier than ever to generate leads and grow your email list. If getting leads for your business is a top priority, then testing out lead generation campaigns should be high on your list. See Figure 26.7 on page 301.

This campaign objective allows you to capture information from Facebook users without the user ever leaving the Facebook ecosystem. Your ad looks just like any other ad except when someone clicks the CTA button on the ad (see Figure 26.8 on page 301), it opens up a form right inside Facebook that gets auto populated with their contact information already mostly filled in!

FIGURE 26.7–Lead Generation Ad

FIGURE 26.8–Lead Generation Form

Not leaving Facebook and hitting a landing page that may or may not convert—not losing a prospect from the time they click your ad until the time they opt-in—is brilliant. No bounce rate here.

Even though the Lead Generation objective is not in the category of Conversion objectives at the time of this writing, we think about it as another one of the Conversion objectives. When you choose this objective, you're essentially telling Facebook to put your ad in front of people who are most likely to opt-into this form. That sounds like a conversion to me!

Speaking of conversions . . .

CONVERSION CAMPAIGN OBJECTIVES

Conversions are the holy grail of Facebook marketing. The ultimate goal is to put a dollar in and get at least a dollar and a penny back out. At the time of this writing, there are three types of conversion campaign objectives to choose from: conversions, product catalog sales, and store visits. (This will change; I can promise you that. But, the core principles here will not.)

Let's start with store visits—this is killer if you have more than one physical location!

The store visits campaign objective combines your physical location(s), geo-targeting, and people with location services enabled on their cell phones. You decide the radius around your location that you want to serve the ad to and choose CTA buttons for your ad.

The first thing you'll need to do when using the store visits campaign objective is set up all of your business locations in Facebook. If you have several locations, Facebook has an option to bulk upload all of your locations. See Figure 26.9 on page 303.

When setting up your campaign, you have the option to target based on a specific mile radius around your location or the radius can be dynamically updated based upon your desired reach (see Figure 26.10 on page 303). Regardless of what you choose, Facebook will automatically pull in all of the locations you added under business locations. You can then overlay custom audiences, interest, and demographic targeting within the designated radius of each location.

Your ads are then dynamically updated for each location with whatever page fields you choose to include in your copy.

The conversion campaign objectives are when you want to be able to track and measure conversions on your website, Facebook, or mobile app. In order to use the conversions campaign objective, you need to have the Facebook pixel installed. For more on the Facebook pixel, refer back to Chapter 25.

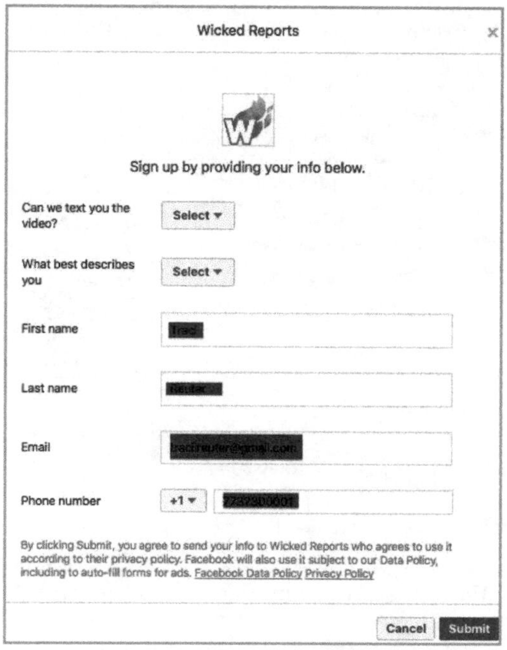

Wicked Reports   ✕

Sign up by providing your info below.

Can we text you the video?	Select ▼
What best describes you	Select ▼
First name	[redacted]
Last name	[redacted]
Email	[redacted]@gmail.com
Phone number	+1 ▼ [redacted]

By clicking Submit, you agree to send your info to Wicked Reports who agrees to use it according to their privacy policy. Facebook will also use it subject to our Data Policy, including to auto-fill forms for ads. Facebook Data Policy Privacy Policy

Cancel   Submit

FIGURE 26.9–Setting Up Business Locations in Facebook

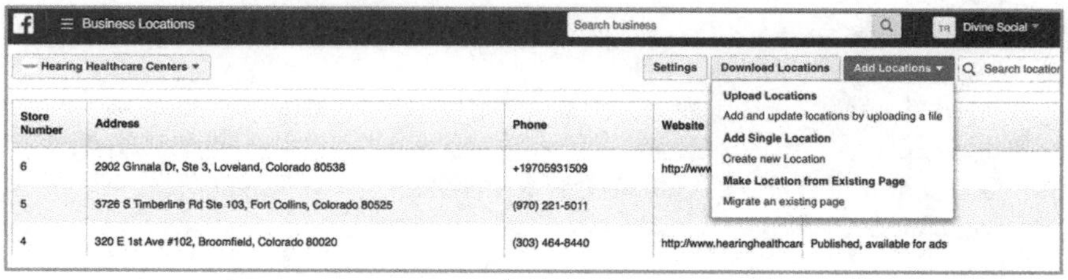

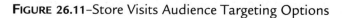

FIGURE 26.10– Setting Up

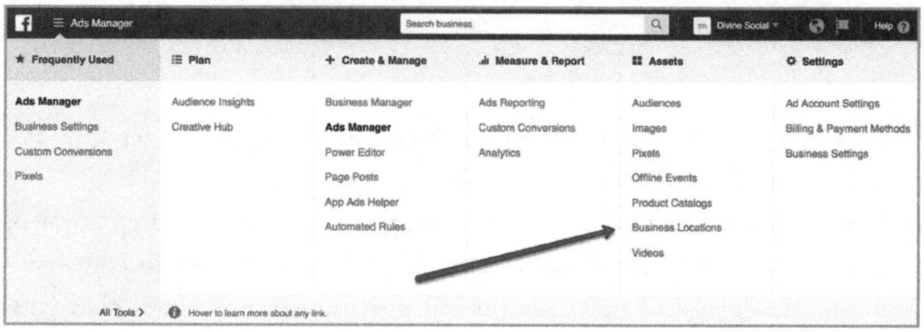

FIGURE 26.11–Store Visits Audience Targeting Options

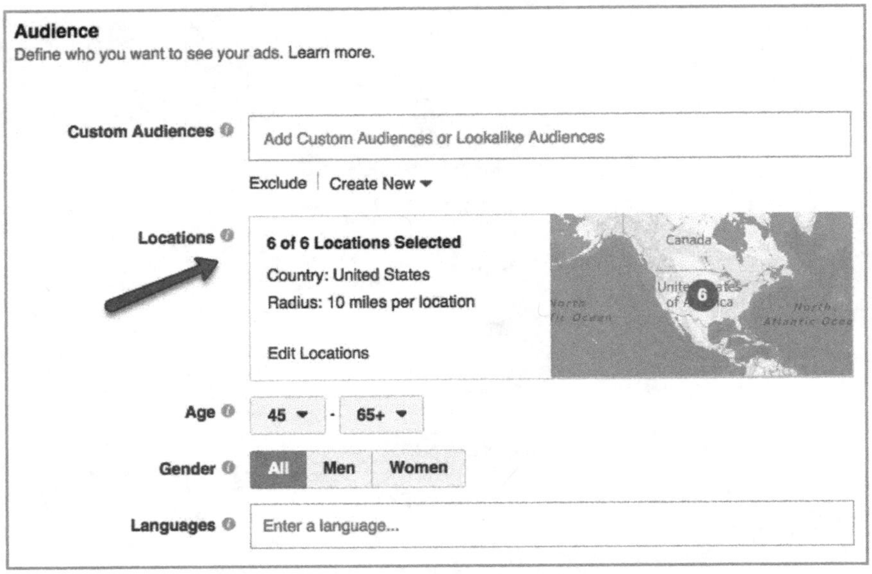

FIGURE 26.12–Copy Page Field Variations

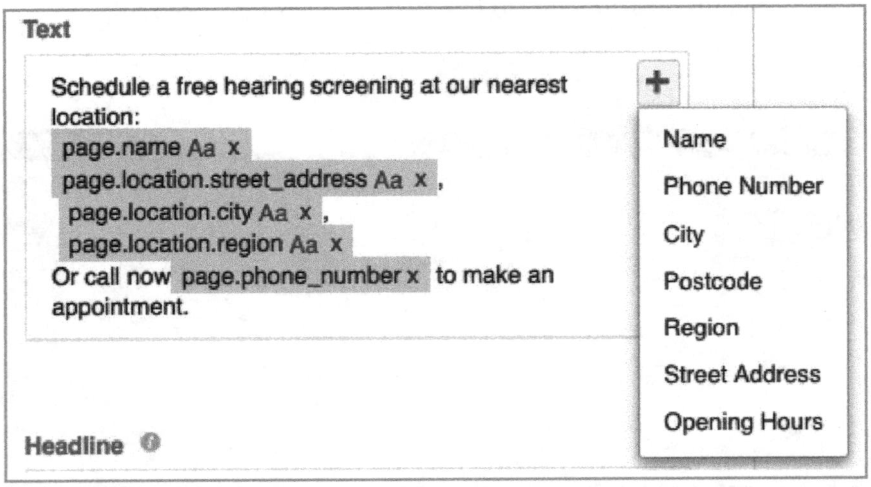

FIGURE 26.13–Store Visits Objective Ad with Page Fields Dynamically Updated

When you use the conversion campaign objectives, you're basically telling Facebook, "put my ad in front of people who are highly likely to convert."

With the standard event pixel, you can set up conversion campaigns that optimize for any of the nine standard website actions. If you're using custom conversions, you can set up your campaign to optimize for any custom website action that you set up. Facebook currently allows you to have up to 40 custom conversions per account.

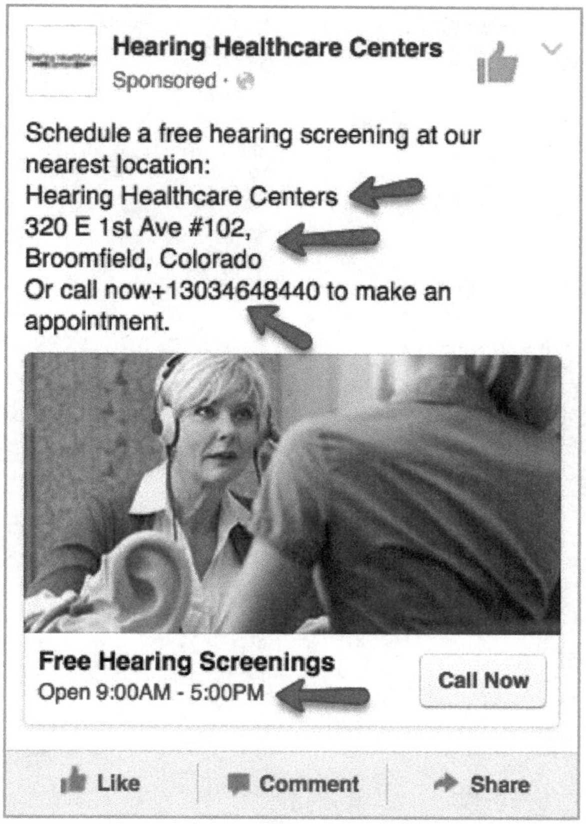

FIGURE 26.14–Choosing the Conversion Event for Your Campaign

Your campaign reporting will then allow you to see the results of your campaign based upon the event you optimized your campaign for. In Figure 26.14, we've optimized this campaign to generate leads, and we're able to not just see how many leads our campaign generated, we're also able to see what our cost per conversion (in this case lead) is for our campaign! See Figure 26.15 on page 306.

You also have the option with this campaign objective to determine the time period that Facebook will count your conversion results. There are four options to choose from (see Figure 26.16 on page 306).

What you choose will depend upon the type of results you're looking for. If you're looking to see if an audience or ad creative converts quickly, then choose one-day conversion. If you have a little bit more time, the seven-day click option will get you better data over time.

If you have an online store or are an ecommerce company, then the product catalog campaign objective may be your most favorite thing of all!

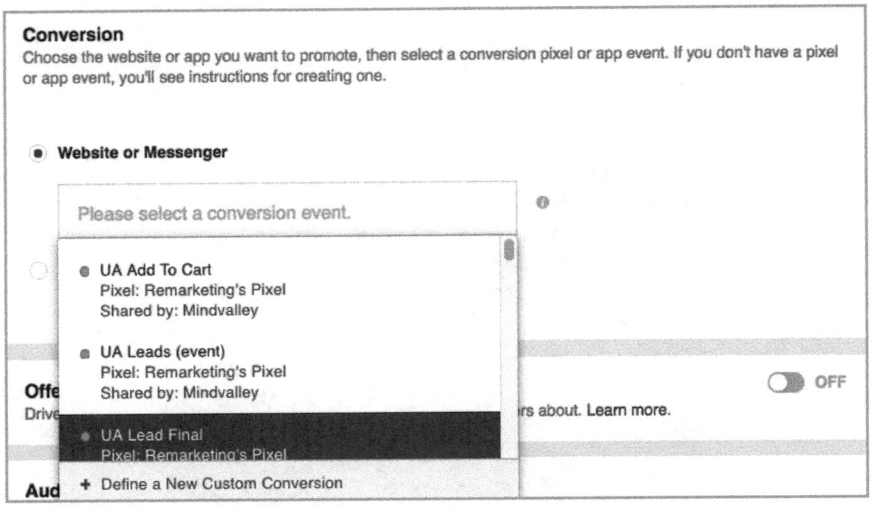

FIGURE 26.15–Conversion Campaign Results

Results ⓘ	Reach ⓘ	Cost per Result ⓘ ▲
214 UA Leads (event)	113,174	$3.06 Per UA Leads (event)
215 UA Leads (event)	104,357	$3.05 Per UA Leads (event)
203 UA Leads (event)	57,462	$3.21 Per UA Leads (event)
188 UA Leads (event)	60,371	$3.48 Per UA Leads (event)
185 UA Leads (event)	48,220	$3.55 Per UA Leads (event)

FIGURE 26.16–Conversion Window Options

This campaign objective is simply designed to get people to purchase more of your products!

This objective really shines with something called dynamic ads. Dynamic product ads (DPA's) look like a regular carousel ad at first glance; except they're anything but regular. With the dynamic ad feature in the product catalog objective, you create an ad template that automatically uses images and details from your product catalog that you would like to advertise.

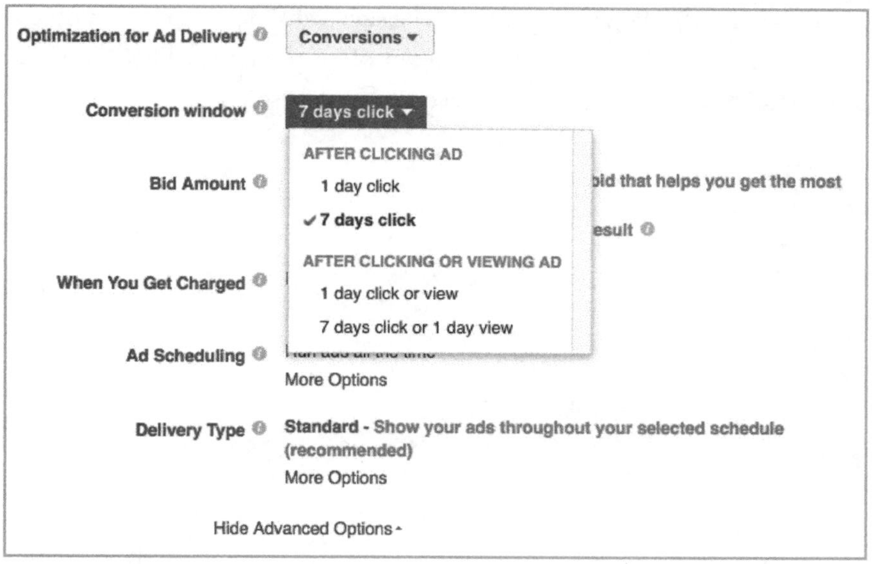

FIGURE 26.17–Dynamic Product Ads (DPA's) Using Catalog Details

Using this campaign objective gives you a few advantages if you're in ecommerce or you have multiple items you're selling (like travel). You can promote your product catalog with unique ads without manually configuring each ad. Find potential new customers by highlighting the right products at the right time. You can show the most relevant products from your catalog based upon products people have viewed on your website. Best of all, you can reach people anywhere. This objective runs on all of the Facebook advertising platforms.

WHICH CAMPAIGN OBJECTIVE IS RIGHT FOR ME?

That's the question we get asked over and over again, "What is the best campaign objective to run for my business or my campaign?"

The truth is, it depends. As you now know, each campaign objective accomplishes something different in each situation. Every business is unique, and every campaign is unique. That's why we recommend before you launch a campaign that you take the time and think through what EXACTLY you want to accomplish and then choose the objective that most fits. And as we mentioned earlier in this chapter, in some cases, it depends on the quality of your specific ad. There will be times where you might have two or more campaign objectives that could work for your situation. In this case, if you have the budget, test them. See which one ultimately gives you the best results that you are after for your unique campaign. If you don't have the excess budget or excess time, then just go with the objective you have the best feeling about. Most likely, if you have a great ad and a great offer, your campaign will be successful no matter what objective you choose. And if you have a sub-par ad or sub-par offer, then most likely your campaign will not be successful, no matter what objective you choose.

Chapter 27

Building and Structuring Your Ad Sets

Guest Author Traci Reuter

You've decided upon the right objective for your campaign, and now, it's time to get to the good stuff! This is the sweet spot in running your campaigns. Building and structuring your ad sets is all about making sure your ad hits your target audience. In this chapter, we'll cover the fundamentals of building your ad sets and some strategies you can use to optimize your campaigns.

> *"The odds of hitting your target go up dramatically when you aim at it."*
>
> —Mal Pancoast

The ad set level is where we make most of the ongoing changes and modifications to our campaign as time goes on. The majority of the testing of different variables takes place at the ad set level.

For some larger ad accounts, it's not uncommon to have hundreds, sometimes thousands, of ad sets per campaign. If you're new to running Facebook ads, that may seem like an awful lot of ad sets. Once you understand all the flexibility and variable as available to you at the ad set level, you'll understand why that is!

PUTTING OUT AN A.P.B FOR YOUR TARGET AUDIENCE

When law enforcement puts out an A.P.B., they're broadcasting information to other officers about the details of a suspect that needs to be detained. Setting up your ad sets is very similar. You're telling Facebook the details about the "suspect" or prospect that you want to be "detained" or to engage with!

When it comes to Facebook ad sets, A.P.B. stands for something other than "all-points bulletin." When we talk about A.P.B. in Facebook ads, we mean, "Audience, Placement, and Budget."

AUDIENCE, PLACEMENT, AND BUDGET

No matter the campaign objective you choose; audience, placement, and budget will be the next things you'll need to decide upon. Some campaign objectives may have additional components involved at the ad set level. We'll cover what those are later in this chapter.

Setting Up Your Audiences

Chapter 23 went into the process involved in the audience research phase of building your campaign. Once you're ready to build your ad set, this is where you'll put that into play.

You have three choices when choosing your audience in each ad set:

1. Use an existing saved audience,
2. Use an existing custom audience, or
3. Create a new audience.

A saved audience is when you take that audience research you did earlier, and you set up and save the audience in your asset library. When you set up saved audiences with interest and demographic targeting, you can pull those into your ad sets.

Keep in mind that if you need to make any changes to the audience targeting once you've chosen to use a saved audience, you'll have to edit the original saved audience (see Figure 27.1 on page 311). Also, you can only use one saved audience at a time. If you want to combine saved audiences, you'll have to create an entirely new saved audience (see Figure 27.2 on page 311).

Your next option is to choose a custom audience. It's grouped by all custom audiences, lookalike audiences, or just custom audiences (see Figure 27.3 on page 312). The cool part about using custom audiences is that you are not limited to using only one as with saved audiences. There may be times where it makes sense to target multiple custom audiences all at once. A good example of that would be when you want to retarget your

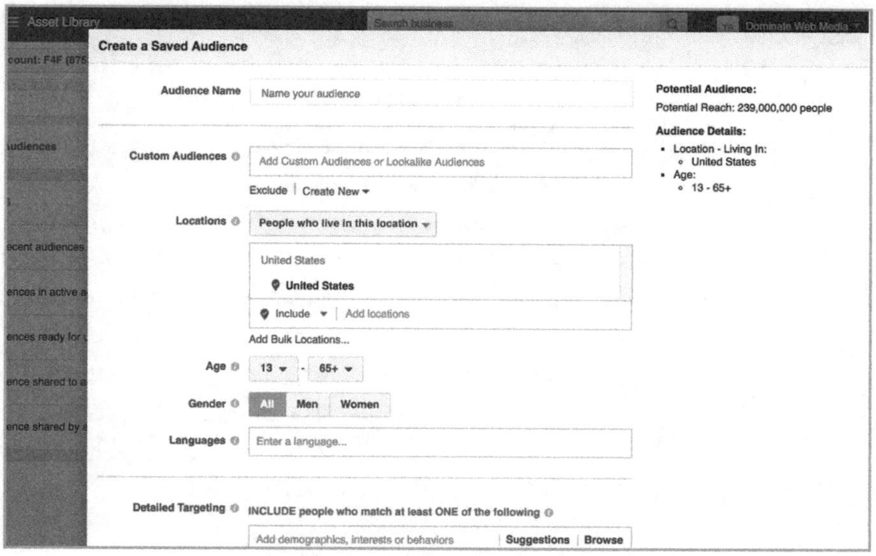

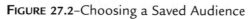

FIGURE 27.1–Saved Audience

FIGURE 27.2–Choosing a Saved Audience

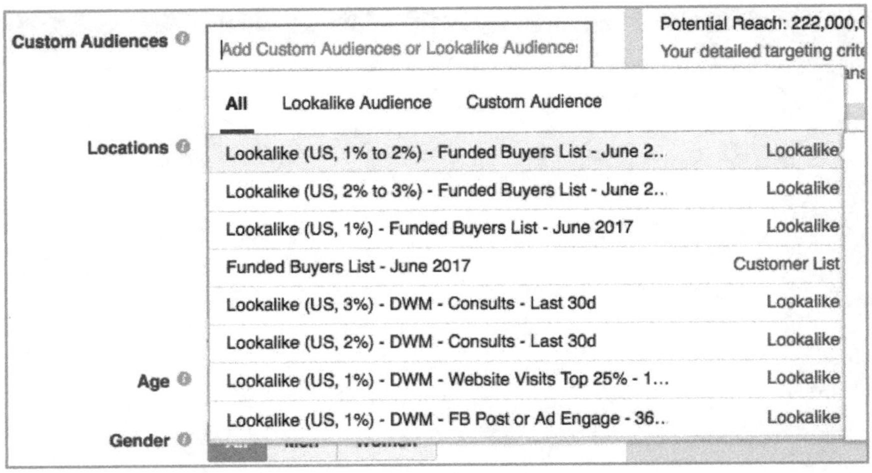

FIGURE 27.3–Choosing a Custom Audience

FIGURE 27.4–Combining Multiple Custom Audiences into One Ad Set

entire warm audience with one ad. You can combine all of your custom audiences into one ad set, as seen in Figure 27.4.

The third option is to create an entirely new audience. This would be just as if you had created a saved audience in your audience assets, except you're doing it as you create the ad set. This is where you'd use interest targeting and demographic targeting to create a new audience.

With custom audiences and new audience creation, you have the option to change the geographic targeting, the age and gender demographics, as well as the detailed targeting. You also have the option to add in connection types to your audiences. This is where you would add in fans of your Facebook page, friends of fans, app users, friends of app users, as well as people who have responded to your events. The connections option is not an option if you're choosing a saved audience as that is something that you would need to add when creating the saved audience.

The next decision you need to make is your geographic targeting, as seen in Figure 27.5. You can target by country, state or province, city, congressional districts, zip codes, or postcodes. There's also the option to target worldwide, regions, free trade areas, and other areas, like iTunes app store countries, emerging markets, and more! Facebook also allows you to drop a pin on the map and target a precise radius around that exact location. The minimum and maximum radius varies by location targeting anywhere from 1 to 50 miles, as seen in Figure 27.6.

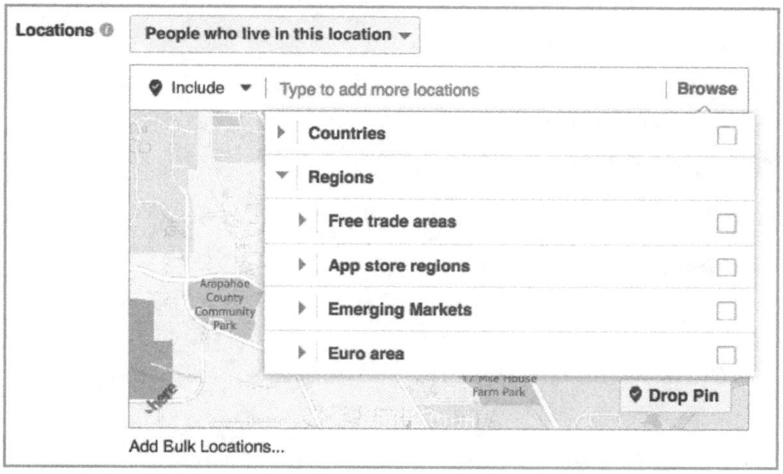

FIGURE 27.5–Geographic Targeting Options

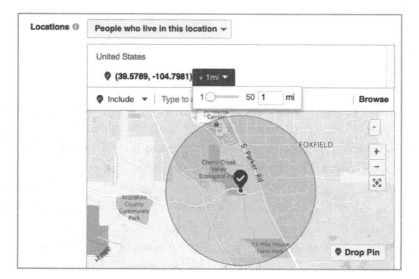

FIGURE 27.6–Precise Geo-Targeting

When selecting your geographic targets, you have four options to refine your targeting even more. (See Figure 27.7) The default is to target "everyone in this location." This means you'll reach people who are currently within your geographic area. "People who live in this location" are people who have indicated by their Facebook profile where they live, but also, it's based upon their device connection (Facebook knows more about us than most people realize!!). "People recently in this location" will reach people based upon location services on their phone. This is incredibly powerful for local businesses to target people while they're in the area of your store or location. "People traveling in this location" are people that Facebook determines are more than 125 miles away from their home location. This option is great for travel related companies or any business that relies on tourists.

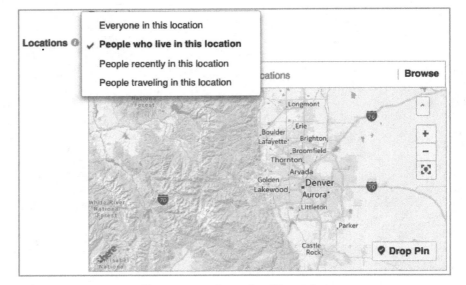

FIGURE 27.7–Location Targeting

Once you've set up your geographic targeting, then you have the options for age, gender, and languages. You also have the option to use detailed targeting. In Figure 27.8 on page 315, you will see detailed targeting provides additional demographic information, interests, and behaviors. The targeting options are based on people's activities, both on and off Facebook. Use the browse feature to get a full list of the options available.

One of the more useful features of detailed targeting is the ability to choose "or" targeting or "and" targeting. If you add criteria to the "include people," your audience will include people who meet at least one of the criteria but not all of them. If you add people who are:

- Homeowners

FIGURE 27.8–Detailed Targeting Category Options

- Interested in cooking
- Parents

You could possibly end up targeting a person who likes cooking but isn't a parent and doesn't own a home because they will be in this audience. This is an example of "or" targeting. These are people who are homeowners or like cooking or are parents.

If you wanted to target people who met all of your criteria, you can use the "audience narrowing" feature and take advantage of "and" targeting. In Figure 27.9, you have an

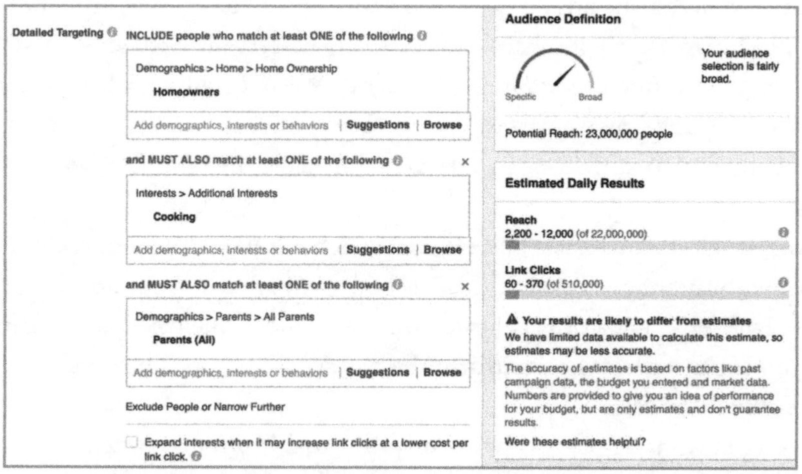

FIGURE 27.9–Detailed Targeting with Audience Narrowing

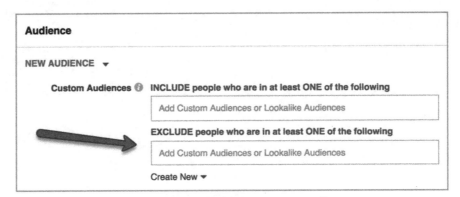

FIGURE 27.10–Excluding Custom Audiences

example of the targeting of people who own a home, are interested in cooking, and are parents.

We can't talk about setting up your audience without talking about the "Exclusion" options available. This can be a huge benefit when running campaigns, especially conversion campaigns. We will use the "Exclude" option for audiences. For example, when we are running a lead generation campaign and want to exclude existing leads or customers. This is a great way to optimize your ad spend and not serve up an ad to people who have already seen your ad or shouldn't be seeing the ad you are running. (See Figure 27.10)

You can also exclude geographic locations, detailed interests, and connections. A common exclusion with connections is to exclude your fans if you are trying to serve your ad to a truly cold audience.

Choosing Your Placements

Placements is where your ads are going to show up to your target audience. You have multiple platforms that your Facebook ads can be served. Facebook, Instagram, the Audience Network, and Sponsored Messages. When deciding how to choose your placements, you have two options: let Facebook choose for you or you pick where you want your ads to show up. Figure 27.11 on page 317 shows how it looks inside Facebook.

When you select Automatic placements, which Facebook recommends even though that may not always be the best choice, Facebook will serve up your ads to the platforms where the Facebook algorithm believes your ad is most likely to get the most results. You have no control over what platform the ads are served on. The Facebook algorithm makes the choice for you.

Choosing automatic placements can be a valuable strategy when you are running a new campaign to cold traffic. It allows you to see where your audience is responding

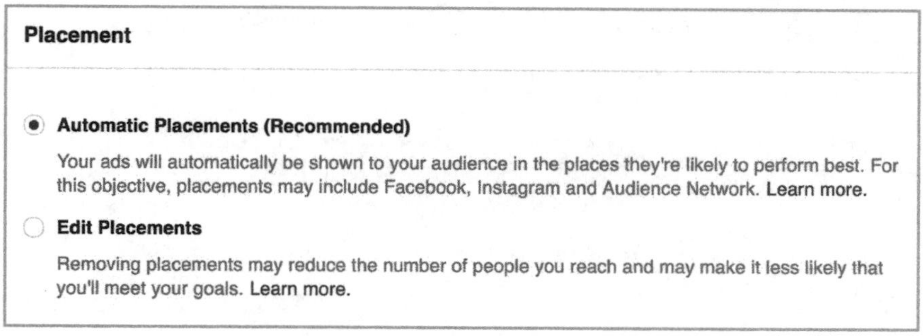

Placement

○ **Automatic Placements (Recommended)**

Your ads will automatically be shown to your audience in the places they're likely to perform best. For this objective, placements may include Facebook, Instagram and Audience Network. Learn more.

○ **Edit Placements**

Removing placements may reduce the number of people you reach and may make it less likely that you'll meet your goals. Learn more.

FIGURE 27.11–Ad Set Placement Choices

the most, and in the future, you can use that information in future campaigns when selecting your placements.

When you choose edit placements, you get to control exactly where your ads will be served. Choosing automatic placements means your ads will potentially run on all platforms, but with edit placements, you choose what platforms to include or exclude. Figure 27.12 shows the placement options at the time of this writing.

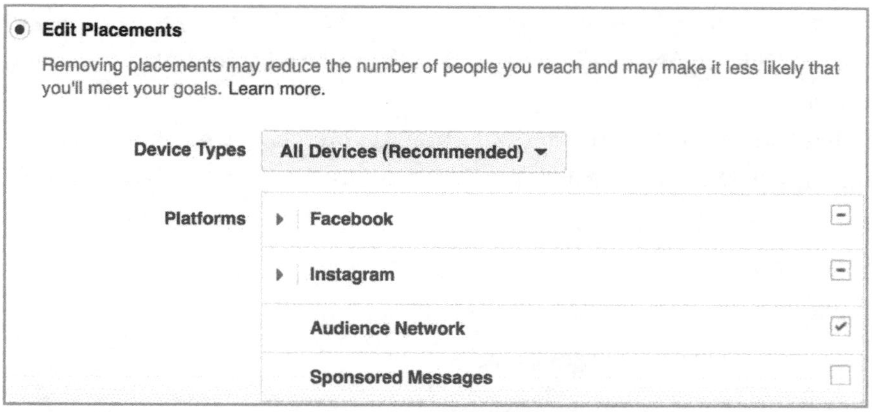

● **Edit Placements**

Removing placements may reduce the number of people you reach and may make it less likely that you'll meet your goals. Learn more.

Device Types	All Devices (Recommended) ▼	
Platforms	▶ Facebook	⊟
	▶ Instagram	⊟
	Audience Network	☑
	Sponsored Messages	☐

FIGURE 27.12–Edit Placement Options

The first thing you need to decide is whether you will run your ads on all devices or on a mobile or desktop only. Depending upon your choice, the platform options will change. For example, if you choose desktop only, using Instagram no longer becomes a placement option because Instagram is a mobile-only platform. Figure 27.13 on page 318 shows device type placement options.

Once you've decided on the device type options, you get to choose your platform options. Not only does the device type you choose determine what platform options you have, the campaign objective you choose also will determine what platform options you have. On Facebook, you have: feeds, instant articles, in-stream videos, right column, and

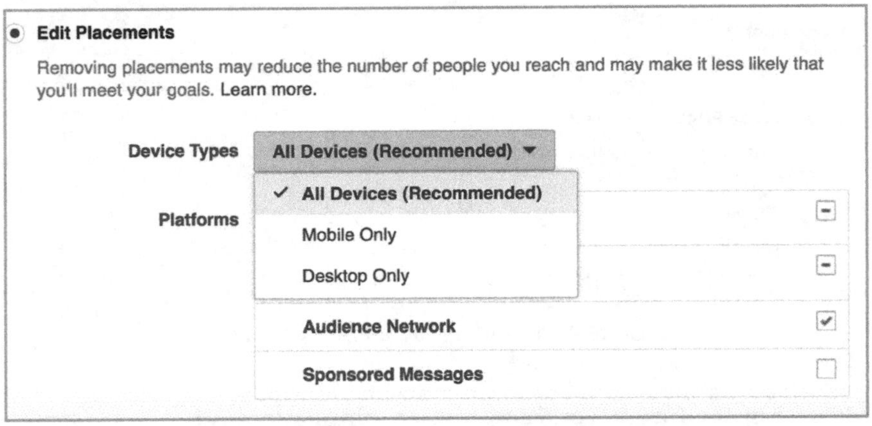

FIGURE 27.13–Device Type Placement Options

suggested videos. Instagram gives you the options for their feed or Instagram stories. See Figure 27.14 for platform placement options.

Finally, you also have some advanced placement options. Your first option is to choose specific mobile devices and operating systems. This gives you the flexibility to run ads to all mobile devices, Android, or iOS only devices and to run your ads only to people connected to Wifi. Figure 27.15 on page 319 shows the advanced placement options for mobile devices.

Facebook also gives you the options to block your ads from running next to certain types of content. With the exclude categories option, you can exclude certain types of

FIGURE 27.14–Platform Placement Options

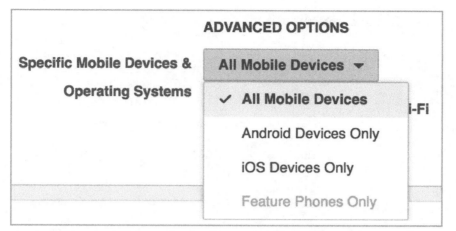

FIGURE 27.15–Advanced Placement Options—Mobile Devices and Operating Systems

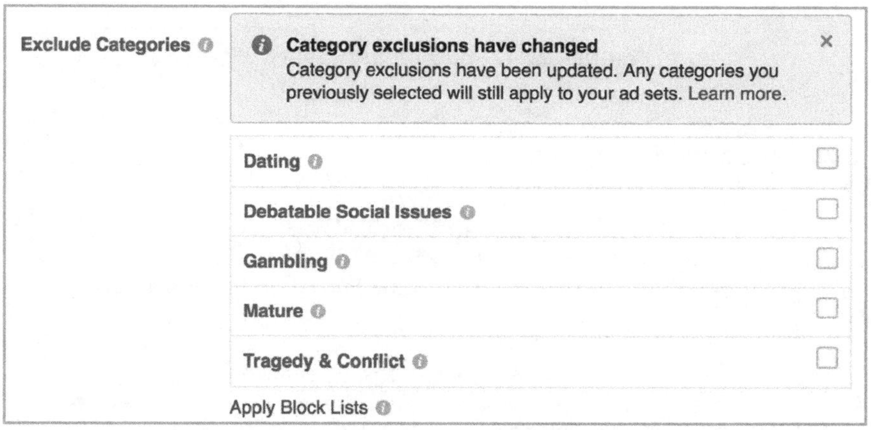

FIGURE 27.16–Category Exclusion Options

content from your ads that are running on the in-stream video placements, the audience network, and instant articles. For many businesses, this is extremely important as some of these categories are in extreme conflict with their brand or messaging. Figure 27.16 shows category exclusion options.

The final advanced placement option is to use block lists. Block lists allow you to block your ads from running on specific websites or apps within the audience network or on the instant articles of specific publishers. Once you create and upload a block list, you then have the option to use that same list across multiple campaigns.

Budget and Schedule

The ad set level is where you decide the budget for your ads, as you can see in Figure 27.17 on page 320. In Figure 27.18 on page 320, you will see that you can choose a daily

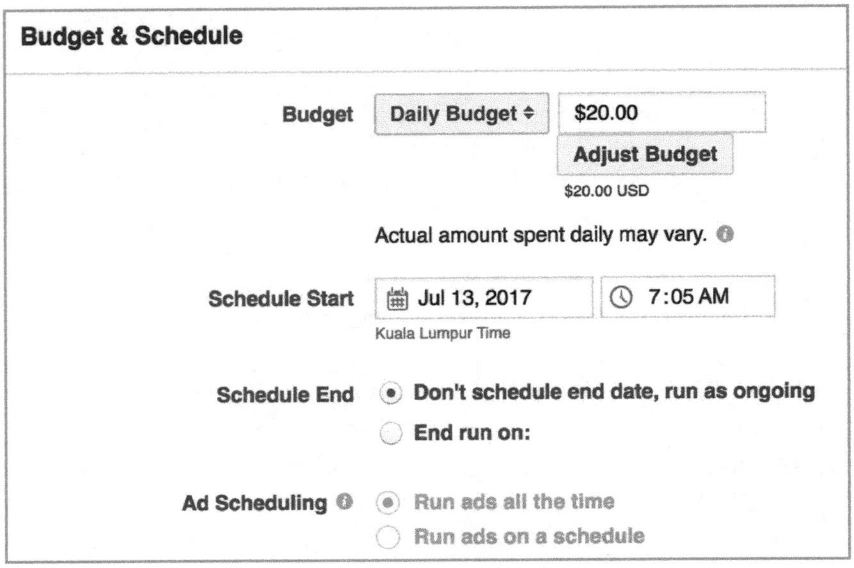

FIGURE 27.17–Budget and Schedule

FIGURE 27.18–Daily vs. Lifetime Budget

budget or a lifetime budget. In most cases, choosing a daily budget is recommended since that gives you more control over your ad sets over time. A lifetime budget is recommended if you are running your campaign for a specific period of time and you have an absolute budget to work within. When you pick daily budget, your actual daily spend may vary. Facebook looks at your daily budget as an average and will optimize your results by spending more one day over another if that will mean getting you better results. The maximum Facebook will overspend in a day is 25 percent over your daily budget. The Facebook algorithm will use this flexibility to spend your ad budget as efficiently and effectively as possible. Even though you might have overspending one day, your ad spend will average out over the course of seven days so you never have to be concerned that you're overspending your budget.

Use the scheduled start and end dates if you have campaigns that must start and stop at certain times. We often don't like to launch campaigns at the end of or late in a day, so we will use the scheduled start time to launch the campaigns early the next day. The scheduled end is useful when you have a campaign that has a finite ending. Utilize this scheduled end date to ensure your ad stops serving when you want it to.

When choosing lifetime budget, you also have the option to run the ads all the time or run the ads on a schedule. (See Figure 27.19) We have found that running the ads all the time works best because the Facebook algorithm is always looking to serve your ads during the times that are most likely to get the most results. However, there may be instances where you want to be able to control the times your ads are shown and running on a lifetime budget with a schedule is how you do it.

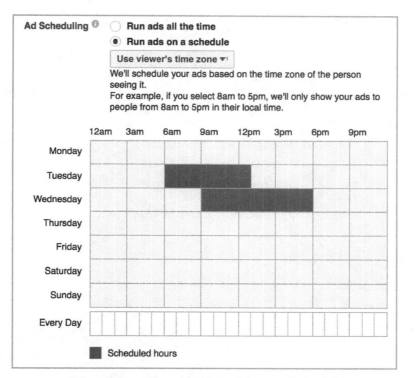

FIGURE 27.19–Running Your Ads on a Schedule

OTHER AD SET OPTIONS

Once you have your A.P.B set up, the other options in your ad set will vary depending upon the campaign objective that you've chosen.

Brand awareness, post engagement, event response, video views, and store visits campaigns all have only the audience, placement, and budget to set up. If using the reach, page likes, or lead generation objectives, you'll need to choose the page associated with your ad campaign. The app installs campaign objective will have you choose your app, and the product catalog campaign objective will have you choose your products.

If you're using the traffic campaign objective, you'll also have to decide where you want to send your traffic—either to a website, Facebook messenger, or an app. You also have the option to add an offer to your traffic ad, as seen in Figure 27.20. If you choose this option, you must choose the Facebook page you want the offer to run from, and then, you can either choose an existing offer or create one, as seen in Figure 27.21.

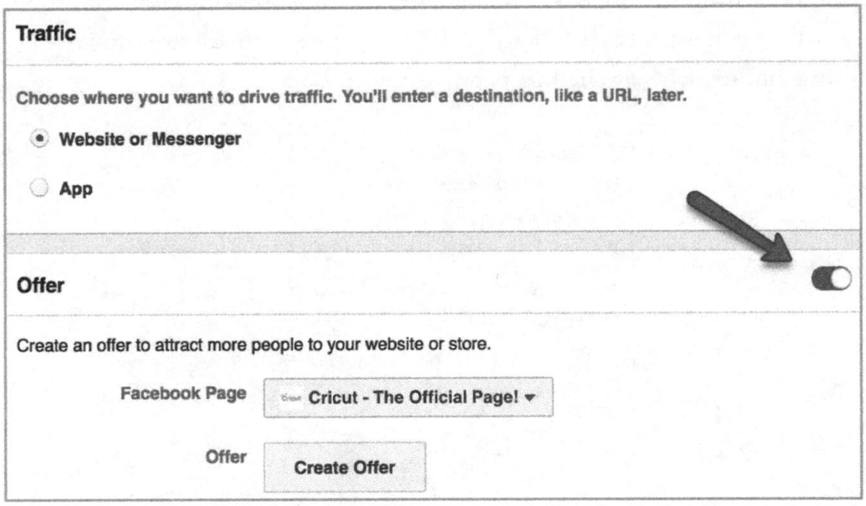

FIGURE 27.20–Add an Offer to Your Campaign

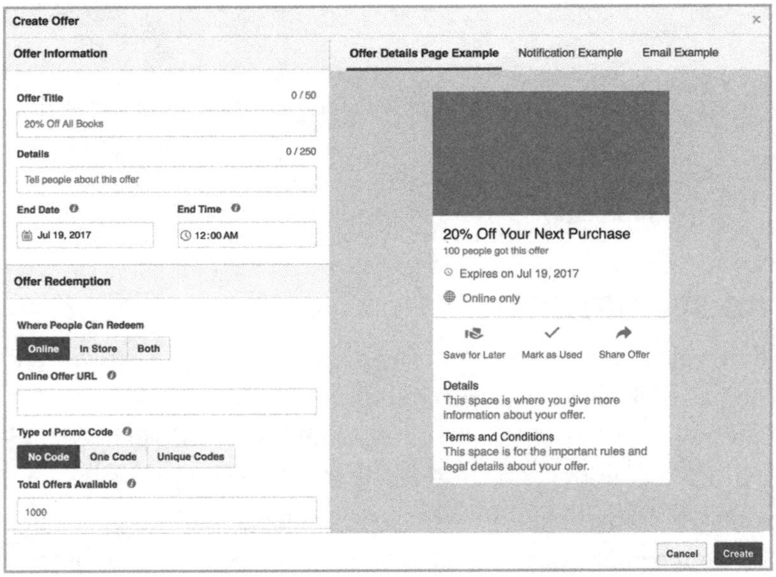

FIGURE 27.21–Creating an Offer

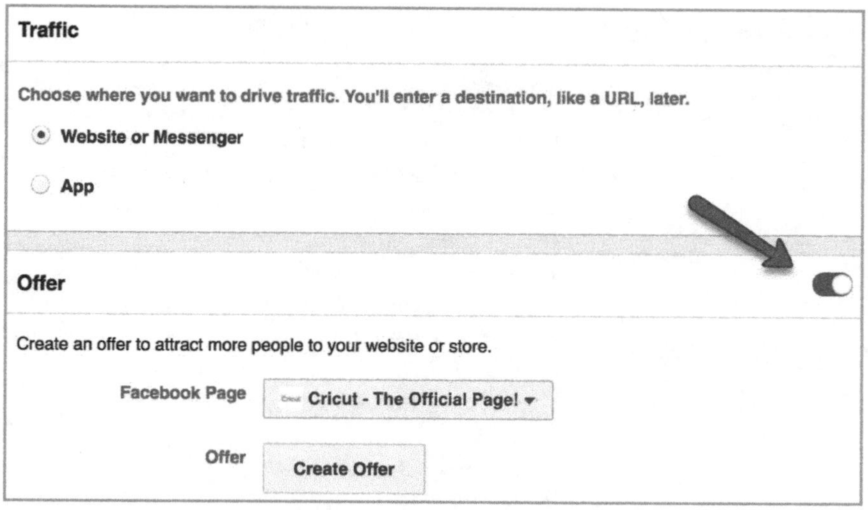

FIGURE 27.22–Choosing Conversion Event for an Ad Set

When running a conversion campaign, you need to choose the conversion event you are optimizing your campaign for at the ad set level as in Figure 27.22.

OPTIMIZATION AND DELIVERY

The final part of building and structuring your ad set is optimization and delivery. This is where you tell Facebook what you want them to optimize for. Typically, the automatic choice will be based upon the campaign objective you've chosen, however, you have the option to choose other optimization events. The majority of the time, it's recommended to go with the conversion optimization that Facebook automatically recommends. There are times where you may need to adjust that. One example is with retargeting ads. For example, we might run a retargeting ad with a "video views" objective, but instead of letting Facebook optimize for video views, we may choose "impressions" for the ad delivery goal (as seen in Figure 27.23 on page 324) instead to make sure we get that retargeting video in front of as many people as many times as possible.

Optimization and delivery is also where you get to pick your bid amount. There are two options, automatic and manual bid. Automatic bid lets Facebook set the bid that will allow you to get the most results. More often than not, we go with automatic bid. Manual bidding allows you to set your target cost per result. With manual bidding, you have the option to choose average or maximum bid amount. If you know you have a limit to what you will spend per result, using manual bid maximum will allow you to tell Facebook what you're willing to spend to get those results.

If you are running conversion campaigns, the last thing you need to choose is your conversion window. You can choose from one day or seven days after clicking your ad,

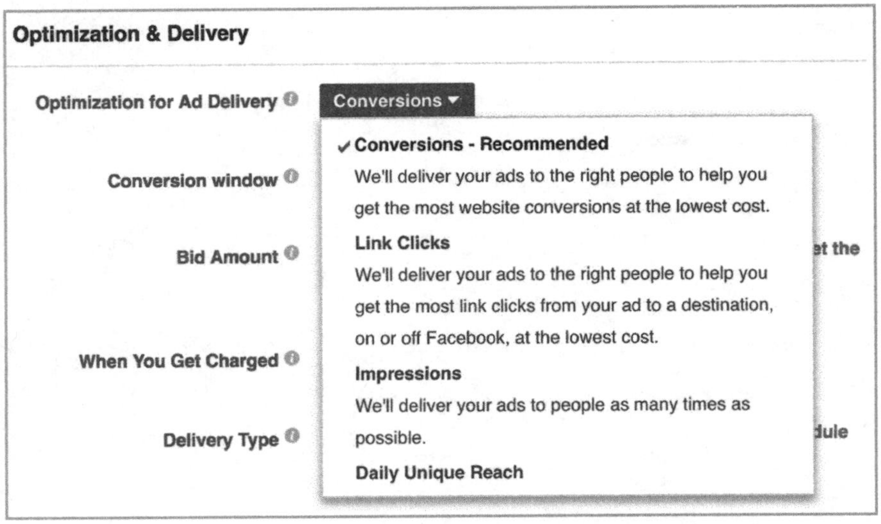

FIGURE 27.23–Optimization Ad Delivery Selection

or one or seven days after clicking or viewing your ad. If you know that people purchase or take action on your offer quickly, then a one-day conversion window might be your best bet. We like to choose the seven-day window when we have a little time to allow the Facebook algorithm to work. When choosing the seven-day window for optimization, you might not get as many conversions out of the gate, but quite often, you will get better results over time because the Facebook algorithm is pulling a larger amount of data in a seven-day conversion window. The debate over one day vs. seven-day conversion window continues. We always test this in our campaigns, and we suggest that when building and structuring your ad sets, you do the same as well!

Chapter 28

Creating Your Ads

Guest Author Vladimir Gonzales

Most of the content from this chapter was pulled from the *Ad Creation Standard Operating Procedure* written by Vladimir Gonzales for our agency. (Like all Standard Operating Procedure's at DWM, the active version is updated online on a monthly basis in order to remain current and relevant.)

After you create your ad set, click "Continue," and this will take you to the ad creation page. See Figure 28.1.

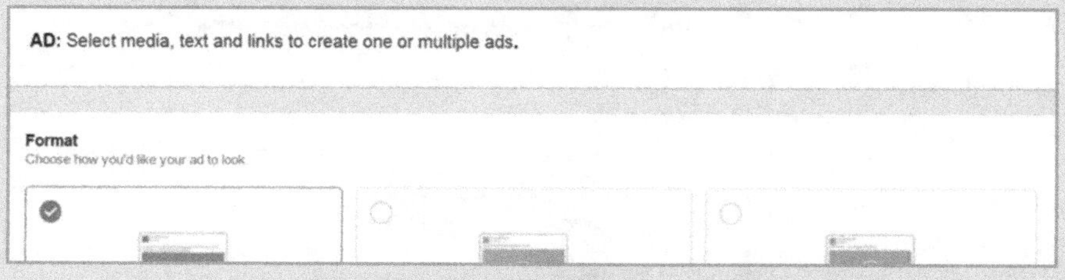

In the Format section (Figure 28.2 on page 326), you have five options to

> *"Many a small thing has been made large by the right kind of advertising."*
>
> —MARK TWAIN

AD: Select media, text and links to create one or multiple ads.

Format
Choose how you'd like your ad to look

FIGURE 28.1–Ad Format Section

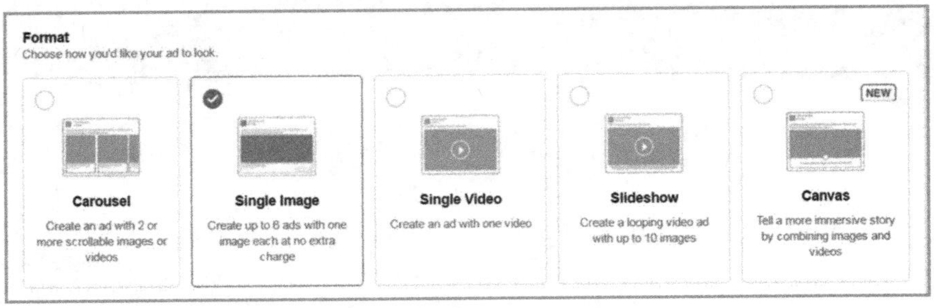

FIGURE 28.2–Single Image Ad Format

choose (Carousel, Single Image, Single Video, Slideshow, and Canvas). Let us use Single Image for now.

Under Images, you can upload a new image, use previously uploaded images, or use the free stock images (see Figure 28.3). If you are uploading a new image, use the Recommended Image Specs as a guide.

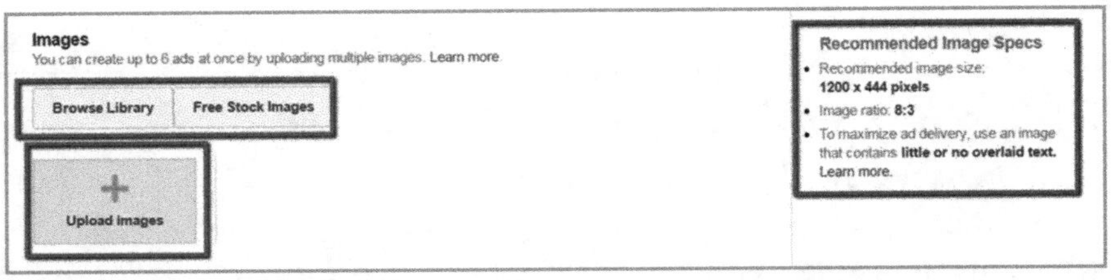

FIGURE 28.3–Upload Images

In Figure 28.4, under Page and Links, select your Facebook page. If you have an Instagram account, you can add it here as well.

FIGURE 28.4–Page and Links

Enter your Website URL and ad copy in the provided boxes. Also, it's good practice to take advantage of the "Call to Action" button. (See Figure 28.5)

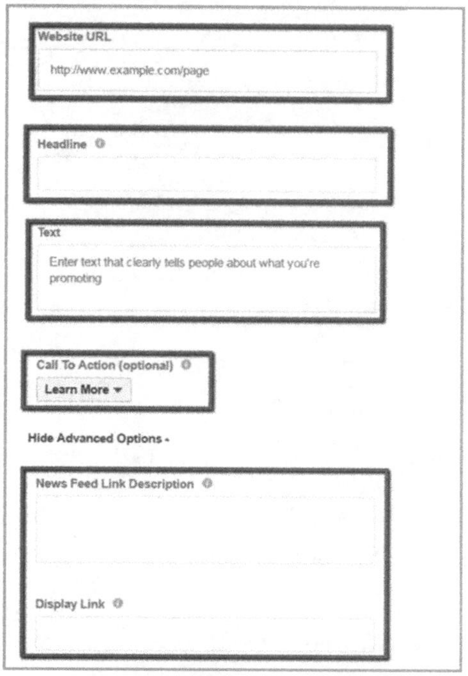

FIGURE 28.5–Ad Copy Section

Once all is complete, clicking "Review Order" will take you to a window to finish creating the campaign, ad set, and ad. (See Figure 28.6.)

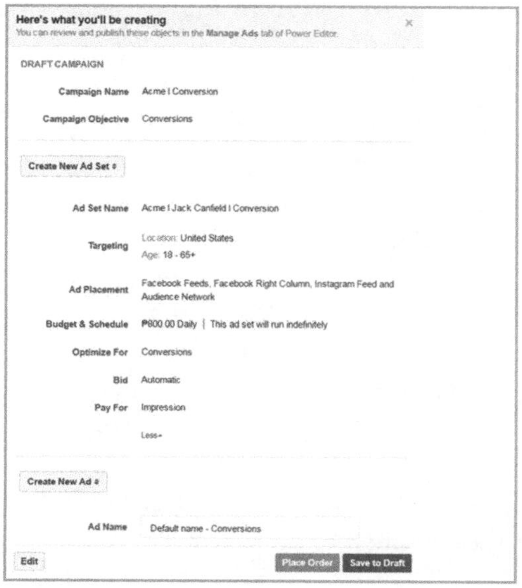

FIGURE 28.6–Review Order

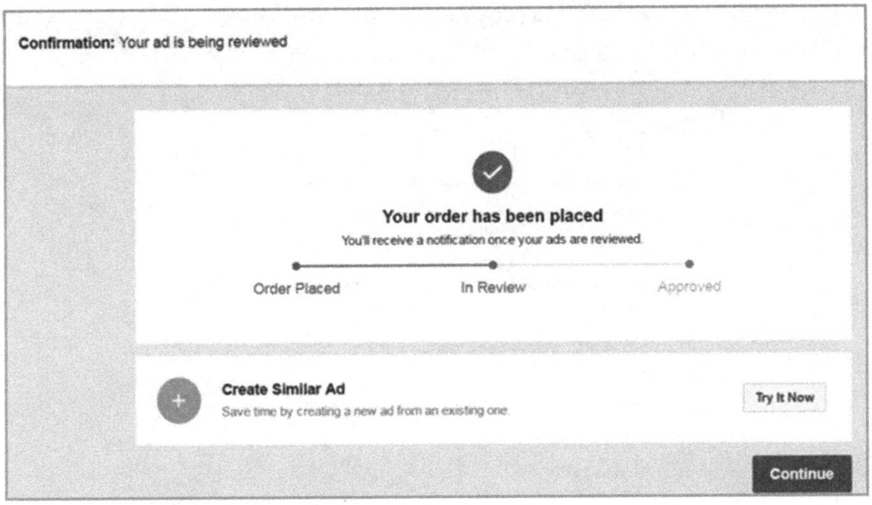

FIGURE 28.7–Place Order

By clicking the green "Place Order" button (Figure 28.7), Facebook will then review your campaign, ad set, and ad. Simply click on the blue "Continue" button to finish.

After confirmation, you can create a new ad using the same window (you see in Figure 28.8) to test out different images or copy.

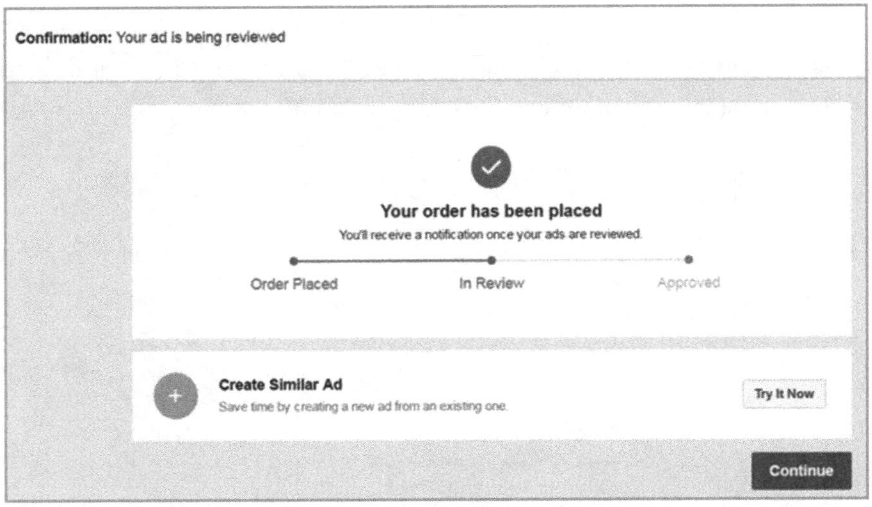

FIGURE 28.8–Order Confirmation

Once all is done, you will be taken to the campaign view page, pausing the new campaign temporarily. (See Figure 28.9 on page 329.)

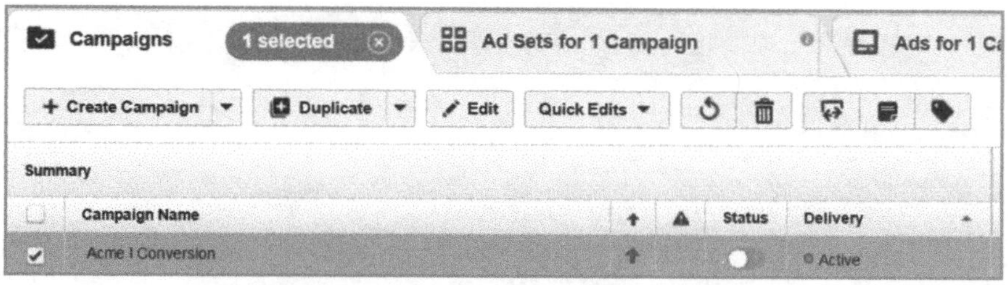

FIGURE 28.9–Clicking Into Ad Campaign

To create a new ad set using a different targeting or placement, click on your paused campaign (see Figure 28.9), and you will be taken to the ad sets tab, as seen in Figure 28.10.

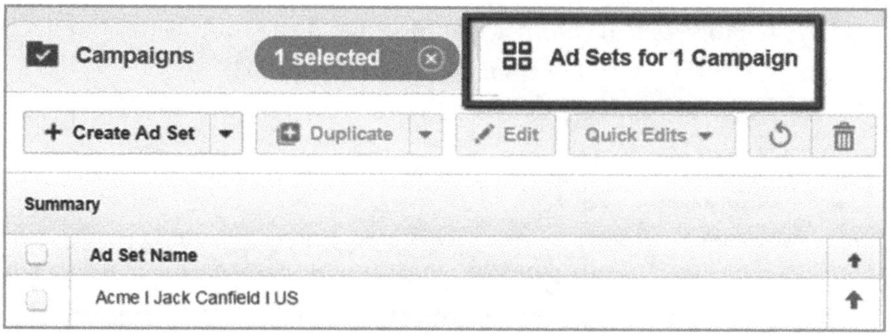

FIGURE 28.10–Ad Sets Tab

Note: This is a Power User Tip. This will help you save time creating new ad sets targeting different interests.

Select the first ad set you created and then click the "Duplicate" button, as seen in Figure 28.11.

FIGURE 28.11–Duplicate Ad Set

Duplicate Ad Set   ×

CHOOSE A CAMPAIGN

◉ Keep Same Campaign

○ Use Existing

○ Create New

FIGURE 28.12–Keep Same Campaign

When the duplicate window pops-up, use the default "Keep Same Campaign," as seen in Figure 28.12.

If you have ten interests in your list, put nine under the "number of duplicates." For status options, select the second option. (as seen in Figure 28.13).

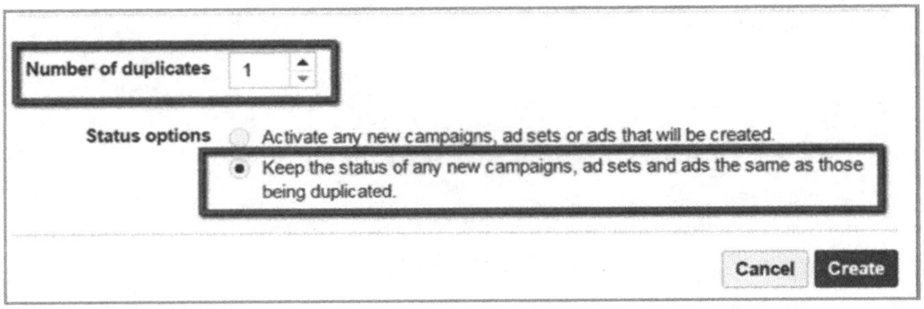

Number of duplicates   1   ▲▼

Status options   ○ Activate any new campaigns, ad sets or ads that will be created.

◉ Keep the status of any new campaigns, ad sets and ads the same as those being duplicated.

Cancel   **Create**

FIGURE 28.13–Keep Campaign Status Same as Duplicated

The duplicated ad sets will appear with the word "Copy" at the end. You just have to select it, hit the "edit" button (see Figure 28.14), and then just add a new audience to that ad set.

FIGURE 28.14–Duplicate Ad Set

Chapter 29

Reporting, Analysis, Action

Guest Author Angela Ponsford

There's a whole lot to look at in Facebook ads reporting, so I'm going to try and simplify things for you here. Otherwise, you'll end up overwhelmed and fed up!

WHAT'S THE BEST WAY TO MEASURE SUCCESS?

This may sound like a very simple question but it's vital for interpreting your Facebook results correctly. If you look at the wrong metric, you may be totally reading the wrong story. So, what should you be looking at? The answer is your Cost Per Acquisition (CPA).

> *"Analysis is the critical starting point of strategic thinking."*
>
> —Kenichi Ohmae

For different funnels, your CPA may be different. For example, it could be Cost Per Lead (CPL), Cost Per Registration (CPR), or Cost Per Sale (CPS). It really depends on how well you know your numbers and how quickly you're looking for positive ROI. For example, some businesses are OK with an initial negative ROI because they know their follow-up sequences are effective and are effective and will earn ROI in the near future. For this type of funnel, a CPA a CPL may be appropriate. Others may need to ROI right away so their CPA would be CPS.

The reason we focus on CPA and not other common online paid advertising metrics like Click Through Rate (CTR), Cost Per Click (CPC), or Cost Per Impressions (CPM) is because they don't consider your entire funnel. For example, in Google AdWords, where the format of each ad is basically the same, the above metrics are important metrics for ad performance because you're basically comparing apples to apples.

On Facebook, you have all sorts of ad formats and content choices (e.g., short copy, long copy, video) that you're really comparing apples to oranges. For example, an extremely well written short copy ad may have a higher CTR than a video ad because you've created curiosity in the short copy. The CTR for your video ad may be lower but the person clicking is more qualified because you've provide value before asking them to take action. So, in this example, you may be okay with a lower CTR from your video ad because they are more qualified and therefore more likely to opt-in or purchase. That's why it's so important to measure the actual result that you want to achieve.

This is not to say that CTR, CPC, and CPM aren't important because they are. But they should be used as a secondary measure to help troubleshoot where your funnel is breaking down in case you aren't reaching your desired CPA.

WHERE CAN I SEE MY RESULTS?

The easiest way to see how your campaigns have performed is in Ads Manager. There's a LOT of information in there, so you need to be clear on the objective of the ad and what the main metric is that will determine success. If you look at the wrong metric, you'll either think your ads are tanking or you'll think they're doing amazing. But when you go check the ACTUAL results, you'll be bitterly disappointed.

Figure 29.1 shows the default Performance column view that you see when you first go into Ads Manager.

The Results and Cost per Result columns will show you the main metrics that are relevant to the type of campaign you're running. For example:

- If you're running an engagement ad to get page likes, you'll see the number of page likes and the cost per like.
- If you're running an ad to get traffic to your website, you'll see how many link clicks and the cost per link click there are.

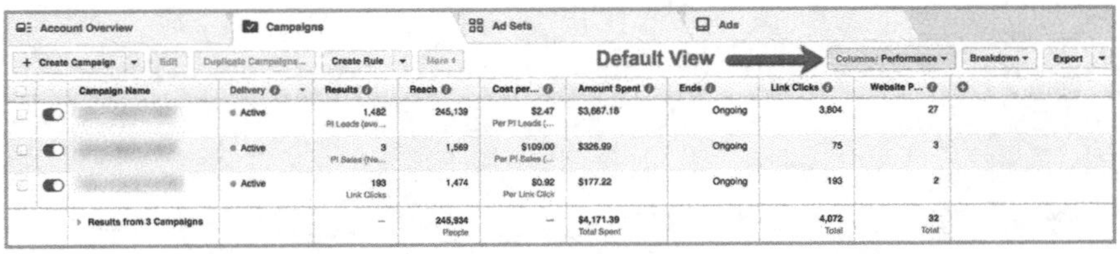

FIGURE 29.1–Default View in Ads Manager

- If you're running a conversion campaign, you'll see how many conversions and the cost per conversions there are.

Looking at these metrics at the campaign level gives you an overall picture of how well the campaign is performing. You can then delve deeper into other metrics and into the performance of individual ad sets and ads after that.

So, let's take the example shown in Figure 29.1 and work through the results of the conversion campaign. When you click through to the Ad Set level, you'll see all the different ad sets you have running. Once again, you'll see the results at the default Performance column view.

The image in Figure 29.2 shows the results of four ad sets. On this view, it seems like two of the ad sets are doing really well, one is doing OK, and one is really not performing well.

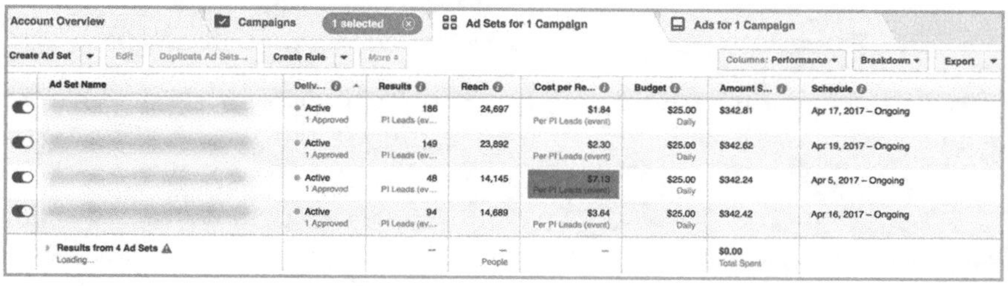

FIGURE 29.2–Results at Ad Set Level

To delve deeper into why some of the ad sets are doing well and why some aren't, then you need to customize your columns to show more metrics.

Click on the dropdown icon in the Columns menu (next to Performance), and you'll see there's some preset column views in there. Figure 29.3 shows the options available.

Performance and clicks is a good starting point for traffic and conversion campaigns, but if you have any custom conversions or customized tracking set up, you need to go to customize columns and create your own view. Figure 29.4 on page 334 shows some of the many options available to you in the Conversions > Website section.

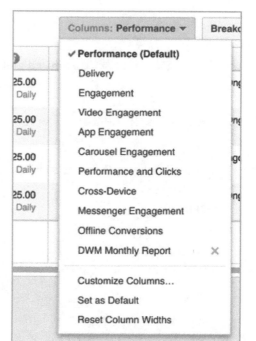

FIGURE 29.3–Column Views

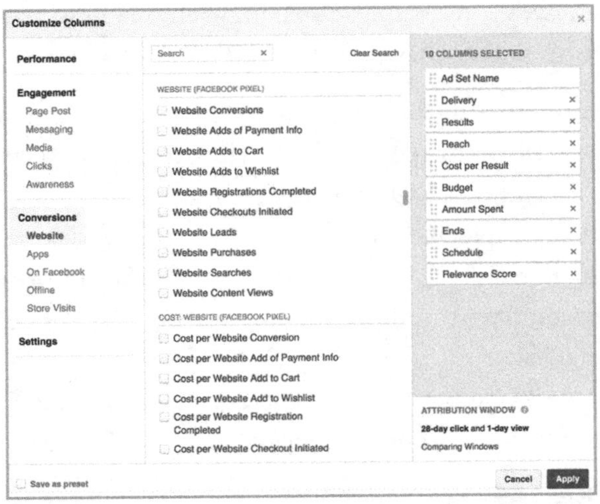

FIGURE 29.4–Conversions > Website Column Options

Figure 29.5 shows the custom columns chosen to view the performance of this campaign.

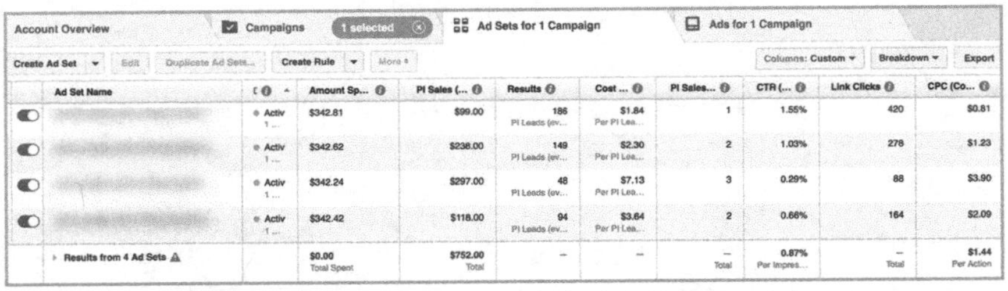

FIGURE 29.5–Customized Column View for Website Conversion Campaign Measuring Leads and Sales

For this specific campaign, I'm interested in

- No. of Leads (Results)
- Cost Per Lead (Cost Per Result)
- CTR (Link Clicks)
- Link Clicks
- CPC (Cost per link Click)
- Number of Sales
- Sales Conversion Value

So even though the main goal of this campaign is to generate leads, I'm also able to look at how many people are buying my product as a result of seeing the ads. Facebook has a default Attribution Window that will show you actions/conversions that have occurred one day after someone has viewed the ad or 28 days after clicking on an ad. You can change the settings for this when you're customizing your column view if you wanted to increase the view-through window or reduce the click-through window.

So looking at the results in Figure 29.5, we can see that the third ad set has a much higher lead cost than the other three, a much lower CTR, and a higher CPC. So these combined numbers indicate that the ad creative being used in this ad set is probably not interesting to the audience that it is being shown to.

However, the number of sales and revenue generated by this ad set is higher than all the others. So even though the leads are costing more, it seems that they are higher quality leads, because they're actually buying at a higher rate than the other leads.

So the combined information we can get from looking at several of the relevant metrics can lead us to making a decision as whether we're willing to accept a higher lead cost knowing that we're making more revenue from those more expensive leads. I know what choice I would make every time!

BREAKDOWN

In addition to the metrics you can see in the column views, Facebook also provides you with many more options in the Breakdown menu. Figure 29.6 shows some of the options available.

By selecting these options, you can see which age groups performed the best, whether males or females engaged more, which countries gave the best results, plus many more options.

Figure 29.7 on page 336 shows the age breakdown for our example campaign.

We can see that ages 25 to 34 gave us the cheapest leads and that ages 55 to 64 are delivering the most revenue. We would then use that information to add in some new audiences and demographic targeting so as to maximize the ad budget we have.

EXPORT TO EXCEL

You also have the option to export your results into Excel and perform some more detailed analysis of what you're seeing. This can be useful when you have a lot of data to sort through and also when you have additional

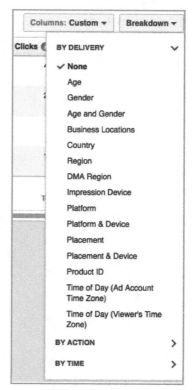

FIGURE 29.6–Breakdown of Campaign Results

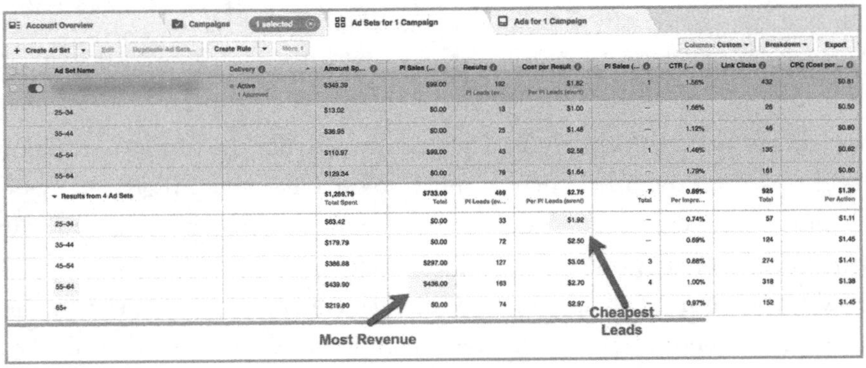

FIGURE 29.7–Age Breakdown

calculations that you need to make to the campaign. Simply click on the "Export" button next to the Breakdown button and choose where you want to save the file.

The reporting of Facebook ads may seem overwhelming when you first begin, but if you take the time to work your way around each section, after a while, you'll be more confident to make decisions on the data you're seeing. You'll also get a better understanding of how different metrics are good indicators of the overall performance of your campaign.

Chapter 30

Troubleshooting

Guest Author Traci Reuter

You've followed all the steps—you've got a hook, you've researched your audience, you've created the images, you've built all the campaigns, and you set them live. You've got great hopes. You just know they're winners, and then they tank.

What do you do? Give up? Decide Facebook Ads don't work? Heck no! It's time to troubleshoot!

> *"We cannot solve our problems with the same thinking we used when we created them."*
>
> —Albert Einstein

THE FIVE MOST COMMON TROUBLESHOOTING SCENARIOS, AND WHAT TO DO ABOUT THEM

In this chapter, we'll cover the five most common troubleshooting scenarios we see over and over again when running campaigns and what you need to do in order to try and salvage them.

The five common troubleshooting scenarios:

1. Zero conversions
2. CPAs are too high

3. CTR is high—CPC is low

4. Social shares are high—conversions are low

5. Relevance score drops or is low

Zero Conversions

You launch your campaign, 24 to 48 hours go by, and you've got nothing. Nada. Zilch. Zip. Goose egg. Alarms start to go off in your head. This is the worst of all scenarios.

First things first, verify that the Facebook pixel is on every single page. This may seem obvious, but you'd be surprised at how often this happens. This is where having the Facebook Pixel Helper installed on your chrome browser comes in handy. Start by checking every URL in your funnel. Click on the URL in every ad that has zero conversions, and verify that the pixel is there. See Figure 30.1.

FIGURE 30.1–Facebook Pixel Installed

The next thing you'll want to look at is whether you have the CORRECT pixel on every page. There are times when you may have more than one pixel on a website. This can be because a client has multiple ad accounts, multiple companies—it happens. The key is making sure that the pixels on the URL's are the pixels you're running conversion ads for.

To verify you have the correct pixel on every page, go to Ads Manager, select all tools in the dropdown menu, and then go to pixels (see Figure 30.2 on page 339). Once you're there, you'll find your ad account Pixel ID on the right side (see Figure 30.3 on page 339). Then, you'll want to cross reference that Pixel ID with the pixel the Facebook Pixel Helper is listing (see Figure 30.4 on page 339). Make sure these two numbers match up on every page of your funnel.

Next, make sure that you're optimizing for the right conversion event and that your reporting columns match. This can be easily overlooked because depending upon the

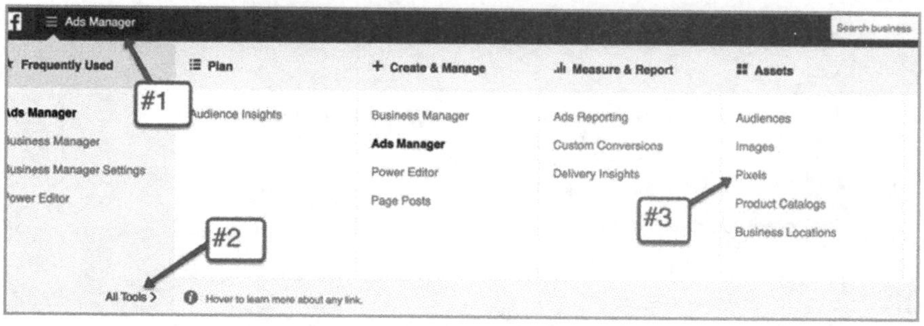

FIGURE 30.2–Pixel Assets in Ads Manager

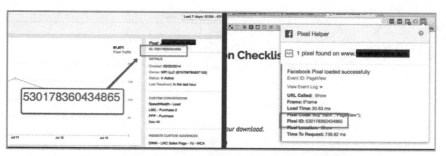

FIGURE 30.3–Ad Account Pixel ID

FIGURE 30.4–Checking Pixel ID in FB Pixel Helper

event that you are optimizing for, it may not show up in your standard Facebook report in Ads Manager.

You can verify the conversion event you are optimizing for at the ad set level See Figure 30.5 on page 340.

Once you've verified that you're optimizing for the correct conversion event, go back to your reporting columns and make sure that is what is being shown. If it isn't being shown, you'll want to customize your ad report columns to show the correct conversion event. Simply select the correct conversion event that you want to show up in your reporting, and then save this reporting view as a preset. Name it something that makes sense to your campaign, and then save it as a default view so that it will be the first thing you see in your reporting. See Figures 30.6 to 30.10 on pages340 to 341.

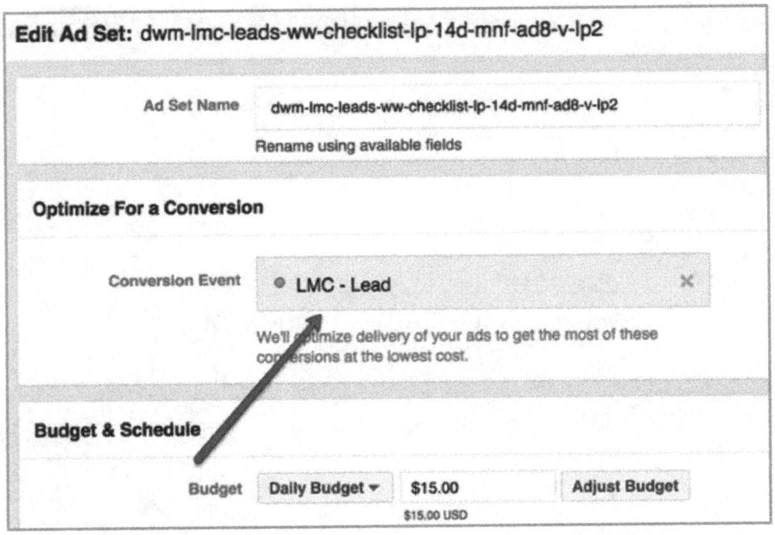

Edit Ad Set: dwm-lmc-leads-ww-checklist-lp-14d-mnf-ad8-v-lp2

Ad Set Name   dwm-lmc-leads-ww-checklist-lp-14d-mnf-ad8-v-lp2

Rename using available fields

Optimize For a Conversion

Conversion Event   ● LMC - Lead   ✕

We'll optimize delivery of your ads to get the most of these conversions at the lowest cost.

Budget & Schedule

Budget   Daily Budget ▾ $15.00   **Adjust Budget**

$15.00 USD

FIGURE 30.5–Conversion Event Being Optimized For

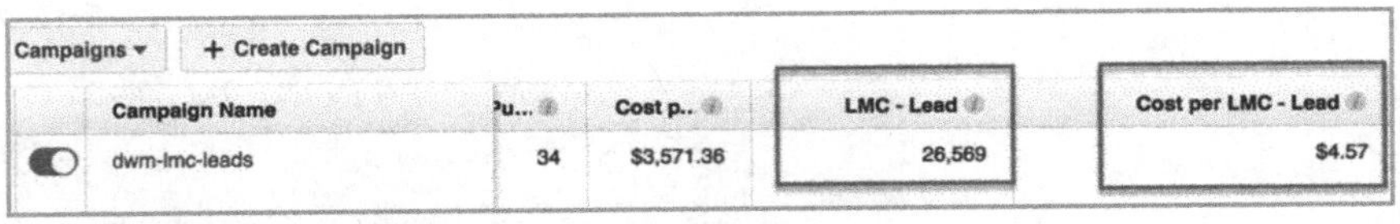

Campaigns ▾ + Create Campaign				
Campaign Name	Pu...	Cost p..	**LMC - Lead**	**Cost per LMC - Lead**
◯ dwm-lmc-leads	34	$3,571.36	26,569	$4.57

FIGURE 30.6–Reporting Columns

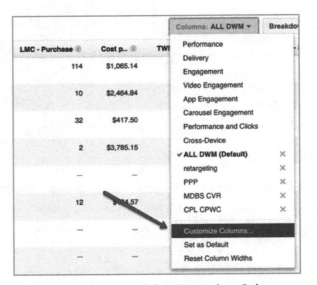

FIGURE 30.7–Customizing Reporting Columns

FIGURE 30.8–Customizing Reporting Columns

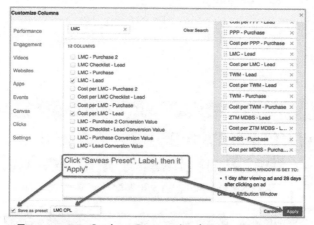

FIGURE 30.9–Saving Customized Report as Preset

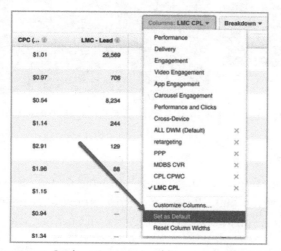

FIGURE 30.10–Saving Customized Report as Default View

After you've verified that all the pixels are on the right pages, check and make sure all the URLs in your funnel are loading. You could have a page load speed issue, a caching issue, or something else interfering with the load speed. If you suspect that may be an issue, you can check your site load speed at https://gtmetrix.com.

If this turns out to be the case, then you'll need to have someone who can clean up the technical issues involved come in and resolve what is making the URLs load slowly.

If you've made it this far and still haven't found the culprit behind your ads that are tanking, it's time to move on to the landing pages themselves. Again, as mentioned earlier, this may seem obvious, but make sure that all the call to action (CTA) buttons on all your URLs are working properly (see Figure 30.11). Click on every single CTA button or link and make sure they are going where they are supposed to go.

The final thing to look for in this process is to make sure that your landing pages actually have a CTA button or link (see Figure 30.12 on page 343). It really has happened where we've had a client want us to run traffic to a page for conversions, and there wasn't even a button or link anywhere to be seen on the page! Again, it's the little things that can be overlooked.

FIGURE 30.11–Check That CTA Links/Buttons Work

CPAs Are Too High

This isn't as bad as getting zero conversions, but what do you do when the conversions you're getting are just too high? First, you need to know what your target CPA is. Your CPA is your Cost Per Acquisition (e.g., Cost Per Lead, Cost Per Sale, etc.) Once you know

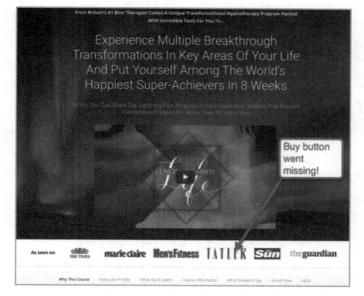

FIGURE 30.12–Verify That CTA Link/Button Exists on the Page

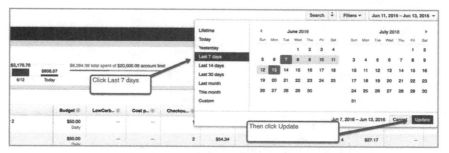

FIGURE 30.13–Sort Reporting by the Last Seven Days

what your target CPA is, the first thing to do is pause every ad set that is converting at two to three times your target CPA. We recommend first sorting your reporting view by the last seven days (see Figure 30.13).

Once you have this view, sort your ad sets by the cost of your conversion from the greatest to the least (see Figure 30.14 on page 344), and then start turning off any ad set that is two to three times your target CPA (see Figure 30.15 on page 344). Also, look at any ad set that has zero conversions over the last seven days and shut those off as well. The easiest way to do this is to sort your ad sets by the amount spent column, and then sort from the greatest to least (see Figure 30.16 on page 344). Look for any ad sets that have spent two times your CPA and have had zero conversions and turn them off right away.

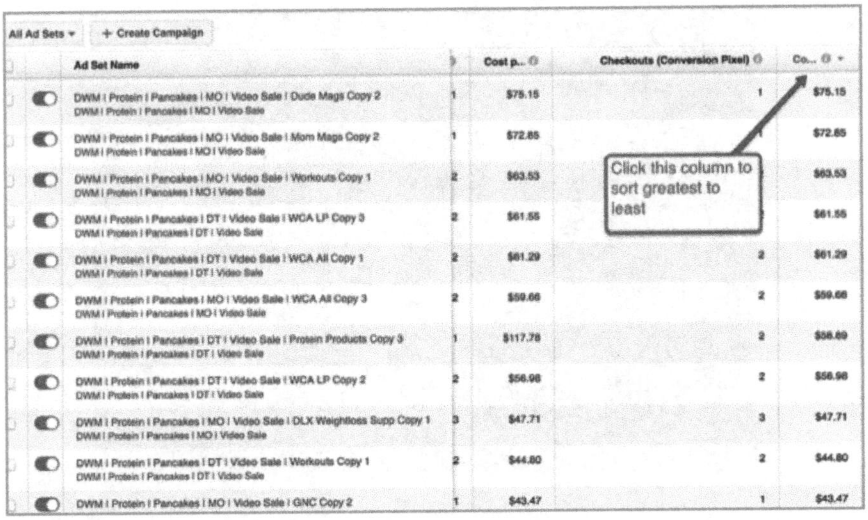

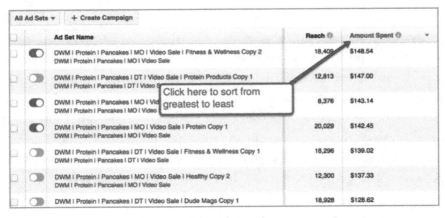

FIGURE 30.14–Sorting Cost Per Conversion from Greatest to Least

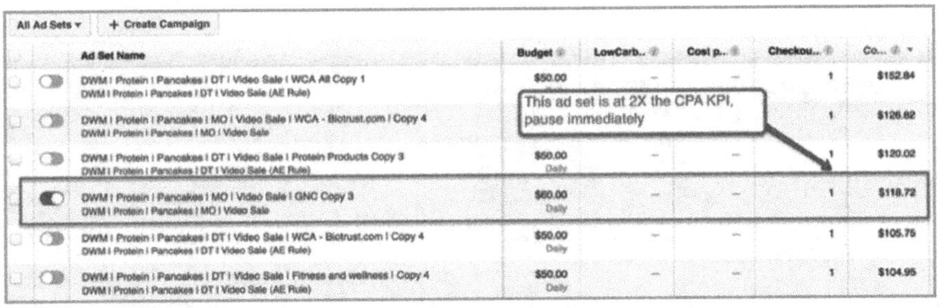

FIGURE 30.15–Pausing Ad Sets That Are Two to Three Times Your Target CPA

FIGURE 30.16–Sorting Ad Sets by Amount Spent

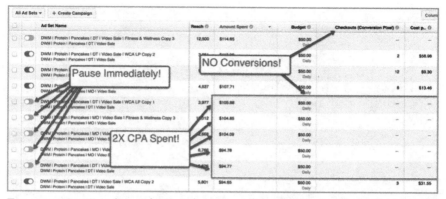

FIGURE 30.17–Pausing Ad Sets That Have Spent Two to Three Times Your CPA with Zero Conversions

CTR Is High–CPC Is Low

CTR, or click-through rate, is the percent of people who see your ad who actually click through to it. In this case, we're referring to the link CTR, and not the general CTR, which measures any clicks on your ad. CPC is the cost per click each time someone clicks through from your ad to your URL.

A CTR over 1 percent is typically considered high, a low CPC targeting consumers is typically under $0.50, and a low CPC in the business to business area is usually $1 or less. This can vary from business to business, but it a good general rule of thumb.

You might be thinking, "seems like a high CTR and a low CPC would be a good thing" but not if you're not getting any conversions or your CPAs are high.

There are three potential issues in this case—landing page, ad scent, and targeting.

If it's your landing page, people are clicking on the page but not converting. They're not opting in, they're not signing up, and they're not buying. If it's your ad scent, you don't have any scent between your ad and your landing page. There's just no smell. If it's your targeting, you've been sending unqualified traffic to your page, and it's time to take another look at your targeting.

If your landing page is the culprit, this is when you want to consider split testing your landing page. Take a look at your landing page conversion rates (see Figure 30.18 on page 346). Average conversion rates for a landing page are around 20 percent, and if you're running below 10 percent, you've got a problem. We've listed in the table in Figure 30.18 some landing page conversion rate benchmarks you can use as a guideline. Rework your landing page, your registration page, and your sales page and see if you can increase your page conversion rates.

Ad scent is easy to overlook but pretty easy to fix. Look at your ad and look at your landing page—are there any similarities or familiar components? Figure 30.19 on page 346 is an example of an ad and landing page that have excellent ad scent.

	Landing Page Conversion Rate	Tripwire Page Conversion Rate	Core Offer Page Conversion Rate
Above Average	40%+	20%	20%
Average	20%	10%	10%
Below Average	10%	5%	5%

FIGURE 30.18–Landing Page Conversion Rate Benchmarks

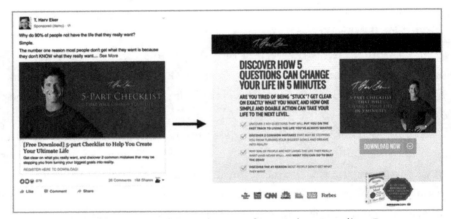

FIGURE 30.19–Excellent Ad Scent from Ad to Landing Page

Interest targeting seems like something you'd get right, but we've often seen people where people target an audience that really has no correlation with their target market. Just because someone likes Oprah doesn't mean they read books. Take a little time, and make sure you're putting your ad in front of the right people.

Social Shares Are High–Conversions Are Low

You might expect that if you have an ad that gets super crazy social engagement—people liking, commenting, and sharing—that you'd get great conversions. That's not always the case. If this happens, especially if your ad is getting lots of social shares, the first thing you should do is re-evaluate your campaign objective (see Figure 30.20 on page 347).

If you're running a campaign with a traffic or page post engagement as the objective, that's what the Facebook algorithm will give you—traffic or engagement but not conversions.

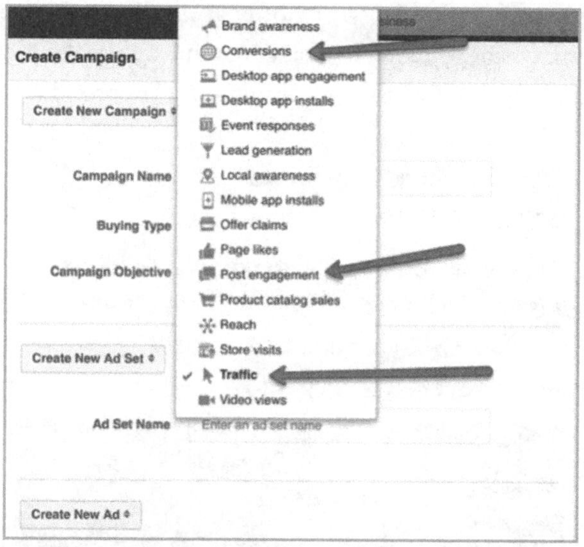

FIGURE 30.20–Re-evaluate Your Campaign Objective

The next thing to look at is your ad copy. Is your hook strong? Is the copy leading to the next step in the customer journey?

The ad in Figure 30.21 is a great example of an ad that had really high social shares, but just wasn't converting.

FIGURE 30.21–Ad with High Social Shares Not Converting

We revamped the copy, created a strong offer and call to action, and added a URL in the copy. This ad started converting like crazy. You have to make it clear to people what the next step in the journey is. The first ad didn't, but the second ad did in a big way.

FIGURE 30.22–Revamped Ad with Strong, Relevant Calls to Action

Another possible solution to high social shares with low conversions is to rework your offer. If you're getting high social shares, your ad is resonating with your audience and you've got a solid hook. It's most likely the offer that is missing the mark.

The final thing to consider in this scenario is your ad copy and creative. It's possible that your ad is engaging people for the wrong reasons, and they totally miss your point that would lead them to convert because they're focused on the wrong thing.

Relevance Score Drops or Is Low

Before you can begin troubleshooting this scenario, you've got to really understand what relevance score is. Facebook is all about the user experience, and it's a huge priority for them to only show ads to people who are the most relevant to them. Facebook determines relevance score based upon the positive and negative feedback they expect an ad to receive from its target audience. As people interact and provide feedback on the ad (both positive and negative), Facebook adjusts the relevance score of the ad. Relevance scores range from 1 to 10, with 10 being the best and 1 being the worst.

While relevance score isn't the only factor in a poor performing campaign, it can impact your CPA's and your conversions.

A low relevance score is ultimately the result of a poor message to market match. The first thing you should do is make sure your offer is what people want. The best way to do that is to rewrite your ad copy to better connect with your target audience. Make sure your copy is hitting on their biggest pains, their desires, and their biggest fears. Focus on taking your prospect from their undesirable before state to their desirable after state. Remember, good ad copy can literally turn around just about any poor performing campaign.

Keep in mind, those aren't the only troubleshooting scenarios you might run into when running Facebook ad campaigns. There are several more including: low click through rate (CTR), high cost per click (CPC), high CPA with large target audiences, ads not getting impressions from Facebook, and having your CPA rise as you scale your campaigns.

For more detailed information on these scenarios as well as detailed case studies, please visit www.perrymarshall.com/fbtools.

Chapter 31

The Five-Tier Scaling System

Guest Author Ralph Burns

You've done all the hard work—performed your market research, defined your avatar, created a killer hook and offer, written your ad copy, found the perfect creative, built your campaigns, and launched it out into the world. Now comes the moment of truth.

The nervousness, the excitement, the OCD-like symptoms, the feverishly checking your reporting every few minutes to see if you've made a sale and then like magic a sale registers in your dashboard—was it a fluke? You're not sure.

> "*Most people spend more time and energy going around problems than in trying to solve them.*"
>
> —HENRY FORD

You wait . . . a second sale registers . . . quickly followed by a third . . . then another . . . and another.

Wow! You've got a winner on your hands. What a rush!

You decide it's time to go big, but there's a problem.

Theoretically, it should be relatively straightforward to scale on Facebook. For example, if you're running an ad for $10 per day, just increase the budget to $100 per day, and you should see a ten-fold increase in revenues while retaining your desired Cost Per Acquisition (CPA).

But if you've been around for a little while, you know that unfortunately Facebook doesn't behave like that. Trying to scale by increasing the budget often feels like a crazy jerky rollercoaster ride rather than a simple smooth ascending linear graph. Your results may go up. They may go down . . . get stuck . . . sometimes recover . . . sometimes not . . . sometimes, Facebook won't even show your Ads, and often, your conversion costs skyrocket.

The exact reason for this haywire is unknown. It's potentially a quirk of the Facebook algorithm. It kind of reminds me of *Seinfeld*'s Soup Nazi—once your order is in, there's no going back. If you try to change your order, the Soup Nazi might yell "NO SOUP FOR YOU!"

Yet scaling is a vital part of building large, successful advertising campaigns on Facebook—so how should you do it?

INTRODUCING "THE FIVE-TIER SCALING SYSTEM"

In this guide, we'll show our best strategy for turning small successful campaigns into large, even massive, successful campaigns. We call it the five-tier scaling system.

The five tiers are:

1. Duplication Scaling
2. Audience Scaling
3. Alteration Scaling
4. Large Budget Scaling
5. Small Budget Scaling

The reason we have five tiers is because there's no one size fits all when it comes to scaling. Together, these five methods will give you all the tools you need to reach large audiences without having to fasten your seatbelt for Facebook's crazy broken rollercoaster.

These methods are purposely listed in order. Try method one before trying method two. Try method two before trying method three. Try method three before trying method four, and so on. These methods also work best when used in conjunction with our proprietary campaign building process called the Michigan Method.

MICHIGAN METHOD

In a nutshell, the Michigan Method is a campaign structure that uses a lot of ad sets all with small budgets. Sometimes as many as 180. There's only one ad per ad set. For the Michigan Method to work optimally, you must target larger audiences (between 400,000 to 2 million). This helps insure your ad sets don't cannibalize one another or saturate the market.

THE POWER OF TARGETING LARGE AUDIENCES

Facebook changes fast, and so do our strategies. Recently we discovered that using large audiences is one of the best ways to leverage the power of Facebook's amazing algorithm. This might mean four or five million people in an audience, or in some cases, our best audiences might have 40 to 50 million people in it. However, the only way you can be successful targeting large audiences like this is when you are generating at least 20 to 30 (at the bare minimum) conversions per week per ad set. When you are using the "Website Conversions" objective and you are sending lots of Facebook conversion data (preferably 10 to 20 or more per day), then Facebook will do the heavy lifting for you. They will only put your ads in front of the people who have most similarities to your customers, subscribers, engaged audiences, etc. Please visit www.perrymarshall.com/fbtools, and listen to our podcast to get the latest updates on how the algorithm works, and what our Partner Manager over at Facebook, who we talk with every two weeks and visit in-person at their Austin corporate office several times a year.

One caveat, this recommendation is for targeting the U.S. In smaller population countries, take Australia for example, finding a great-targeted audience that size might be challenging. In these scenarios, use an audience of 100,000 to 500,000.

The beauty of the Michigan Method is that within a short period of time, you can see which ad sets are failing and which are bringing in an awesome CPA. We kill off the ad sets that suck and build on the ones doing well. We call it "Killing the Ponies, and Feeding the Stallions." (Yeah, we're brutal that way.)

The five-tier scaling system is all about bulking-up your stallions.

DUPLICATION SCALING

When looking to scale, the first method to consider is Duplication Scaling. It works best if your CPA is $100 or lower. Duplication Scaling involves identifying an ad set performing well and making an exact copy of it. We define "Performing Well" as having at least ten conversions in an ad set below your desired CPA. Please make sure you have enough data and feel confident before starting to scale.

Now remember for Duplication Scaling to work, you need to be targeting large audiences, but it works even better if you can target an audience greater than a 1 million.

For smaller audiences, you can still use the same principles but just realize there's a much lower ceiling for how many ad sets a smaller audience can support. Plus, the frequency for how often people see your ads will increase more quickly and could potentially cause higher ad costs.

For smaller audiences, we recommend having multiple ad variations in rotation inside your ad set, but only have one ad live at a time. This is the only time we recommend more than one ad per ad set. That way, you can turn an ad on and off when frequency gets too high and CPA starts to increase.

BEFORE GETTING STARTED

As you know, the Facebook Ads Platform updates regularly, so the screenshots I'm sharing are current at the time of writing.

VITAL STEP

Just going off topic for a moment—whenever you create an ad in Facebook, you create two identifiers: the Ad ID Number and a Post ID Number. The Post ID refers to the content inside the ad. So, if you create two different ads with the exact same copy and creative, Facebook will consider them to be two different posts and assign them their own unique Post ID.

Why is this important? Because if not set up correctly Duplication Scaling can quickly become a community management nightmare.

Here's what I mean.

Just say you make nine duplications of your winning ad set. What you've also done is created nine new posts that people can like, share and leave a comment on. So even though it looks like the same post, now you have to moderate ten different posts (the nine duplications and the original). Plus, you're thinning out your social proof because your social engagement is spread over ten different posts.

The solution: use the same Post ID (the original ad) in all duplicates (Figures 31.1 and 31.2 on page 355).

Your Ad ID Number will be different for each ad, but you use the same Post ID (Figure 31.2). This collects all your comments, likes, and shares in the one location, which makes it easier to manage plus Facebook will reward you with more impressions at a lower cost if the reaction to your ad is favorable.

THE PROCESS FOR SCALING VIA DUPLICATING AD SETS

1. In Ads Manager, set calendar to the last seven days. See Figures 31.3 and 31.4 on page 355.

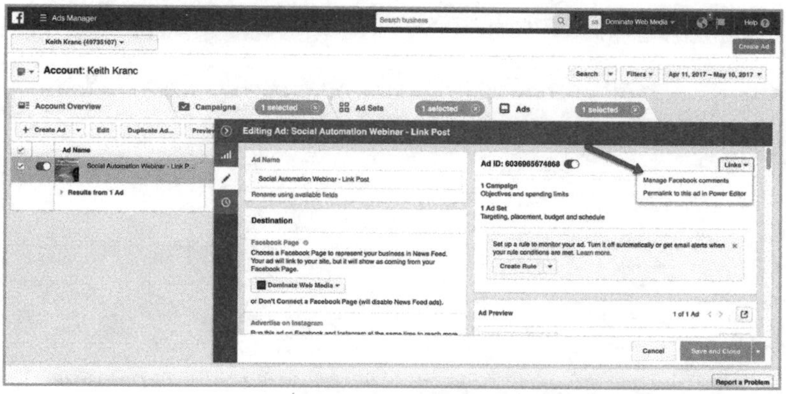

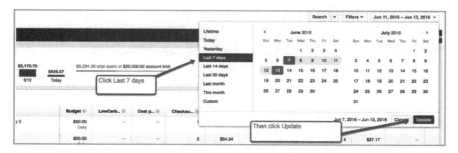

FIGURE 31.1–Post ID

FIGURE 31.2–Post ID

FIGURE 31.3–Duplicating Ad Sets

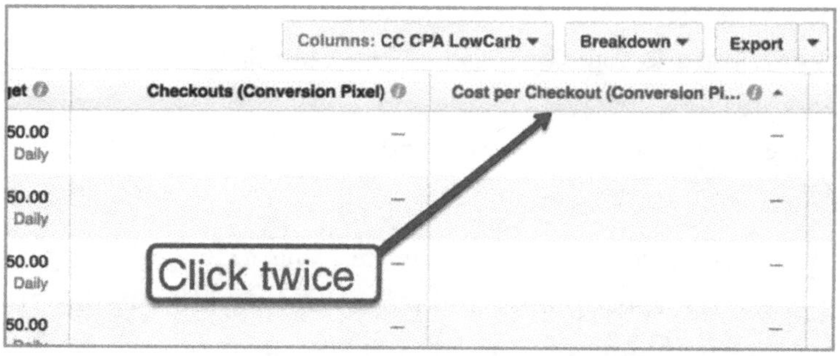

FIGURE 31.4–Duplicating Ad Sets

2. Sort ad sets by CPA—order from smallest to largest. See Figure 31.5.

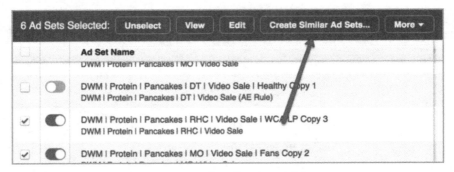

6 Ad Sets Selected:	Unselect	View	Edit	Create Similar Ad Sets...	More ▾				
		Ad Set Name				Budget	LowCarb..	Cost p..	Checkou..	Co... ▲
	⬤	DWM I Protein I Pancakes I DT I Video Sale I Healthy Copy 1 DWM I Protein I Pancakes I DT I Video Sale (AE Rule)				$50.00 Daily	–	–	–	–
✓	⬤	DWM I Protein I Pancakes I RHC I Video Sale I WCA LP Copy 3 DWM I Protein I Pancakes I RHC I Video Sale				$50.00 Daily	–	–	19	$4.46
✓	⬤	DWM I Protein I Pancakes I MO I Video Sale I Fans Copy 2 DWM I Protein I Pancakes I MO I Video Sale				$60.00 Daily	–	–	7	$5.55
✓	⬤	DWM I Protein I Pancakes I RHC I Video Sale I Fitness & Wellness Copy 3 DWM I Protein I Pancakes I RHC I Video Sale				$70.00 Daily	–	–	2	$7.07
	⬤	DWM I Protein I Pancakes I RHC I Video Sale I Healthy Copy 1 DWM I Protein I Pancakes I RHC I Video Sale				$50.00 Daily	–	–	1	$7.90
✓	⬤	DWM I Protein I Pancakes I RHC I Video Sale I WCA LP Copy 2 DWM I Protein I Pancakes I RHC I Video Sale				$70.00 Daily	3	$65.20	22	$8.89
	⬤	DWM I Protein I Pancakes I RHC I Video Sale I LA WCA - Biotrust.com Copy 2 DWM I Protein I Pancakes I RHC I Video Sale				$50.00 Daily	–	–	2	$11.59
	⬤	DWM I Protein I Pancakes I RHC I Video Sale I WCA LP Copy 1 DWM I Protein I Pancakes I RHC I Video Sale				$70.00 Daily	–	–	2	$12.97
✓	⬤	DWM I Protein I Pancakes I MO I Video Sale I LA WCA - Biotrust.com Copy 2 DWM I Protein I Pancakes I MO I Video Sale				$50.00 Daily	–	–	18	$14.09
✓	⬤	DWM I Protein I Pancakes I RHC I Video Sale I WCA - Biotrust.com I Copy 4 DWM I Protein I Pancakes I RHC I Video Sale				$50.00 Daily	–	–	9	$15.88
	⬤	DWM I Protein I Pancakes I RHC I Video Sale I WCA All Copy 3 DWM I Protein I Pancakes I RHC I Video Sale				$70.00 Daily	–	–	2	$16.75

FIGURE 31.5–Duplicating Ad Sets

3. Screen by volume of conversions, scroll down to the conversions that have signifi-cant amounts of conversions and select all the ads that have the most conversions at or below your CPA. See Figure 31.6.

6 Ad Sets Selected:	Unselect	View	Edit	Create Similar Ad Sets...	More ▾
		Ad Set Name			
		DWM I Protein I Pancakes I MO I Video Sale			
	⬤	DWM I Protein I Pancakes I DT I Video Sale I Healthy Copy 1 DWM I Protein I Pancakes I DT I Video Sale (AE Rule)			
✓	⬤	DWM I Protein I Pancakes I RHC I Video Sale I WCA LP Copy 3 DWM I Protein I Pancakes I RHC I Video Sale			
✓	⬤	DWM I Protein I Pancakes I MO I Video Sale I Fans Copy 2			

FIGURE 31.6–Duplicating Ad Sets

4. Highlight those ads, and then click "Create Similar Ad Set." See Figure 31.7 on page 357.
5. When a new window opens, review and press "Place Order." See Figure 31.8 on page 357.

When you create your copies, Facebook will automatically Add "– copy" to the names of your ad sets. Search for that phrase, and rename them all by entering "DUP" and the date or perhaps a version number. That lets you keep track of your duplicated ads. The

FIGURE 31.7–Duplicating Ad Sets

FIGURE 31.8–Duplicating Ad Sets

more you can name your ads logically, the better. It's extremely important when you're duplicating at scale. See Figure 31.8.

Once you've created your duplicates, move on to the budget. Hit "Edit," scroll down to "Budget and Schedule," and enter the daily budget. See Figure 31.9.

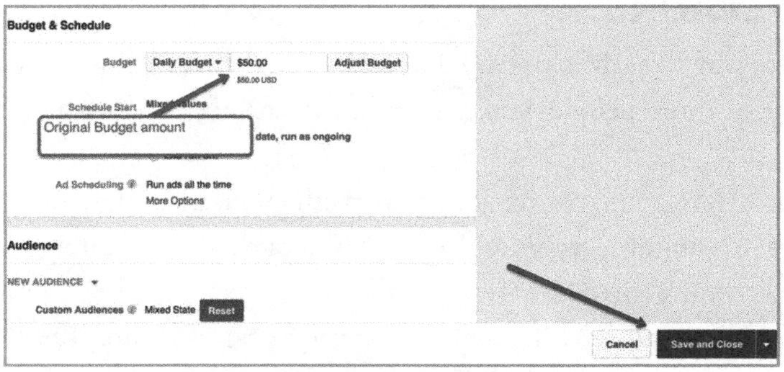

FIGURE 31.9–Duplicating Ad Sets

Note: If you've altered the budget of the original ad, start the duplicate ads with the same budget you initially used for the original. It's really important. We've found that if you duplicate an ad set with an increased budget, the results aren't as good.

For example, if you initially used a budget of $10 a day in the original ad, but after seeing it do well, you increased it to $20 a day, then when you duplicate the ad set make sure the duplicates have a budget of $10 a day and not $20 a day.

Once you've saved those ads, you'll need to make sure that you have entered the Post ID of the original ad. Select all your duplicates; click "Enter Post ID," insert the ID, and press "Submit." See Figure 31.10.

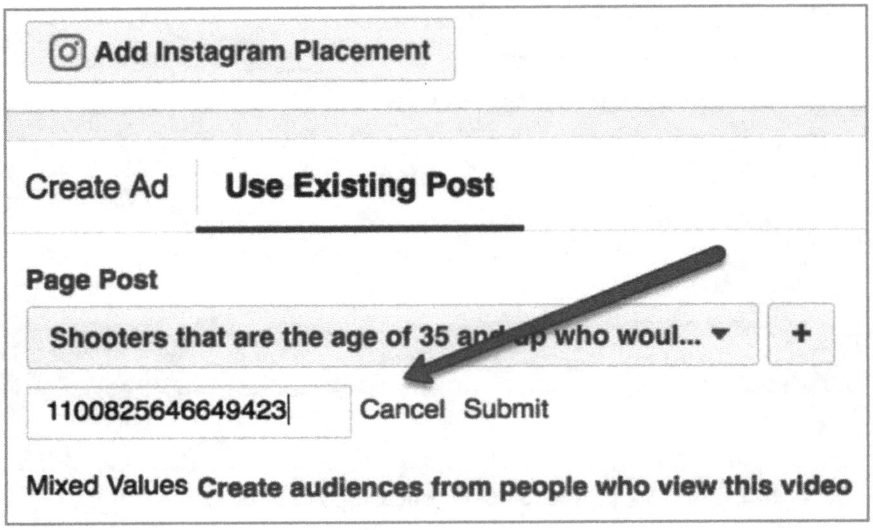

FIGURE 31.10–Duplicating Ad Sets

And that's it—that's really all there is to it.

AUDIENCE SCALING

The second-best way to scale is to use what we call Audience Scaling. In other words, get our ad in front of more people who are similar to the audiences you're already having success with.

Now, this is not about using lookalike audiences, although that is one way to Audience Scale. It's about leveraging Facebook's data to identify interests and behaviors that are similar to your current targeting.

For example, if an ad set with the interest targeting of "Frank Kern" is performing well, there's a good chance that a similar interest, such as "Ryan Deiss," might also do well. That's because the two sell similar products to people with similar needs.

Two quick points to remember:

1. When performing your audience research, you might find highly relevant audiences that don't meet the Potential Reach Requirement of 400,000 to 2 million. Record these anyway as you can group several similar interests together to make up the numbers.

2. Start looking at your ad sets in a new way. Begin by looking at what the targeting of successful ad sets have in-common and how they might differ from poor performing ad sets. Then, use the positive attributes to figure out who else you should target.

As you know, Facebook has an incredible amount of data about their users and as an advertiser you have access to this amazing wealth of information via Facebook's research tools. The two Facebook research tools we recommend for Audience Scaling are the Power Editor Suggestion Tool and Audience Insight.

How to Perform Audience Scaling Using Audience Insight

1. In Ads Manager, set calendar to last seven days.
2. Sort ad sets by CPA—order from smallest to largest.
3. Screen by volume of conversions, scroll down to the conversions that have significant amounts of conversions and lowest CPA.
4. Review your targeting for those ad sets and record in spreadsheet.
5. Insert your interest targeting into audience insights.
6. Choose "Page Likes." (See Figure 31.11.)

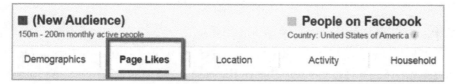

FIGURE 31.11–Audience Insights

7. Record in new relevant interests in spreadsheet.
8. Open Power Editor and enter new interests into the detailed targeting section to confirm if it's a targetable interest and record potential reach.

How to Perform Audience Scaling Using the Power Editor Suggestion Tool

1. In Ads Manager, set calendar to last seven days.
2. Sort ad sets by CPA—order from smallest to largest.

3. Screen by volume of conversion, scroll down to the conversions that have significant amounts of conversions and lowest CPA.

4. Review your targeting for those ad sets and record in spreadsheet.

5. Open Power Editor and in the detailed targeting section insert your interest targeting.

6. Click the "Suggestion" button. (See Figure 31.12)

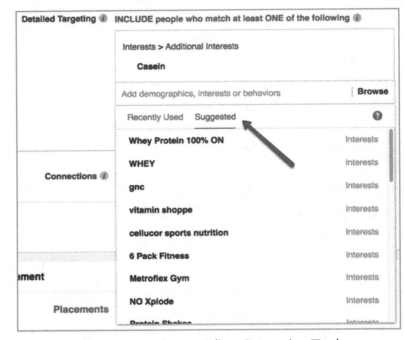

FIGURE 31.12–Power Editor Suggestion Tool

7. Record in relevant interests in spreadsheet.

The biggest advantage of using the Power Editor is it only lists interests that are targetable. That is not always the case in audience insights. As for which of these two ways we recommend, the answer is both. Start by using the "Suggestion Tool" and then move onto audience insights to find additional ideas.

Once you've identified 5 to 20 new highly-relevant appropriate sized potential interests here are the next steps:

8. In Power Editor, highlight the ad sets from the campaign you want to scale, and press "Duplicate." See Figure 31.13 on page 361.

9. Insert the new interests into duplicated ad sets.

For example, let's say your initial interest is "Robert Kiyosaki." You might make three duplicates. In each of the duplicate ad sets, replace the "Robert Kiyosaki" targeting

FIGURE 31.13–Power Editor Suggestion Tool

with your newfound related interests e.g., Tony Robbins, Brendan Burchard, and Dave Ramsey.

Lastly, don't forget to do the housekeeping by changing the names of each of the ad sets to reflect the new interest. Double check the audience size potential reach, and make sure you are always in the sweet spot of between 400,000 and two million. And finally, insert the Post ID to keep your social proof.

ALTERATION SCALING

Alteration Scaling is a lot like Duplication Scaling except you make minor changes to your ad. The idea is to give your ad a fresh look without changing the ad significantly.

For example, inside your ad copy you could change a statement into a question, you could insert brackets or emojis, you could combine the image from one winning ad with the copy of another winning ad, or you could switch out your image for a similar themed image. See Figure 31.14 on page 362.

Whatever you change, make sure you base your decision on data. You want to use your best performing content, including hook and offer, and just present it in a slightly different way.

How to Perform Alteration Scaling

1. In Ads Manager, set calendar to last seven days.
2. Sort ad sets by CPA—order from smallest to largest.
3. Screen by volume of conversion, scroll down to the conversions that have significant amounts of conversions and lowest CPA.
4. Highlight those ads and then click "Create Similar Ad Set."
5. Enter new images or new copy.
6. Rename the ad, using a name that reflects the variation. (For example "[name] Copy 7 Img 3").
7. Hit "Review Changes," and place order.

In summary, the purpose of Alteration Scaling is to get more of your ads in front of the same audience but with slight variations. Keep your audiences large so the different

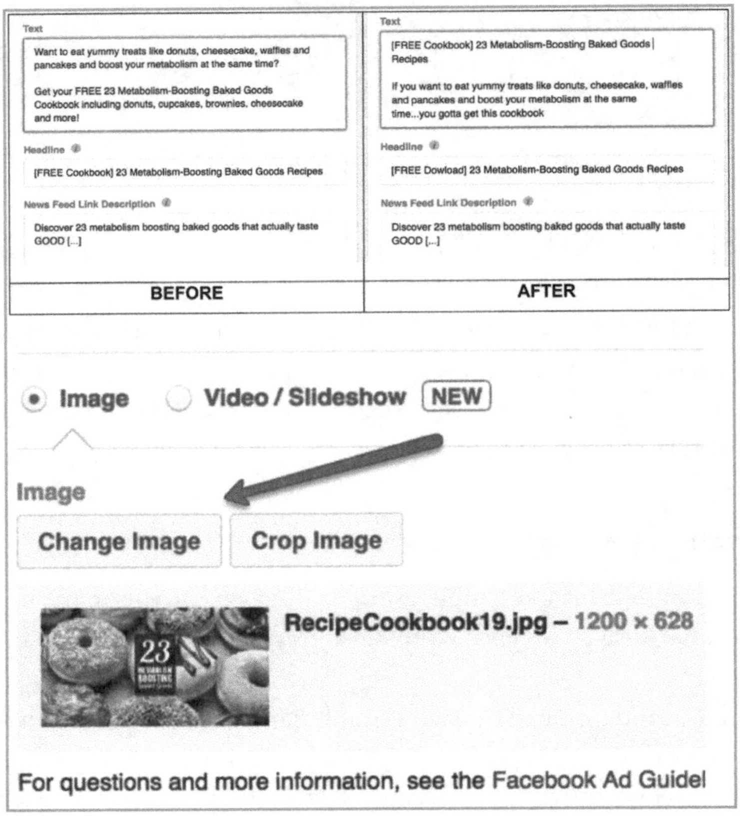

FIGURE 31.14–Alteration Scaling

ads aren't seen too frequently, and because they contain different content, it tends to keep your ad out of their "seen that" blind spot.

LARGE BUDGET SCALING

The fourth tier is the one that comes closest to what you'd expect from scaling.

Basically, you take successful ad sets, duplicate them into new campaigns, and increase the budget by a considerable amount—5 to 20 times the original budget.

But be warned: you must be extremely cautious when performing large budget scaling because not only are you spending a lot more money, but sometimes ramping up budgets causes havoc with the Facebook algorithm.

In our experience, we find setting the daily budget to two to three times your target CPA works best. So, if your established CPA is $25 and your budget per ad set is $10 per day, then create a new campaign with an ad set daily budget between $50 to $75.

Sometimes, you get lucky with larger increases, but our tests have consistently found that two to three times CPA produces good results. For many of our clients, the CPA is $100 so our daily budget is three times that: $300.

How to Perform Large Scale Scaling

You can perform large scale scaling with two simple steps:

1. Duplicate your lowest CPA ad sets, and insert into a new campaign.
2. Increase your daily budget to your level of comfort, ideally 2 to 3X CPA.

Here's a ninja trick—when increasing daily budgets by large amounts, e.g., increasing from $100 to $300, change the lower end of your age range by "one year." Facebook considers this to be a different audience and will not view your ads in competition with your other ads. See Figure 31.15.

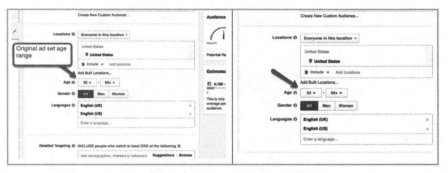

FIGURE 31.15–Large Scale Scaling

In fairness of full disclosure, we know of one advertiser that always starts with a budget of $300 per day and usually ends up with a $3 cost per lead, but they also have really amazing offers. So, our recommendation is based more on our experience than anything set in stone. These guidelines work for most campaigns but not all.

While we usually scale up to three times CPA, you can be more aggressive and set budgets higher and see if it works. As a rule of thumb, we've found it works about one time in five. It might be worth trying if you have an offer that's really really hot.

As for when to start your new campaigns, mornings are usually best, but there's not a great deal of difference between midnight and first thing in the morning. Just avoid starting the campaign in the evening because Facebook will only spend a small portion of your daily budget before the end of the day, and it can skew your results.

SMALL BUDGET SCALING

The last tier is number five for a reason. It's a much more conservative version of large budget scaling.

Instead of ramping the budget up to two to three times your CPA, you just increase the budget by 20 percent every three days until you reach the point of no return—when you exceed your desired CPA—you scale back a couple of steps.

It's a useful tool to have if you're working with a tight budget, but it's very labor intensive. If you're small budget scaling more than ten ad sets, it soon becomes unmanageable. But if budgets and the number of ads are small, it can be a good method and a solution to Facebook's dislike of sudden large jumps in the budget.

Bear in mind results may be skewed for 72 hours because Facebook takes time to adjust to the new budget. Use three days as a guide, but if you find that the campaign settles faster, you can increase the speed of the increments.

So, if your budget is ten dollars a day, you'd first go up to $12 a day, and you'd wait three days to see how it performs. At the end of the three days, you look back over those three days of results, then add another 20 percent if doing well. Three days later you could again try to be a little cocky and double it to see how that turns out, but the principle is to keep rising 20 percent every three days, keep an eye on your CPA, and if you exceed your target CPA, roll the budget back two increments.

How to Perform Small Budget Scaling

If, on the other hand, you want to perform small budget scaling, you'd do this:

1. In Ads Manager, set calendar to last seven days.
2. Sort ad sets by CPA—order from smallest to largest.
3. Screen by volume of conversion, scroll down to the conversions that have significant amounts of conversions and lowest CPA.
4. Click "Edit" and increase the daily budget by 15 to 20 percent. Hit "Save" and close. See Figure 31.16 on page 365.
5. Check every three days to make sure your CPA is below the target CPA. If it is below the target CPA, repeat the process by increasing the daily budget another 15 to 20 percent.
6. When target CPA is exceeded, roll back by at least two increments by opening Ads Manager and entering a lower budget.

You can find the history of each increase in Ads Manager under the individual ad set by clicking on the amount spent. If you hover over the green line, you can see what the budget was before you exceeded your target CPA. It's a very helpful tool that shows you what you did and when you did it (see Figure 31.17 on page 365).

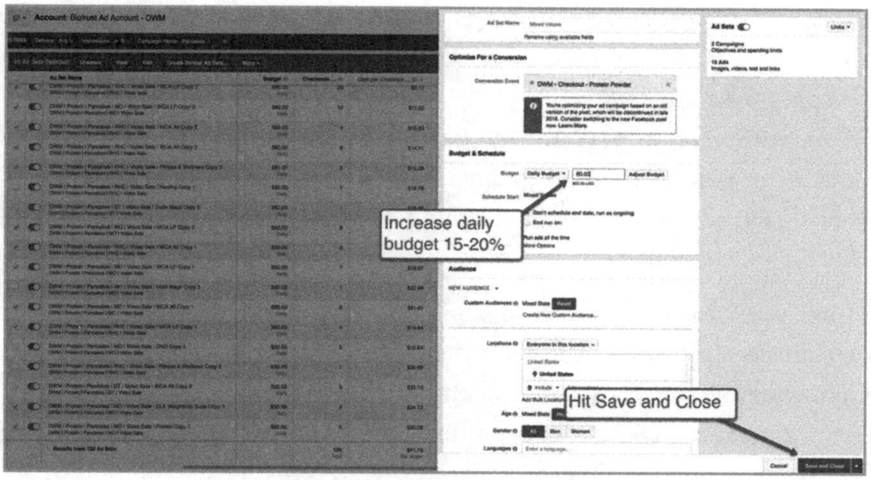

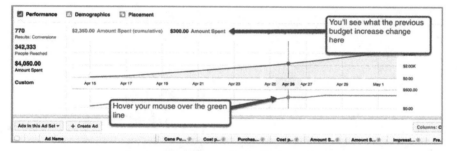

FIGURE 31.16–Small Budget Scaling

FIGURE 31.17–Small Budget Scaling

MASSIVE RAPID SCALING

All of these strategies work great in isolation, but if you want to put your campaigns on steroids and go really big, really fast, try combining them all at once or what we call Massive Rapid Scaling.

For example, you can use duplication scaling to increase the number of ad sets in the same campaign and use it to create a brand-new campaign. You can use audience scaling to broaden your potential reach into new audiences. You can create other ads, ad sets, and campaigns by using alteration scaling . . . plus further increase your ad spend by using large budget scaling.

I hope you're starting to get the picture!

Additional Scaling Tip

- *Duplication Scaling.* Always remember to duplicate the original ad and not the duplicate ad sets.

■ *Audience Scaling.* For advanced Audience Scaling, duplicate your entire Michigan Method campaign—then change the original 20 interests with 20 new interests, keeping the same creative.

■ *Alteration Scaling.* After you've duplicated your campaign, create three new creative and three new pieces of Ad copy. Now, you can make nine different ad variations, each ad copy with each creative. Use the original 20 interests in the original Michigan Method campaign.

So there you have it—the secret to scaling on Facebook.

In conclusion, remember there's no one-fits-all method when it comes to scaling, but by following the five-tier scaling system, you have the power to either slowly increase your ad spend or turbo-charge your results in a very big fast way, growing your business and taking it to a whole new level all while staying in control and maintaining your CPA.

Chapter 32

Career Opportunities
The Desperate Search for Quality Facebook and Social Media Marketers

There is a gold mine right now for highly trained social media marketing and Facebook advertising specialists. The number of different job titles related to this career path seems to be endless—you have the social media manager, social media advertising specialist, Facebook advertising specialist, Facebook ads manager, Facebook account manager, Facebook marketing specialist, Facebook ads consultant, media buyer, online media buyer, social media marketing manager, marketing manager, and the list goes on and on.

> *"Control your own destiny or someone else will."*
>
> —Jack Welch

At the agency, we call this position a Facebook Ads Account Manager and this is also the position we train entrepreneurs to be qualified as through our certification programs and events. We have a "Facebook Ads Account Manager Certification" program. The reason we use the term "account manager" is because we want people who really have the chops to leverage the Facebook platform to go out and acquire new customers for clients on demand. As you have probably realized by now, after reading this book, the level of success or failure of a paid traffic campaign on Facebook or any other social network, is dependent on a lot more than just turning levers inside the Facebook ads manager. You gotta understand the big picture.

When you develop the skills and reputation as a master craftsman in the world of customer acquisition, especially focusing on the digital marketing world specializing in channels like Facebook and Instagram, where the most customers are hanging out and 90 percent of businesses are scrambling like mad to try and figure out how to actually leverage these platforms to acquire those potential customers, you become very, very valuable.

This is especially true if you have an easy way to let the world know about those skills, which is very rare. This conundrum is one of the biggest reasons why we put so much time, effort, and resources into running such a top tier certification program, modeled after the airline industry, which has the best training and certification programs in the world. (Since peoples' lives literally depend on the quality of the flight training.) Since we know the quality of our certification training, along with the rigorous written exam and individualized practical exam testing we do to ensure every certification graduate is proficient and up to our level of standards in every phase of the Facebook ads account management process, produces the highest quality Facebook ads account managers—we actively promote our graduates, because we know they can provide an amazing solution for our customers who need this incredibly complex stuff taken off their hands!

There are tons of opportunities to build a consulting business, an agency, or become a digital marketing or Facebook ads specialist inside a fast-growing company. Just go to Upwork and do a few searches for the wanted ads.

If you want to jump into a hot market, build a consulting business, and take control of your own destiny then I say jump in and do it!

If you would like some help becoming a master craftsman, or if you would like to send some of your team members or employees through our high-end coaching programs or certifications, then we'd love to help you even more. Visit www.perrymarshall.com/fbtools to learn more.

And if you want to take what you learned from this book and start pounding the pavement on your own, then I encourage you to do that, too. Just get started baby!

More Boosted Posts

Guest Author Dennis Yu

This appendix is a continuation of the discussion of boosted posts in Chapter 6 on page 35. To see some more great examples of boosts and unicorn babies, check out www.perrymarshall. com/fbtools. There, we have featured examples on how you can get more engagement with customer feedback, PR, lead generation, post engagement tips, and more.

> "*A*re you a PPC Unicorn or a
> PPC Donkey?"
>
> —Larry Kim

The following are some Larry Kim recommends going all-in on "unicorns" to put all your ad dollars against content that is "hot" to get even more engagement. He tests each post with a $50 budget, while we like to do "dollar a day" for seven days.

It is crucial to only boost successful posts. Boosting a post is just like multiplying a post. If you boost a video with bad results, you are going to get terrible results when pushed out to more people. If you boost a video with great results, your numbers are going to be through-the-roof.

Figure A.1 on page 370 is an example "unicorn," identified by one of many triggers, such as an engagement rate greater than 10 percent.

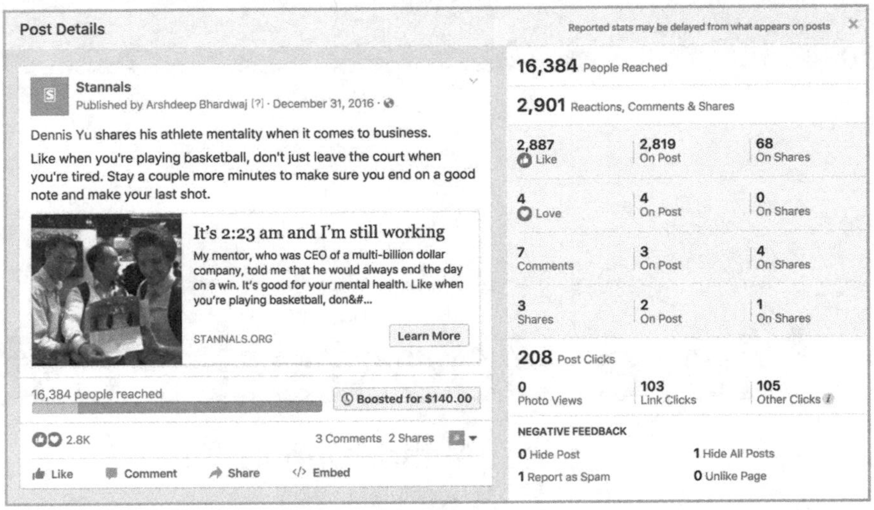

FIGURE A.1

2,901 reactions divided by 16,384 reach is 18 percent—almost double the threshold

Sometimes, content is almost a unicorn, but you've boosted to the wrong audience. The audience won't be the same for every post—sometimes, for us, the right audience has fans of Social Media Marketing World, Digital Marketer, or whatever audience is most relevant.

In this case, from the "hustle" nature of the article—and that it's 2:23 A.M., and I'm still working—I chose Gary Vaynerchuk fans.

I spent $98.86 to drive 2,703 likes, which works out to 3.6 cents a like. This is not great, but not terrible for this type of boost.

The numbers do not account for secondary effects, however. If your friend shares your post and their friend likes it, it won't be counted. Your numbers are actually better than your results say they are. A share is worth 13 times more than a "like" on Facebook. A "like" is a dead-end when one person enjoys your post, and it stops there. A "share" multiplies your numbers, when a person "promotes" your post to everyone they are connected with and extends your reach.

GET THE RESULTS

Now I have some social proof, which means not only is there high engagement, but also that it's the right fans. **So, it's time to switch-boost to a media inception audience to create a unicorn baby**. See Figure A.2 on page 371.

Let's break this down:

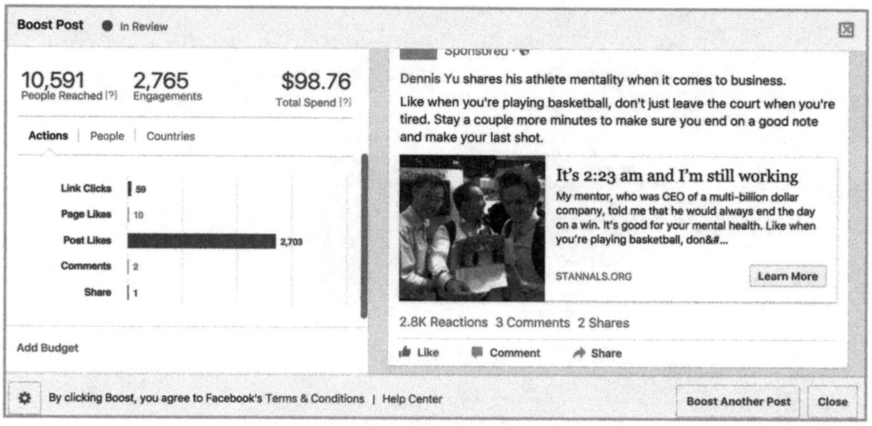

FIGURE A.2

Switch-boost. I originally boosted to a broader interest or behavioral target. I want not only high engagement for cheap to stimulate the algorithm love on this post, but I also want to create social proof. So I'm switching the audience of the boosted post to an influencer audience.

Media inception audience. The influencer audience I've switched to is a media workplace audience. I'm targeting all the people that WORK at *Forbes, CNN, The Wall Street Journal*, and so forth—not people who read these publications.

If they find the content compelling and "newsworthy" (viral counts as newsworthy), then they may write about it or share my post. And when we get coverage by these outlets, we share their posts and boost again to media inception targets, creating "unicorn babies."

Unicorn baby. Once I've got one unicorn, I want to create many variants, which we call unicorn babies. We can create these babies by switching the audience of the boost or even duplicating the ad set, so we're running against two at the same time. We can create derivative (similar or related) pieces of content, to replicate the effect of the initial unicorn.

Got these three components (switch-boost, media inception audience, and unicorn baby), and how they fit together? Great! Let's dive into the mechanics.

Figure A.3 on page 371 is the boosted post after I switch-boosted to the media inception audience:

Notice I created a *saved* audience called "mega media inception"? It's one I reuse often. Even though I can create one of these audiences straight from the boosted post in just ten minutes, I prefer to keep things clean.

If I have other people managing the account, they must use the audiences we've already created, which eliminates the mess most people have. There's no law against

FIGURE A.3

switch-boosting multiple times to test or take advantage of current events. For example, let's say I'm speaking at Social Media Marketing World in a couple weeks. Then I would take a few older boosted posts and switch to Social Media Examiner fans for a couple weeks. See Figure A.4.

FIGURE A.4

SWITCH-BOOST

When I switch-boost, the post keeps all the existing social proof it's built up over time.

So I get this rolling snowball effect that I can redirect wherever I want.

If we don't have something we're currently promoting—a book, event, product, or sale—I'll keep it on the media inception audience.

If the post is amazing, I'll duplicate the ad set in Ads Manager so that I might keep it going at a dollar a day against social media marketers, a dollar a day against fans of Mari Smith, and then whatever audience I'm currently using in the boosted post itself.

Yes, you get only one audience at a time when you boost from the timeline of the page, but there's no law against choosing "page post engagement" from Ads Manager so I can run multiple audiences against this post.

I happen to be lazy and like to avoid having to go to the Ads Manager or Power Editor. I spend 90 percent of my time in the page's timeline and the insights tab where I can see organic and paid stats together.

Ads Manager and Power Editor don't show organic data, so if your post is going "viral" you might miss it if you aren't looking elsewhere.

And most of what we do in tuning ads is trying different audience combos for posts, as opposed to creating tons of new posts. We believe in quality instead of quantity—a key distinction between ROI-driven social marketers and the "just post X times per day" social marketers. Larry Kim and I believe in spending the bulk of our time cultivating winners (unicorns), rather than trying to coax donkeys to fly.

GREATEST HITS

You've listened to your favorite song more than once in your lifetime. Just like music, create a "greatest hits" that lists your most successful posts. Boosting isn't a one-time action. If something worked well in the past, **it is going to work in the future.** Imagine what would happen if the greatest bands sang a song once and then moved on?

After all, if you have your "greatest hits," why not keep playing them over and over (plus creating similar versions) instead of trying to make new stuff from scratch over and over again?

Unless you like self-inflicted punishment, you should be looking at what's done well over the last 24 months and switch-boosting. It's so much less effort to boost a winner (as long as the content is evergreen) than trying a moonshot each day.

When you've finally assembled a herd of unicorns, you have a pretty good idea of what's working in your business, which allows you to:

- *Boost articles you have on third-party publications*—the more guest articles, quotes, and mentions you get, the more items to boost.
- *Track your articles, quotes, and mentions in your content library*—a simple Google sheet lets you track which content bits you can link to in new articles, sprinkle in marketing content, and use for boosting.
- *Set up triggers for conversion parts of your funnel*—you can switch-boost to remarketing audiences. If you're in B2B lead gen or have a product/service with a lengthy consideration phase, some high authority mentions can increase your conversion rate. The pros know that increasing conversion rates is less about tweaking button color and more about persuading the user by overcoming various objections.

Let's go deeper:

Boosting to third party publications is usually more powerful than boosting to your own site.

I wrote an article for Stannals, which is a community of young entrepreneurs, perfect for this content. Another article I wrote about developing people belongs better on Influencive, so I put it there and promoted the Influencive link from my public figure page. See Figure A.5.

CONTENT LIBRARY

Track your articles, quotes, and mentions in your content library—you don't need a fancy tool. Figure A.6 is our content library, shared out with our internal and extended team:

FIGURE A.5

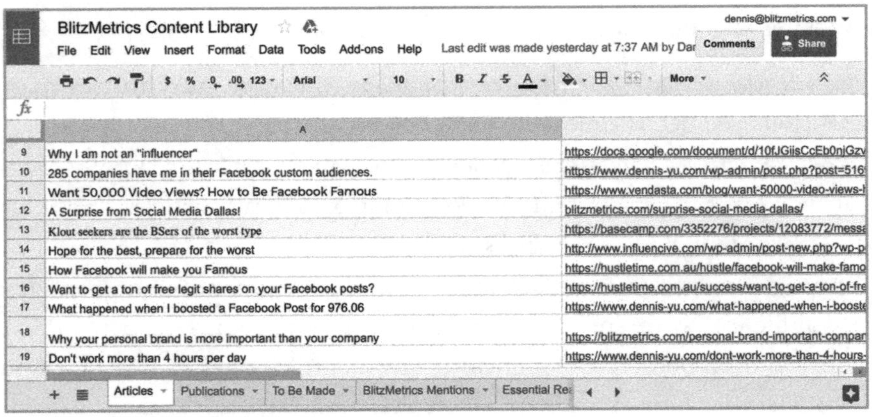

FIGURE A.6

We have tabs for the several thousands of articles we've written, a list of publications we write for, mentions, pictures with influencers, and so forth. Then anyone who is writing an article knows what they can link to, what images they can handily insert, and who we can reach out to for quotes.

We do this not for SEO purposes but because we know that eager readers will want to dig further if they like our articles. And that's why we're OK with spending our ad dollars to send people to someone else's site, since if the article is good, **they'll eventually follow links back to our paid courses**.

FUNNEL

Set up triggers for conversion parts of your funnel—a truly powerful funnel has many sequences, which are IF/THEN statements.

Many Facebook advertisers confuse sophisticated with being complicated:

- *Complicated* is having tons of remarketing (custom), lookalike, and interest/behavior audiences being used in a ton of ad sets.
- *Sophisticated* is having most of your campaigns being driven by remarketing, instead of static demographic and interest targets. The graphic in Figure A.7, which we call the "Bow Tie Formula" is an example of a sophisticated strategy

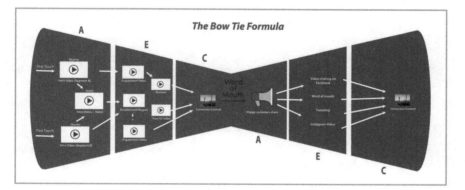

FIGURE A.7

When we develop relationships over many touches, we have more opportunities to build value in the funnel, which increases the LTV of the user and allows us to spend more to acquire leads.

Having a "value, value, value, offer" strategy (like what Michael Hunter teaches in his sequences for Brendon Burchard), also generates goodwill with the community. It doesn't look or feel like selling—more like a trusted friend that you've known for years who is making a recommendation based on what they know about your needs. So when we "think like journalists," our articles have authority, allowing us to share our expertise on high profile sites. And that's where we create unicorn babies that we amplify via switch-boosting to media inception targets.

> ***Don't forget! To see some great examples of boosts and unicorn babies, check out www.blitzmetrics.com/soe. There, we have featured examples on how you can get more engagement with customer feedback , PR, lead generation, post engagement tips, and more.***

Remember, not every boost is going to become a unicorn. Measure organically first; then stack worthy posts on top of each other by boosting each of them for a dollar a day over seven days. Compare their reach and engagement. Put more spending against your winners. Once you have your business goal selected, you need to find the content that matches up with it. Choose a target when you boost the post. Then watch how Goals → Content → Targeting will lead you to success on Facebook.

About the Authors

PERRY MARSHALL

Perry Marshall is the number-one author and world's most quoted authority on pay-per-click advertising. He is the author of the best-selling guide to Google advertising, the *Ultimate Guide to Google AdWords* , and the biggest-selling guide to Facebook advertising, the *Ultimate Guide to Facebook Advertising*.

His company, Perry S. Marshall & Associates, consults with companies in over 300 industries on generating sales leads, web traffic, and maximizing advertising results.

Prior to his consulting career, he helped grow a tech company in Chicago from $200,000 to $4 million in sales in four years, and the firm was sold to a public company for $18 million.

Like direct marketing pioneer Claude Hopkins, Perry has both an engineering degree and a love for persuasive copywriting.

He's led marketing seminars, spoken at conferences around the world, and consulted in hundreds of industries from computer hardware and software to high–end consulting, from health and fitness to corporate finance.

He's published hundreds of articles on sales, marketing, and technology, and his works also include *80/20 Sales and Marketing* (Entrepreneur Press, 2013), *Ultimate Guide to Google AdWords* (Entrepreneur Press, 2017), and two technical books, *Industrial Ethernet* (ISA, Third Edition, 2017) and *Evolution 2.0* (BenBella Books, 2015).

He's spoken at conferences around the world and consulted in over 200 industries, from computer hardware and software to high–end consulting, from health and fitness to corporate finance.

KEITH KRANCE

Keith Krance is the CEO and founder of Dominate Web Media, which provides Facebook ads education courses, certifications, coaching, and full-agency ads management services to small businesses and large companies all over the world.

Overseeing over $60 million in total ad spend (currently averaging $2.5 to $3 million per month in over 100 ad accounts), which has generated over 15 billion impressions, 500 million video views, 250 million clicks, millions of leads, and hundreds of millions of dollars in revenue, with either full-service agency or coaching/consulting clients. Keith's super power is helping businesses architect customer attraction systems that produce perpetual traffic. Leads, sales, and massive brand equity and awareness are also Keith's specialty.

He is the host of the top-rated podcast "Perpetual Traffic," published by Digital Marketer, along with co-hosts Molly Pittman and Ralph Burns.

Prior to transitioning 100 percent into the digital marketing world, Keith was an airline pilot for Horizon Air (subsidiary of Alaska Airlines) for six years, racking up over 4,000 hours. He also owns and operates multiple retail locations as a franchisee of two different franchises in Washington State—Emerald City Smoothie and Desert Sun Tanning, where they use more traditional off-line direct response and brand marketing such as direct mail, newspaper, radio, TV, outdoor, etc.

Keith leverages his flying experience using normal and abnormal checklists and SOPs with his retail sales and marketing experience to create the system for turning social media users into customers and brand advocates.

THOMAS MELOCHE

At the age of 38, Meloche along with three partners founded Menlo Innovations, a software consultancy and development firm. The immediate challenges he and his partners faced were staggering: a software industry in a quality crisis, the collapse of the internet bubble, the beginning of the offshore movement, and an economy in free-fall after the terrorist attacks of 9/11. Most would not believe it possible to start a software consultancy in the midst of such monumental turmoil. The circumstances, however, do reflect many of the same day-to-day struggles organizations face today—a world dominated by change. Meloche lead Menlo Innovations' marketing initiatives implementing techniques he learned from Perry Marshall.

Menlo is now world famous. Last year executives from over 200 corporations around the world traveled to Menlo to tour the facility and observe their operations first-hand. A book on Menlo, *Joy Inc. How We Built a Workplace People Love* (Portfolio, 2015), has become a best seller. "Don't forget," Meloche reminds his audiences, "My success with Menlo and dozens of other companies is because of direct marketing fundamentals. The details of how to best leverage Facebook may change, but the direct marketing fundamentals never do."

Thomas Meloche is president and chief-dishwasher of Meloche Consulting Inc., consulting on Facebook advertising and organizational transformation.

GUEST AUTHORS

ANGELA PONSFORD is the co-owner of Dotti Media Facebook Ad Agency and also an Account Manager with Dominate Web Media. She's a former Forensic Scientist and loves geeking out over clients ad campaigns and figuring out how to get the best results. For questions or consulting inquiries please contact her at angela@dottimedia.com or www.DottiMedia.com.

TRACI REUTER is the founder of Divine Social, a Facebook Advertising Agency and also an Account Manager with Dominate Web Media. She brings a unique strategic perspective to her client campaigns with her vast background in sales and marketing with a Fortune 10 company. For questions or consulting inquiries, please contact her at traci@divinesocial.com or www.divinesocial.com.

RALPH BURNS is the owner and CEO of the DWM Agency, a Facebook advertising agency managing $2.5 to $3 million per month in ad spend, serving businesses all over the world from ecommerce companies selling physical products, software, and services, to digital products, coaching, and consulting. He can be reached at Ralph@dominatewebmedia.com or www.DominateWebMedia.com.

ANDREW TWEITO is the founder of Funnel Boom, specializing in digital marketing strategies, engineering profitable sales funnels, and tracking implementation services dedicated to improving return on ad spend. He can be reached at www.Funnel Boom.com.

RYAN DEISS is the founder and CEO of DigitalMarketer.com. Over the last 36 months Ryan and his team have invested over $15 million on marketing tests, generated tens of millions of unique visitors, sent well over a BILLION emails, and run approximately 3,000 split and multi-variant tests.

MOLLY PITTMAN is Digital Marketer's Vice President and Traffic Manager, as well as a Digital Marketing Consultant. She uses her wide range of business, communication, and deep understanding of the customer journey to create profitable, scalable traffic campaigns. She can be reached at molly@mollypittman.com.

DENNIS YU is the founder and Chief Technology Officer of BlitzMetrics.com, a digital marketing company that partners with schools to train young adults. Dennis' program centers around mentorship, helping students grow their expertise to manage social campaigns for enterprise clients, such as the Golden State Warriors, Nike, and Rosetta Stone.

Index